AFTER NEWMAN

AFTER NEWMAN

A Eulogy for Anglo-Catholics, 1845–1965

Aidan Nichols, OP

GRACEWING

First published in England in 2025
by
Gracewing
2 Southern Avenue
Leominster
Herefordshire HR6 0QF
United Kingdom
www.gracewing.co.uk

All rights reserved.
No part of this publication may be reproduced, stored in a retrieval system, or transmitted in any form or by any means, electronic, mechanical, photocopying, recording or otherwise, without the written permission of the publisher.

The rights of Aidan Nichols to be identified as the author of this work have been asserted in accordance with the Copyright, Designs and Patents Act 1988.

© 2025 The Dominican Council
as sole corporate Trustees of
The English Province of the Order of Preachers

ISBN 978 085244 788 8

Cover image: 'The Hour of Glory'
St Cyprian's, Clarence Gate
Photo by Fr Lawrence Lew, OP
Cover design by Bernardita Peña Hurtado
Typeset by Word and Page, Chester, UK

CONTENTS

	Acknowledgement	vii
	Preface	ix
1.	Leadership after Newman	1
2.	What happened next?	15
3.	Rites and Ceremonies	33
4.	Brighton and Beyond	49
5.	Monasticism and Religious Life	61
6.	Social Movements	85
7.	The Theologians	103
8.	The Inner-Church Struggle	129
9.	Anglo-Catholics and the Arts	147
10.	Ecumenism and Mission	179
11.	Conclusion	203
	Select Bibliography	205
	Notes	213

Anglo-Catholicism ... commanded spiritual and pastoral success, reinforced by ... academic and scholarly plausibility... [through] leading Oxford and Cambridge academics, biblical scholars and theologians ... intellectuals, artists, writers, and architects.

Anthony Symondson, SJ

The English Roman Catholics for the most part disliked and derided the Movement.

Sidney Leslie Ollard

ACKNOWLEDGEMENT

I should like to thank Benjamin Eadon, Priest-Director of the Shrine of Our Lady of Walsingham, for giving me access to the Shrine's Eric Kemp Library, which gave me an initial orientation for the writing of this book, and also to Mehmet Cifci, Librarian of Pusey House, and Michael Yelton, Secretary of the Anglo-Catholic History Society, for their help in enabling me to consult the Society's admirable publications.

PREFACE

This book has been written for Roman Catholics who may—I would say, who *should*—wish to know something about the body of Christians closest spiritually, liturgically, theologically, artistically, to themselves. That is so, at any rate, if the Roman Catholics in question belong to the Latin—as distinct from the Oriental Catholic—churches of the papal Communion. It is unapologetically a eulogy—and also something of an elegy, since much of the corporate life I describe is no more.

In a brief account of my own writing, produced for the website 'Christendom Awake', I described my theological outlook as inscribed within a triangle of which the defining points were the Roman magisterium, Constantinople, and the thought of 'Christians formed by the Anglican patrimony'. Since that time, the limpid waters of the magisterium have become a trifle muddied, and, after the schism with Moscow over autocephaly in Ukraine, 'Constantinople' can no longer stand alone for the Orthodox world. 'Christians formed by the Anglican patrimony' was always a rather mealy-mouthed expression, though in *The Panther and the Hind* I suggested that elements from the three main post-Reformation sub-traditions in the Church of England could be judiciously extracted in some future Uniate church. The three elements were: the rational theology of Christian Platonist metaphysics (Latitudinarian, or Broad), a full-blooded theology of the Atonement (Evangelical, or Low), and a thoroughly incarnational Christology, ecclesiology, and theology of the sacraments (High, or Catholic).[1] The model of the Uniate churches which I made my own had already been adopted, incidentally, by the 1920 Anglo-Catholic Congress for future relations between a thoroughly Catholicized Canterbury and Rome.

But obviously enough, a scanning of those various Anglican elements, if it be adjudicated by criteria furnished by Rome and the Orthodox, is always going to produce an overall account that is more favourable to traditional Anglo-Catholicism than to any other Church of England grouping. That 'Catholic Anglican' tradition was already split at the time of my writing—above all, over issues of theological anthropology, namely the Ordination of women and the ethics of sexuality and marriage. To those has since been added the question of transgenderism, now seemingly acknowledged as a non-negotiable element in diversity, inclusion, equality.[2] Since 1990, 'Affirming Catholics', who correspond in almost every particular to 'Progressive Catholics' in the Roman Catholic Church, stand over against the rest, who, for want of a better name, I shall call the 'classical Anglo-Catholics'.

The creation of the Ordinariate of Our Lady of Walsingham by Pope Benedict XVI offered, in terms that were generous, but not over-generous, an opportunity for classical Anglo-Catholics to realise a corporate reunion that for some of them—the Anglo-Papalists—had always been described as all-important, while for others—those who were not Papalists—it was at least a major goal, along with (but not in preference to) union with the Orthodoxy of the East.[3] In the Ordinariate, as things turned out, the 'take-up' was very limited, and the 'refuseniks' have since done well, preserving their distinctive identity as parishes and Societies, under the umbrella of the bishops of the 'Society under the patronage of St Wilfrid and St Hilda': 'The Society' for short. The impossibility of bringing into an 'Ordinariate' Anglo-Catholic parish churches—they are, after all, property of the Established Church to its entirety, explains much in the rather feeble response (the option of leasing, on some agreed basis, does not seem to have been explored).

But that was not the only factor. As a former Anglican myself, I am painfully conscious of the lack of comprehension, and indeed of basic historical knowledge, that typified many Roman Catholics, including priests and bishops, when faced with the promulgation of *Anglicanorum coetibus*. That incomprehension, and even ignorance, surmised by Anglicans, also played its part in the *déroulement* of events in 2009. It still persists, inasmuch as thought is ever given to them, in regard to the 'holy remnant' of the classical Anglo-Catholics today.

So what I would like to do in this book is to present historic Anglo-Catholicism to a (Roman) Catholic readership, and, by that means, bring home the achievements, so eminently worthy of respect, that are described in these pages. Here they will find within one cover material about the Oxford Fathers (Newman aside), the Ritualists and liturgists, founders of Sisterhoods and monasteries, social thinkers, creators of Church societies, guilds, schools and newspapers, organizers of Congresses, theologians, architects and artists, poets and novelists, hymnographers and musicians, ecumenists and missionaries. In a word, everything that made Anglo-Catholicism, in Geoffrey Rowell's words, a 'vision glorious' in the religious and cultural history of England.[4] The material is hardly unknown to students of the period but its presentation by a Roman Catholic author may give it a certain piquancy.

The present circumstances of the Church of Rome, at a time of considerable confusion, not seen since the pontificate of Paul VI, are not

Preface

especially propitious for any further advance in the Reunionist cause.[5] But the ground can still be prepared for any future eventuality in which the heirs of Dr Pusey and Mr Keble, and the other 'greats', might wish to look toward the Apostolic See, and this time with the possibility of a more informed reception. The Anglo-Catholic hope of 'taking over' the entire English Church, common in the glory days of the Catholic Revival (the late 1920s and early 1930s), has gone forever. The Ordination of women, and the consequent loss of a ministry that could (in principle, granted new factors—revision of the Ordinals and participation of Old Catholics in Anglican consecrations) be recognized by the Latin Church, has shattered the ecclesiology of the Oxford Movement. But that does not mean that Anglo-Catholics of 'The Society' have no role yet to be played in the destinies of Christendom—if, that is, they are faithful to their history. I think of a Western Catholicism, patriarchally unified yet denuded of hyper-papalism, and leavened by strong sympathy with the Orthodoxy of the East.

St Dominic's Priory,
Haverstock Hill,
London
Eastertide, 2025

Note: The dates of birth and death, where available, of figures key to this study will be given either at the first mention of their names or in the case of persons to whom a section of the text is devoted where such more sustained reference occurs.

1

Leadership after Newman

As the Preface explained, this is chiefly a book for Catholics about what happened 'After Newman'. The Roman Catholic assumption runs: Newman's conversion was the pearl produced by the Oxford Movement. From a jeweller's perspective, oysters cease to be of interest once they have put forth their pearl. And so it has been here. As an American student of the Movement has put it (for reasons of human drama rather than theology): 'At this point [John Shelton Reed is speaking of 1845], the Oxford Movement, properly speaking, was over. Disgraced in Oxford, its enemies' suspicions wholly confirmed, abandoned by its greatest spokesman and by the many lesser figures who preceded and followed him — the curtain should fall, or we risk bathos.'[1]

But speaking of oysters, marine biologists are interested in oysters for their own sake. So there is nothing necessarily conclusive — certainly, not anything *concluding* — about events at Littlemore in that fateful year.

It was in any case true that by the late 1830s disciples of the 'Oxford Movement' were known in Oxford itself not as 'Newmanians' but as 'Puseyites' — even if, on one judgment, '[e]very Oxford man knew better. Newman commanded and Pusey followed'.[2] It was also becoming clear that 'Tractarians' at large were not simply a reiteration of the old 'high church' component in Anglicanism, a tradition dating from the Laudian, Caroline, and Restoration divines, persisting through the 'long eighteenth century', and with a minor renaissance during the years of the governments of Robert Banks Jenkinson, Earl of Liverpool (1770–1828), between 1812 and 1827. Historical scholarship had always been vaguely aware of this. The research of Peter Nockles of Manchester University, at once wide-ranging and exactingly minute, has amply confirmed it.[3]

Not the least reason for the innovatory character of Tractarianism was that new times demanded new policies. As Owen Chadwick, doyen of historians of the 'Victorian Church', wrote in his book of that name, it could well be argued that 'in the English scene of 1840 a demand for church authority was inevitable, that a Church which by Parliament's action was ceasing to be national must be more aware of the universal

Christian (as opposed to the national) inheritance; that the romantic literature and religious sentiment of the age must find expression in Catholic modes of prayer and mortification—in short, that Rome needed no stimulus from Puseyites to attract, and that Puseyites guided souls into a safer port'.[4] The guides were, for Anglo-Catholics, the 'Oxford Fathers', and, after Newman, that meant Pusey and Keble. To understand where Anglo-Catholics 'were coming from' is impossible without taking into the account their pre-1845 as well as post-1845 story.

Mr Keble

John Keble (1792–1866) belonged to a family of minor gentry in rural Gloucestershire.[5] Home-schooled by his clergyman father, he was astonishingly well prepared for studying Classics at Oxford. Taking a spectacular Double First landed him with a Fellowship at Oriel College at the age of eighteen—and Oriel was the only College where Fellowships were awarded competitively, by examination.[6] The Oriel Common Room was known for its clerical high-flyers, to whose number Newman would eventually be added.

Keble proved a pioneer in expecting the role of an Oxford tutor to be pastorally as well as academically demanding. He was also a critical voice, insisting that the University of Oxford was intended by its mediaeval progenitors not for idle playboys but for poor students with a craving for sound learning. That was the daring theme of his 1839 'Creweian Oration' when William Wordsworth (1770–1850) received an honorary doctorate.

Keble's own teaching is to be found principally in his sermons,[7] *Tracts*,[8] and the lectures on poetry that he gave in pursuit of his duties as the University's Professor of Poetry.[9] His *Christian Year*, once a feature of every high church household, had baptized the Romantic Movement in a best-selling collection of liturgically oriented devotional verse, where, characteristically, emotion is robust and yet controlled.[10] All these texts are infused with a patristically nourished spiritual exegesis of the Bible. For Keble, the ideal reader of Holy Writ will not only take seriously the religious value of its poetic expressiveness. He or she will also be engaged on a moral journey, for which desirable project he took over from the Greeks—and popularised among the Tractarians—a quite distinctive word.

The word is 'ethos', which is not just an alternative term for ethics since it stakes out a distinctive claim. Moral judgment, taught Keble, has an intellectual foundation, just as intellectual judgment, at any rate in ethical and spiritual matters, has its moral preconditions.[11]

This emphasis on the inseparable unity of theological sensibility and spiritual growth was crucial for the Oxford Fathers, and explains much in later Anglo-Catholicism, not least the strongly devotional element which accompanies the argumentative elements in its doctrinal preaching.[12] Except on the special public occasions when major figures gave lengthy expositions, usually turned into pamphlet-length publications, the Tractarians were keen that parochial sermons should be 'plain' and 'practical', which meant calculated to foster a prayerful and virtuous way of life. The Evangelical Movement, the background of some, not least Newman, had left its mark. 'The vision of the devotional life which emerges from consideration of these sermons is one in which the earnestness of Evangelical "heart" religion has been translated into a no less earnest and attentive series of daily practices, guided by reflection on the Church's year, and designed to deepen the believer's understanding of, and dependence on, the Christian gospel.'[13]

Keble was convinced that the poetic mode was indispensable for both nurturing and challenging religious feeling,[14] a view he had come to, based on his reading of Joseph Butler (1692–1752), even before the 'Lake Poets', Wordsworth and Coleridge (1772–1834), got there—though the work of the latter certainly helped.[15] 'The typological exegesis of Scripture and the strong sacramentalism of the Fathers commended themselves to men who had already begun to criticize the evidence theology of the eighteenth century, under the influence of the work of Bishop Butler and the rediscovery of the symbolic and imaginative character of language in the literature of Romanticism.'[16] If the first Tractarians found in Wordsworth confirmation of their conviction that cosmic nature is a disclosure of the divine, Coleridge's role is rather more complex and, consequently, less easy to adjudicate. On one view, giving a central role to the posthumous *Confessions of an Enquiring Spirit*, Coleridge had opposed not only 'Scripturalism' (belief in the verbal inspiration of a self-interpreting Bible) but also its apparent opposite, religious rationalism. But these were the very habits of thought most criticized by supporters of the Oxford Movement. Coleridge had sought instead to base biblical authority on the way the Scriptures have been experientially tested in the life of the Church. 'By the long trial of the Christian centuries it was made clear that other books were to this Book but as subordinate spiritual luminaries… It was this corporate consciousness of the Church, becoming ever more articulate and definite, that attested to the divine message.'[17] The Tractarian affinities of such a conclusion are undeniable.

Alertness to symbol—a common trait in the Fathers, Butler, and the Romantics—would persist in Anglo-Catholicism in a second, extra-biblical, way as well. Anglo-Catholicism became known for the highly charged symbolism of its ritual worship. With that might be linked its tendency to produce or attract poets such as Christina Rossetti or, in the following century, T. S. Eliot, and poetically inclined novelists like

After Newman

Eliot's friend, Charles Williams. Its theologians, too, showed an inclination to fuse argument and symbolism, as, for instance, in the later work of Lionel Thornton, who belonged to one of the Oxford Movement's monastic foundations, and the writings of Austin Farrer, Warden of the College named for John Keble by grateful disciples.

And doctrinally it was Keble who rediscovered not just the Caroline and Restoration divines—the most 'Catholic' of the post-Reformation English divines, writers who, in Eliot's language, preceded a damaging 'disassociation of sensibility' between reason and feeling—but the non-Jurors too, those schismatics from the Williamite church in the wake of the 'Glorious Revolution' of 1688 that sent packing the anointed king, James II (reigned 1685–8). The more radical of the non-Jurors led Keble's mind to a wild surmise. The work of the English Reformers, as with all interpreters of Holy Writ, would have to be placed under the judgment of Christian Antiquity, whereupon that work might (conceivably) be found wanting.

Among the first Tractarians, Pusey had been a comparatively late arrival whereas Keble had some claim to be the initiator of the entire Movement. At any rate that is how Newman remembered things, seeing Keble's 1833 sermon on 'National Apostasy' to judges in Oxford's University Church as a call to spiritual arms which the *Tracts* and all that followed from them served to answer.[18] And leaving aside the question as to whether the significance of that sermon has been overestimated,[19] Pusey's own move in a 'high church' direction, if initially owing to the influence of his bishop, Charles Lloyd of Oxford (1784–1829), came about chiefly through the 'influence of Keble, either directly or as mediated by Newman'.[20]

Why, then, we might wonder, were Anglo-Catholics called 'Puseyites' and not, 'Kebelians'? Keble's desire to be, like his father, a country clergyman, albeit one who took the greatest pains over preaching and kept up a personal ministry of contact and counsel, *viva voce* or by letter, was the ruling passion in his life. It was also the answer to the question just posed. Keble was in every way a retiring man. Yet in its own manner his parish at Hursley, near Winchester, with its school, Sunday school, and careful oversight of the welfare of its villagers, was itself a lived—and efficacious—'icon' of the Catholic Movement. In this it was aided by the (admittedly, rather ruthless) way the squire, Sir William Heathcote (1801–81), refused tenancy agreements with Dissenters—unless, that is, they agreed to send any children they might have to Keble's church school. The parish was a Victorian dream, recreating in one little space the homogenously harmonious Anglican civil society envisaged by Late Elizabethan Anglicanism' s greatest exponent, Richard Hooker (1554–1600).

Hursley's message for the increasingly urbanized society that was the England of the middle and later years of Victoria's reign (1837–1901) was, accordingly, far from obvious. That, however, did not disable the stimulus Keble was able to give through his occasional writings,[21] and his even rarer polemical interventions, forwarding the advance of a 'high' ecclesiology, based on Apostolic Succession, and a similarly 'high' sacramental doctrine notably in regard to Baptism, the Holy Eucharist, and Penance. Nor did it prevent Keble's star schoolmistress, Charlotte Yonge, from becoming *par excellence* the novelist of the Oxford Movement. She will be visited in Chapter 9 below.

Dr Pusey

Edward Bouverie Pusey (1800–82) was born into a Berkshire family with aristocratic connexions. He had travelled an archetypally upper-class educational route—Eton and Christ Church—but via an unusual detour to the University of Göttingen. Ordination, marriage, and appointment to the Regius Chair of Hebrew at Oxford all took place in his *annus mirabilis* of 1828 when he also became a canon of Christ Church, Oxford's cathedral, housed within the college of that name.

His Teutonic immersion marked him out. Despite the example of Coleridge, few Englishmen at that time learned the German language, important though it was for philosophy and theology at the turn of the eighteenth and nineteenth centuries. In Germany the young Mr Pusey had discovered Pietists struggling to find a satisfactory compromise—a kinder phrase was a 'theology of mediation' (*Vermittlungstheologie*)—with theological rationalists formed by the European Enlightenment. While he defended them on his return, the unstable equilibrium they represented prompted a need for further evaluation of what real Christian orthodoxy was. That was how Pusey became drawn to the *Tracts for the Times* as they appeared.[22] In Germany, or when defending the Germans once back home, Tradition had not been a factor in his thinking—in which regard he was as remote from the old 'high churchmen' as he was from the budding 'new' or 'apostolical' school.

Though Pusey had offered the editors a brief essay on the topic of fasting (number 18 of the *Tracts*, 'On the Benefits of the System of Fasting enjoined by our Church'), an early sign of the ascetical tendencies so pronounced after his wife died, it was not till the mid- to later 1830s that he fully aligned with the Tractarian Movement. Pusey's offering was the first not to be entirely anonymous (he appended his initials), probably because he was not yet ready to be identified with the series as whole. The decision to make common cause was signalled in number 67 of the *Tracts* (it spilt over into numbers 68 and 69), *Scriptural Views of Holy Baptism*, a publication which led one Evangelical newspaper to comment that Dr Pusey would surely be better employed at Maynooth or in the Vatican than on the Isis (Oxford's name for the Thames). Sour grapes: the treatise was the most patristically learned ever written in England on its topic. One thing, however, soon became clear. The objective reality of Baptismal regeneration would be a constant theme of the Oxford Movement, and it was asserted over against Reformed Protestants in particular.

The date of publication of *Scriptural Views of Holy Baptism*, 1836, was also, not altogether coincidentally, the year of a bitter campaign to clip the wings of Oxford's new Regius Professor of Divinity, Renn Dickson Hampden (1793–1868), a doctrinal minimalist. Pusey knew from Germany where that path led, with inherited doctrine sidelined as 'orthodoxism' or 'scholasticism'. He was confirmed in his new direction by the intense editorial work he undertook for the 'Library of the Fathers': the Fathers, that is, in modern English translation for contemporary Anglican reading.

Henceforth for Pusey the criterion was to be Scripture interpreted by the ancient Fathers, after the manner of the Caroline and Restoration divines. Pusey still laboured under the misapprehension that the Reformers, by this exacting standard, came through in every instance with flying colours.

Pusey might not have cared for the idiom Newman used in Number 90, the last of the *Tracts for the Times*, the bombshell, detonated in January 1841, driving Newman both from Oxford and out of the Church of England. But, like Keble, Pusey supported its overall case. The text of the Thirty-Nine Articles could be read in a sense that renders them compatible with historic Catholic doctrine in the pre-Reformation Church. That was Newman's highly controversial claim. If anything, Pusey would go further than Newman and argue that the 'Articles' were *actually intended* by their framers to be so read.

Meanwhile, he had his own trials, and not only the premature deaths of his wife and his daughter Lucy. In 1843 he was suspended from preaching in the University for two years. That was owing to his support for the doctrine of the Real Presence in the Eucharist, a conviction he found in Cyril of Alexandria—not needing, then, to wait for the Fathers of Trent to give it utterance. Thus ran the sermon *The Holy Eucharist a Comfort to the Penitent*, which sold twenty thousand copies, to the chagrin, one imagines, of the other canons in the Christ Church chapter.[23]

1843 was also the year when Pusey received the Religious vows of Marian Rebecca Hughes, the foundress, some eight years later, of the Society of the Holy and Undivided Trinity, who thus became the first woman to profess such vows in the post-Reformation Church of

England. (*Faute de mieux*, Pusey used the rite for the Consecration of a Virgin from the Roman Pontifical.) Though there was no Religious community of which Hughes could be a member, this was nonetheless a harbinger of the future. There would be a veritable explosion of such Sisterhoods under Tractarian auspices, followed in time by a more modest appearance of Religious communities for men. Nor was this confined, in due course, to England. In the words of one later twentieth century commentator, 'insofar as in the century since Pusey's death the colonial Church has derived much of her strength from the vitality of her religious communities, her sisterhoods, her bush brotherhoods and monastic orders, she owes Pusey a debt she has never repaid.'[24] Southern Africa, Australia and the Pacific: the reverberations were felt far from Carfax Tower, the notional centre of the city of Oxford. The topic of Religious life, as placed on the agenda by the Oxford Fathers, will be examined in Chapter 5, and some reference made to its missionary contribution both there and in Chapter 10, 'Ecumenism and Mission'.

Baptism and the Holy Eucharist were not the only sacraments Pusey handled. Once he had recovered his University 'voice', he preached two sermons entitled *Entire Absolution of the Penitent*, giving a boost to the recovery of auricular Confession—for Victorian Protestants, by far the most controversial of the causes he supported.[25] The *Tract* on Baptism explained how every act of mortal sin so weakens Baptismal grace that the individual lacks ordinary means with which to restore it. And that is precisely why—so Pusey now argued—the extraordinary means of another sacrament, Confession, or (to use its more correct name) Penance, is needful. Yet despite certain references in the Book of Common Prayer the English public were convinced that confessing to a priest was a Popish practice, and they were repelled by it.

Pusey did not exactly initiate its revival. For the most part, he was a passive recipient of requests from others. Overwhelmingly, these were young adults in Tractarian circles who had become more sensitive to the full connotations of the word 'sin'—sometimes through Evangelical, not Anglo-Catholic, churchgoing.[26] Resistance to the idea of repeated or even habitual Confession was the reason Bishop Samuel Wilberforce (1805–73) of Oxford proceeded to inhibit Pusey's preaching—the second such humiliation, then—in 1850. 'You seem to me to be habitually assuming the place and doing the work of a Roman confessor, and not that of an English clergyman.'[27] And again, 'I so firmly believe that of all the curses of Popery this [regular confession] is the crowning curse, that I cannot allow voluntarily within my charge the continuance of any ministry that is infected by it'.[28]

Critics generally add that Pusey cannot be entirely exonerated from giving exaggerated advice about physical mortification—though recommending heavy serge as a form of hairshirt seems less than draconian and he did have the problem of over-zealous clients. Less justified were complaints that he sought to adapt Continental works of devotion for the use of, especially, Sisters. To Wilberforce, adaptations or otherwise (Pusey was not beyond recommending the unexpurgated texts), they weaned people away from the 'earnest sobriety of our own Prayer Book'.[29] To Pusey's mind, such English insularity was contrary to Catholicity. Whatever God had given to Christ's Church he must have given to the Church universal.

Not till 1853 did Pusey venture again into the realm of Eucharistic teaching with his sermon on 'The Presence of Christ in the Holy Eucharist'. That showed no mitigation of his earlier doctrine, and copious patristic data covered his back.[30] The recovery of traditional doctrine on the Eucharistic Presence—and the Eucharistic Sacrifice—would soon trigger the liturgical or ceremonial revival known in this context as 'Ritualism'. In contrast to the case of many later Anglo-Catholics, however, Pusey's horse, like Keble's, shied at the fence of Transubstantiation, considering it, in Rowell's phrase, an 'over-definition' of doctrine, intruding philosophical language into the sphere of the mystery.[31]

This entire history sufficed to mark out Pusey, after 1845, as the natural leader of Newman's erstwhile disciples. It was a position for which he was in any case socially and professionally qualified thanks to his seniority in the University as professor of Hebrew and 'Student' (meaning Fellow) of Christ Church, its cathedral-connected and in that sense ecclesiastically premier College. And after all, by general consent, he was the most learned Orientalist (expert in Hebrew, Arabic, Syriac) in England.

That was a pertinent consideration since as yet Tractarianism was chiefly an academic thing, only just beginning to go out to the parishes, though many parochial clergymen knew of it—through the *Tracts* themselves as well as the report of Newman's mesmeric preaching. Sharing Newman's fine scholarship but lacking his brilliance and flair, Pusey grasped readily enough what was at stake in the Tractarian emphasis on the Holy Catholic Church as the 'pillar and ground of the truth' (First Timothy, 3:15), its founding documents to be scanned, as both Newman and Keble had recognized, in humility of heart. For Pusey too that distinctive moral-cum-intellectual 'ethos' was altogether crucial.

That did not make him temperamentally a leader. He was the 'hermit of Tom Quad', preferring to keep to his Christ Church study than to enter the world of the court, Government, or national organizations. A qualification must be entered, however, for his detailed counterplans to the Liberal Government's scheme for reforming the University of

Oxford in the early 1850s. In the upshot he became a member of the reconstituted 'Hebdomadal Board', to be made up of Heads of Houses along with holders of Chairs, successor to the body which had so harried Newman and the don who preceded him to Rome, William George Ward. It was ironic, and a turnaround that puzzled Keble. But at least that reform kept (for the moment) the University's Anglican 'Tests', though now they were re-expressed in negative form: an undertaking not to undermine the doctrine and discipline of the Established Church. Still, quite against Pusey's wishes lay Professors had arrived, the clerical monopoly vanquished.

If Pusey's energies, like Keble's, were given for preference to persons rather than organizations—and his letters of spiritual counsel and spiritual direction suggest as much, he would not in any case have been able easily to rally the Tractarian forces, since of its essence this was a nation-wide undertaking. His experience was too limited, one reason why the 'Tractarians justly venerated Pusey's sanctity and disregarded his judgment.'[32] That would change, as his increasing influence with the English Church Union, founded for the defence of Anglo-Catholics within the national Church, would go to show. But seared by bereavement and weighed down by a sense of deep personal unworthiness, if also gifted with a profound awareness of the blessings entailed in Incarnation and Atonement, Pusey remained an entirely God-obsessed man.

It would not be right, however, despite his reported 'heaviness', to call him a God-tormented man. Arthur Macdonald Allchin, who, as historian, could register the distance covered by Tractarianism in the period 1845 to 1965,[33] and, as participant-observer, saw the shoals ahead for classical Anglo-Catholicism in the modern period, summed up the man by taking as epigram the Preface to Pusey's *Parochial Sermons* of 1848. On Allchin's interpretation, in publishing his collected sermons Pusey had two highly positive aims in view. He wanted, firstly, to show Evangelicals that Tractarian concern for the 'sacraments and structures' of the Church did not impugn the 'absolute centrality' of Jesus Christ, just as Tractarian stress on good works did not come at the expense of the doctrine of grace. Despite the calumnies the Evangelical Alliance (later, the Church Association) had uttered against him and his followers, had he not said, 'I love the Evangelicals, because they loved Our Lord'?[34] In the second place, Allchin continued, Pusey wanted to issue a warning to all and sundry in the English-speaking world. 'Man's longing for God... is so ineradicable that if it is not assuaged by an experience and understanding of the perfect union of man with God in Christ through the Spirit, it will search for satisfaction through other and less adequate paths.'[35] Western Christians in the twentieth century would learn the truth of that.

After Newman

The sometime Master of the College of Guardians of the Shrine of our Lady of Walsingham, Peter George Cobb (died 2010), a scion of the key Oxford Anglo-Catholic institutions of Pusey House and St Stephen's House, put matters rather more brutally. Pusey was responsible for the 'lack of direction' of the 'Catholic party in the Church of England'. He was 'its only possible leader but he had no wish to act as such'.[36] He furnished scholarly assistance, yes, but it was not enough. He was 'persecuted' by bishops but simply bore it in silence, rather than turning it to (politically) good use. Cobb was thinking of the embarrassment of his public naming in a Pastoral Charge by Bishop Charles James Blomfield of London (1786–1857) for encouraging inappropriate Continental devotions, as well as the private inhibition from preaching in the Oxford diocese by Wilberforce.

Uneasy about Ritualism, since doctrine and spirituality should come first, and the law be respected in the meanwhile, Pusey's trumpet gave out an uncertain sound—though, admittedly, once the storm broke over their heads, he supported the Ritualist clergy to the best of his ability. Hitherto, in the *bon mot* of a contemporary, he had been 'like a man who has lit a fire, and is surprised and vexed because it does not confine itself to the bottom of the grate'.[37]

Pusey joined no Catholic societies except belatedly the English Church Union, even if he agreed to compose a Rule for the (priestly) Society of the Holy Cross. He held back from the Unionist attempts of his time, except for the curious instance of the *Eirenicon*, that 'olive branch fired from a catapult', written against exaggerated elements in popular Roman Catholic piety, sent formally to Keble, and answered by Newman who coined the witticism just quoted.[38] It was an odd way to set about making friends and influencing people.

Pusey's *Eirenicon*, and the follow-up texts he produced in the light of Newman's reply, will be touched on again in Chapter 10 under the general heading of 'Ecumenism and Mission'. But it may be said at once that what he could have achieved for Reunion in the circumstances of the Canterbury and Roman Communions of the time—or indeed, had he been whisked forward in Dr Who's Tardis to the world of Post-Conciliar Catholicism—is far from clear, even with hindsight. Nevertheless, it was Reunion, on 'Catholic' terms, that Pusey strongly desired. He had written in August 1845 to the still Anglican, and indeed, at that juncture, strongly anti-Roman, Manning, '[A]ll that I have seen of the temper of those engaged in the Reformation makes me feel that there was very much human in it, that it was not done as its ought. Our subsequent history makes me feel that we thus brought in a wrong element into our Church, which has been struggling with Catholicity ever since, and that one or the other must in time be ejected'.[39]

Pusey had no objection to the 'formal decrees of Rome', meaning the teachings of the Council of Trent. His difficulty was with popular Catholicism for which he found Newman's concept of development (useful when applied to the doctrines of the ancient Church in their relation to the apostolic preaching) to be so broad in its exculpation of everything found *de facto* in Latin Catholic theory or practice that it was useless as a tool for discernment and therefore dangerous. He had in mind extravagances in language about the Blessed Virgin, the abuse to which the system of Mass stipends and the quest for indulgences could lend themselves, the withholding of the Cup from the laity, and, not least, the extreme claims put forward by Neo-Ultramontanes for the Pope's universal jurisdiction and his teaching office.

In the *Eirenicon*, Pusey knew what was certain *de fide* at Rome, for Trent had told him. What he wanted was assurance about what was *not* 'of the faith' there and never would be. Newman in his reply would point out how hard the request was to meet. It would entail predicting all future doctrinal crises and attempts to deal with them by papally approved Councils till the end of time. Newman sought to defuse the anxieties about Latin practices by distinguishing between devotion which is free and therefore variable, and doctrine which is not. He did not really come to terms with the ultra-papalism to which Pusey had drawn attention, and which, in the early twenty-first century, still haunts the Roman Catholic Church. Not, that is, until he wrote against Gladstone's *The Vatican Decrees* in an Open Letter of his own, this time to the Duke of Norfolk, and fixed the dragon of *Überpapalismus* to the ground with one thrust of his lance.[40]

The *Eirenicon* was itself a reply to a pamphlet from the now Roman Catholic Manning, denying the Church of England's standing as a branch of the Catholic Church.[41] Pusey's reply, couched in the form of an Open Letter to Keble,[42] looked increasingly to what Rome and the separated Eastern Churches had in common as the true canon of Catholicity (a change from his early exclusive concentration on Christian Antiquity) — while also considering that the primary duty of Anglicans was not to Orientals but to the See of Rome, from which so much of their patrimony, as Western Christians, had come. A reunited West could 'then approach the East to settle differences which were not the same as those separating England from the rest of the Western patriarchate'.[43] It was a noble aspiration. But how was he to carry others with him, whether Anglican or Roman — or indeed, for that matter, the Orthodox? All he could say was: 'The longing for Reunion is supernatural. It is the fruit of the Divine love shed abroad in various hearts'.[44] But in truth that was to say much.

Counter-factual proposals

Counter-factually, there were Tractarians who, in different circumstances, might have occupied the role of leader. It does not say a great deal for Pusey that in the opinion of Richard William Church, Dean of St Paul's, in his classic study of the genesis of the Oxford Movement, Newman's conversion left Oxford at the mercy of the Liberals (the 'Neologians') thereafter.[45] Three possibilities, all of whom left the Canterbury communion for Rome, invite speculation about other directions for a movement deprived in 1845 of its natural head.

William Palmer (1811–79), a Fellow of Magdalen College, Oxford, in deacon's Orders, sought to reconcile the English and Eastern Orthodox Churches, as in his *Harmony of Anglican Doctrine with the Doctrine of the Eastern Church*, published the year after Newman's departure.[46] A decade later, in 1855, he followed in Newman's footsteps, living thereafter as a layman in Rome.[47]

Had Palmer remained an Anglican, and influenced the future development of Tractarianism, the Oxford Movement would clearly have taken a more Orientalising character than it did, though there were later Anglo-Catholics who looked quite as much to the East as to the Latin Church, departing in this respect from Pusey's programme. After Palmer's death Newman edited his 'Notes' on visits to senior Russian clergy and laity in the early 1840s.[48] Their estimate of the heretical character of much contained in the Thirty-Nine Articles was not encouraging.

Frederick Oakeley and William George Ward, both of Balliol College, Oxford, collaborated on running the Tractarian journal *The British Critic* which, however, was obliged to fold when old high churchmen withdrew support. Both men wrote themselves early out of the script. Frederick Oakeley (1802–80), briefly favoured by Lambeth Palace and named Whitehall Preacher,[49] left Oxford to become incumbent of the 'Margaret Chapel' in London's West End, where Gladstone was among his most supportive congregants. Oakeley's 'chapel in London was loved or feared as a pattern of High Anglican worship'.[50] His beautification of the setting of its worship, and notably the altar, is often regarded as the beginning of Tractarian Ritualism, though he might have been copying arrangements introduced by Newman's curate, John Rouse Bloxam (1807–91), in his parish church at Littlemore.[51] Beautification was highly suspect in some quarters. In 1844 a sermon was preached at Cheltenham: 'The Restoration of Churches is the Restoration of Popery'.[52]

As a Roman Catholic, Oakeley went on to write substantial studies of the liturgical rites, one of which was translated into Italian for the benefit of masters of ceremonies. Joining Newman at his Littlemore 'monastery' in 1845, he was ill-at-ease in his Anglican allegiance, having lost his licence in the diocese of London owing to his statement that—basing himself on the arguments surrounding *Tract 90*—he felt at liberty to preach all Roman doctrine. Oakeley preceded Newman into the Roman Communion by a matter of a few weeks. Had he persevered as an Anglican, it would have been harder to allege that the development from Tractarianism to Ritualist Anglo-Catholicism was no natural transition but a betrayal of the original inspiration of the Oxford Fathers, made possible by a leap of generations.[53]

William George Ward (1812–82), the author of the *Ideal of the Christian Church*, had concluded that the only hope of intellectual salvation for the Church of England lay in corporate submission to the Church of Rome,[54] That work had played a decisive role in the difficulties of Tractarians with the University of Oxford, until Ward emulated Oakeley by preceding Newman into Roman communion in September 1845.[55] Debarred in the period as a married man from Ordination in the Roman Catholic Church, his preferred path was that of a lay professor, teaching ethics, metaphysics and, eventually, dogmatic theology, at a Hertfordshire seminary ('Old Hall, Ware') as well as becoming editor of the *Dublin Review*.[56] Ward would turn the *Review* into a formidable engine directed against the theological positions of Liberal Catholics defined over against an uncompromising Neo-Ultramontanism, though even that latter recipe was food for the stomachs of some Anglo-Papalists of the future.[57]

Had Ward survived as a priest of the Church of England, and taken over the leadership of the movement, it would have become much earlier and more widely an Anglo-Papalist movement than in fact it became. Not that the element of Anglo-Papalism was in the longer term insignificant, especially after 1900.[58] On the Centenary of Keble's Assize Sermon, which coincided with the 1933 Holy Year called by Pius XII a petition of Anglo-Papalists, signed by that body's leading clerical and lay figures, asserted that 'union with Rome is the logical and highest goal and the natural consummation of the movement celebrated by the present Centenary'.[59]

And, after naming that trio, what, in conclusion, of Dean Church himself? As the only one of this quartet of figures to remain within the Anglican fold, Richard William Church (1815–90) merits a touch more biography. Son of a wine merchant (his parents settled in Florence), educated at a strict Evangelical school at Bristol, followed by Wadham College, Oxford, he had become a Fellow of Oriel, and taken Anglican Orders, in 1839. Erstwhile disciple of Newman (as junior proctor he persuaded his senior colleague to veto the public censure of *Tract 90* in 1846), he came to 'glory'—his own choice of verb—in the 'inconsistencies' of the English Church. At once despite and owing to his Tractarianism, he was made Dean of St Paul's by the first 'Tractarian' Prime Minister, William Ewart Gladstone. Church's doctrinal and liturgical sobriety has gained from one biographer the sobriquet the 'Anglican response to Newman', the Newman who, on this implied view, was simply too capriciously or at least too subtly brilliant for his own good, or the good of the Church.[60] (One need only think of the uses to which the *Essay on the Development of Christian Doctrine* was put by the late nineteenth century Roman Catholic Modernists and their successors.) But Church, withdrawing into literary and historical pursuits, was not the coming man either. 'Cometh the hour, cometh the man' was not a proverb whose truth Anglo-Catholicism verified.

2

What happened next

For reasons well beyond its deficit of effective leadership Puseyism made no early inroads into the English Establishment—into what remained of England's *ancien régime*, the unitary post-Restoration Church-State complex.¹ Not, that is, until Gladstone became prime minister for the first time in 1868. Sir Robert Peel (1788–1850) had not ventured to promote its adherents and his successor, Lord John Russell (1792–1878), was openly hostile. The sense of urgency of the Tractarian leaders at the Movement's launching in 1833 derived, after all, from a critical juncture in Church-State relations when Whigs such as Russell were precisely the enemy in their intent of re-making the Church (initially in Ireland) through a conscious if gradualist deconfessionalization of the State. It was not to be expected that Whigs, or Tory converts to Liberalism like Peel, would do Tractarians any favours.² But some independent initiatives helped.

In 1846, the year when Russell succeeded Peel, R. W. Church, in tandem with the chancery lawyer Thomas Henry Haddam (1814–73), founded a successor to the *British Critic*. This was *The Guardian*, not to be confused with the modern daily of that name. Surviving till 1951, in the twentieth century it was best known for its serialization of *The Screwtape Letters* by C. S. Lewis (1898–1963). What Puseyites saw as Russell's tyrannical attitude had undermined their confidence in the exercise of the Royal Supremacy to which the early Tractarians had once looked for support over against an unfriendly Whig Parliament. Consolidation of opinion through print media was a characteristically nineteenth century alternative to the loss of influence at the political centre. The Press and news media were that century's 'Fourth Estate'. Anglo-Catholic newspapers were going to be important for the future, as Chapter 8 will explain. A succession of crises would mean their aid was sorely needed.

First crisis: Gorham and the Privy Council

Diminishing confidence in the Royal Supremacy predisposed the Tractarians to the perils of a crisis mentality when the 'Gorham Case' broke. Chronic anxiety was largely justified. Unfortunately for Puseyites, the 'No Popery' outburst which followed the recreation of the Roman hierarchy in 1850, trumpeted forth in the Pastoral Letter 'Out of the Flaminian Gate' by Cardinal Nicholas Wiseman (1802–65), predisposed the British public quite as much against Tractarianism as against a revival of Roman Catholicism. 'Wiseman had not only put Catholic chapels in peril but unwittingly caused an upsurge of English feeling against the disciples of the Oxford Movement.'[3] Rioting at St Barnabas, Pimlico, the most 'advanced' Anglo-Catholic parish in the capital, and so a flagship church, showed how 'No Popery' and 'No Puseyism' went together. 'Papal Aggression' aggravated the English awareness of post-Reformation Protestant identity.[4] 'During the next few years the Anglo-Catholics attained the zenith of their unpopularity, the government of the Church of England moved toward the Evangelicals, the alliance between low churchmen and Dissenters was restored and cemented. Parochial life was subject to strain. Laymen pestered bishops or archdeacon with complaints about their parsons and demanded disciplines. Vicars who wanted to introduce a new and reverent custom into their church looked nervously at their flocks… Observers called spies by the unfriendly were sent to parishes of notorious Tractarians to report on ritual.'[5] This state of affairs proved to be inter-generational, at least until the later 1930s. It did not endear Anglo-Catholics to Roman Catholics. The pity was, it failed to arouse a sense of common cause, for the same fundamental interpretation of Christian tradition was at stake. Admittedly, close association with Papists would have added still further to Anglo-Catholic woes.

The Gorham Case was the first test of Puseyites' mettle. George Cornelius Gorham (1787–1857), by background a Cambridge Evangelical, but now vicar of St Just in Penwith, had advertised in the *Ecclesiastical Gazette* for a curate free of Tractarianism. That alerted his ordinary, Bishop Henry Philpotts (1778–1869) of Exeter, a rare Tractarian sympathizer on the Bench, to trouble ahead. Cornish parishes offered meagre pickings, but Charles Christopher Pepys, Earl of Cottenham (1781–1851), twice Lord Chancellor, presented Gorham to the rich Devonian living of Bramford Speke, close by Philpotts' see city. Philpotts refused to induct him on the ground of his flagrant Calvinistic denial of Baptismal regeneration. Mr Gorham lost his case against the bishop at the Court of Arches and appealed to the Judicial Committee of the Privy Council which promptly overturned the ecclesiastical judgment. (A decade or so previously, the Committee had recently extended its remit, replacing the High Court of Delegates, a crown court but with lawyers trained in both canon and civil law—and at one time with bishop-members who, however, had disappeared in the eighteenth century.) The Church was now in thrall to a body of common lawyers. In Tractarian circles the 'talk of secession and disruption' was, in Owen Chadwick's ominous words, 'no longer vague.'[6]

The Gorham Judgment unsettled consciences—Manning and Robert Isaac Wilberforce (1802–57), both archdeacons, the former a future Archbishop of Westminster and the latter a theologian of considerable stature, were two of its casualties. Yet Puseyites could take comfort from the fact that, after Gorham, high church opinion rallied to the notion that Something Must Be Done. Bishop Richard Bagot (1782–1854), now ensconced at Bath and Wells (he had been Newman's kindly bishop at Oxford), petitioned the Crown, and his fellow bishops, for the setting up of a spiritual court and the right to synodical government—which was as much as to say the restoration of the Convocations of Canterbury and York (composed in each case of two houses, consisting of 'upper' and 'lower' clergy), and held in suspended animation since 1717. That plea found a sympathetic hearing in the ear of the hapless Coalition prime minister George Hamilton-Gordon, the Earl of Aberdeen (1784–1860), who as a Scot had at least the merit that he 'never saw the Church as a mere department of State'.[7]

Yet Aberdeen was worried. If Convocation turned into a General Assembly on the Scottish model, might there not be a 'disruption' in England comparable to the 1843 'Great Disruption' (over lay patronage of ministerial appointments) in Scotland? So while Convocation was brought out of limbo (initially in the Province of Canterbury and a few years later in the Northern Province likewise), for its first decade of revived existence its members were disallowed by the Crown from formulating canons. It remained, accordingly, a talking shop during those years, though Aberdeen need not have worried: agreement in its lower houses to any initiatives of the higher clergy was far from easily secured in the years that followed.

Meanwhile, when the conversion to Rome of Rudolph Fielding, the future Earl of Denbigh (1823–92), led to withdrawing from Anglican hands the church he was building for Tractarian use at Pantasaph in Flintshire and giving it instead to Roman Catholic friars, quite a row ensued in which Anglicans started 'talking of oaths, and tests' and 'binding assurances' that certain persons 'would not join the Church of Rome'.[8] In the end other strategies prevailed. Bishop Bagot and some who thought like him joined with Anglo-Catholics in signing a letter that reaffirmed Baptismal Regeneration and denied the authority of the

Privy Council in spiritual matters. A copy was deposited at St Alban's, Holborn, one of the 'Slum Ritualist' churches (to be described in Chapter 3) and exhibited in a symbolically well-chosen spot above the Baptismal font. Behind the framed document was placed an inscription which ran, 'I acknowledge one Baptism for the forgiveness of sins.'[9]

Yet old 'high and dry' bishops like Bagot were disappearing, and Tractarians were not happy under a new Archbishop of Canterbury, John Bird Sumner (1780–1862), an Evangelical and 'bitter opponent of the Oxford Movement'.[10] Aberdeen wangled Walter Kerr Hamilton (1808–69) into place in Salisbury, the first Anglican bishop to carry a crozier. Otherwise, Queen Victoria had her way in banning Tractarians from preferment till Gladstone became her nemesis. The Prince Consort, doubtless speaking for his wife, advised Aberdeen: 'A system of marked disfavour should be adopted and steadily persevered in towards those who promulgated "principles likely to disturb the peace of the Church"'. And Albert went on cynically to observe that 'even the most active, ambitious and talented of the High Church party were not likely long to hold principles which permanently excluded them from preferment'.[11] The Prince could presume on the support of public opinion. Evangelicals, by contrast, were popular in the country. They were also popular with Aberdeen's successor as prime minister, Lord Palmerston (1784–1865), who preferred simple Godly men, those least like himself. In 1847 Palmerston threatened to override the Bishop of London (and any bishop) who refused to withdrew licence to minister from overseas chaplains whose (modest) ceremonial changes had irritated expatriates.[12]

Pusey himself was dead set against all Parliamentary intervention in Church affairs—and even against Crown appointments if handled by whatever minister of the Crown who could best secure a following in Parliament. At least in the Colonies, where for the most part the State did not subsidise the Church, senior bishops, he thought, could furnish a *terna* of names for the Crown to choose among without undermining its Supremacy. For Pusey's 'theo-political' objection was above all to a religiously mixed Parliament, not to the role of the king. 'Pusey was so critical of ministerial interference in church matters both in the past and present, precisely because he felt that it stifled and checked the true role of the Crown as a "nursing father".'[13] He defended his wish for a church veto on 'bad' nominations on the grounds that 'His Majesty's Prerogative would gain more than it would lose by taking from him the nominal appointment and giving the real one to that party who we know are always surest to stand by him'.[14] Like Keble, he held no brief for Becket and the Gregorian Reform, unlike in this Richard Hurrell Froude (1803–36), early Tractarianism's sharpest critic of the English

Reformation—not to mention the 'Romanisers', beginning with Ward and Newman.[15]

Appellate royal jurisdiction, intended for the defence of persons against wrongful decisions by episcopal courts, was not, to Pusey's mind, itself Erastian. But before the Gorham Judgment, the Crown had never previously taken it upon itself to adjudicate heresy. Thus Pusey's 1850 treatise *The Royal Supremacy not an Arbitrary Authority*,[16] which offered the measuring rod of not just pre-Reformation but more specifically pre-Conquest practice. He did not have Keble's veneration for Charles I, the 'Royal Martyr (reigned 1625–49).[17] But neither had he yet noticed Victoria's visceral disapproval of the theological doctrine, and the associated sacramental and devotional practice, for which he stood.

Civil life in Victorian England was moving inexorably further away from the Caroline order of things. The State, Pusey told Gladstone reprovingly in April 1849, was now assuming a 'nondescript' character which would end up by being 'infidel'—a prophecy the correctness of which can hardly be doubted.[18] And if a Parliament of laypersons of all beliefs and none could not rule the Church, neither, in Pusey's view, could a gathering of believers not all of whom were in the apostolic succession with its exclusively episcopal 'charism of truth'. On the eve of the restoration of Convocation, Pusey was writing to Gladstone in January 1852 to warn him against any notion of introducing laypeople into synodical gatherings, never mind giving them, as had happened in the former American colonies, a veto over episcopal appointments.[19] The result had been—among other things—the abolition in the United States of the use in church of the Athanasian Creed.[20] 'I look with terror on any admission of laity into Synods. It at once invests them with an ecclesiastical office, which will develop itself sooner or later, I believe, to the destruction of the Faith.'[21]

The role of Gladstone

William Ewart Gladstone (1809–98) was plainly significant in this narrative, being key to the rise of Anglo-Catholics to positions of influence in the Church. But at the time of Newman's secession Gladstone was undergoing a slow conversion of his own, from belief in the confessional State to acceptance of a neutral State—which, he profoundly hoped, would not live down to Pusey's prediction. As with Keble and Pusey some retrospect is necessary to understand the direction of Gladstone's journey.

As a serious, and religiously sensitive, young man, Gladstone had read himself into a position favourable to the Fathers and the seventeenth century Anglican divines, especially on the question of Holy

Baptism. (Once again, as in the still future Gorham Case, the Calvinist theology of Reformation-minded Anglicans, favoured by female members of Gladstone's family, was the obvious systematic alternative to 'Catholicism'.) He came to see the continuity of the Prayer Book with the Catholic past, having observed liturgical forms in use in Belgium and France, during Continental tours that ended in Rome where for the first time he felt the pain of Christian disunity.[22] In Perry Butler's view, though Gladstone had read Number 2 of the *Tracts* (Newman, on 'The Catholic Church'), his view of Church, ministry, and sacraments owed more to old high churchmen such as the Irish layman Alexander Knox (1757–1831) and his co-national William Palmer of Worcester College, Oxford (1803–85, not to be confused with the namesake at Magdalen). And Gladstone's doctrine of salvation was always strongly Augustinian (and thus remained *relatively* close to Calvin's).[23] Not an 'advanced' Anglo-Catholic, then, he never seems to have made use of auricular Confession—which does not imply opposition to the practice. Many Tractarians said of recourse to the sacrament, 'All may, some should, none must'. And he had occasional scruples about prayers for the dead, an echo perhaps of that radically Augustinian doctrine of grace.

Nevertheless, from 1841 onwards Gladstone regularly attended the principal Tractarian worship centre in London, the Margaret Street Chapel (later All Saints, Margaret Street), Catholicized by Frederick Oakeley, with a round of daily offices and Eucharistic celebrations on Sundays and holydays. He wrote out his own prayers in English and Latin for Holy Communion, prayers that expressed a distinctly Catholic understanding of the Eucharistic Presence. He belonged to a fraternity with a Rule set out by Keble, prescribing regular works of charity and almsgiving as well as a rhythm of prayer for Church fasts and feasts. He would have seen St Margaret's gloriously rebuilt in polychrome by William Butterfield and watched as the All Saints Sisters of the Poor, one of the most successful of the new Anglican Sisterhoods, made their foundation there. Tractarian architecture and art, Tractarian Sisterhoods (to be discussed in Chapters 5 and 9 respectively): these were familiar features of his world.

In 1838, some five years after entering Parliament, he wrote his book on Church and State—this at a time when he looked, optimistically, to an Oxford Movement empowered to renew Anglicanism, making it capable not only of absorbing Dissent but of forming the basis for a truly national Catholic church. In *The State in its Relations with the Church*, Gladstone argued that the State has a conscience, and that conscience demands support for whatever religion it may deem best for the country.[24] Reviewing the book in the *British Critic*, Keble was unconvinced. Too much turned on appeal to natural law rather than to what the inspired prophets had to say about the 'foster fathers and nursing mothers' (thus Isaiah 49:23) who would be Christian kings and queens under the New and Everlasting Covenant. Gladstone had rehearsed what were largely secular considerations while ignoring the way the British State was actually usurping ecclesiastical authority.

Keble's tones, Butler assures us, were authentically those of the 'new' or 'apostolical' high churchmanship. Only the spiritual integrity of the Church ultimately matters.[25] Yet at this juncture Gladstone could not accept it was more important for the Church to be free than for the nation to be Christian. He thought the State could rightly 'interfere with' the Church in regard to 'temporalities' and even, for that matter, the 'external' aspects of ecclesiastical discipline as well. In 1841 Gladstone published an expanded, if also revised, edition of *The State in its Relations with the Church*.[26]

His ideal fell apart with the Maynooth Grant of 1845 — the concession whereby the government to which he belonged began to support financially the training of Roman Catholic priests in Ireland. It triggered a short-lived resignation from Peel's cabinet. And when at the end of that year Gladstone agreed to return to Peel's government as Secretary of State for the Colonies, his developing administrative experience gave him further pause. Only with the greatest difficulty could his general theory be extended to those overseas possessions where the Church of England was beginning to expand into an 'Anglican Communion'.[27] There was more to come. A debate on education for factory children showed him how unrealistic was his expectation that Protestant Dissenters would rally to a reinvigorated Church of England. And dealing with the 'Dissenters and Chapels Bill', which gave Unitarians legal rights to chapels they had inherited from English Presbyterians (many of the latter had abandoned Trinitarianism in the eighteenth century), 'heightened his churchmanship' but lowered the level of his 'church-and-statemanship'.[28]

The concept of a Church Establishment had to be adapted, Gladstone now thought, to a modern representative governmental system. In March 1845 he had already written to the still Anglican Newman about the problems involved. The Christian 'figure' of the English polity still endured in the civic institutions, so one must use what opportunities for good that allowed, 'however they may be surrounded with violent moral contradictions'. Where the State still acts 'as if' it has a religious conscience, then keep up Christian criteria in judgment and action. Otherwise, take 'social justice according to the lower, but now prevalent, idea for a guide'.[29]

This policy would, in effect, be Gladstone's own version of life 'after Newman' and license his use of the Crown prerogative to promote

After Newman

Puseyites, thus extending the Anglo-Catholic outlook in a Church otherwise condemned by history to ultimate uncoupling from rule by the State. By 1848 his 'remedy' was patient confidence in the 'gradual but inevitable spread of the Catholic ethos within the Church [and] the call for greater freedom to rule and order itself in doctrinal matters'.[30]

As Prime Minister in four Liberal administrations (1868–74; 1880–5; 1886; 1892–4), Gladstone engineered numerous Tractarian appointments. He made George Moberley (1803–85) Bishop of Winchester in 1869. He appointed Pusey's biographer Henry Parry Liddon, the chief dogmatician left to the Movement after Robert Wilberforce had left it, a canon of St Paul's in 1870 and Chancellor of the cathedral in 1886. Richard William Church became its Dean in 1871. James Bowling Mozley (1813–78), two of whose brothers had married two of Newman's sisters, Gladstone made a canon of Worcester and then Regius Professor of Divinity at Oxford in 1871. James Russell Woodford (1820–85), one of Archdeacon Denison's defenders against his condemnation by Archbishop Sumner, became Bishop of Ely in 1873, Edward King (1829–1910) — with some claim to be the first Tractarian saint[31] — Professor of Moral and Pastoral Theology at Oxford in 1873, and Bishop of Lincoln in 1895. George Howard Wilkinson (1833–1907), later Primus of the Scottish Episcopal Church, Gladstone had appointed Bishop of Truro in 1883. The founder of the Christian Social Union Henry Scott Holland was made a canon of St Paul's in 1884, and William Stubbs (1825–1901), sometime Regius Professor of Modern History at Oxford, Bishop of Chester in 1884. Stubbs would be translated to the see of Oxford in 1888, though this was the doing of Robert Gascoyne-Cecil, Marquis of Salisbury (1830–1903), Gladstone's Conservative successor. Edward Talbot (1844–1934), the first Warden of Keble College, Oxford, and thus a notable keeper of the Tractarian flame, became Bishop of Rochester in 1895.[32]

These appointments were pushed through despite the disapproval of the monarch whose preference was for scholarly clergymen without too pronounced views. Victoria reserving her special enmity for the 'extremes' of Evangelicalism and Tractarianism. The latter's rise to intra-ecclesial influence by the time the twentieth century opened is, without Gladstone, simply unthinkable.

New crisis: the threat from Liberalism

After Gorham, Pusey's next crisis was the *furore* over the 1860 publication of *Essays and Reviews*, a collection of Anglican essays that argued for treating the Bible as 'any other book' — in other words, not through the lens, and with the presuppositions, of a properly ecclesial hermeneutic, but by applying the scholarly methods of the 'higher criticism' as that would be practiced in, for example, Oxford's 'Greats' School when reading pagan texts inherited from antiquity.[33] Pusey knew from his early exposure to German theological scholarship what the problems with that were—and had already had a brush or two with minimalists over the 'Hampden Controversy', both when Renn Hampden, who had Latitudinarian inclinations, became Regius Professor of Theology at Oxford in 1836 and on his elevation to the see of Hereford by Russell—a deliberate smack in the face to Puseyites—in 1847. The attack on the supernatural inspiration of the sacred writers, on the historicity of miracles, on the possible compatibility of the opening chapters of Genesis with scientific cosmology, and on the eschatology of Scripture: these were commonplaces in the German Protestant faculties but not among the general reading public in England. For one contributor, H. B. Wilson, the very idea of a National Church implies a latitude as broad as the nation, with an indefinitely extended range of opinion in matters of belief—even using what could be considered a version of Newman's *Tract 90* when it came to the Thirty-Nine Articles: 'when a man "alloweth" or "acknowledgeth" the Book of Articles to be true and agreeable to the Word of God, he may with perfect propriety allow or acknowledge that which he does not approve or that which he is merely unprepared to contradict'.[34] Where did it leave the patristic orthodoxy of the Church if authors of this school were to be considered Anglicans in good standing?[35] Not that the essayists cared what Anglo-Catholics thought. *Essays and Reviews* dismissed them as 'this last monster out of the deep', threatening to bring back to Protestant Europe the 'shadows of the twelfth century'.[36]

Pusey's principal anxiety was not, however, the book itself, for which his bishop, Samuel Wilberforce, managed to elicit a vote of disapproval from the Convocation of Canterbury. Rather, it was the decision of the Crown, within the decade, to appoint one of the clerical essayists, Frederick Temple (1821–1902), to the see of Exeter. Writing to *The Guardian* in October 1869, Pusey thought Temple's consecration raised the possibility of irresponsibly selected bishops becoming a 'curse' to the Church, a prospect for which Disestablishment would be the only possible remedy. His was not the only voice raised in protest and in 1870, Temple withdrew the offending article. That the *Church Times* had not supported Pusey in the matter might be taken as an indicator for the future. Unlike the Oxford Fathers, Anglo-Catholics could be willing to accept heterodox bishops if only they practiced toleration. In that case, the silence was significant, even ominous: an early warning sign of a future Anglo-Catholicism amounting to 'Congregationalism with bishops'.

Fortunately for his peace of mind, Pusey did not live long enough to witness a second essay collection, this time—cruellest cut—from those who considered themselves the original Tractarians' spiritual children. It might have been thought that Pusey's death in 1882 left his biographer Henry Liddon, recently retired Dean Ireland's Professor of Exegesis at Oxford, Chancellor of St Paul's Cathedral, and a priest who had refused more than one offer of a bishopric, in a strong position to defend the Puseyite theological heritage. In that heritage nothing was more important than the trustworthiness of the Gospels as received by the patristic Church.

Before the decade was over, this proved too optimistic an assessment. Not so easy to ignore were the more-than-ever audible siren voices of Germanic scholarship—and the possibilities opened for a reconciliation of theology and philosophy by the rise of English Idealism, itself a pup from the sire of its German originators, notably Hegel, as mediated through the Balliol philosopher Thomas Hill Green (1836–82). In 1889 *Lux Mundi*, edited by Charles Gore, future Bishop of, successively, Worcester, Birmingham, and Oxford, renewed the debate over biblical inspiration and raised questions about the credibility of the Conciliar Christology constructed from the New Testament witness in the Church of the Fathers.[37] 'Liberal Catholicism', in its intellectual (rather than political) and Anglican (as distinct from Roman) embodiment, was about to be born.

Inter alia, Gore had thought Jesus mistaken about the authorship of Psalm 110 (a crucial psalm for the Messianic claims). It was not actually the work of the historical King David. He explained this disparity by a self-limitation in the knowledge of the incarnate Word—brought about by his 'kenosis' or act of self-humiliation in the Incarnation. This was to take a sledge-hammer to smash a nut: 'David', on the lips of Jesus in the exchange reported, may mean the literary persona of a quintessentially Davidic king quite as much as the physical son of Jesse. But Liddon, for his part, did not think in terms of rhetorical tropes and literary genres. The only relevant distinction he was willing to allow was that between limitedness in the knowledge of Jesus (acceptable) and fallibility (unacceptable). Moreover, Liddon was distressed as much by Gore's 'solution' as by the problem Gore meant it to solve. 'He willed so to restrain the beams of Deity as to observe the limits of the science of His age, and He puts Himself in the same relation to its historical knowledge.'[38] The notion that the Logos, in becoming man, might have partially divested himself of an attribute of Divinity made worse, not better, the claim that parts of the Scriptures could be untrustworthy. It was neither historically patristic nor faithfully biblical. The doctrine of the divine simplicity, an indispensable doctrine for any rationally warrantable concept of God, requires that everything God *has* by way of attributes that God necessarily *is*.

What happened next

In Owen Chadwick's words: 'Liddon regarded *Lux Mundi* as the betrayal of everything for which Pusey and the Tractarians stood.'[39] This was an over-reaction. It was because the Late Tractarians thinkers were, as 'Catholics', not exponents of *sola scriptura* in an unqualified sense of that phrase that they felt able to allow for dubieties on such matters as mythopoeisis, idealization, and historical retrospection as factors in the making of the Bible—a Bible which should always be read in the illuminating context of the Church's tradition.

But Liddon was by no means wholly wrong. The original Tractarians were fully committed to the plenary (which does not necessarily imply verbal) inspiration of Scripture, and forewarned their readers (through, for example, *Tract* 13) against any concessions to the mind of an 'irreverent presumptuous age on this most sacred of all subjects'.[40] What must Liddon have felt, he who had put forward Gore as first Principal of Pusey House? Liddon died the September of the year Gore's essay was published. There were those who said *Lux Mundi* killed him.

Editor as well as contributor, founder of the Community of the Resurrection, and nominal guardian of Pusey's patrimony at Oxford's 'Pusey House', it took Gore quite some time to recover from the *débâcle* that followed *Lux Mundi*. George Anthony Denison (1805–96), Archdeacon of Taunton (sometime fellow of Oriel College, Oxford, he had been one of the chief objectors to Temple's appointment at Exeter), left the English Church Union when the latter declined to act. The Trustees of Pusey House debated whether Gore should be asked to resign. They were persuaded of the opposite course by Edward Talbot, the only conservative Tractarian on the Bench.[41] Gore sought to make amends by writing a new Preface to *Lux Mundi* as well as his Bampton Lectures on the Incarnation, a work that satisfied some opponents though by no means all.[42] He came to distinguish between what the incarnate Word had positively taught, and what, in talking with Jews of his day, he merely let pass in speaking. But when in 1901 Gore was made Bishop of Worcester after some years as a canon of Westminster, the protests were renewed.

The protesters need not have worried. Gore had always thought there were limits to historical criticism. As bishop he became a model of Catholic orthodoxy, a defender of the Creeds, including the most disputed of supernaturalist Gospel claims—the Virginal Conception and Bodily Resurrection of Jesus (and was willing to call for the expulsion of clergy who denied these tenets).[43] He proved a doughty supporter of union not only with the Orthodox but even, at the time of the Malines Conversations, with the See of Rome. His sticking point was really the same with both, though he was more inclined to press it with Roman Catholics: treating Tradition as not only illuminating Scripture (accept-

After Newman

able) but complementing it (unacceptable).⁴⁴ If more evidence were needed of Gore's capacity for resistance to the *Zeitgeist*, perhaps his outrage at the decision of the 1930 Lambeth Conference to reverse the ban of its 1920 predecessor on Contraception may do as well as any.⁴⁵

Hopeful signs

Meanwhile, a sign of a brighter future to come was the immensely learned and robustly orthodox Darwell Stone's appointment in 1888 as Principal of the strongly Anglo-Catholic 'Dorchester Missionary College', in the historic village of that name just south of Oxford. Stone (1859–1941) would be Gore's successor (after two *interregna*) at Pusey House. During a long tenure, from 1909 to 1934, with a firm hand and a quasi-omniscient historical erudition, Stone consciously maintained the theological tradition of Pusey, Church, and Liddon. Gore's immediate successor, Robert Ottley (1856–1933) had himself produced a Christological textbook which, though published the year after *The Incarnation of the Son of God*, made grateful mention in its foreword of Liddon whilst ignoring Gore—though this may be an accident of publishing history for the two books did come out close together.⁴⁶ (Ottley's own successor and Stone's immediate predecessor, Vincent Stuckey Stratton Coles [1845–1929], interrupted the line of theologian-principals by chiefly confining himself to pastoral care of the undergraduates and the writing of hymns.)

In the last decades of the century, Anglo-Catholics were heartened too by the publication of what became the standard Tractarian history of the English Reformation. This was the work of Richard Watson Dixon (1833–1900), not a professional historian (the concept was only just emerging) but a gifted amateur. A minor figure—both poet and painter—in the Pre-Raphaelite Brotherhood before his ordination in 1858, and thereafter a teacher at Highgate School where Gerard Manley Hopkins (1844–89) was one of his pupils, Dixon's ministry was largely spent in the diocese of Carlisle and, at the end of his life, in the newly created diocese of Newcastle. His *History of the Church of England from the Abolition of the Roman Jurisdiction* was published in six volumes between 1877 and 1890.⁴⁷ It emphasized the distinction between the disputable theology of the Reformers and the serendipitous way in which the fundamentally Catholic structures of the pre-Reformation Church, reflected in the Prayer Book and Ordinal, managed nonetheless to survive their shortcomings. This would become a standard Anglo-Catholic trope, somewhat dented in later twentieth century and early twenty-first century scholarship.⁴⁸ To the charge that the Tractarians were losing sight of the distinctive doctrines of the Reformers, the *Church Times* had made pugnacious reply in a leader of 28 January 1870. 'We do not lose sight of them at all. We are busy in hunting them down, and have no intention of foregoing the chase until we have extirpated them.'[49]

That went beyond the usual claim for a wider continuity with the ancient British, Anglo-Saxon, and mediaeval Church as put forward by such historians as William Stubbs and Mandell Creighton (1843–1901), both of whom were simultaneously clerics and academics. But the continuity theme was sounded frequently enough for one student of 'Historians and the Church of England' to claim that the predominant later nineteenth century Anglican historiography, far from asserting a Protestant national identity, 'promoted a Catholic, albeit anti-papal, idea of Englishness'.[50] At a time when the historian's craft was held in enormously high esteem—*A Short History of the English People* by John Richard Green (1837–83) easily outsold both the novels of George Eliot (1819–80) and the epoch-making *Origin of Species* by Charles Darwin (1809–82),[51] this silent revolution would surely have its future effects.

Best of all, for the Anglo-Catholic cause, those convinced of the truth of Tractarianism were moving out into the parishes, bringing a message once carried to parsonages on horseback or circulated among the restricted readership of Church periodicals. Hurrell Froude had urged the Movement to go to the urban masses, whom Evangelicalism had barely touched. Pusey gave the lead by the anonymous benefaction which created St Saviour's, Leeds, with its 'college' of priests, to serve the working population of that booming Victorian commercial and industrial city. The church was consecrated within a month of Newman's secession, though the hostility it encountered from the Ripon diocese, including the Vicar of Leeds, presaged a bumpy ride ahead.[52] But Tractarians persisted. '[H]owever small the Oxford Movement might have been demographically, it was emphatically a growing force. In 1840 it boasted just eighty-one incumbents; by 1870 that had risen to 442, much greater than the expansion of the Church of England at large during the same period. In 1840, in parochial terms the Oxford Movement was miniscule; by 1870 it was still a small but clearly expanding minority within Anglicanism'.[53]

In sometimes unlikely spots, Tractarian churchmanship appeared overnight like mushrooms, instead of putting out lateral shoots from Oxford in the manner of strawberry runners.[54] Cambridge graduates appear to have been more numerous among the second generation of Tractarians than their Oxford equivalents, and a considerable number of Tractarian clergy were unbeneficed—leading to the likelihood of much itinerancy. Tractarian churchwardens—a category usually occupied by shopkeepers and farmers—could crop up anywhere, without benefit of Oxonian connexions. And of course when new churches were built or old ones reordered in a 'Camden Society' style, it might be architects rather than clergy, lay patrons, or churchwardens, who set the tone.[55]

Typically, where 'Catholicization' of parishes took place it meant the introduction of daily non-Eucharistic offices, a weekly Eucharistic celebration, and—usually discreet—encouragement of Confession at any rate on occasions that seemed especially to demand it. The early Tractarian doctrines of 'reserve' and 'economy' played their part in reducing outright opposition, whether external or internal, to this Catholicizing process. Those who expected to attend Mattins on a Sunday morning in the parish church but in the afternoon a prayer-meeting in a Dissenting chapel (recent research suggests these too were likely to be farmers and tradesmen), would not rally lightly to the new Anglo-Catholic concept of parochial life. But through a gradual osmosis even parishes of this stamp could become communities where the possession of 'full Catholic privileges' was eventually esteemed a mark of honour.

Changes afoot

Meanwhile large organizational changes were taking place in the wider Church of England. These changes transformed the scene the first Tractarians had looked upon and required a new response. 'Lay Readers' were instituted from the end of the 1860s, allowing missions in remote hamlets where there was no vicar, though for forty years the dioceses were few where they were permitted to preach—a permission that ate into the 'prophetic office' of presbyters in the apostolic ministry. The duties, and privileges, of the latter had been, after all, the topic of the trail-blazing opening *Tract* of the *Tracts for the Times*. More favourable to Anglo-Catholic interests was the 1868 legislation whereby church rates were abolished, for now the citizen qua citizen ceased to have power in his parish church—and this at a time when the layman qua churchman had no constitutional power either, a situation that would persist until the Parochial Church Councils Measure of 1921. In this blessed interval Tractarian incumbents had less to fear from 'No Puseyites' sentiment among locals, or even from their own possibly Protestant-minded congregants. In 1871 the Irish Church, whose 'temporalities' issue had triggered the Oxford Movement, was disestablished. Unlike in Wales half a century later, since the political, social, and religious context was very different, that greatly weakened the now independent 'Church of Ireland'. But there had never been much prospect for its Puseyite Catholicization in the first place.

In the same year, the Universities Test Act initiated the loss of Anglican hegemony at Oxbridge and in Durham, the third and most recent of the Church of England's Universities. Clerical Fellowships were now abolished at Oxford and Cambridge. The combined academic/pastoral ministry of tutors in priest's orders, so dear to Newman and Pusey, was more-or-less at an end. After 1871 there was no need for Oxbridge dons to be in Holy Orders. The unintended consequence was that clerical learning declined. Henceforth only private means or a comfy benefice could bolster its chances. There was some compensation in the setting up of the Honours School of Theology at Oxford and the Theological Tripos at Cambridge (King's College, London, an Anglican foundation, managed to retain ecclesiastical tests in its School of Theology). But University theology would not now necessarily be Church theology — as became apparent in the later twentieth century with the transformation of Faculties of Theology into schools of 'Religious Studies', adrift from Christianity at large.

Belief that Royal Commissions would continue to secularise the old universities gave an impetus to the creation of Theological Colleges such as Cuddesdon, just outside Oxford, whose bishop, Samuel Wilberforce, initially entrusted it to Pusey's premier disciple Liddon, a highly energetic Vice-Principal until Wilberforce was accused of succouring Popery and got cold feet. But eventually such colleges as Chichester and Ely would become strongholds of Anglo-Catholic thinking and feeling, and the same could be said, to a greater or lesser degree, of others: Lincoln, Salisbury, Wells, as well as some in University contexts, not only Cuddesdon but also St Stephen's House in Oxford, St Chad's in Durham, as well as the afore mentioned King's College, London..

In another change: by the 1880s assault has begun on the parson's freehold, a legal tenure that guaranteed a degree of independence for Tractarian clergy faced with bishops unsympathetic to the Oxford Movement. In 1898 the ending of the sale of advowsons by auction cut off one route to increasing the number of Anglo-Catholic parishes, though still unimaginable was the later twentieth century possibility of episcopal 'suspension' of patronage which has loosened the hold of Catholic-minded individual patrons or indeed the corporate patrons that were the Catholic 'Societies'. (Advowsons were, after all, a form of property, and technically they still are.) In itself, patronage had both helped and hindered the spread of Tractarianism into parishes: episcopal control of patronage in most of Wales prevented Anglo-Catholic advance, while, in an isolated but not atypical example, the Kentish benefice of St Barnabas, Tunbridge Wells, was handed to a Tractarian incumbent by the Warden and Fellows of Keble College, Oxford in the teeth of opposition from the rural Dean, an Evangelical.[56]

In the 1890s conversion of vestries into Parochial Church Councils, leaving elected (secular) 'Parish Councils' to deal with civil affairs, reduced the direct influence of the Church on English society but not necessarily its indirect influence. Diocesan Conferences, adorned with the name of 'synods', began to arise, taking as their model the 'Church Congresses' of the 1860s, 1870s, and 1880s. The latter would prove a devastatingly effective means of Tractarian mobilization when they were imitated by the Anglo-Catholic Movement of the twentieth century. But, despite the increasing number of dioceses, few (perhaps only Truro) ever became so coherently Anglo-Catholic as to repeat that triumph in the 'particular'—meaning, the diocesan—church.

In 1885 the Convocation of Canterbury accepted the notion of adding a House of Laity and was followed in this decision in 1892 by the Convocation of York. The House in question was integrated with Convocations to form a 'Representative Church Council' in 1903. But a lay gathering had no right to be consulted on matters of doctrine, something which would change when the Council morphed into the General Synod of the Church of England, via the interim measure of a 'Church Assembly', from the years following the First World War. In the Assembly (but not the Synod, itself instituted in 1970 and thus after the period studied in this book), the bishops retained, however, certain powers in relation to issues of doctrine. With the coming of 'Synod', Pusey's worst fears would become a reality. That said, the institution of a House of Laity, voting for which was confined to baptized Anglicans who attested they were not also members of some other religious body, at least scotched the notion that Parliament was the real 'House of Laity' of a Church by law established. Nevertheless, owing to their high view of the sacerdotal office of the clergy some Anglo-Catholics were unwilling to be co-opted into the new system, with its elaborate organization of parochial church councils, and ruridecanal and diocesan conferences, all leading up to election to the Assembly proper.[57] But it was brought home to them, not least by the English Church Union, that failure to vote, or to stand, at any of these levels of participation would, by default, enable Evangelicals and Liberals to take control of the Church.

And the 1919 'Enabling Act' whereby Parliament brought the Church Assembly into being was useful to the Union as an opportunity to consolidate Anglo-Catholic feeling, not least through setting up a Central Council of Catholic Societies intended to 'coordinate their aims at elections and their voting in the Assembly'.[58]

Historic advance, and a setback

The Anglo-Catholic Movement continued to make steady progress from the High Victorian age, with its Gladstone-enabled rise to high office, till the eve of the Second World War. Essentially, it won the battles over Liturgy and ritual to be described in the next two chapters. Its Religious houses continued to flourish, even if some Sisterhoods died out and were replaced by others. Its network of Societies, shrines, schools, and newspapers impressed outsiders. It organized hugely well-attended congresses. It maintained a high profile in the world of the arts, and its voice was heard on questions of social reconstruction. Its influence spilled over into other parties in the Church of England, and it extended its dominion over various missionary Provinces of the Church, notably in East and Central Africa and in the Western Pacific. Its consent was required in any ecumenical negotiations with which the Church of England was involved.

Or was it? The seemingly unstoppable rise of Anglo-Catholicism to hegemony in the Church of England faced a challenge which its forces proved insufficient to meet. The issue of the 'Church of South India', announced just before the Second World War, held in cold storage in the years 1939 to 1945, and after that an open sore on its body politic, made some observers wonder. If any event 'after Newman' went clean counter to the primary thrust of the *Tracts for the Times* it was the deliberate surrender of four Anglican dioceses to form part of a new Church not all of whose clergy would belong, in its first generation, to an episcopally ordered ministerial succession. Madras, Dornakal, Tinnivelly, and Travancore were far from Tunbridge Wells. Yet in the comfortable rectories of high church archdeacons, or gaunt vicarages in slum parishes devastated by the 'Blitz', and among well-informed Anglo-Catholic laity in the West End (for whom T. S. Eliot may stand proxy[59]), alarm bells began ringing. At Oxford, the Superior General of the Cowley Fathers, William Braithwaite O'Brien, deemed it the 'most serious threat to Anglican unity that has arisen for many years'.[60]

The formation of the Church of South India, finalized in September 1947, was the occasion when a further unspecified number of Anglo-Catholics jumped ship.[61] Assurances that, in the nature of the case, the unsatisfactory ecclesiastical arrangements were temporary, an example of what the Eastern Orthodox might call *oikonomia*, cut little by way of ice. In fact, no unconditional promise could be given of such provisionality.[62] After a thirty-year interval, the new body was to decide whether to continue with exclusively episcopal Ordination or not. Impassioned attempts by Archbishop William Temple (1881–1944) to quell Anglo-Catholic anxieties—efforts dismissed as apologia for 'reunion by destruction'—did not, then, succeed.[63]

After the 1955 vote of Convocations in favour of Archbishop Geoffrey Fisher's carefully crafted compromise document, a defiant 'Annunciation Group continued to maintain that 'Affirming our loyalty to the Catholic principles of the Church of England, we reiterate that we remain unconvinced as to the orthodoxy of the Church of South India and of the validity of its Orders, which in any case we regard as irregular. Consequently we repudiate the resolutions of the Convocations of Canterbury and York on this matter, and refuse to implement them or be bound by them, and we propose to take active steps to enrol further supporters, both from the clergy and the laity of the Church of England'.[64]

In 1964 dissidents in the Sub-continent would not wait for the thirty-year rule to end but broke away to found the 'Anglican Church of India': ironically enough, not a recognised part of the Communion. That mini-crisis reflected in advance what would happen later, in the 1990s and beyond, not only in the Ordination of women to presbyterate and episcopate but also in arrangements for shared Eucharistic communion, including exchange of ministers, between Anglicans on the one hand and, on the other, both Continental Protestants abroad and Nonconformists at home.

The ecclesiology of the Oxford Movement could not easily survive these metamorphoses, and their effect was to drive Anglo-Catholics ever deeper into a state of affairs the Oxford Fathers had neither anticipated nor intended. 'Congregationalism with bishops' was a strategy that enabled Anglo-Catholic parishes to conserve the maximum possible from the gains of the Movement. But it was also, when compared with the ambitions of the Oxford Fathers, or indeed the fair hopes of the Inter War years, very definitely a second best.

— 3 —

Rites and Ceremonies

THE PREVIOUS CHAPTER included no cameo of a 'crisis' over rites and ceremonies since the word seems out of place in the case of a chronic, rather than episodic, difficulty. But the way Puseyism impinged most obviously on the general public lay in the developing ceremonial practice—known to its critics as 'Ritualism'—ordinary Englishmen encountered in their parish churches or heard spoken of, usually with a sense of affront, whenever there was talk of 'goings-on' in the chapels and oratories of Dr Pusey's Sisterhoods.[1] The Liturgy is the best teacher of doctrine, at any rate if people do not disempower the rites by insisting on their didactic function, stressing solely their purely verbal quality— apart, that is, from the most minimal 'manual acts' in handling bread and wine. The liturgical expression of doctrine—if the doctrine concerned is the sacramentalism of the Oxford Fathers—necessarily meant for priests and people a transformation of 'Hanoverian' habits of behaviour in church. And yet the Tractarian 'principle of reserve' (the desirability of following the cue of the divine revelatory process by a gradualist, incremental disclosure of supernatural truth to human recipients) sounded a cautionary note. '[M]ost early Tractarians believed that the clergy should not introduce liturgical practices which their parishioners were not familiar with before preparing them doctrinally and liturgically.'[2]

That warning note was not universally heeded. 'The ritualists, however, thought otherwise: they would teach their parishioners the truths of the Catholic faith through liturgical manifestations which reflected them.'[3]

Trouble ahead

But what *did* the 'Catholic faith' actually teach? In 1853 Archdeacon Denison, preached two sermons in Wells Cathedral in which he reminded ordinands that the inward reality of the Eucharistic sacrament is received by all, whether faithful or wicked. Had not Paul taught it could be taken for condemnation as well as for salvation (First Corinthians 11:29)? The Evangelical Alliance (later the 'Church Association') brought him before an ecclesiastical court. Had he not denied Article 29 of the Thirty-Nine Articles? For the framers of the Article had declared about the 'Wicked and such as be devoid of a lively faith': 'in no wise are they partakers of Christ'.[4] By way of protest, Pusey, Keble, and other Tractarians came to Denison's aid. Meanwhile books of theology from the Tractarian School were openly teaching an objective Presence in the Eucharistic elements, over against the 'receptionism' favoured by more mainstream Anglicans. Robert Wilberforce, an excellent systematician and the most underrated of Tractarian writers, brought out, to this effect, his *The Doctrine of the Holy Eucharist* in 1853.[5] In 1855 Pusey published with the benefit of six hundred pages of notes (not for nothing had he studied in Germany) his celebrated, even infamous, sermon on the topic, now presented as *The Doctrine of the Real Presence as contained in the Fathers and set forth by the Divines and Others of the English Church since the Reformation*.[6] That was followed by John Keble's *On Eucharistical Adoration* in 1859.[7]

The Denison case took two years to go through the church courts. During that period 'younger men in the parishes were busy translating this high sacramental language into external symbol and ritual'—with results that occasioned riots at parish churches and eventually imprisonment, not for affray but for 'Ritual Offences', and not for the disruptors but for the ministering clergy.[8] In *Ritualism and the Real Presence*, an 1866 Open Letter to the Bishop of Gloucester and Bristol, Denison defended the Ceremonial Men. While 'under the circumstances of the Church', Denison averred in an echo of the language of the Tractarian leaders, he himself would rather keep ornament and ceremony rudimentary (Pusey had spoken frankly of the appropriateness to the Church of England of garments of penitence), he was, he claimed, 'one with [Ritualists] in what they teach'.

That Ritualism was mere Aestheticism is the 'surface view of the matter: what the newspaper world are asked to believe, and do believe'. That judgment, Denison wrote, neglected a 'very obvious consideration'. It was 'hardly likely that men should peril position and name and reputation, should incur obloquy and reproach and tumult, and alienation of friends, for a colour or a ceremony or a dress, if the colour and ceremony and dress mean nothing'.[9] Perhaps he protested too much. A generation earlier, in his *Origines liturgicae*, William Palmer of Worcester College, Oxford, a very moderate Tractarian (if indeed, aside from writing an early *Tract*, he could be called a Tractarian at all), had already argued that the Ornaments Rubric of the 1662 Prayer Book positively required ministers to wear alb, stole, and chasuble—the controversial vestments—at the Eucharist.[10] Palmer had shown, in effect, that any 'lawlessness' lay with the anti-Ceremonialists. But then who among the ultra-Protestants of the mid-Victorian church (typically these were

Rites and Ceremonies

'Recordites', subscribers to the hyper-Evangelical magazine *The Record*) read books with Latin titles from the reign of William IV?

Riotous times

No one, certainly, in proletarian districts of the British capital. Riots at St Barnabas, Pimlico, a chapel of ease to St Paul's, Knightsbridge, and at St George's-in-the-East, Stepney, two 'hot spots' of London Ritualism, were prompted both by fear of Popery and detestation of Puseyites as traitors within the gates. Such tumult would not have occurred outside Pusey's canonry-house in Christ Church or Keble's rural vicarage at Hursley. Disturbances took place in densely populated and largely poverty-stricken areas. They were occasioned by the feast of ceremonial and ornament that was becoming characteristic of the 'Slum Parishes'.

As Palmer had noted, the Ornaments Rubric of the 1662 Prayer Book was crucial. Referring as it did in positive not to say prescriptive language to what had been the case in the second year of Edward VI's reign (1547–53) — that is, *prior* to the introduction of the First (1549) Prayer Book — the Rubric seemed to license all the objects in the inventory of a pre-Reformation parish church and, therefore, presumably, the gestures and movement that went with those objects, as well as their architectural placing within the building. The re-introduction of the apparatus of late mediaeval worship was found to draw the unchurched working-class population in a way the bleak scenario of standard Anglican Protestantism had failed to do. Newman had had an inkling of this, and not just for Marx's proletariat, when writing to Manning while both were still Anglicans: 'You must make the Church more suitable to the needs of the heart.... Give us more services, more vestments and decorations in worship; give us the signs of an apostle, the pledges that the Spouse of Christ is among us.'[11]

William Bennett (1804–86), Perpetual Curate of St Paul's, Knightsbridge, when establishing a chapel of ease at St Barnabas, Pimlico, acted on Newman's advice. In the process he created one of the jewels of the Gothic Revival and provided a liturgy to match. In 1851, a public protest, combined with the censures of Bishop Blomfield of London, obliged him to flee. Not that this was the end of his troubles: in 1869 as Vicar of Frome in Somerset (wags asked if the placename rhymed with 'Rome'), Bennett would be brought before the ecclesiastical courts for speaking of the 'real, actual, and visible Presence of the Lord upon the Altars of our Churches', thus rendering the consecrated species 'adorable', and asserting, further, that the Eucharist is a Sacrifice, offered by the ministerial priest. When the Court of Arches acquitted him of contravening the formularies of the English Church the Church Association appealed to the Privy Council who declined to overturn the judgment. Pusey, who had not approved the word 'visible' in Bennett's text (whereupon Bennett removed it), told Gladstone that if the decision had gone the other way he would have been condemned too, since all Bennett had said was taken from Pusey's work.[12]

Meanwhile the ritual innovations persisted. In 1857 the Judicial Committee of the Privy Council, required to pronounce on the goings-on at St Barnabas, Pimlico, determined that the following, at any rate, were legal: 'credence tables, coloured altar cloths, candles (if lit only when required for light), and a cross (but not a crucifix) behind (but not on) the altar (which must be movable)'.[13] This 'Liddell Judgment', named for Bennett's successor, was notable for the decision to warrant changes of custom by appeal to the criterion of the afore-mentioned Ornaments Rubric. It opened a field day for theologically minded antiquarians interested in 'advancing' ritual practice with a view to supporting newly recovered Catholic beliefs.

It also confirmed the opening of riotous times. In Pimlico, a 'local body calling itself the Anti-Puseyite League met at the Wesleyan schoolroom on Tuesday evenings to plan interruptions and stimulate Protestant piety'.[14] Charles Lowder (1820–80) and Alexander Heriot Mackonochie (1825–87), curates, were up to the challenge. As an undergraduate Lowder was inspired to become a priest through hearing Newman preach at St Mary the Virgin. Wanting to work in a more demanding area than rural Gloucestershire, and with Pusey's blessing, he accepted a curacy at St Barnabas. There, under the influence of the seventeenth century French mission priest St Vincent de Paul (1581–1660) and his followers, the early 'Lazarists', he conceived the idea of the 'Society of the Holy Cross', a group of clergy vowed to spread the Catholic faith, especially to the poor (celibacy was recommended, though not required). In 1855 Lowder became its first Master.

The following year (the Judicial Committee decision was still pending) Lowder arrived at the old London parish church of St George's-in-the-East, also riven by Ritual disputes since the arrival of its first Tractarian vicar, Bryan King (1811–95) in 1842.[15] There had been colourful, if unsettling, events. One preacher reported 'shouting, stamping of feet, slamming of doors, whistling and striking of lucifer matches' as well as the throwing of 'walnut shells, orange peels, and small detonating crackers'.[16] The aim of the young and zealous clergyman was to start a new mission, directed specifically at the unchurched masses of London's dockland where in 1857 Lowder was joined by an equally new Community, the Sisters of the Holy Cross, running houses for prostitutes and schools for poor girls under the leadership of Elizabeth Neale (1823–1901), sister of the Tractarian hymn-writer John Mason Neale.

Lowder, unlike King, who had reached the end of his tether, was not inclined to concede defeat. His view was well expressed by another Anglo-Catholic clergyman, the magnificently named Mayow Wynell-Mayow (1810–95), while addressing a public meeting at Brighton in 1865. Anti-Ritualist agitation was intended 'not merely to put down vestments, or put out candles, or extinguish incense, but to drive out of the Church of England the whole doctrine which these things represent; to expel everyone, whether Ritualist or not, who holds and teaches it; to run riot in the destruction of every vestige of faith in the Real Presence, in the Priesthood, the Altar, and the Sacrifice'.[17]

In 1866 Lowder founded St Peter's, London Docks, a church that remains a bastion of the Catholic Movement today.[18] After a long and distinguished ministry, in 1880, during his final appeal for subscriptions, he had described the parish as by then existing. It had, *inter alia*, a school for six hundred children, a hostel for the elderly, 'St Peter's Club and Dining Room' providing meals for working men and their families at a 'moderate cost', a 'Friend of Labour Society' making loans to working men, a Penny Bank, a convalescent home at Reigate, Benefit and Burial Clubs, three Mothers' Meeting Clubs, Clothing and Boot Clubs, and a 'Society for the employment of poor needlewomen'.[19] It was not surprising he was (and remains) recognized locally as a confessor of the faith.[20]

Social historians have sometimes queried how many of the poor who benefited from the exertions of Lowder, and other slum priests like him, were actually found in church. It is true that the census numbers of 1886 suggest chairs were far from all taken, and some sitting on them may have been carriage-folk, attracted by ritual and reputation. Nevertheless, the poor who came were steadfast. 'Working men who embraced Anglo-Catholicism seem to have been an exceptionally convinced or hardy lot, perhaps because prevailing working-class sentiment was against them.'[21]

With Lowder's name is connected that of Alexander Heriot Mackonochie, born in Hampshire to a Low Church family, his father a retired official of the East India Company. Alexander Mackonochie was educated at Edinburgh University and Wadham College, Oxford, in which period he heard Pusey preaching — presumed to be the occasion for his rallying to the Tractarian cause, though he was also friendly with Charles Marriott (1811–58): Marriott had taken over Newman's brainchild the *Library of the Fathers* in 1842 and from 1850 till his premature death in 1858 would be vicar of the University church, St Mary the Virgin. After ordination in 1849, Mackonochie served as curate to William John Butler (1818–94), founder of the Community of St Mary the Virgin at Wantage, prior to acting as a mission priest at St George's-in-the-East from 1856. In 1862 he left St George's for St Alban's, Holborn, with which place his name will always be linked.

At Holborn, the daily Eucharist, accompanied with chant and 'advanced' ritual, and availability of regular (and, unusually, *advertised*) Confessions, combined with the humanitarian and educational work of a slum parish, were continually disturbed by legal assaults mounted by the Church Association, beginning in 1867 and continuing till the eve of his death. Mackonochie was suspended briefly for ritual offences in 1870 and then again for three years in 1878. In 1882 a new round of attacks began whereupon, consenting to his bishop's wish, strongly seconded by Archbishop Archibald Campbell Tait of Canterbury (1811–82, one of the four Oxford tutors who began proceedings against Newman for *Tract 90*),[22] Mackonochie left St Alban's for St Peter's, London Docks. There his health broke down, and he took refuge with his friend Alexander Chinnery-Haldane (1840–1906), the Scottish Episcopal bishop of Argyll, at Ballachulish, by Loch Leven. On 15 December 1887 his body was found in the surrounding forest, guarded by his dogs. A special train would be required to take parishioners and other followers from London to Woking for his interment.[23] Mackonochie had succeeded Lowder as Master of the Society of the Holy Cross. Much involved with the Confraternity of the Blessed Sacrament, the 'martyr of St Alban's' had been a great devotee of the Holy Eucharist.

Intermittent physical assaults and periodic attempts at sacrilege in these three churches were a kind of purging fire through which the Ritualist Movement passed and by which it emerged steeled as a result. In Chadwick's words: 'The older Puseyite austerity and fear of ceremonial began to vanish for restraint was now associated with cowardice and lack of principle. The riots ensured that in the long run, unless Parliament devised some form of high commission to maintain discipline, chasuble and incense and roods and tabernacles would establish themselves more widely in the Church of England than any early Victorian could have predicted.'[24]

The Daily Offices

The service of Holy Communion (the 'Mass'), celebrated by Anglo-Catholics as a weekly event, or even several times weekly, or indeed daily, occupied the eye of the storm, owing to the disputed questions of the Eucharistic Sacrifice and Presence and the 'sacrificing' nature of the ministerial priesthood. Yet the Tractarians had also been concerned to assert the importance of the regular (and not merely Sunday) celebration of the Offices of Mattins and Evensong. Soon Ritualists found inadequate the Prayer Book provision of only two such Offices (the Roman rite had eight, if one treats Matins and Lauds as separate Offices and includes the Office of Prime, which was rather later in emerging than the rest).

Rites and Ceremonies

A fuller schedule, spread throughout the day, had been attempted in the English Church by John Cosin, a seventeenth century divine (his dates are 1594–1672), but that was rather a long time ago. In any case, its purview was restricted: the aim was for Anglican ladies at the court of Charles I's queen to have something comparable to the Books of Hours sported by their Catholic counterparts. Even more esoteric were the 'hours' in Archbishop William Laud's personal book of devotions (Laud was born in 1573), only published after his execution in 1645.

In 1858 *The Day Hours of the Church of England* appeared: an adaptation of the Sarum Use, though the editors confined themselves to the holydays named in the Prayer Book and, at least in the early editions of their book, omitted the direct invocation of saints.[25] This book was used by, for instance, Sisters of the Community of St John Baptist at Clewer, near Windsor, which claimed a background in the Augustinian tradition of canonesses, monastic women dedicated to the singing of the choral Office. The book had evolved out of a vernacular diurnal, *Occasional Offices for the Hours of Prayer*, put together by the combined efforts of 'Dr Lee of Lambeth' and Henry Parry Liddon. Its shaping hand was, however, a layman, another of those invaluable Anglo-Catholic aristocrats, Sir Francis Lygon, later Lord Beauchamp (1830–91), one of the founders of Oxford's Pusey House. In 1898 a Supplement was published under the title *The Service for Certain Holy Days*, an innocuous title which rather deflected attention from the fact that, for the first time, there was included a direct appeal to saints. By that year over twenty-seven thousand copies of the five printings to date had been sold. There was also a truncated form, consisting of the Little Hours (Prime, Terce, Sext, None), which the customer, should he or she so wish, could also purchase bound up with the Prayer Book Offices for Morning Prayer (Cranmer's fusion of Matins and Lauds) and Evening Prayer (the parallel combination of Vespers and Compline, as Cranmer had left it). In 1950, a final edition of *The Day Hours of the Church* adjusted its calendar from Sarum to Roman use, not scrupling to incorporate some festivals, like that of the Sacred Heart, introduced by the Post-Reformation Papacy.[26]

Marian Hughes, the foundress of the Society of the Holy Undivided Trinity at Oxford, the first woman to take Religious vows in the Church of England, went a step further. She began a translation of the Roman Breviary proper, and Pusey's son, Philip Edward Pusey (1830–80), completed it where she had left off. When that book, in edited form, was printed it came before the public under the somewhat misleading title of *The Day Office of the Church. According to the Kalendar of the Church of England*. It was really a translation of the Roman diurnal based on the Mechlin (Malines) editions of the *Breviarum Romanum* of 1852 and 1862.[27]

Thanks to the translating talents of Maria Rossetti (1827–76), sister of the painter and the poetess, the Community of All Saints, as founded at the Margaret Steet Chapel by its incumbent, Upton Richards, Frederick Oakeley's successor, used their own manuscript version of these Roman archetypes. That too was published in the 1870s under the title *The Day Hours and Other Offices as used by the Sisters of All Saints*. In 1922 a revised version, *A Book of Day Hours for the Use of Religious Sisters*, reflected the changes made to liturgical use of the Psalter by Pope Pius X.

The Society of St Margaret, which was Neale's creation, prayed a Breviary based on Sarum but enriched with material from the Roman and various French Breviaries, as did Elizabeth Neale's Community of the Holy Cross.[28] Of course these last Sisterhoods had the services of the erudite and industrious Neale at their disposal. The Sisters of Saint Margaret were thus able to publish in 1870 *The Night Office of the Church* (in three volumes), and in 1877 *Breviary Offices from Lauds to Compline*. According to Peter Anson, their books actually anticipated Pius X's reform of the Roman Liturgy of the Hours (rather than simply reflecting them, as with the later work of the All Saints Sisters) by ensuring that the Psalter's weekly recitation was interrupted as little as possible by other commemorations. A revised version did, however, appear in 1914, and soon after a supplement including such modern Roman Rite feasts as Christ the King and the Precious Blood (since the Post-Conciliar liturgical reform in the Church of Rome the latter is now incorporated into 'Corpus Christi', a mediaeval celebration).[29]

A strictly Sarum diurnal, based on an early Tudor printed text from 1531, also emerged from the Community of St Mary the Virgin at Wantage and was preferred by some other Sisterhoods, notably the Community of the Holy Name at Malvern Link, in Worcestershire. That would be not least because its constituent books had been 'noted', that is, set to the music of the chant, which was done in a gradually accumulated trio of volumes: *Lauds and Day Hours, The Order of Vespers* and *The Order of Compline throughout the Year*.[30]

All this translating, publishing, and—who can doubt it?—*praying* activity should strike Roman Catholics as hugely impressive—not least because many Sisterhoods of an 'apostolic' ('active') kind in the Catholic Church of the nineteenth century revival and onwards contented themselves with the easier, if also far more rudimentary, Office of the Blessed Virgin Mary, a 'Little Office' which would have been used as a pious supplement, not an alternative to the 'Great Office', in the Church of the Middle Ages and beyond.

Protestant reaction

In 1865 the Church Association was founded by Evangelicals to impede, and if possible reverse, the spread of Anglo-Catholic ritual practice, by force of law if necessary. Its aim was to 'counteract the efforts now being made to pervert' the teaching of the Church of England, on 'essential points of the Christian faith', and to 'assimilate her services to those of the Church of Rome'.[31] If the rubrics allowed such assimilation, then the rubrics should go was the opinion of the incorrigibly Evangelical Earl of Shaftesbury and Queen Victoria agreed. If the law allowed the Church to be so comprehensive, the law should be changed to disallow it.

The Parliamentary provision in question was the work of Benjamin Disraeli (1804–81) during his Second Ministry. The timing of the Public Worship Regulation Act of 1874 was not by chance. The First Vatican Council had considerably intensified the 'No Popery' cry. Gladstone's promotion of Irish Disestablishment had caused agitation. The place of the Church of England in the national educational system was bitterly contested by Nonconformists.

What did the Act say? Clergy could be brought before a judge in a special court created for the purpose, where the judge might be a nominee of the archbishops but only if the Crown gave its assent. Charges could be laid on one of three grounds: altering or adding to the fabric, ornaments, or furniture of the church without lawful authority, or adding an ornament forbidden by law; the minister's personal use of an unlawful ornament (meaning thereby some item of clothing) or neglecting to use any such prescribed ornament, and, lastly, his failing to observe the directions of the Prayer Book for the performance of services whether by omission or addition. The bishop could veto a prosecution, giving reasons in writing. Otherwise, the case would come before the court with, on conviction, a possible appeal to the Judicial Committee of the Privy Council. If convicted the guilty cleric would be inhibited from ministering. But the Act failed to allow for disobedience to the inhibition, which in due course was deemed to count as contempt of court, and thus to incur the usual penalty, namely, imprisonment.[32] 'The ritualists could not accept the system of courts as settling this issue: if Parliament made vestments illegal by an act, they would disobey, for in their eyes an non-Anglican Parliament had no more right than the emperor of Japan to determine their clothes in church.'[33] But behind the clothes, and the other ornaments, there were of course the doctrines they implied. For '[a]bove all, [Ritualism] was an expression of a high sacramental theology- a theology in which the adornment of worship was seen as both intrinsically appropriate and a logical means of teaching men and women the glory of Christ's presence in His Church and in the sacraments.'[34]

Under the provisions of the Act five clergymen were imprisoned for contempt of court in denying the right of English law to impose restrictions on liturgical practice. These are the 'Martyrs of Ritualism'. Arthur Tooth (1839–1931) of St James, Hatcham, had been before ordination a round-the-world traveller. His lasting legacy to the Anglo-Catholic Movement was his foundation of the Guild of All Souls, a national society for reviving prayer for the departed, begun in his parish in 1873. After release from prison he acquired a property in Surrey (now Ashburton Park) where he established a chapel, convent, and orphanage. Thomas Pelham Dale (1821–92), of St Vedast's, Foster Lane, in the City, an alumnus of King's College, London and Sidney Sussex College, Cambridge, was a former Evangelical, one of whose daughters edited his life and letters.[35] Richard Enraght (1837–98) of Holy Trinity, Bordesley, Birmingham, a graduate of Trinity College, Dublin, was ordained priest in 1862 at St Paul's, Brighton, on which Mecca of Anglo-Catholicism more anon. After prison Enraght worked in the East End of London before retiring to a Norfolk vicarage at Bintree, some ten miles to the south of Little Walsingham, a place still awaiting the revival of its historic Shrine. Sidney Faithorn Green (1841–1916) of St John the Evangelist, Miles Platting, Manchester, eventually became rector of a living in the gift of Keble College, Oxford, at Charlton-by-Dover in Kent.[36] James Bell Cox (1828–1923) was Perpetual Curate at St Margaret of Antioch, Toxteth Park, Liverpool, the epicentre of Liverpudlian Anglo-Catholicism in a markedly Low Church diocese. The prosecutions of these figures spanned the decade between 1877 and 1887.

The bishops of the Church of England soon discovered that the tribulations of the 'Ritual Martyrs' only increased the popularity of their practices. Over seventy churches had permanent Eucharistic Reservation by the end of Victoria's reign, and nearly four hundred used incense at the Holy Communion.[37] In the circumstances, faced with dissent on this scale, the only viable course was for bishops to invoke their power of veto, given them by the Act for any individual case. In 1878 Archbishop Tait, a Low Churchman, vetoed, through gritted teeth, the prosecution of Lowder at St Peter's, London Docks.

Anglo-Catholic demands

Although there would always be places where the 1662 Prayer Book was used in its textual integrity but with every visual appearance of a Roman (or Sarum) Mass, it was more customary to find Anglo-Catholic clergy seeking substantial revision of the Prayer Book service—until, that is, such revision became a serious possibility, with the likelihood it would not, in all respects, correspond to their demands.

In 1873 Lowder's Society of the Holy Cross presented to the Upper Convocation of Canterbury a petition asking for the 1549 Prayer Book (more Catholic than its 1552 and 1662 successors) to be the approved model for Prayer Book revision,[38] with restoration of the ancient Propers and Commons, provision for the 'decent and reverent' reservation of the Eucharistic species, the restoration of anointing in Baptism, Confirmation, and the Anointing of the Sick, a rite for the consecration of churches, and the restoration of what the petitioners described as the 'ancient and edifying ceremonies' for various feast days from Candlemas to Holy Week and the Rogation days.

Most spectacularly, the petitioners asked that in 'view of the widespread and increasing use of Sacramental Confession, your venerable house may consider the advisability of providing for the education, selection, and licensing of duly qualified confessors, in accordance with the provisions of canon law'.[39] Though Pusey began hearing the Confessions of individuals as early as 1838 and never abandoned the practice, and Keble had urged Confession quite generally on his flock at Hursley, this request really put the cat among the pigeons. Quasi-unanimously—the views of Richard Durnford of Chichester (1802–95) were uncertain—the Bench of Bishops condemned any habitual system of Confession along with the assumption that Confession was sacramental while also ignoring the rest of the Society's recommendations. Where Confession was concerned, their concern was how to curb it, not how to provide for it. Indeed, the two Archbishops released a letter declaring that 'through the system of the Confessional great evil has been wrought in the Church of Rome and that our Reformers acted wisely in allowing it no place in our reformed Church, and we take this opportunity of expressing our entire disapproval of any such innovation, and our firm determination to do all in our power to discourage it'.[40]

But what *was* it in their power to do? If the battle over Eucharistic vestments were anything to go by, not very much. 'Tait began to prefer allowing vestments to risking contempt of court and imprisonment.'[41] In 1882, in cahoots with John Jackson (1811–85), Bishop of London, Tait had managed to persuade Mackonochie to resign his charge at St Alban's, Holborn, but the two prelates had already decided, in the event of non-cooperation on the part of the culprit, to veto any further legal proceedings. In effect, the bishops were expanding their discretionary powers at the cost of sometimes protecting illegality. The only alternative was, at the churches in question, to refuse to confirm children (or adults) or to license curates, not a prospect that would lead decent pastors to sleep easy at night.

Meanwhile, from the Evangelical side, the Church Association was determined to fight all compromise: the episcopal veto on prosecution could not in the nature of things, or so it was argued, be absolute. The practices of Anglo-Catholic clergy at the Holy Communion on which their opponents had their eye included some or all of the following: the wearing of Eucharistic vestments (and not just gown, surplice and black scarf); the use of unleavened wafer-bread; the mixing of water with wine in the chalice; the use of the sign of the cross in blessing or absolving the congregation; the placing of lighted candles on the altar; the priest's occupation at the altar of the Eastward position; the singing of the Lamb of God after the consecration; the elevation of the paten and chalice at the Consecration of the elements, and the carrying out of the ablutions (the washing of the Eucharistic vessels) at the altar.

Most if not all these traditional features of the Western rite were recommended in George Rundle Prynne's *Eucharistic Manual* of 1865 (it reached a tenth edition in 1895), a book that Archbishop Longley of Canterbury, Tait's predecessor, had been quick to censure. Prynne (1818–1903) was a Cornishman, for fifty-five years Vicar of St Peter's, Plymouth where the young Joseph Leycester Lyne, a major if eccentric figure of the monastic revival, was, when a deacon, his curate.[42] Prynne was a great supporter of Priscilla Lydia Sellon and the Sisters of Mercy at nearby Davenport, sharing in their work with the sick and hearing confessions of the girls in their orphanage. Need it be said that there were riots at his church? Prynne left his hearers (or readers) in no doubt that the ceremonies he introduced were dogmatically founded, as attested by his 1894 *Truth and Reality of the Eucharistic Sacrifice*, and, in 1903, *Devotional Instructions on the Eucharistic Office*.[43] He was to become Vice-President of the English Church Union in 1901, not long before his death.

Back in the Home Counties, by the end of the 1870s, Thomas Thellusson Carter (1808–1901), vicar of Clewer, near Windsor, did at the Liturgy what Prynne's *Manual* required. In 1875 the English Church Union had settled on 'Six Points' of liturgical practice, deemed to be essential expressions of a proper Eucharistic sensibility: the Eucharistic vestments, the Eastward position, altar lights, the mixed chalice, wafer bread, and incense, 'thereby making formal what had become a consensus on the points of ceremony worth fighting for'.[44] All were anathema to the Ultras. But Bishop John Fielder Mackarness of Oxford (1820–89) refused to allow Carter's prosecution, despite a parishioner's equally formal complaint. The Court of Queen's Bench overruled the bishop, but further courts of appeal (culminating in a hearing in the House of Lords) reversed that verdict.

Another damned close-run thing concerned George Frederick Bodley's 1883 design for a new high altar, with crucifix, at St Paul's Cathedral,

Rites and Ceremonies

estimated to be the 'largest crucifix to appear in an Anglican church since the Reformation'.[45] Archbishop Frederick Temple vetoed a prosecution of the Dean and chapter, and in 1891 (so slow do grind the mills of God) the House of Lords ruled that Temple could not be compelled to allow the suit. Decisions such as these may have averted a schism.

Upping anti-Ritualist pressure

In 1888, however, the Church Association changed tactics and decided to prosecute a bishop directly—not for use of the veto (an impossibility, given the state of the law) but for his own ritual irregularities. Their chosen target was Edward King of Lincoln, first bishop of the English Church to wear the Eucharistic vestments since the Reformation. Archbishop Edward White Benson (1829–96—he succeeded Tait on St Augustine's chair and preceded Temple), might have tried to use the veto furnished him in the case of priests by Disraeli's legislation. But Benson suspected that, in this novel situation of a suffragan bishop hauled before the civil courts, he lacked the power to do so. The Judicial Committee of the Privy Council gave him leave to try the case in his own archiepiscopal court—a tribunal last convened in the reign of William III (reigned 1688–1702) when its claims were considered dubious. King himself would have preferred to be tried before the Upper House of Convocation, since, as his supporters argued, a primate acting alone was hardly different from a Canterbury papacy. King's first biographer thought Benson had indulged a love of the theatrical. 'The delightful prospect of presiding over an ecclesiastical pageant, with all the attendant "pomp and circumstance" of legal and religious millinery—scarlet robes and silver maces and full-bottomed wigs—of sitting in the chair of St Augustine, surrounded by comprovincial prelates, and solemnly passing judgment on the successor of St Hugh [of Lincoln], proved fatally attractive'.[46] In the event, Benson allowed some practices but forbade others, notably blessing with the sign of the cross and the mixed chalice. The Church Association appealed to the Judicial Committee (whose authority in the matter, however, Bishop King did not acknowledge). But the question of King's imprisonment (for contempt) never arose since the Committee upheld the Archbishop's verdict in all but one rather small particular.[47]

Thus frustrated, Evangelicals went for direct action instead. Such action, after all, had not been wholly ineffectual decades earlier, at Pimlico or St George's-in-the-East. The first sign of the new policy was when in 1897 John Kensit (1853–1902), founder of the Protestant Truth Society, publicly objected at the official confirmation, at St Mary-le-Bow, of the new bishop of London, Mandell Creighton. Creighton had been Dixie Professor of Ecclesiastical History at Cambridge. He had also, when bishop of Peterborough, worn a mitre, and 'failed' to intervene against Tractarian preaching.[48]

The public were sympathetic to Kensit owing to Lord Halifax's recent overtures to Rome on behalf of the English Church Union. That body was seeking — unsuccessfully, as things turned out — the approval of Anglican Orders by the pope. National exasperation was intensified by the publication of Walter Walsh's scabrous and much read *The Secret History for the Oxford Movement* (Walsh was assistant editor of the Evangelical paper *The English Churchman*). Described as evidence from an Anglo-Catholic 'underworld', it smelt of 'Romanizing and secrecy and bad faith'.[49]

A major campaign of disruption of Ritualist churches was mounted in 1888–9, with a special emphasis on stamping out advertisements of auricular Confession. (Readers of Rosemary Macaulay may remember how, in a later generation, 'Protestant Stormtroopers' in the London scenes of *The Towers of Trebizond* defaced the notice-board of the — fictitious — Father Chantry-Pigg's church where this sacrament was offered.) Priests who heard Confessions were often under pressure, in fact, to keep the matter secret owing to opposition from parents, spouses, or bishops. Members of these widespread constituencies were disturbed by what they heard of Confession. Yet the Prayer Book had allowed it, both at the Visitation of the Sick and, by implication and without reference to the dying, in the Ordinal. Charles Lindley Wood, Viscount Halifax (1839–1934), the lay leader of the Anglo-Catholics at century's end, was defiant on all fronts and advised no concessions.[50]

This extended beyond the issue of the sacrament of Penance. In 1899–1900 the two archbishops met at Lambeth and declared both incense and Eucharistic Reservation to be illicit in the Church of England. Appealing in the matter to moral rather than legal authority, this Lambeth Declaration had some at least temporary effect. But the continual spread of liturgical actions typical of the mediaeval Latin Church and its Tridentine successor could not be systematically inhibited owing to the diocesan bishop's right of veto as accorded by Disraeli's Act. In September 1898 the London *Times* opined that the time had come. Parliament must do for the Church what the Church would plainly not do for itself. Further attempts to rein in Ritualists were consistently lost in the Lower Houses of Convocation, so Parliamentary Bills to that effect began to surface in the Commons. In 1899 a new Church Discipline Bill (the existing Act of that name did not envisage the Ritual controversies dating as it did from 1840) proposed a blanket prohibition on publicly calling the Holy Communion service 'The Mass' and any encouragement to regular Confession.

More compendious was a 1903 Bill to abolish the bishop's veto on prosecution for Ritual offences of every kind. That led to the appointment of a Royal Commission on Ecclesiastical Discipline (1904–6) and, more remotely, the quest for a new Prayer Book which would come to a head in the years 1926 to 1929. Preoccupation with the aftermath of the Second Boer War (1899–1902) put a temporary end to further projected legislation. But debates about Welsh Disestablishment and Irish Home Rule as well as the education question, pitting the established Church against the rest, fed the ill feeling of that hour.[51] An irresistible force was meeting with an immoveable object. In 1906 the Royal Commission in Ecclesiastical Discipline came at last to its historic conclusion. 'The judgments of the Judicial Committee cannot practically be enforced.'[52]

4

Brighton and Beyond

THE SUSSEX COASTAL TOWN OF BRIGHTON serves as an egregious instance of how Anglo-Catholicism fared in matters of the sacred Liturgy. It is not a chance example. Following on the name of the London, Brighton and South Coast Railway (one of the original pre-nationalisation British railway companies), Anglo-Catholicism was jocularly called 'London, Brighton and South Coast religion'. That reflected its peculiar strength in the region.

The Wagners of Brighton

In 1846 Henry Michell Wagner (1792–1870), product of a wealthy mercantile family—originally Huguenot immigrants, they were hatters in Pall Mall—and Vicar of Brighton from 1824,[1] built St Paul's, West Street, as a subsidiary place of worship. This was for the sake of his son, Arthur Douglas Wagner (1824–1902), a Tractarian, whom Wagner *père* then 'presented' as Perpetual Curate of this 'proprietary chapel'. Wagner *fils*, thus released from parental bondage, soon provided it with a Sisterhood of its own, to which he gave the name 'The Community of the Blessed Virgin Mary', and an address at Numbers 3 and 4 of Brighton's Queen Square. Both Keble and the still Anglican Manning preached at the newly opened St Paul's and Gladstone attended its services when taking the sea air.

The younger Wagner's education had been at Eton and Trinity, Cambridge. His family were friends of the Puseys as well as of the Wellesley Dukes of Wellington. So even apart from the riches of Croesus he was not lacking in useful contacts. Wagner became nationally known in 1865 when the alleged child-murderess Constance Kent (1844–1944) was encouraged by him to give herself up to the police. According to public rumour: under pressure from her confessor she had wrongly owned up to the murder of her half-brother whose horribly savaged body had been found in an outhouse. The said confessor, Arthur Wagner, declined to disclose the contents of her Confession in court. In the ensuing outcry,

Protestant bodies called on local officials to bring before Parliament the scandal of degrading confessional practices carried out by renegades in the National Church. A riot followed, in which Wagner was assaulted in the street. Police protection was accorded to Wagner's vicarage, the church, and St Mary's House of the Penitent where Kent, already arrested at least once in her native Somerset, had been in residence.

In 1873 St Paul's became a parish where Wagner remained incumbent until 1902. There he employed his vast inheritance on a combination of organized almsgiving (notably in the form of subsidised social housing) with the building of other Anglo-Catholic churches in or around Brighton. They ranged from the bijou to the gigantic. At St Mary's, Buxted, intrigued by recent excavations at Little Walsingham in Norfolk which had uncovered the site of the medieval Marian shrine with its 'Holy House' (an attempted replica of the house of the Holy Family at Nazareth), Wagner created a 'Walsingham Chapel' which in time would inspire the restorer of the once celebrated Marian shrine of that name, a young lad called Alfred Hope Patten.

One of the many curates whom the younger Wagner provided for his churches was John Purchas (1823–72), educated at Rugby School and Christ's, Cambridge, and a curate in that county until he entered Wagner's employ at St Paul's, Brighton, in 1861. Purchas was the original editor of the *Directorium Anglicanum*, a primer in Sarum Use liturgical practice supplemented where necessary by Roman texts or practices and intended for immediate practical application in churches and chapels.[2] In Purchas' argument, the authors of the Book of Common Prayer, having left out so much about the practicalities of worship—not unusual, he pointed out, for even Roman liturgical books require ceremonialists and rubricians to become usable, he himself had stepped forward to fill the gap. It would retain its importance until chased from the market by the even more popular if wholly anonymous *Ritual Notes*.[3]

In 1866 Purchas bought the proprietary chapel of St James's, Brighton, and, taking a leaf from the book of the elder Wagner, presented himself to his own property as Perpetual Curate thereof. The 'advanced' ritual practices at St James's, together with the open advertising of hours for the hearing of Confessions, led to further rioting in 1868. The Church Association persuaded an outraged military man, Charles James Elphinstone, to take Purchas before the Court of Arches which found against him on some but not all points, whereupon Elphinstone's seconder (Elphinstone having inconveniently died) took the matter to the Privy Council with the customary results. Purchas was found guilty on all points, and suspended, but ignored the suspension, having prudently taken steps to place his monies in the hands of others. No fines had been levied by the time of his premature demise. The Purchas Judgment is generally regarded as crucial background for Disraeli's ill-fated Public Worship Regulation Act in 1874.

The feeble spluttering out of Disraeli's firecracker gives, in turn, some credence to another opinion. The historian of the Purchas riot, John Hawes, would link the Church Association's spectacular failure in Brighton with the 1900 decision of John Kensit to stand for Parliament as an Independent Conservative on a platform of 'draconian methods to discipline Ritualistic clergy'.[4] By that date—century's end, and the vigil of Victoria's death—the nugatory character of the 1874 Act (the Martyrs of Ritualism notwithstanding) was plain for all to see.

1874 was also the year when the Wagner fortune made possible the opening of the enormous new church of St Bartholomew's, Brighton, whose schools, guilds, musical tradition (operatic Masses with Palestrina for the more solemn feasts), support for missionary work (The Universities' Mission to Central Africa, the Poona Mission, the Bloemfontein Association), and Sisterhoods (Sisters of the Community of St Thomas-the-Martyr, Oxford, to be described in Chapter 5, followed by the Society of Sisters of Bethany, founded by Etheldreda Anna Bennett, 1824–1913, under Pusey's inspiration, for the holding of Retreats[5]), made a huge impact over the succeeding half-century. The evidence is laid out in the ample Jubilee brochure produced for the parish in 1924: *St Bartholomew's, Brighton. A Short History of the Last Fifty Years on the Occasion of the Jubilee*.[6] The span of St Bartholomew's resources and activities are another icon, fit to set beside Keble's Hursley, of the Anglo-Catholic movement of that time.

The *cause célèbre* at the heart of the Purchas and Wagner episodes was not forgotten. In the course of the year 1898, so the anonymous chronicler of St Bartholomew's noted (while suitably recognizing that sacramental arithmetic is no index of quality), nearly ten thousand Confessions had been heard at St Bartholomew's, Brighton, some seven hundred in the run-up to Christmas alone. In the Holy Week immediately following, the more precise, and attractively symmetrical figure, of 888 had been recorded.[7] It was not likely that, in 1900, and despite Kensit's combination of Parliamentary and extra-Parliamentary tactics—much would be heard in the succeeding century of his strong-arm methods[8]—the Archbishops' dissuader, as issued at Lambeth, could turn back so great a tide.

In the wider England

As the cases of the 'Martyrs of Ritualism' demonstrate, the Ritualist or 'Ceremonial' movement—which might also with equal justice be called in its theological character a 'Sacramental' movement—was not confined to London, or indeed to Brighton, or even to the south-east of

England, though London and the Sussex coast had the most important concentrations. John Shelton Reed offers an early vignette. At Helston in Cornwall, a churchwarden complained to Bishop Philpotts of Exeter that under their vicar, Walter Blunt (1809–82), worshippers were deterred from attendance as they 'are not able to rid themselves of the fear that some strongly exciting event is about to take place'. He knew, he said, of many 'ladies who have been incapacitated from performing their religion and other duties for the rest of the day in consequence of the excitement that have been subjected to in church'. In this case, the bishop, who was sympathetic to Tractarians, was not convinced, scenting the 'lamentable delusion… which can discern nothing but popery in every attempt to restore sound Church principles'.[9]

It would be, then, a mistake to think that Tractarianism did not disturb old ways in market towns, or indeed in the villages of deep England.[10] Geographical considerations took second place to questions of cultural allegiance. Reed allowed himself the generalization that, in the country as a whole, 'Many Anglo-Catholics had themselves emerged from the commercial class; others felt that the growing influence of that class threatened their social standing. In either case, their new mode of religious expression distanced them from the world of commerce, rebuked that world's pretensions, and subverted many of its values.'[11] This was not a social *couche* confined to any one region.

Within London itself there is some dispute as to who, in sociological terms, the Ceremonial Movement attracted. '[E]ven though the ritualistic churches began by aiming at the working man, they succeeded especially among the middle class. In the sixties their leaders talked much of the artisan's interest in high worship. Over thirty years later a religious census of South London proved what was not expected, that the middle class, believed to be puritan by tradition and conservative by habit, attended them in large numbers. Across South London, from St Stephen's Lewisham (1443 attendants) to St Peter's West Norwood (1420 attendants) ran a belt of high Anglican churches, most of them flourishing.'[12]

London is not, of course, synonymous with England. The slum parishes could be replicated in the provinces such as—to take the most celebrated instance—St Agatha's, Landport, where on the South Coast, Robert Radclyffe Dolling (1851–1902), son of an Irish land agent, educated at Harrow and Trinity, Cambridge, ministered to the proletariat in Portsmouth's own Dockland district.[13] The Cornish south-west, source of Reed's amusing anecdote, would eventually have a swathe of Anglo-Catholic parishes straddling, at any rate in the towns, such as Truro or Bodmin, the divisions between the classes. The new diocese of Truro, established in 1876, gradually acquired the reputation of an Anglo-Catholic fiefdom. East from Portsmouth, the Mecca of southern

Anglo-Catholicism that was Brighton has already been described. Its parishes boasted a wide social diversity, from labourers to carriage-folk.

The North of England, or the Northern Province generally, was, at any rate initially, less propitious terrain. Bishop Brooke Foss Westcott of Durham (1825–1901) believed the hold of the Oxford Movement on the North to be restricted to the clergy. St Saviour's, Leeds, was an obvious exception, though as a fruit of Pusey's personal initiative it was also unique. In time, however, the exceptional became less rare, especially in the industrial towns of the West Riding, and across the Pennines, the eastern part of Lancashire. In these areas, new sees—for the West Riding the diocese of Wakefield, created in 1888, and, rather later, for Lancashire north of the Ribble, the diocese of Blackburn, formed in 1926—would count as Anglo-Catholic strongholds. And well-supported individual parishes of an 'advanced' character could be found even in unpropitious ecclesiastical surroundings, as with St Margaret of Antioch, Toxteth, in Liverpool, or All Saints, Middlesbrough, in the North Riding of Yorkshire.

British Museum religion or Roman ways?

In 1899 Percy Dearmer (1867–1936) published the first edition of *The Parson's Handbook* which offered a different way ahead from that proposed by liturgical 'Romanisers'.[14] Or, rather, it took with full seriousness the Society of the Holy Cross petition to the bishops that the 1549 Prayer Book should be the model for future Anglican worship. Dearmer was able to capitalize on those incessant references to the Ornaments Rubric in the Ceremonialist controversy, and to do so not by aping Rome but, on the contrary, by directing attention away from what Continental Europeans were currently doing in Latin Europe to what the English had once been doing on the eve of the sixteenth century Reformation.[15] Had he known of it, Dearmer would have warmed to—but also been disturbed by—Professor Eamon Duffy's celebrated *The Stripping of the Altars*, a study of immediately pre-Reformation English religion (and its Henrician, Edwardine, and Elizabethan undoing).[16] Dearmer was opposed to an inherited Anglican anti-Ceremonialism, the result, he claimed, of reading the Prayer Book through 'Hanoverian spectacles', and thus the legacy of a 'period of exceptional sloth and worldliness'.[17] The Ornaments Rubric was, he maintained, the 'interpretation clause of the Prayer Book', the meta-rule governing any and every suggestion for the means of worship the Book might make.

But Dearmer warned against not only 'lawlessness' but also 'vulgarity', the 'senseless imitation of those meretricious ornaments, both of the Church and of its Ministers, with which ignorant and indiscreet persons have ruined the ancient beauty of Roman Catholic churches'.[18] Bad music turns people away from bad churches. So likewise does bad art. The son of a London artist, Dearmer proposed what, in the early twenty-first century, a Roman pope would call the *via pulchritudinis*—a 'way of beauty', which in practice was a reprise of medieval English things seen through the eyes of John Ruskin (1819–1900), William Morris (1834–96), and the Arts and Crafts Revival.

Dearmer had a proper Anglo-Catholic pedigree. While reading Modern History at Christ Church he had acted as Charles Gore's secretary at Pusey House. But when in 1901 he became Vicar of St Mary the Virgin, Primrose Hill, he set about devising ways to avoid the Church Association's initiation of legal action in Tractarian parishes—and divert the Kensitite attacks which physically disrupted Ritualist worship. He used his own congregation (not least the servers[19]) as a kind of laboratory where he could refine, in successive editions of the *Handbook*, materials he had acquired from historical research. Hence the sobriquet 'British Museum religion' attached to his efforts by Anglo-Papalists. In this he had scholarly collaborators thanks to the Alcuin Club, founded in 1897 for liturgical historians. The Club would come to play a major part in twentieth century attempts to revise the Book of Common Prayer, especially at the time of the Prayer Book Crisis of the later 1920s.

In 1912 Dearmer set up the Warham Guild—a craft guild named for the last pre-Reformation archbishop of Canterbury—for making well-produced accoutrements of strictly *English* Catholic worship, and that in 'fair conditions of labour'. This last requirement stemmed from the social radicalism exemplified (along with a strong dash of hierarchical management) in Ruskin's Late Victorian 'Guild of St George' (founded in 1871), which in turn might be conjoined with the influence of Stewart Headlam's Guild of St Matthew (it flourished from 1877 to 1909)—though Headlam did not share Ruskin's combination of artistic and social concerns, except insofar as he sought to render actors and actresses, as well as music hall artistes, respectable. At the heart of the Establishment, Dearmer would use the Westminster canonry somewhat grudgingly allotted him towards the end of his life to set up a canteen for the unemployed—probably not to the total satisfaction of all worshippers if John Betjeman's *In Westminster Abbey* is anything to go by. 'Think of what our Nation stands for,/ Books from Boots' and country lanes,/ Free speech, free passes, class distinction,/ Democracy and proper drains.' Readers of the poem can probably infer from the text's reference to the imminent *Blitzkrieg* that Betjeman (1906–84) wrote it in 1940, so it post-dates Dearmer by a whisker.[20]

The twelfth edition of *The Parson's Handbook* came out in 1932, four years before Dearmer's death. The thirteenth edition, from 1965, revised and partially rewritten by Cyril Pocknee (1906–80), an expert on the liturgical arts and sacramental theologian, largely simplified Dearmer's ceremonial, partly in light of the Continental 'Liturgical Movement', while defending, over against more radical spirits in that Movement, his fundamental options. Its date of publication coincides, appropriately enough, with the end of the epoch defined by the present book. [21]

Back to Baroque

An exactly contrary strategy was proposed by the (1911) Society of SS Peter and Paul. On the understanding that, had the Marian reaction succeeded, England would have looked rather like the Spanish Netherlands (a political union was envisaged in Mary's marriage settlement, in the event of offspring), the Society turned to contemporary Belgium for its preferred Neo-Baroque aesthetic style. The less Protestant the better was the mind-set of the Society's founders, which included the future Mgr Ronald Knox (1888–1957) though there had of course been such a thing as English Baroque, with Nicholas Hawksmoor (1661–1736) and Christopher Wren (1632–1723). That fitted with the way Anglo-Papalists, led by Lord Halifax, were seeking, by an ongoing 'Forward Movement', fully to imitate Continental practice in the Tridentine Church—with such devotions as Stations of the Cross, Benediction of the Blessed Sacrament, the recitation of the Rosary, and the public veneration of images and relics.

In 1921 the Society published *The Anglican Missal*, with a 'rite drawn from Anglican and Roman sources but with Roman rubrics'.[22] As the introduction to its High Mass volume explained, the result could be said to approximate to the 1549 Prayer Book but with ceremonial 'prescribed by the only authority which legislates on such matters, namely the Congregation of Rites in Rome'.[23] As S. L. Ollard commented, official opposition did not 'arrest the ceremonial advance, but it checked the older and more scholarly men, with the result that younger men took the lead, who turned for their models, not to libraries, and to the records of the English Church, but to the ceremonial they found existing as a living rite in the Churches of France and Belgium'.[24] Referring directly to 'Rome' added insult to injury. As Dearmer had written, the 'court of Rome... has no authority in this country, and can only be followed here by a violent exercise of that private judgment which is essentially Protestant, under whatever name it may mask itself'.[25]

The ceremonies of Exposition and Benediction of the Reserved Sacrament might be described as an obvious sequel to resuming Eucharistic Reservation itself. In 1918, accordingly, a Benediction Defence Fund was established, to help defray any financial costs incurred by prosecution. Its classic apology was the 1919 *Benediction and the Bishops* by the Anglo-Papalist Alban Baverstock (1871–1950).[26] Baverstock pushed the clergy to go beyond simple Reservation to a full extra-liturgical cultus of the Blessed Sacrament. The argument was that, *qua* extra-liturgical, it lay beyond the power of the bishops to ban it, whereas pastorally and spiritually it was well within the responsibilities of parish priests to promote it.[27] How could one have the very Body and Blood of the Redeemer in one's church, albeit in the order of sacramental signs, and then carry on with the weekly round of services just as though the *Sanctissimum* were absent?

In this context as in others, London and Brighton were still at the forefront of such radical Traditionalism. The role of Brighton was highlighted once more by a provincial Anglo-Catholic Congress which met there in 1922. Owing to the unexpected scale of attendance, it met both in the Brighton Dome, named for the central cupola of its concert hall, and at the Royal Pavilion, the Prince Regent's Indo-Saracenic extravaganza. The great majority of Brighton churches were now Anglo-Catholic, even the old parish church of St Nicholas.

As to London, in 1929 Kensit wrote an Open Letter to its bishop, Arthur Winnington-Ingram (1858–1946). 'Undiluted Romanism: A Call to Action' brought to his lordship's attention the sheer number of parishes in his jurisdiction where idolatrous worship was perpetrated perfectly openly. Winnington-Ingram's attempt to control (meaning stamp out) the cultus of the Reserved Sacrament produced something rather different: the 'Rebellion of the Twenty-One', an argued statement of 'Non possumus' by parish priests who refused to surrender. The great majority came from slum parishes in the East End (Stepney, Poplar, Bethnal Green, Hackney, Haggerston, the Isle of Dogs, and Limehouse), making them more difficult, morally speaking, to challenge. Some upper class churches were involved (St Augustine's, Queen's Gate; St John the Baptist, Holland Road; St Stephen's, Gloucester Road—T. S. Eliot's church; St Mary's Bourne Street—where Halifax worshipped when not on his Yorkshire estate). A few were in more socially mixed areas of Central London (Paddington, Fulham, Shepherds Bush), while a couple lay in darkest suburbia, in Teddington and Acton Green.[28]

Saints galore

Whether liturgical enthusiasms were neo-mediaeval, as in *The Parson's Handbook* or among devotees of the full Sarum Use, or, contrastingly, neo-patristic, as with those who opted for the Roman Rite as, in all fundamentals, the Mass of St Gregory the Great, one consequence might be 'menological', from the (Greek-derived) Latin word for a listing of holy persons to be 'remembered' in the liturgical calendar. (The oldest in the West, tentatively ascribed to a monk of Ramsey Abbey, is a prologue to the Anglo-Saxon Chronicle.) Anglican Catholics, like nineteenth century Roman Catholics, wished to extend the Church Calendar to include the more obscure saints of the pre-Reformation British Isles.[29] A goodly number of Anglo-Saxon figures could, in this antiquarian spirit, be recalled to life. But research soon showed they were far outclassed by the Cornish.

Gilbert Hunter Doble (1880–1945) was born at Penzance and after local schooling read Modern History at Exeter College, Oxford, from which base he attended all the Anglo-Catholic shrines: Pusey House, the Community House of the Society of St John the Evangelist on the Cowley Road, and the Anglo-Papalist bastion of St Paul's, Walton Street. After ordination training at Ely he returned to Cornwall to become vicar of Wendron, a lonely hamlet on the north coast (three miles from Walter Blunt's Helston), and organizing secretary of the English Church Union. Edward White Benson, as first bishop of Truro (between 1877 and 1883), had encouraged Anglicans to take an interest in Cornish saints but it is doubtful he realized what energies he was releasing. Doble's huge capacity for scholarly work, which earned him a honorary doctorate in Divinity at Oxford (though no one could be found with the necessary erudition to critique his scholarly output), engaged with the cultural impetus of the Cornish Revival led by Henry Jenner (1848–1934), the first Grand Bard of the Cornish Gorsedd (his 1904 *Handbook of the Cornish Language* was a key text),[30] and Robert Morton Nance, his successor (1873–1959, a prime mover in the development of 'Unified Cornish').[31] Cornish Methodism, the dominant religiosity in the Duchy, was strongly anti-Catholic, and Doble had to face down accusations that the Anglo-Catholic movement he represented stood for fetishistic sacramentalism, the setting up of a sacerdotal trade union, and a cult of the saints that amounted in practice to an 'Arian polytheism'.[32] This was not propitious ground for a menologist. It says much for his irenicism that he found himself able to compare John Wesley to St Francis Xavier, treating him as a precursor of Pusey and (somewhat hopefully) a teacher of Transubstantiation.[33] Doble's series of booklets on Cornish saints pieced together the tiniest fragments of historical data. The saints were already known from their Cornish church dedications but the majority had passed through on their way to or from Wales, Ireland, or Brittany, leaving very little other trace, though their (much) later acts and miracle legends could be copious enough. Doble's pamphlets evolved with his scholarship, moving from the kind of simple, straightforward account suited to the casual buyer in a village post office or the worshipper thumbing through tracts at the rear of a church to complex and tentative presentations readable only by the learned. The 'imagined audience changed from a communal world and the parish to the gathered church of international scholarship'.[34] Certainly he was no charming eccentric like his Victorian Cornish near-contemporary Parson Robert Stephen Hawker of Morwenstow (1803–75) who 'paced his parish in a purple cassock, a blue jersey, high wading boots, and an assortment of headgear that included a pink cap resembling a fez'.[35] Hawker regarded the ensemble as the proper dress of a presbyter of the ancient Celtic Church with which he considered himself aligned. Not that he should be written off. Tennyson judged Hawker's unfinished Arthurian poem, 'The Quest of the Sangraal' better than his own 'Idylls of the King'. Hawker was also a man of action, leading a number of successful rescues of shipwrecked sailors on the north Cornish coast.

Doble's crowning achievement was his 1927 *Cornish Church Kalendar*, from whose throng of saints Walter Frere of Truro—co-founder with Gore of the Community of the Resurrection, and as such a *bona fide* Anglo-Catholic though, like Doble himself, a moderate Ceremonialist—permitted the selection of five names for special mention. Days were to be appointed for veneration in the churches of his diocese. Doble had included in his Kalendar formal prayers for the blessing of a holy well, and midsummer fires (surviving remnants of popular Cornish Catholicism), but Frere added a note forbidding unauthorized liturgies of any kind (the Prayer Book Crisis had made the topic especially neuralgic in Parliament, and among the public at large). Doble died appropriately enough at Helston where that early Ritual controversy was played out in the long-suffering Bishop Philpotts' time.

The Prayer Book Crisis

After the close of the Great War there was an attempt to find a pacific solution for the continuing tensions over Liturgy and rite. The solution sought was intended to recreate a lost homogeneity in Anglican practice—possibly a mythical concept, if one bears in mind the discrepancy between cathedral practice and that of the parish church, yet a typical desideratum of ecclesiastical bureaucracies, as with their civil counterparts. It led the Church of England's bishops to sponsor, if with some misgivings, an official revision of the Prayer Book, the Restoration Settlement book of 1662.

The aim was to meet the sensibilities of the ever-growing Catholic party in the Church without alienating their most determined adversaries, the Evangelicals (and for that matter, the other competing party, that of Broad Churchmen). Like all compromises, it would entail each party abandoning something, and the question on all lips was, But how much? Eucharistic Reservation (by episcopal licence) would be permitted but only (probably) for the sick; an 'epiclesis', suggestive of Real Presence, would be introduced into the Great Prayer, but *after* the Words of Institution (contrary to Western Catholic practice);[36] prayer for the departed would be introduced, if discreetly worded. Considerable resources of diplomacy in both argumentative and persuasive modes were deployed, as well as much skirmishing in church newspapers and public meetings. Parliament turned out to have its own ideas. In what proved to be historically its last but also most dramatic, display of Erastian temper, the House of Commons fired off the cannonball that scuttled the ship. The *Manchester Guardian* reported via another metaphor, 'The Protestant watchdog has barked, and has proved to be a bigger dog than was perhaps expected in these Laodicean days'.[37] An adverse vote in 1927 was repeated when a modified version of the scheme came before Parliament the following year. As in Victoria's reign so under George V (reigned 1910–36), 'No Popery here' was the cry of the hour.

For quite opposite reasons, faced with the resultant wreckage, Evangelicals and 'advanced' Anglo-Catholics, notably those fully committed to the 'Western Rite', were relieved. The Evangelicals were pleased that no official concessions would be made to Catholics. Many Anglo-Catholics were pleased that an attempt to define the final limit of any such concessions had been thwarted. The proposed Liturgy, so it was witheringly remarked, was 'intended as a *ne plus ultra*, the extreme limit of innovation, the Prayer Book of King Canute'.[38] The Federation of Catholic Priests had announced that its fourteen hundred members would in any case defy the provisions about Reservation laid down in the 'Deposited Book'.[39] Yet other Anglo-Catholics, of whom Frere may be taken as typical (and his position was strong, by virtue of his liturgical learning),[40] thought an opportunity had been missed. Percy Dearmer went further, printing at his own expense an encomium that described the new Book as 'exceedingly good'.[41] The *Church Times* preserved a delicate neutrality between these dissonant Anglo-Catholic opinions. Those keen on 'political' analysis detected a decisive shift of power in the 'party' toward its 'Western' rather than its Dearmer-esque 'Sarum' or 'English' wing. The further attempt to push through a revised Bill, which included banning not only Eucharistic tabernacles ('Western') but the hanging Eucharistic pyx ('English') — the latter was deemed to denote a more 'pervasive' than 'localised' Eucharistic presence — left even Frere outside. But when in 1929 some bishops authorized the amended 1928 text for use in their dioceses Frere was among them. He had it specially bound up with copies of *Hymns Ancient and Modern* for regular services in Truro cathedral.

The uneasy truce over liturgical and ritual pluralism continued till the end of the period with which this book is concerned. It might also be said that the division within the Movement over the wisdom or otherwise of the 'Deposited Book' anticipated the rupture—over quite other issues—which, by the end of the twentieth century, would divide Catholic Anglicans into two camps: 'Affirming' Catholics, who accepted the agenda of Progressive Roman Catholicism, fed as it is, in matters of anthropology, by secular Liberalism, and the 'classical' Anglo-Catholics of whom *After Newman* is a eulogy.

— 5 —

Monasticism and Religious Life

THE REVIVAL OF MONASTICISM, especially in its active or 'apostolic' form—covered by that capacious term (in modern Roman Catholic usage) the 'Religious life'—was one of the more unexpected fruits of the Oxford Movement. Pusey and Keble, after all, were married men. Among the clerical Fellows of Oxford Colleges, celibacy was a condition to be endured until such time as a parish, generally a College living, beckoned and with it a new existence. But Newman had already conceived the notion of the peculiar congruence between celibacy and a total Christian commitment, though he meant it initially only as an autobiographical—even an idiosyncratic—observation.

Some wider range of application became inescapable as soon as the saints of the Pre-Reformation period were held up for veneration. Once an interest in historic Christian sanctity was awakened, the time-line could hardly stop there. Charles Lowder's exercise of priesthood was inseparable from the discovery of a Counter-Reformation giant, St Vincent de Paul, and the celibacy of the founder of the 'Company of the Mission'—Vincentians or Lazarists—was undoubtedly taken for granted. 'Devotional' and 'romantic' considerations, to use Owen Chadwick's epithets, now meshed with 'pastoral'. 'This pastoral motive derived strength from the sight of Roman Catholic nuns in slums or hospitals or orphanages; not only nuns in French or Belgian parishes, but nuns who fled to England from the French Revolution, and nuns from a growing number of convents in resurgent English Catholicism.'[1]

The Sisterhoods

The popularity of Tractarian Sisterhoods has puzzled historians. The numbers are not easy to crunch but it is by no means impossible that there were more women in Anglican Sisterhoods at the end of the nineteenth century than there were nuns in England on the eve of the Reformation. Among the historians of this 'silent rebellion' opinion as to the significance of this is divided. For Michael Hill, the motivation behind the development of the Sisterhoods was 'virtuoso and feminist', offering an extension of the woman's sphere beyond the domestic world, sometimes dramatically so—slums were no place for ladies, and the military hospitals of the Crimea no place for Englishwomen.[2] For John Shelton Reed, a close linkage to Victorian Feminism is not so plausible. Religious life 'embodied some of the same values, but in such a limited and tentative way, and incorporating so many of the patriarchal assumptions of the time, that it might be better to regard it as an alternative to feminism'. And yet, he added, the movement unquestionably 'responded to and benefited from some real strains resulting from the prevailing views of appropriate activities for women'.[3]

The first such Sisterhood hove into view in 1841 with—as noted in Chapter 1—Dr Pusey's receiving the vows of Marian Hughes (1817–1912), the daughter of a Gloucestershire clergyman.[4] It took a decade, though, before she became foundress at Oxford of the 'Society of the Holy and Undivided Trinity': suitable title for use by a *dirigée* of so doughty a supporter of the Athanasian Creed. In fact, her Sisterhood, despite its grandiose name, would be essentially a parochial affair—though not in the parish that might have been expected. For Hughes was cousin to Thomas Chamberlain (1810–92),[5] Vicar of St Thomas-the-Martyr, Becket Street, the first Anglo-Catholic parish where a chasuble was used at the Eucharist, sewn by her from two silk academic hoods gifted by Oxford masters-of-arts. Chamberlain wanted—and he got—a Sisterhood, the 'Community of St Thomas-the-Martyr', with good results for the illiterate poor, the housebound, orphans, and girls in want of training for domestic service in west Oxford, around the soon-to- be-built railway station.[6] But it was not with his cousin's aid.

Hughes' problem lay in her conviction that she could only belong to a community that was not merely 'Puseyite' but 'Puseyan': namely, one under the direction of the man who in 1841 had received her vows. While her foundation would be in Oxford, the site of Pusey's canon-professorship, it would not be at St Thomas's.

Much of inner Oxford, north of the former city wall, belonged to the non-Tractarian parish of St Giles, and it was there that, in due course, Marian Hughes built a magnificent convent (now St Anthony's College), leasing land on the Woodstock Road. Parochial Sisterhoods required sympathetic parishes, so it was fortunate that out of this parish was carved a trio of Anglo-Catholic centres: St Barnabas, Jericho; St Paul's, Walton Street; and SS Philip and James, close by the Society's convent. Experience was already showing it was generally more fruitful when Sisterhoods and parishes worked together.

Mother Marian chose a rule close to that of the Ursulines of Blois, a community she encountered on a journey through France in the year of her vows to Pusey. By 1861 she had defined the aims of her Sisters: 'to instruct and protect young girls, to visit the poor and ignorant, to nurse in hospitals or otherwise, and to pray for the preservation and increase of the true Faith, and by acts of mercy and charity to testify their love and obedience to our Lord and Saviour Jesus Christ'.[7]

But this is to get ahead of the wider story. In 1844 Lord John Manners (1820–74), later Duke of Rutland, who had in mind a fitting memorial to the poet Robert Southey (1774–1843) — Southey hit on the idea of Sisterhoods even before Pusey[8] — persuaded a reluctant Bishop Blomfield of London to allow the opening of a Sisterhood in the vicinity of Regent's Park. Linked to Christ Church, Albany Street, where a Tractarian, William Dodsworth (1798–1861), was Perpetual Curate,[9] the members were known as the Sisters of the Holy Cross, or, more colloquially, 'Park Village West'. They were to teach pauper children, run an orphanage, and visit the poor in the slums on the Euston Road.[10] A comparison with Roman Catholic 'Sisters of Charity', as active Sisterhoods were generically known in Catholic Europe, immediately suggests itself. Britons, military and otherwise, had been impressed by the work of such *Soeurs de la Charité* during the Napoleonic Wars — an impression Southey's plea for a Church of England version plainly reflected.[11] Both Pusey and Keble helped Dodsworth compose its customary, drawn from a variety of sources and used in conjunction with the Rule of St Augustine. Marian Hughes was headhunted to be the first Superior, but an aged parent vetoed the proposal. Her time was not yet.

Park Village West was adversely affected by secessions to Rome and fell victim in due course to the empire-building proclivities of another foundress, in faraway Devonport, as will be told.[12] Meanwhile, Pusey arranged for the Sisters to occupy a neo-mediaeval conventual building, created for them by William Butterfield at St Saviour's, Osnaburgh Street, close to a major centre of Tractarian worship, St Mary Magdalene, Munster Square.

Next came the Vicar of Wantage, William John Butler (1818–94), who, in 1848 started a community of teaching nuns in his parish under the title, The Community of St Mary the Virgin.[13] Butler consulted Archdeacon Manning about suggestions for a Superior and the choice fell on Elizabeth Crawford Lockhart (1811–70), the sister of William Lockhart (1820–92), one of Newman's community at Littlemore. It was Lockhart whose departure for Rome occasioned Newman's memorable 1843 sermon 'The Parting of Friends', since become emblematic of the separation of the 'Oxford Fathers' from the 'Oxford Converts'.[14] The 'Wantage Sisters' now added a 'House of Mercy' for prostitutes — or unmarried mothers: possibly, in a sexually censorious age, there was a difficulty in distinguishing.

The Gorham Judgment reduced the Community of St Mary the Virgin to a two-some (Elizabeth joined her brother in going to Rome) but Bishop Wilberforce told Butler to soldier on. A second choice of Superior picked out a diamond. Harriet Day (1811–92), a farmer's daughter, became, for all practical purposes, the real foundress if always in tandem with Butler himself. The Wantage Rule as eventually formulated turned out to be eclectic. After enumerating its sources, Peter Anson, historian of the monastic revival in the Church of England, summed it up as best he could: mostly 'traditional Benedictinism with a dash of the spirit of some of the older communities of Canonesses Regular'.[15] The Wantage Sisters would make themselves known as learned or at any rate highly educated women, with a variety of apostolates in the arts (notably printing plainsong books and wood-carving) and teaching (including training teachers), as well as maternity and parochial work and those near-ubiquitous Victorian 'Houses of Mercy'. C. S. Lewis dedicated his theological science fantasy *Perelandra* to 'some ladies at Wantage'.[16]

Also in 1848, and with at least initially rather warmer episcopal encouragement (the *episkopos* this time was the Tractarian-inclined Philpotts of Exeter), Priscilla Lydia Sellon (1821–76), née Smith (she was the daughter of a naval commander who changed his name to Sellon on receiving a fortune from a maiden aunt) entered Tractarian circles through friendship with the family of a London barrister, churchwarden at Christ Church, Albany Street.[17] In answer to Philpotts' appeal to his diocese to do something about destitution in the maritime towns, Sellon put herself forward for philanthropic activity. As she began work among the poor in the seaports of Plymouth and Devonport, Pusey encouraged her to think in terms of forming a Sisterhood, and so she did.[18]

She was versatile, creating not only an orphanage but homes for delinquent boys and old sailors, a school for teaching girls fine needlework, model lodging houses, a soup kitchen, and much else. At the time, the counties of Devon and Cornwall contained only a single Roman Catholic convent: the enclosed Carmelites at Lanherne. That gives her achievement even higher relief. On the debit side, her disciplinarian outlook and abbatial bearing did not win her universal sympathy, even among her own Sisters. Then in the years 1854 to 1856 Mother Lydia (as she had become) took over what remained of the Manners community originally domiciled in Regents Park. It was probably at this time that, in the fashion of a lady abbess in European monasteries, she began to make use of a ceremonial pastoral staff. She had been inducted as abbess of the two foundations on the feast of St Benedict, 1857, for 'Pusey toyed with a dream of Miss Sellon as abbess-general of all religious communities in Britain.'[19] All *female* Religious, presumably, though mediaeval abbesses had occasionally ruled double monasteries. But the day for reviving male monasticism was not quite yet.

Sellon's 'Society of the Most Holy Trinity' was unusual in generating wheels within wheels—one cadre of Sisters (the First Order), wearing black, for active works of charity, another (the Second Order), wearing white, as more or less cloistered contemplatives, and a Third Order, wearing grey, to assist in the manner of Tertiaries the life and work of the other two. This elaborate organization which extended to plans for the constitutional amalgamation of all Anglican Sisterhoods as well as schemes for sets of missionary Sisters overseas, suggested to Anson the mind-set of a 'born legislator', not content to 'muddle through' in the usual English fashion.[20] But the sheer complexity of Mother Lydia's 'Seven Great Rules', drawn up in 1861, rather belies the suggestion of efficiency.

In 1863, making use of an inheritance passed to them by Pusey on his mother's death, the Society opened for its contemplative branch the splendid Ascot Priory, in Berkshire, another Butterfield commission. By this point the cloistered Sisters resembled Poor Clares more than any other Catholic Order or Congregation, though their white habits had turned purple rather than Franciscan brown. Mother Lydia died at Ascot, fittingly enough, since in the grounds stood the hermitage where Pusey too would die six years on.

Contemporaneous with the founding of the Society of the Most Holy Trinity, a Community of Nursing Sisters of St John the Divine was established, at least in incipient form, in London's Fitzroy Square.[21] Trained in the Middlesex and Westminster hospitals these generous women soon took over all nursing activity at King's College Hospital, where they also set up the training school for what was to be in future their principal activity. They were unique among Sisterhoods in receiving massive episcopal support (twelve diocesans stated their approval, including the two primates). There was a reason for that. The support was forthcoming on condition that no Religious vows were ever pronounced—anathema as such vows were to almost all Anglican bishops at this date, and to many for much longer. The Clewer Sisters, to be described below, met with Samuel Wilberforce's encouragement until they proposed changing their Constitutions to enable vows for life. Thomas Carter, their founder, supported them 'It has always been the feeling of the Sisters that their purpose and conviction is a life-long dedication of themselves'[22]), while admitting that historically, the taking of vows was a product of monasticism rather than its precondition.

Only in 1932, when the first of the perduring Anglo-Catholic monastic initiatives for men, the Society of St John the Evangelist, took the Community of the Nursing Sisters of St John the Divine under their wing was it possible for its members to live in the proper sense a *vowed* life, commenced through a regular novitiate where the promise of consecration until the natural end of biological existence was kept determinedly in view.

In 1851, the year when Thomas Chamberlain, founded (without cousin Marian) his own parish Sisterhood, another foundress, Harriet Brownlow Byron (1818–87), took as her collaborator William Upton Richards (1811–73), minister of the Margaret Street Chapel where he succeeded Frederick Oakeley when the latter absconded to Rome. The two of them set up the Community of All Saints Sisters of the Poor, initially housing homeless children and tubercular women, with Byron modelling the life of her Sisters on the Daughters of Charity in Paris's Rue du Bac.[23] On the feast of St Dominic, 1856, Miss Monsell received a ring of profession from Bishop Wilberforce, acting for Blomfield of London and, now Mother Harriet, was made Superior for life. Sir William Jenner (1815–98), the pioneer of smallpox vaccination, asked the All Saints Sisters to take responsibility for two wards of University College Hospital—the beginning of a long commitment to nursing and convalescent care, including the building of the first ever seaside convalescent home, at Eastbourne, in Sussex. Foundations followed in Edinburgh; Baltimore, Maryland; Cape Town (with a leprosarium on Robben Island in Table Bay); in the docklands of Bombay as well as at various locations in England itself. After Mother Harriet's death in 1887 a new mother house was established at Colney Park, near St Albans, superseding Margaret Street itself. At 'London Colney' the chapel was finished by John Ninian Comper in his characteristic manner, with chromatically wonderful painted glass and a classic gilded civory or 'ciborium'. No matter what drudgery these Sisterhoods took on, they kept as their maxim 'Worship the Lord in the beauty of holiness' (a version of Psalm 96:9).

Then in 1852 Thomas Thellusson Carter (1808–91), Vicar of Clewer in Berkshire, in collaboration with a clergyman's widow, Harriet Monsell (1811–83), set up the Community of St John the Baptist.[24] A mile from the chief residence of a disapproving monarch at Windsor, 'Clewer' was designed by Henry Woodyer (1816–96), a pupil of Butterfield, in a romantically mediaeval style evoking 'memories of Pre-Raphaelite paintings, with which it was more or less contemporary'.[25] Its chief task was to be reclamation of London's women of the street, estimated at some ten thousand souls. Care of such women was (to put it mildly) an 'extremely unconventional task for a lady'.[26] From these beginnings in Houses of Mercy (a gentler name than State officialdom's 'Penitentiaries') Clewer branched out into nursing and education, the provision of almshouses and rest-homes for the aged, and, when transplanted into the world of the Raj, a sanatorium at Darjeeling in the Himalayan foothills.

As with all these Sisterhoods, the liturgical Hours provided the stable rhythm of the day. Where Clewer seems to have been exceptional was in managing without reference to pre-existing models in Catholic Europe. It proved to be especially fast-growing, numbering three hundred at the time of Carter's death.[27] For some reason it acquired a distinctly high-caste membership. From the 1860s onwards a number of the professed 'had discarded their aristocratic titles—but not necessarily their social standing—when they took the veil'. [28]

For statisticians one of the most successful of the early Sisterhoods was the Society of Saint Margaret, founded by the hymnographer and novelist John Mason Neale (1818–66).[29] The Sisters of the Society of Saint Margaret began by nursing in parishes around East Grinstead, on the edge of the Ashdown Forest. Later they added schools, and houses of refuge for those women of the street. Neale's 1843 *Ayton Priory, or the Restored Monastery* is a novelistic account of what it was like to begin or, on the Continuity Thesis beloved of the high church party in general, to *resume* Religious life in the Church of England.[30] Not that Neale proposed to live such a life himself (he was a married man with five children.) Yet he recognized its value for a Catholic version of the Church. A Church with no form of consecrated life was only half a Church.

The idea of writing a novel to commend it suggests a romantic amateur. Yet there was nothing amateur about the way Neale went about critically considering models for his Society. He studied the efforts of the new Religious at Park Village West, at Wantage, and at Devonport, as well as the most recent, created by Thomas Carter, the Vicar of Clewer, in 1851. Then he extended his explorations to France where there was, or should have been, the wisdom of experience to guide—though much Religious life in Continental Europe was itself a new start after the dispersions of the Revolutionary and Napoleonic eras. The rule Neale produced for the Sisterhood was in effect a conflation of the rule composed by St Francis de Sales (1567–1622) for his Visitandine nuns (the 'Order of the Visitation of Holy Mary') with that of the Daughters of Charity of St Vincent de Paul.[31] Seventeenth century models were rarely far away in the Anglo-Catholic Sisterhoods of Victoria's reign.[32]

In 1857 the fledgling Society endured a riot of its own at the Lewes funeral of one of its Sisters. For once the bone of contention was not the sacraments or the Liturgy. Neale had been accused of persuading a nun from a wealthy family to hand over her money, and setting her to work (with murderous intent, or at any rate fatal results) nursing those suffering from scarlet fever. A mob of 150 people tried to burn his house down, and the bishop of Chichester pleaded with him to leave the diocese. Naturally he refused and, undaunted, extended his efforts north of the Border, with an 1864 foundation at St Margaret's Aberdeen, the first autonomous filiation of his Society.[33]

Strangely (or not if sibling rivalry were in question), his own sister by blood did not enter the Society of St Margaret but began her own. Elizabeth Neale's (died 1901) Community of the Holy Cross—its members co-workers with the slum priests at St George's-in-the-East—was originally modelled (once again) on the Daughers of Charity of St Vincent de Paul, Charles Lowder's hero.[34] Her Sisters too opened a refuge for prostitutes, which moved to the more salubrious setting of Sutton, in rural Surrey, in 1858. Training former prostitutes for domestic work, the home was also a refuge for destitute girls—aiming at prevention rather than cure. In 1869 the difficulty of finding a large enough house for the growing Community in the East End led Mother Elizabeth to accept an invitation from the Vicar of St Paul's, Lorrimore Square, to move the Sisterhood to Walworth. But they continued to receive girl clients from Dockland with its massive social and economic problems. 'The Docks' would be a suppurating sore till the end of the Victorian age: their traditional occupation, the building of sailing ships, with its ancillary trades of sail- and rope-making, had wholly collapsed.

The Community of the Holy Cross had always been, thanks to Lowder, more 'Western' than 'Prayer Book'. In time (but still within the lifetime of the foundress) it gave up its active works and adopted the Benedictine principle that 'nothing is to be preferred to the Work of God'. In 1886 it determined to carry out that *opus Dei* on Hayward's Heath in Sussex, in a version of German Gothic designed, along with the glass of its windows, by Charles Eamer Kempe. In 1955 Peter Anson could report that the Sisters 'carry out the Divine Office according to the Monastic Breviary in the Latin tongue with a perfection that would surprise most Roman Catholic communities', rating their efforts alongside those of the nuns of Stanbrook, at that time the gold standard of the Chant in England, comparable to the monks of Solesmes in France.[35] This quite dramatic evolution of Mother Elizabeth's community at least showed that the efflorescence of Religious life in Anglo-Catholicism is not solely to be understood as a somewhat extreme reaction to perceived social needs.

In the 1840s and 50s, the life of women Religious was deemed unnatural, their autonomy and professionalism out of place. Their occasional tendency to abscond to Rome (true of the first Superiors of Park Village West and Wantage) had been predictable since it was happening already on a wider scale among groups of priests living together but without formal vows. That included Newman's group at Littlemore, Frederick William Faber's (1814–63) at Elton, in Huntingdonshire, and most of the celibate clergymen brought together by Pusey's munificence in a common clergy-house at St Saviour's Leeds. Yet the Sisterhoods had survived the No Popery outbursts after 1850, and their reputation was enhanced by reports of their nursing activities among the wounded and dying of the Crimean War—a war opposed by Neale, who thought it reasonable for the Russian Tsar to be official protector of Orthodox Christians in the Ottoman Empire. Lord Palmerston, an early practitioner of Bismarckian *Realpolitik*, had little time for such Churchy considerations.

For the following decade, between 1860 and 1870, Peter Anson, the chronicler of their many foundations, listed ten new Orders of Sisters. The process of multiplication continued steadily until century's end: between 1870 and 1900 Anson discusses fifteen. In the next century, conveniently opening in the year of Victoria's death, Anson totted up a total of twenty-one new foundations. And these numbers do not take into account the many communities that came into existence as remote offshoots of English (or, occasionally, Scottish) foundations overseas.

It did not take much, however, to shake the confidence of bishops in Sisters. The Bishop of London withdraw recognition from Park Village West because the Sisters used Pusey's bowdlerized book of Roman devotions. His brother of Chichester followed suit after the Lewes Riot, frightened by the popular outbursts. Their colleague at Exeter abandoned Mother Lydia's foundation since he thought the Sisters under too great moral pressure to keep their Community promises. At Clewer, Bishop Wilberforce of Oxford banned all crucifixes, as well as Roman manuals of spiritual theology, though on balance he appears to have been more of a friend than a foe, defending the Sisterhoods against critics, including no doubt his episcopal confreres.[36]

But by the turn of the century a majority of bishops were likely to agree they were an enhancement to Church life, even if the issue of life vows still stuck in the maw for some. In 1883 Wilkinson of Truro had become the first diocesan actually to found a Sisterhood, the Community of the Epiphany in his see-city.[37] In 1890 the Upper House of the Convocations of Canterbury, by way of an oversight in drafting, allowed for life-vows, not noticing that 'what had originally been described as a promise to the Bishop became a promise in the presence of the Bishop' which could only mean a promise to God.[38] Colonial bishops, as the last Lambeth Conference of the nineteenth century indicated, were even more likely to assent, having discovered their invaluable missionary role in young churches. Church authorities could, however, still sustain shocks as when in 1908 a London branch of the Society of St Margaret, situated at Queen Square, Bloomsbury, made their corporate submission to Rome.

The monasteries: a rocky road

Purely contemplative—and therefore in the strictest sense, monastic—Sisterhoods (like the transmogrified Community of the Holy Cross) were late in coming, whereas for men they were the vanguard of advance, a somewhat faltering advance though it might be.

There were two attempts to re-create Benedictine life. Joseph Leycester Lyne's would begin in East Anglia, first at Claydon, in a rural setting on the edge of Ipswich, and then at Elm Hill, Norwich, from which city he was chased out by its bishop. Father Ignatius picked up the pieces and continued his efforts, eventually settling in 1869 at Llanthony, in the Black Mountains. Benjamin Fearnly Carlyle's monastery started in a slum parish on the Isle of Dogs. Subsequently, after perambulation through Gloucestershire and Yorkshire (where Viscount Halifax befriended him), Abbot Aelred hit on the 'extra-diocesan' site of Caldey Island, off the Pembrokeshire coast opposite Tenby. The lifestyle of the first of these foundations was necessarily mitigated, not to say disabled, by the activities of a much-in-demand charismatic preacher and speaker who might have been more at home in early Methodism. But the work of the second was undeniably that of a Benedictine founder albeit on a late mediaeval model—as could be seen, not least, from the grandeur of the abbot's princely dwelling, the *abbatiale*.

Father Ignatius Leycester Lyne (1837–1908) was the son of a City of London merchant, educated at St Paul's School, and subsequently at Trinity College, Glenalmond, where his religion teacher was William Bright (1824–1901), a future Regius Professor of Ecclesiastical History at Oxford.[39] The Lynes were originally a Cornish family who had made their fortune in glassmaking (they re-glazed much of Lisbon after the 1755 earthquake) while the Leycesters were minor gentry settled at Cookham in Berkshire. Mrs Leycester Lyne encouraged the youthful Joseph's ecclesiastical bent. A kinsman of hers was Bishop of Moray, Ross and Caithness who kindly arranged for her son's place at the Scottish church's boarding school for boys, Trinity College, Glenalmond. That explains how Joseph came to be ordained deacon by the Scottish Episcopal Bishop of Perth, though he made sure of returning to England for his first curacy, at St Peter's, Plymouth, where the vicar was already celebrated as a model Anglo-Catholic priest. And, as it happened, George Prynne himself had once been curate to a Lyne—at Tywardreath, across the Tamar into Cornwall.[40]

Leycester Lyne's conviction that he had a vocation to re-found monasticism in the Church of England, or, as he put it, 'come before the world as a monk', allegedly had the backing of both Pusey and Mother Lydia, alias Miss Sellon.[41] An initial attempt at Stoke Damerel, between Devonport and Plymouth, proved abortive, though around that time he made his first visit to the Honddu Valley, and glimpsed the tantalizing ruins of the twelfth-century Augustinian priory at Llanthony. A further pastoral appointment at St George's-in-the-East (he had met the Rector, Bryan King, while on holiday with his family at Bruges) was also short-lived. But while in Stepney he read the Rule of St Benedict and, despite misgivings on the part of Charles Lowder, now arrived at that Ritualist hotbed, began to wear a modified version of the Benedictine habit, adding a Franciscan rope-girdle and rosary as well as sandals, worn on bare feet.

Leycester Lyne's two attempts at a Benedictine foundation in East Anglia (1863–4 at Claydon, 1864–6 at Norwich) lay somewhere between fiasco and farce, from which only retreat to London—a suburban house in Stoke Newington, followed by a more substantial property at Laleham, then still a Middlesex village—salvaged his reputation. Where, however, he was somewhat more successful was with the formation of a community of Benedictine nuns in the nearby village of Feltham. There he installed as prioress a physician's daughter from Plymouth, Harriet Stewart (died 1906), who thereby became Mother Hilda. After a row that split their community in two, the faction who fled back to the founder (by then Abbot of Llanthony) did not prosper, but the rest flourished, moving first, in 1893, to West Malling in Kent and then to Milford Haven in Pembrokeshire where in 1913 they were received into the Church of Rome. Their Kentish buildings were taken over by another group of nuns associated with Aelred Carlyle. Adopting the Rule of St Benedict under his influence, the newcomers thus became the well-respected Anglican house that is Malling Abbey, on the main road between London and the Kent coast.

The anarchism of Leycester Lyne's male monastery, with its dabblings in infant oblateship and whiff of adolescent homo-eroticism at Norwich and romantic mediaevalism mixed in with Celtic revivalism at Llanthony, was compounded in the eyes of ecclesiastical officialdom by the founder's canonically illegal acceptance of Orders from an *episcopus vagans*. Joseph-René Vilatte (1854–1929), the son of a Paris butcher, had received orders from a Latin-rite cleric in Ceylon who himself had been consecrated a bishop by Syrian Orthodox hierarchs from the Monophysite patriarchate of Antioch.[42] Vilatte, domiciled in the region of the Great Lakes, had turned up unannounced at Llanthony—possibly a result of connections made during its abbot's preaching tour in America in 1890 and 1891. The decision to accept Orders from this source was the consequence of repeated refusals to advance Ignatius from diaconate to priesthood, depriving the monks of any but the rarest possibility of Eucharistic celebration. Despite Leycester Lyne's undoubted gifts as an evangelistic preacher (preaching tours up and down the country occupied some twenty weeks of the year[43]), it meant the end of any hope of official recognition by the Church of England.

At his death in 1908 he left Brother Asaph Harris (died 1960) as his successor, but Harris repeated his abbot's mistake in securing Orders in extra-canonical style, and the property of Llanthony passed to the residuary legatee, the Abbot of Caldey.[44] Leycester Lyne's reputation has not weathered well. But justice requires taking note of the positive account of his personality (though not his practicality) recorded by that judicious Welsh pastor Francis Kilvert (1840–79) in his celebrated *Diary*.

Benjamin Fearnley Carlyle (1874–1955) was born in Sheffield, but a year after his birth the family moved to Truro for the sake of his father's work. This was the first move in a highly mobile childhood and youth — including for a period, Argentina, where he had opportunities to renew a nodding acquaintance with the worship of the Latin church. He had first experienced the Roman Liturgy at Cheltenham, where monks of Douai Abbey were the rectors of the mission.[45] Carlyle's education at a prestigious West Country school, Blundell's, in Tiverton, was cut short by his father's death, and the consequent loss of his income. So instead of proceeding to read medicine at Oxford, as planned, he called on the services of a private tutor with whose help he became in 1892 a medical student at London's St Bartholomew's Hospital. Much of the time he should have been giving to medical studies he spent in inspection of the rich tapestry of Anglo-Catholic (and to some extent Roman Catholic) church life, most influentially the convent established at Twickenham by the rebellious remnant from Ignatius Leycester Lyne's female foundation. In 1893 he became an Oblate of that convent, and, taking the name Aelred (after the twelfth century Cistercian abbot of Rievaulx), was invested by its chaplain with a form of Benedictine habit tailored by the nuns. Shortly after, his fellow Oblates — a group of idealistic young Anglo-Catholic men — elected him their Superior.

Thus began Aelred Carlyle's monastic life in whose principles and practices he now proceeded to form his charges, alternating consultation of written sources with visits to exiled French monks at Buckfast, in Devon, who were governed *in absentia* by the abbot of La-Pierre-qui-vire on the windswept and barren *plateau du Morvan*. In later life Carlyle described that Abbey and its daughter foundations, fairly enough, as 'a strict almost Trappist Congregation, strictly contemplative but with an ardent missionary spirit'.[46] It gave him his initial idea as a founder: a rigorous monastic life in a physically demanding setting. In 1896, accordingly, he started up his monastic foundation in much the same circumstances as so many Anglican Sisterhoods — in his case, the parish of St John's, Isle of Dogs, where he and his confreres taught catechism and provided recreational space for socially deprived Dockland youths.

But the ultimate aim was a strictly contemplative house—hence the search for a suitable site which took his group on a perambulation through the Cotswolds, with interludes of hospitality from his nun friends, now moved from Twickenham to West Malling, and the 'Cowley Fathers' (yet to be described) both at the latter's London house and in a country cottage they owned in Dorset. In 1902 the monastic neophytes reached a safe if temporary harbour at Painsthorpe, in the East Riding of Yorkshire, a property of Lord Halifax. More streetwise than Leycester Lyne, Aelred Carlyle now obtained ordination from the Anglo-Catholic Bishop of Fond du Lac, Wisconsin, thus acquiring the limited but perfectly regular status of 'clergyman in Colonial Orders'. (Charles Grafton, 1830–1912, wanted to encourage Benedictinism, a form of monasticism that ante-dated the rise of 'Roman errors' and thus was acceptable to strict Tractarians of his ilk.) Carlyle charmed out of Frederick Temple an acknowledgement both of his monastic profession and of his abbatial election, for in Halifax's house his community had grown to a respectable size, well over a score, a total never equalled at Llanthony. The Archbishop of York, in whose Province this monastic experiment was established, appears to have taken a relaxed attitude to the matter, neither recognizing nor inhibiting Carlyle's employment of abbatial insignia or his priestly activities. In 1904 Carlyle launched the journal *Pax*, and in 1905 the Confraternity of the Order of St Benedict with cells in Anglo-Catholic parishes. By 1910 it counted two thousand confraters.

The offer of Caldey Island, allegedly an extra-diocesan territory and, with greater historical certainty, a place hallowed by monastic saints of the ancient British church, was the dream solution. Carlyle had Halifax's moral backing. If only it could be converted into that most useful of commodities, hard cash. And soon, with skilful advertising, funds began to accrue.

The acquisition of Caldey Island in 1906 gave Carlyle a very different canvas on which to paint. His extravagance on Caldey where neither patrons nor bishops stayed his arm was made possible by a highly specific combination of factors. The dramatic clarity of his personal vision meshed with the fervent desire of highly placed Anglo-Catholics to see English Benedictinism revive in the Canterbury Communion. He was much in demand in 'advanced' parishes, and when he ceased accepting such engagements, better-off parishioners, as well as clergymen and students from the ancient Universities, could flock to the island's guesthouse instead. There was certainly much to see: the abbey buildings with their impressive range of towers and turrets, the peacocks spreading their fans in the landscaped gardens, the oaken misericords in the chapel, the ebony and filigreed silver candlesticks on the high altar with its lapis lazuli crucifix, and at pontifical Mass the gem-encrusted abbatial mitres.⁴⁷ The opulence damaged not only his funds but also his memory.⁴⁸

Worse was to come—from the viewpoint of the English Church Union and Carlyle's other Anglo-Catholic supporters. The Abbot, supported by a Community vote, refused to compromise with episcopal demands not to use Roman-Benedictine books in public worship, or keep Marian feasts based on the Roman doctrinal tradition, or maintain the extra-liturgical cultus of the Blessed Sacrament: three points on which Charles Gore, the delegate of Temple's successor, Archbishop Randall Davidson (1848–1930), was adamant.

For its late date in the Ritualist culture wars, 1913, Gore's stance on these matters, it must be said, was remarkably intransigent. But as that rarity an Anglo-Catholic diocesan bishop, he had a vested interest in keeping other Anglo-Catholics within church-legal limits. So perhaps his inflexibility was understandable after all.

The other principal issue in his ultimatum, namely, the immediate transfer of the property from a private trust to the Anglican authorities, confronted the monks with the possibility that, even in case of compliance, they might lose everything. The impasse led to the secession of the majority of the Caldey community on 5 March 1913 and their subsequent Roman Catholic relocation to a more affordable site at Prinknash in Gloucestershire.⁴⁹

English Roman Catholics had been hard on the Anglican Caldey. An exception was Dom Bede Camm (1864–1942) of Erdington Abbey who told John Cuthbert Hedley (1837–1915), Bishop of Newport, 'What amazes me so much is their faith and devotion. They might have been Catholics for years'.⁵⁰ Carlyle's statement of monastic theology and practice, *Our Purpose and Method*, was entirely wholesome, and remains in use in the Catholic daughter houses of Caldey to this day.

The Caldey minority, who voted against leaving the Church of England, began slowly to pick up the pieces of a common life, initially at Pershore in Worcestershire.⁵¹ Only a priest-oblate, Denys Prideaux (1864–1934), was left of those in Orders, and inevitably, despite reluctance to make solemn profession as a monk, he had to fall on his sword, becoming at first 'warden' and then in 1922 abbot, of which task he made a surprisingly good job.⁵² Expansion suggested the acquisition of a new property, Nashdom in Buckinghamshire, a Lutyens house in the Neo-Georgian style put on the market by the emigré Russian aristocrats who had built it.

Perhaps the building retained some ghostly Russian presence. At any rate Prideaux's interests turned East, somewhat in the spirit of William Palmer of Magdalen. Under the presidency of Athelstan Riley (1858–1945), a leading Anglo-Catholic layman determined that the

Caldey inheritance at Pershore/Nashdom should at all costs survive, Abbot Denys agreed to be vice-president of the Anglican and Eastern Churches Association. From this came a curious development. Sergei Bolshakoff (1901–90), author of a standard study of Russian mystical writers,[53] had formed a religious society of his own (the 'Devotees of the Logos') at an Estonian university. In 1924, he decided it should become a Benedictine confraternity spiritually attached to Nashdom. Bolshakoff was then given the Benedictine habit *in absentia* by the émigré Bishop Tikhon (Lyashchenko, 1878–1945) of Berlin, a hierarch of the Synodal Church, alias the Russian Church in Exile.[54] It was an extraordinary meeting of worlds which must have delighted readers of the *Church Times*. Such openings to the Orthodox in no way diminished Dom Denys' Anglo-Papalism, which was carried with a remarkable insouciance towards both the Roman and the Canterbury authorities. 'He did not think that a politico-economic wrangle between the Court of St James and the Court of Rome disturbed the real, divinely ordained, unity of the Church.'[55]

As the only abbot in the Church of England Prideaux was in some demand, especially from other Religious. He was chaplain general to the Sisters of the Church, founded by Mother Emily Ayckbowm (1836–1900) in 1864, for the care of disabled and sick children, but with communities at various English locations, including at Squire's Gate in the present writer's hometown, Lytham St Anne's.[56] He encouraged the Community of St Mary of the Cross at Edgware (originally Shoreditch) to adopt the Benedictine Rule, which they did in 1935 re-christening their superior as the first abbess.[57] He was also able to assist the Society of the Precious Blood at Burnham Abbey, at a Buckinghamshire location and therefore not far from Nashdom. Founded by Mother Millicent Taylor (1869–1956) as an apostolic group at St Jude's, Birmingham (it moved later, but not very far, to Kings Heath), the Society had transmogrified into a contemplative Sisterhood, albeit in the Augustinian, rather than Benedictine, tradition.[58] There was also an attempt to run a seminary, exploiting the great talents of Dom Gregory Dix who would have been its director of studies. It was the route that had been successfully taken by Mirfield and Kelham. Dix himself was at this point a simple Oblate, only simply professed in 1937, solemnly in 1940.

By then Prideaux had been succeeded by the second abbot, Martin Collett, who sought to direct Nashdom's energies towards the ecumenical movement. It was not a propitious time, after the failure of the Malines Conversations, Pius XI's discouraging encyclical *Mortalium animos*, and the Prayer Book Crisis which, inevitably, had drawn attention to the Babylonian Captivity of the Church of England to Parliament. Despite his Orthodox connexions, Prideaux had believed Anglo-Catholicism's chief priority should be its own strengthening, and in Nashdom's case the ensuring of the survival of Anglican Benedictinism. Not 'chasing dreams of corporate reunion'.[59]

In actuality, however, Martin Collett (1880–1948) found time to continue his predecessor's work of drawing women's communities into Nashdom's orbit. He encouraged Edgware Abbey to give refuge to Sisterhoods in difficulty: the Canonesses Regular of Our Lady of Victory and the Sisters of the Transfiguration came under their umbrella.[60] He helped the Sisters of the Good Shepherd, founded among the poor on Canvey Island, to move toward Benedictine observance (they were originally under the Neo-Franciscan 'Society of the Divine Compassion'.)[61] But this drive to empire, with ambitious plans for an Anglican Benedictine Congregation, with houses of both monks and nuns, never achieved fruition.

That did not prevent Nashdom attaining a high level of liturgical and conventual life. It was a classic monastery with a fully Roman Liturgy (in Latin), indistinguishable in outward appearance from monasteries on the European Continent (or, in England, the Solesmes Congregation house of Quarr Abbey, on the Isle of Wight). Only it was a bit odd to hold a Solemn High Mass in what had been a ballroom.

The Communities: 'surrounded with variety'

Thomas Aquinas had defended the plurality of new Orders in the Latin Christendom of the twelfth and thirteenth centuries by reference to the Epithalamium Psalm, Psalm 44, where the queen at her wedding (Aquinas is thinking typologically of the Church) is 'surrounded by variety', the variety of her attendants. That recipe for pluralism in Religious life was reflected in the widely differing male Religious houses that emerged from the Church of England's Catholic Revival.

More influential on the wider Church than the attempts to recreate the Black Monk life of medieval Benedictines were four non-monastic Brotherhoods, all of which, however, had recognisably monastic elements—unlike, say, the 'regular clerks' of Counter-Reformation Catholicism which spurned the choral celebration of the Divine Office. Four of these Anglo-Catholic foundations were outstanding: the Society of St John the Evangelist, originally (and throughout our period) based at Cowley, Oxford's 'East End'; the Community of the Resurrection at Mirfield, in Yorkshire; the Society of the Sacred Mission with a mother house at Kelham in Nottinghamshire, and the Anglican Franciscans. I tack on to this account a Brotherhood which was, for the most part, not in any obvious sense a Community at all: the collection of celibate clergy living an occasionally corporate life but otherwise functioning as dispersed celibates that was (and is) the Oratory of the Good Shepherd.

The Society of St John the Evangelist was founded in 1865 by a mid-Victorian Vicar of Cowley, and since it lasted in England for a century and a quarter has a good claim to be the first fully stable Brotherhood of the Tractarian Revival. 'Tractarian' is certainly the word, since Richard Meux Benson (1824–1915), the son of a London merchant married to the heiress of the Meux brewing fortune, was strongly influenced by Pusey. So much can be seen from the Rule of his Society, which emphasized frequent Retreats and days or times of silence, along with regular Confession, as well as the choir office and a ministry to those outside the house.[62]

Benson's own Retreat material, drawn partly from Ignatius of Loyola, admired by Pusey, would influence C. S. Lewis, to whom it was mediated through St Edward's House, the Society's London establishment. Its community included Lewis's confessor, Walter Adams (died 1952), who had that role from 1940 until his death.[63]

What could not be deduced from such circumstantial considerations was the biographical connexion: it was Pusey who secured for Benson nomination as a Student (that is, Fellow) of Christ Church, a position he retained till the end of his life. Pusey also helped Benson organize, initially for undergraduates, the 'Brotherhood of the Holy Trinity', a guild for serious, prayerful, and studious Tractarian junior members of the University—we shall encounter it when considering the Anglo-Catholic 'Societies' in Chapter 8.

Once ordained, Benson had a nucleic presence in East Oxford at his first incumbency, St James, Stockmore Street, an inexpensive and provisional 'iron church' of the kind that cash-strapped Roman Catholics were busily erecting in this period all over the country. Some time in the summer of 1865 he wrote to Bishop Wilberforce of Oxford proposing a Community of clergy and laymen to give missions and addresses, whilst also running a 'House in Oxford for scholars who wish to live by rule while getting a University education, for Students in Theology, [and] for clergy who wish to retire for a time of study'.[64] Granted the expansion of the city, a new parish was needed and now came into existence as St Mary and St John, Cowley—known colloquially as 'Cowley St John'.

On Oxford's Marston Street, between the Cowley and Iffley Roads, the Society erected a major complex with a mission church as well as a trio of chapels, a song school, a guest wing for Retreatants and of course accommodation for the Brothers—in quarters famous for their singular bareness. Under Benson's successor as Superior General the worship in the newly consecrated church consisted of the 'Roman use so far as it can be adapted to our present Prayer Book service'.[65] The architect was George Frederick Bodley, with a great east window by Charles Eamer

Kempe—two figures who will enter this 'Eulogy' more fully in Chapter 9. The window, apart from depicting the church's patron, St John, in his exile on island of Patmos, showed the Crucified topped by the iconographic pelican, symbol of sacrifice, with, below the Christ-figure, a Tree of Life carrying twelve fruits (compare Apocalypse 22:2). The fruits in question were: Basil, Benedict, Columba, Augustine, Aidan, Bede, Boniface, Bruno, Bernard, Dominic, Francis. In the West window at the opposite end Kempe added four great missionary saints: Martin, Ansgar, Patrick, Birinus. It was a splendid testimony to a lively sense of the Communion of Saints.

Wherever Cowley Fathers went they encouraged members of the Anglo-Catholic Sisterhoods to go with them. That was true of their implantation in Massachusetts which, however, soon acquired autonomy (the Episcopal authorities did not look kindly on a foundation redolent of British hegemony in the pre-Revolutionary past). It was true of their mission work in the 'Global South', whether in South Africa, where they were chiefly concentrated in Cape Province (mainly among Cape Malays) and the Transkei, or in India, a more ambitious setting for their efforts to be described in Chapter 10. The work in South Africa was made possible by the episcopate of Robert Gray (1809–72) as bishop of Cape Town, and eventually metropolitan. A Tractarian-inclined bishop, not afraid of decisive action (hence the arraigning for heresy of one of his suffragans, the 'higher critic' John William Colenso, 1814–83), Gray asked for batches of the new Anglo-Catholic Religious, both women and men, to come as missionaries. His successors continued that policy, which explains the confluence on South African soil of a variety of English-originated foundations, generally based on male/female cooperation, in the later nineteenth century and the greater part of its twentieth century successor.[66]

So far as Cowley was concerned, the relation with the All Saints Sisters of the Poor was especially close. Benson had enticed them to Oxford in 1873, and they established a convent with, in due course, a chapel by Comper. In India they also worked alongside members of the Community of St Mary the Virgin. The Society's interest in women's Religious life was not merely a hunt for auxiliaries. A Cowley Father, George Seymour Hollings (1845–1914), was responsible for the founding of a purely contemplative Sisterhood with a Carmelite spirituality, the Community of the Sisters of the Love of God, at Fairacres, Oxford, in 1906.

A London house, long envisaged, opened that same year at College Street, Westminster, considered by Benson far too grand to suit the Society's deliberately modest beginnings. For the 'SSJE' was not just 'Puseyite'. It was also 'Puseyan' in its entirely sober, highly austere, and (in consequence) somewhat forbidding spiritual profile.

The beginnings of Mirfield, alias the Community of the Resurrection, were more than a trifle unsteady.[67] At Oxford's Pusey House, the first Principal, Charles Gore, gathered around him a small group of priests keen to lead a common life, punctuated by prayer, study, and a degree of pastoral involvement. That was under the title 'The Society of the Resurrection' ('SR')—not yet in any sense a Religious Order but an 'association', with outliers, some of them as far off as in India, for members of the Oxford Mission to Calcutta had been encouraged to treat Pusey House as their home base. Gore thought it might become in time an 'Oratorian sort of community'.[68] At any rate he did not want it to resemble too closely the Cowley Fathers where the Superior was autocratic (this lay behind the disastrous attempt to retain the allegiance of the first American members of the Society),[69] and the spirituality tinged with Jansenism. Benson thought Religious should be 'dead unto the world', a misreading of St Paul who had written 'dead to sin' (Romans 6:11), something rather different.[70]

In 1893 a move to a country vicarage in South Oxfordshire (the patron of St James the Great, Radley, was the nearby Radley College, a Tractarian foundation) furnished the core group—from 1892 entitled the 'Community' or 'CR'—with a more suitable building. Unfortunately, Gore found the parish work at Radley crushing—not because objective demand made it so but because any and every pastoral disappointment struck him as a disaster. His spiritually elitist view of the Church was confounded. 'In Radley for the first time he was confronted by Anglican lay religion which is largely implicit and unarticulated and for which the church (as Gore understood it) is tangential, even dispensable for much of the time.'[71] Soon enough the first members of the Community of the Resurrection mislaid their Father Superior or, as Gore preferred to be known, the 'Senior'. In 1895 he accepted a canonry of Westminster Abbey, the beginning of an ecclesiastical career that took him to be in turn Bishop of Worcester, Birmingham, and Oxford.

In his absence a common life of a recognizably monastic—and liturgically Anglo-Catholic—kind continued at Radley for some while. The Day Hours and Compline were added to the Prayer Book offices, though the State Prayers (additional collects for the Royal Family) were deleted from Evensong, an 'Anglo-Catholic gesture against erastianism'.[72] The parish itself appears to have been kept in blissful ignorance of the Oxford Movement trajectory. In consequence, no riots were expected.

Meanwhile Gore's reputation at the Abbey as a preacher and social commentator was soaring. For his part, the Marquis of Salisbury, prime minister for a second time, wanted to see the new generation of Tractarians represented on the Bench. Gore's opposition to the Boer War was not held against him once the British were victorious. It was not surprising that in 1901 he was named Bishop of Worcester. He resigned from the English Church Union and the Confraternity of the Blessed Sacrament so as to accept the post, foreseeing conflicts of interest.

In effect, the real founder of the Community of the Resurrection was Gore's assistant and successor, the liturgist Walter Frere (1863–1938), who took the opportunity of the appointment to carry out the long-expressed wishes of the majority and move north. Under a Christian Socialist impulse of a kind that followed from the fledgling social concern of the early Tractarians, sharpened by Gore's close friendship with Henry Scott Holland, founder of the 'Christian Social Union', the members of the Community had discussed even in Oxford days the possibility of a move to the industrial North of England. Mirfield, in the West Riding of Yorkshire, was situated in the 'Heavy Woollen District', a series of townships specializing in the manufacture of a heavy-weight woollen cloth. A millowner's attempt at a mansion, set in twenty acres of ground, seemed to fit the bill.

Frere too would become a bishop, but not till 1923, which left him the greater part of two decades (1902–13, 1916–23) to set his ship on course.[73] Under his guidance the House of the Resurrection would launch out on a formidable programme of parish missionizing, complemented by publication of 'Mirfield Manuals', inexpensive books of instruction (over two and a half million copies were sold by the 1920s).[74] The monastic character of its life intensified: a fine church, described as Byzantine without, Romanesque within, helped in this, though shortage of money truncated the design. But Mirfield's defining act was its founding, in 1903, the 'College of the Resurrection', a school of theology for Ordination candidates of limited financial means.

The College, with its fine library, attracted to the Community talented men combining pastoral and intellectual gifts. That in turn enabled it to send out priest-teachers or pastors to a variety of sites in the wider Anglican Communion, notably in the Transvaal, Southern Rhodesia, and Sarawak, before the War of 1939–45, and to Cape Province and (for a short time) Barbados after it. In South Africa they made a notable contribution to black emancipation through their schools, teachers' training college, theological college for ordinands, and, in the wake of the electoral victory of the Nationalist party of D. F. Malan (1874–1959) in 1948, public opposition to apartheid (where the name of Trevor Huddleston, 1913–98, later Bishop of Masasi in Tanzania, then of Stepney, is preeminent).[75] At the cultural as well as geographical antipodes, their London house, first in South Kensington and then in Holland Park, acted as a centre for a metropolitan version of its Retreats and missions—in a certain degree of competition, then, with the Cowley Fathers who also had their place in the capital city.

'Kelham' was entirely *sui generis*.[76] Founded as the Society of the Sacred Mission in Kennington, in South London, in 1893, its initial project was to prepare missionaries for Korea. It soon became diverted to serving (for the most part) the home mission of the Church of England. A common life of prayer and fellowship could be exploited for various ends but Herbert Hamilton Kelly (1860–1950), the most outstanding of the trio of the Society's founders, had very definite intellectual passions. That made it likely the running of theological colleges would be a priority.[77] Kelham was unlike any other. It took boys as young as 15 (they could enter the Army at that age, or government service); it stressed dogmatics and history (neither prominent hitherto in training courses for clergymen, and the two connected since history, for Kelly, is what God does); it taught not through lectures as in a University system but through a combination of duplicated handouts and free time for the reading of carefully selected books, with questions suggested by the handouts in mind.[78] Kelham's historian noted of its peculiar pedagogic method: 'The student is always sent back to ask questions. It may be also that, because these are merely typescript notes, something of the risk of a new canonized authority line was avoided.'[79]

Herbert Kelly's idea of a study programme, once matured in the Inter-War years, was unique in Anglicanism, not least because it emphasized philosophy — not a feature of Anglican theology since Hooker, whereas it was deemed an essential of Roman Catholic Ordination training, as of theology itself. More specifically, he proposed as its two leading masters Thomas Aquinas (for natural theology) and F. D. Maurice (for 'revealed' theology).[80] That sort of combination could find favour at the turn of the twenty-first century, in a 'post-Modern' theology keen to make unusual juxtapositions, but in the period it was unheard of. Kelly himself taught the crucial subjects: dogmatics and Church history; the combination hit off his distinctive theological approach: to learn from the plan of God what God is doing with the Church in the world. At other hands, that formula might conceal an activist horizontalism, but Kelly's vision of Religious life required a high level of liturgical observance and, for those in formation, recognition of the importance of strategic distance from the world. To learn how to see the world truly, it must initially be seen from afar.

The English college of the Society was created the year after its foundation, but only in 1903 with the purchase of Kelham Hall, in Nottinghamshire, an enormous Gothic pile designed by Giles Gilbert Scott with strong stylistic affinities to St Pancras' Station, a London railway terminal, was its future assured. (Assured, that is, until the disastrous down-turn for Anglo-Catholicism that was the 1960s.) Lit exclusively by oil, with open fires for heating and no running water above ground level, it made for a strenuous environment. Run on somewhat military lines, it carried echoes of Kelly's time at Sandhurst, the British Army Officers' Training School. In 1928 the great domed chapel was finished, a numinous building dominated in the interior by a massive stone altar, sheltered by the second largest concrete dome in England. In 1947 the Society replicated its success at Kelham by founding a priory and theological college in the Anglican diocese of Adelaide, in South Australia. At its height, the Brotherhood had eighty professed members, in England, Australia, and South Africa where they had established a beachhead early on, in 1902.

The Anglican Franciscans have a mixed origin. At least three initiatives conjoined. In 1921 George Charles Montagu (1874–1962), Earl of Sandwich, offered a farm and farmhouse near Cerne Abbas, in Dorset, where Donald Downes (1878–1957), an Oxford economist in priest's Orders, together with a group of Francis-inspired friends, could run a hostel for the homeless men and boys moving from place to place in search of work at the onset of the Great Depression.[81] In 1924 George Potter (died 1960), Vicar of St Chrysostom's, Hill Street, Peckham, created a Brotherhood of the Holy Cross for serving the poor in a Franciscan spirit.[82] In 1934 Algy Roberston (1894–1955) a member of the Christa Prema Seva Sangha ('Society of Servants of Christ') at Poona, India, returned to England for health reasons. As Vicar of St Ives, in Huntingdonshire, he set up a branch of the Society under the name the 'Brotherhood of the Love of Christ' and made his vicarage a training place for Indian missionaries on the 'Poona Mission' he had left behind. Roberston then joined forces with Brother Douglas at Cerne.[83]

In 1936 the various initiatives came together as the 'Society of St Francis'. In 1937 a Third Order was created for sisters (though an Anglican Franciscan Sisterhood, the 'Community of St Francis' had been active in London's East End since 1905), and in 1950 a Second House was added in the form of a contemplative monastery of nuns at Freelands, near Oxford.

In 1952 the Society of St Francis absorbed the tiny Society of the Divine Compassion, which had worked for half a century in the East End at Plaistow; Henry Ernest Hardy, 'Father Andrew' (1869–1946), had been the last surviving of its three founders and a noted spiritual counsellor.[84] Its best known friar was, however, William Sirr, who set up a hermitage in a stable—all that was left of the gutted manor house of the Winfords of Glasshampton, in Worcestershire, hoping to draw others seeking the contemplative life. They came to 'Father William of Glasshampton' in droves, but none of them stayed.[85]

The Society of St Francis has seeded many foundations in the former British Dominions and colonies, as well as, more surprisingly, in places untouched by English settlement or colonisation, such as Brazil.

Lastly, the Oratory of the Good Shepherd brought together some of the best-known Anglo-Catholic clergy of the day, notably the Church historian Alec Vidler (1899–1991) and the philosophical theologian and dogmatician E. L. Mascall. It was founded in December 1913 at Little Gidding, in Huntingdonshire, the former seat of the semi-monastic community established around the family of Nicholas Ferrar (1592–1637) in the first year of Charles I's reign. In the increasingly embittered atmosphere that led up to the Civil War, Ferrar's household, with its round of Hours, was denounced by Puritans as a Protestant nunnery (and later remembered by Eliot, in the *Four Quartets*, as a place where prayer 'had been valid'). Three Cambridge College chaplains, John How of John's (1881–1961), Edward Wynn of Jesus (1889–1956), and Eric Milner-White of King's (1884–1963) set out in 1913 the 'Provisions of Little Gidding', the basis for the Constitutions of the Oratory, prescribing celibacy, a rule of life, regular accounting for spending (though not a common purse), and, more especially, the 'Labour of the Mind', that is, a serious commitment to study. The title suggested a remote origin in post-Reformation Latin Catholicism, in the 'Oratories' of St Philip Neri (1515–95) and Cardinal Pierre de Bérulle (1575–1629). There was for a while an 'Oratory House' in Cambridge, with a properly common life, but after 1939 the Oratory had no abiding city.[86]

Of the founders two became bishops: Wynn at nearby Ely, where the theological college (of which he was an alumnus) was, with Chichester, the closest to Anglo-Catholicism outside the monastic colleges at Mirfield and Kelham, How in the Scottish Episcopal Church—a law unto itself—at Glasgow, where the see was coupled with an ancient episcopal name for the south-west of Scotland, Galloway. Milner-White, the grandson of a boat-builder at Cowes, left the Isle of Wight for Harrow School before reading History at King's, Cambridge, where he became Dean in 1918. A highly decorated military chaplain on the Western Front, it was not predictable that he should have become best known as a '"choreographer" of Anglican worship', but so it fell out.[87] he introduced the famous Festival of Nine Lessons and Carols, which has since spread to many other places at Christmas, including, occasionally, to Anglophone regions of the Latin church. Subsequently Dean of York, Milner-White's advanced knowledge of stained glass, an Anglo-Catholic specialty, qualified him to be an adviser to London's Victoria and Albert Museum. In a very different capacity he was also an influential figure among the trustees of Woodard Schools in the north of England (another Anglo-Catholic initiative, to be described in Chapter 8). As indicated by his 1929 polemic, *One God and Father of All*, co-authored with his fellow 'Oratorian' Wilfred Knox (1886–1950), brother to the better known Mgr Ronald Knox (1888–1957), he was certainly no Anglo-Papalist. The sharpness with which historically or theologically disputable claims were set forth (St Peter had never even seen the Tiber, and infallibility could not of its nature be an attribute of the Christian *Ecclesia*) is partly to be explained by the secession to Rome of a well-known Anglo-Catholic preacher, Vernon Johnson (1920–99), a former member of the Society of Divine Compassion to whose apologia, *One Lord, One Faith*, the joint book *One God and Father of All* was a hurried response.[88]

For whatever reason, the more successful male foundations in the Anglo-Catholic Revival were not those which sought to recreate mediaeval conditions within modern Anglicanism.[89] They were, rather, those that struck out on a line of their own: Mirfield, not Llanthony, Kelham, not Caldey. The Franciscans were *sui generis*, since, in the context of the notoriously fissiparous Franciscan 'Order', there was no obvious mediaeval 'standard' to follow other than the personal charism of the Poor Man of Assisi himself.

6

Social Movements

I T IS WRONGLY SUPPOSED that the Tractarians had no interest in social questions, or what early Victorians called the 'Condition of England' question. The supposition makes it difficult, if not impossible, to understand how such questions could have been of such consuming interest to their successors, so much so that the Anglo-Catholic movement became effectively identified with both Christian Socialism, in the years leading up to 1914, and 'Christian Sociology', in the periods between the two World Wars.

The Tractarians and the Social Question

The suggestion that first generation Tractarians knew only an 'abstract Incarnationalism'—and left it to their successors in the mid- and late Victorian periods to put flesh on a ghost—ignores the range of materials in sermons, pamphlets, articles in quarterly reviews, as well as 'social novels', which attest their interest in the 'Condition of England Question'. They did not, in point of fact, forget the world.[1] The Centenary of the Movement, in 1933, occasional at any rate two offerings which could have challenged what had become by the 1990s a scholarly consensus. W. G. Peck (1883–1962) wrote *The Social Implications of the Oxford Movement*,[2] and Ruth Kenyon (1879–1943) contributed to the multi-authored *Northern Catholicism* 'The Social Aspect of the Catholic Revival'.[3] Both Peck and Kenyon went on to be to be major players in the movement of Christendom Sociology of the Inter-War years and after.

Ironically, it was the theo-political—theocratic, if one will—notions of the Oxford Fathers that made possible a more incisive social criticism than the old high churchmen had ever managed. The Church, on the Tractarian view, was not only independent of the secular power but superior to it, and able, therefore, to teach it its duty with binding authority.

The concrete manner whereby Tractarians attempted to carry out this task was sometimes spoiled by an unrealistic desire to return to a pre-industrial society. Not for nothing had they read Sir Walter Scott

(1771–1832) and the Lake Poets. But their immersion in practical affairs tells a different story: Simon Skinner instances Keble's sponsoring of allotment schemes and a parochially managed savings bank at Hursley, and Pusey's decision to take on a voluntary curacy at Spitalfields, East London's crowded market quarter, during the 1866 cholera outbreak. These were examples of 'collective exposure' to either chronic or episodically dire social problems, to set alongside the romantic desire for a reinvigoration of a pious and socially benevolent squirearchy.[4]

Attack on the Utilitarian sponsored 'New Poor Law', with its removal of care for the poor from the hands of parishes operating 'outdoor relief' in favour of a Benthamite bureaucracy operating the dreaded 'workhouse' system, was a regular feature of Tractarian criticism. Tractarians saw the ranker aspects of industrialization and the socially disintegrative effects of economic individualism. Some of their panaceas included the encouragement for Sabbath recreation, physical as well as spiritual, the institution of national 'holy days', alias holidays, and communal fairs which could bring all classes together.

There was a historical dimension to this. 'Tractarians had… reinforced their theological distaste for the Reformation by attributing to it a maldistribution of property from which paternal mechanisms never recovered,'[5] in which view they could cite such contemporary 'prophets' as William Cobbett (1763–1835) and Thomas Carlyle (1795–1881) in support. They insisted on a restoration of a sense of the duties of property, and not only, as in the wake of reaction to the French Revolution, its rights. The Church, they held, should act as guardian of the poor, who were entitled, in the words of the *British Critic*, to a 'sufficient and dignified maintenance'.[6] That could be presented as perfectly compatible with belief in the 'providential ordination of social rank', and even, indeed, in the 'ineradicable nature of poverty'.[7] Essentially, the Tractarians called for the parish to resume its rightful place, fuelled by the tithe system, which, further amplified by a continual pulpit pricking of the consciences of the propertied, should suffice to give the poor their rights, over against the philosophically induced miserliness—allegedly required by a sound political economy—of an increasingly de-Christianized Parliamentary State.

Socialists, sacramental and other

Succeeding generations of 'sacramental socialists' were moved initially by the ruminations of Frederick Denison Maurice (1805–72), whose conceptually indefinite but affectively inspirational writings, shared the Incarnation-centred theology of the Tractarians but not the entirety of their ecclesiology or sacramental doctrine.[8] Christian Socialists in the

Anglo-Catholic tradition came to realise that, at any rate in urban areas, solutions via the parochial route were not enough. Maurice himself, it might be pointed out, had little knowledge of parish life. In his Suffolk boyhood and while at Cambridge he was still a Unitarian, his father's religion (and hence unable to take an academic degree). In 1831 he sought Baptism at Oxford from where, on graduation, he proceeded to Orders, but his professional life was lived in London's literary and social scene—until, that is, he became in 1866 Knightbridge Professor at Cambridge. Now the senior chair in philosophy in that University, it was in his time a chair of 'Moral Theology, Casuistical Divinity, and Moral Philosophy', reflecting its late seventeenth century origins.

In his influential *The Kingdom of Christ*, a book which grew considerably in size from the first 1838 edition until the third in 1883, Maurice insisted that from the social implications of the Incarnation, and its product, the Church-body, some more fully corporate—national and even international—corollaries should surely follow. That found expression when he founded in 1854 the Working Men's College in London's Oakley Square, now in the Borough of Camden, and later, after much experience of co-operatives, the Society for Promoting Working Men's Associations as well.

The theological liberalism apparent in Maurice's *Theological Essays* and *What is Revelation?* separated him from Anglo-Catholics to whom, in any case, he had never been fully attached.[9] The Creedless character of his organizing activity for working men had not attracted them. The flurry of controversy aroused by these writings, and not just in high church circles, made advisable his retreat to the Cam and the safer realms of the 'metaphysical and moral' philosophy to which he devoted his final years.[10]

To consider the 'succeeding generations' of sacramentally minded Christian Socialists—essentially, the fifty years from the last quarter of the nineteenth century (Maurice died on its eve) till the decade that followed the Great War, one could do worse than consult a retrospect furnished by the essay collection *Prospect for Christendom*—sub-title, 'Essays in Catholic Social Reconstruction'—published on war time economy paper in 1945. Its author was well-placed to offer a comprehensive overview of organizations and events in the post-Maurice generations.

Percy Widdrington (1873–1959), like Maurice Reckitt, the editor of the collection, had been in on the start of the National Guilds League and was a contributor to the 1922 *Return to Christendom* prefaced by Gore and closed with an epilogue by G. K. Chesterton (1874–1936) in what proved to be the Sage of Beaconsfield's last piece of Anglican writing.[11] He was a Southampton-born Anglo-Catholic priest, educated at Oxford's St Edmund Hall. Widdrington had served his principal curacy at Haltonwith-Aughton, on the outskirts of Lancaster, before becoming Vicar of St Peter's, Coventry in 1906.[12] Coventry and Lancaster were two cities where the ruralist formulae of early Tractarianism would not work. But Widdrington was not unfamiliar with the rural scene: in 1918 he had exchanged his Midlands incumbency for a living at Great Easton, near Dunmow, in Essex. He used an 'Epilogue' to the volume to set out how he saw the Anglo-Catholic social movement developing so far.[13]

His story ran as follows. The Guild of Saint Matthew, and its monthly *The Church Reformer*, founded by Stewart Duckworth Headlam (1847–1924), had been the beginning of a new generation—despite the Guild's comparatively short life, between 1877 and 1910.[14] Though Widdrington is sparse in biographical matters, the historian will want to note that Headlam was born into a wealthy Evangelical family at Wavertree, and after schooling at Eton matriculated at Trinity College, Cambridge, where he came under the powerful influence of F. D. Maurice. It was from this Maurician spring that Headlam considered his Christian Socialism to flow. Headlam had recurring difficulties with bishops, beginning from his first curacy at St John's, Drury Lane, where Jackson of London delayed his priesting, objecting to his political (or 'ecclesio-political') opinions. His second curacy, at St Matthew's, Bethnal Green, was served under a highly sympathetic rector, Septimus Cox Holmes Hansard (1823–95). But whereas the clergy of St Matthew's, a classic slum parish in the Anglo-Catholic tradition, were inclined to live outside the parish boundaries, Headlam rented a flat in a building within those boundaries and inhabited exclusively by proletarians—even if his wealth enabled him to furnish it in what is described, possibly with considerable restraint, as an 'individual' manner.[15]

In his retrospect, Widdrington took it for granted that anger at widespread poverty on the one hand, complacency in the national Church on the other, were the reasons the Guild of St Matthew, created in 1877 under Headlam's leadership, had bound itself so closely to the nascent Labour movement and accepted the sobriquet 'Socialist' as its own. With its request that all members communicate Eucharistically on the great festivals, as well as attending the celebration of the Holy Communion on Sundays and saints' days, the Guild had a good claim to be the origin of 'Sacramental Socialism', a phrase coined by an historian of the Labour movement in the 1960s.[16]

But the Guild of St Matthew had taken up so many causes, from sweated labour to the 'restoration of the land', from extending popular education to removing prejudices against those who worked in theatre and ballet, it was not surprising it had little energy to spare for working out fundamental theological principles to differentiate it more persuasively from those of political Socialism at large.

This for Widdrington had been its weakness. *Prospect for Christendom* had as its epigraph a line from the Middle English allegorical narrative poem *Piers Plowman*: 'Christ's blood on Calvary the spring of Christendom'. It was an indicator that, for Widdrington's own new-found collaborators, a further phase of the social movement would be no doctrinally milksop affair. With 'so many and diverse crusades in hand', Stewart Headlam's Guild had not done its theo-political homework. It 'failed to find out the basis of a recovered Christendom.'[17]

Surprisingly, Widdrington left out of account Henry Scott-Holland's Christian Social Union, founded 1889, despite its connexion to Anglo-Catholics through the clergy of the London slums. That was probably because he wanted to frame his narrative in terms of an eventual rejection of a Labour-allied Christian Socialism that emphasized the adjective ('Christian') much less than the noun it qualified. Scott Holland's Christian Social Union was not, however, to be pooh-poohed. Possibly Widdrington was put off by the 'new aristocracy' background of its founder.[18] Henry Scott Holland (1847–1918) was born in Herefordshire, his father the *chatelain* of Dumbleton Hall, near Evesham, and his mother the daughter of the first Baron Gifford, the Earl of Liverpool's Solicitor-General.[19] Strongly influenced at Balliol by the organic-cum-Idealist social thinking of T. H. Green, Scott Holland had founded the Christian Social Union while a canon of St Paul's Cathedral, in 1889. Its aim was to analyze the causes of contemporary poverty (the main remit of its Oxford branch, much assisted by Scott Holland's appointment as Regius Professor of Divinity in 1910) and to mobilize public opinion with a view to alleviating social ills (the work of its London branch, which collaborated with Anglo-Catholic slum priests in mounting programmes of popular lectures). The Union inherited from the Guild of St Matthew, if in more attenuated form, the connexion between Eucharistic Communion and a change of ethos in social life together.[20]

The year after Scott Holland's death, 1919, the Union, which by then had some five thousand members in branches up and down the country, merged with the Navvy Mission Society to become the Industrial Christian Fellowship. Though its analyses and prescriptions were offered under the rubric of claiming for the 'Christian law the ultimate authority in social practice',[21] the mustard does not seem to have been hot enough for the Christendom thinkers.

The desire of the latter was to go beyond the simple humanitarianism of that outstanding figure among the Late Tractarian social critics, Bishop Gore. Gore, who was Bishop of Oxford during Scott Holland's holding of the Regius chair, had told Widdrington that theologically inspired theorizing, such as that of Maurice, had played little part in his own turn to social involvement. Its real motor force was hands-on experience when Joseph Arch (1826–1919), the agricultural workers' trade unionist leader, took him on a tour of Oxfordshire villages. But by 1945, the date of *Prospect for Christendom*, Widdrington had come to see a danger in such *insouciance* toward doctrine (surprising in Gore as this was), and its concomitant—exclusive attention to a theologically neutral act of social observation and analysis.

In what was in effect a *mea culpa*, since he had been not only a founder of the Oxford University Fabian Society and an early adherent to the Independent Labour Party but an active supporter of the equally Church-non-allied Women's Social and Political Union, Widdrington wrote: 'even in those years [the 1880s to the Great War] we were not altogether unaware of the inadequacy of our background, and we realized that the workers [he meant, in effect, Labour leaders] were apt to regard Christianity as merely instrumental to their programmes of reform'.[22] That was hardly compatible with the Guild of St Matthew's self-proclaimed adherence to the 'Incarnation and the Mass'.[23] Widdrington might have added, but did not, that the official philosophy of the Christian Social Union had already staked out for its own socio-economic explorations a Christological claim of a quite explicit kind.

The formation in 1906, in Morecambe, of the Church Socialist League confirmed these undesirable features of the inherited landscape in re-opened Anglo-Catholic eyes. The new League owed its existence to a perception that the Catholic character of the Guild of Saint Matthew would be especially unwelcome in areas north of the Trent where Protestantism was strong (presumably Widdrington means Protestant Dissent, but—as already noted—Westcott at least considered Tractarianism a largely clerical affair in the Province of York). Powerfully influenced by both the Labour Party and the Independent Labour Party, which the 1906 General Election showed to be advancing in popularity, the Church Socialist League was all too ready to accept the maxim that 'Christianity is the religion of which Socialism is the practice'. Widdrington saw the secularist potential dangerously latent in that formula.[24]

And yet paradoxically, the Church Socialist League was the first organization to propose to its members—admittedly, unsuccessfully—the formation of a 'Christian Sociology'. That defeat was only temporary, and one sign that its day would come lay in a set of Bampton Lectures, *Christian Theology and Social Progress* by Frederick William Bussell (1862–1944), delivered in 1905, and hence prior to the Morecambe jamboree. Widdrington sums up their message as the irreconcilability of Christian revelation with the notion that a 'moral or political system can be set before men with authority, apart from any conception of a Divine Order'.[25] The lectures advised that the Church must criticize from its own proper dogmatic viewpoint. Otherwise, it would be false to its own mission.[26]

In the remaining years before the Great War much pro-Labour agitation may have repaired the reputation of the Church of England as a 'reactionary' organization (what would later be called the 'Tory Party at Prayer'), but it brought precious few people to share in church practice. Widdrington reported increasing 'intellectual confusion and uncertainty' owing to the lack of a 'thought-out theological basis'.[27] That was why, after the Armistice, dissatisfaction with the Church Socialist League's strategies came to a head. Anglo-Catholicism could not make progress with forwarding a social ethos inherited from the Tractarians if it ceased to integrate political economy with orthodox theological doctrine, the liturgical life, and a culture derived from the essentially corporate nature of a genuinely Catholic if also national Church.

One Sacramental Socialist who had certainly made his mark on the Church of England's reputation, and in no merely secularizing manner, was Conrad le Despenser Roden Noel (1869–1942), grandson of the first Earl of Gainsborough and 'Red Vicar' of Thaxted in Essex.[28] Educated (briefly, before rustication) at Corpus Christi College, Cambridge, and Chichester Theological College, Noel's first curacy, at Flowery Field in Cheshire, was cut short by parishioners' objection to his Socialism. In 1904 he was rescued by Percy Dearmer, who made him his assistant at St Mary the Virgin, Primrose Hill. In 1910 he was presented to the living of Thaxted by the Countess of Warwick, Frances Greville (1861–1938), who shared his political outlook. He introduced to his parish a liturgical regime of the modified Sarum variety recommended by Dearmer. It spilled out of church not only in processions but also in Maypole and Morris dancing. There Dearmer's urban church, squeezed into a tiny site, could not compete. Noel's Neo-Mediaevalism, indebted to Morris and Ruskin, was combined with a fervent admiration for Leon Trotsky (1879–1940) as well as a 'full-fat' Catholicism.

This was a heady cocktail of ingredients whose outcome was his 1918 foundation of the 'Catholic Crusade of the Servants of the Precious Blood'. The Crusade's aims were to 'create the demand for the Catholic Faith, the whole Catholic Faith, and nothing but the Catholic Faith', and to 'encourage the rising of the people in the might of the risen Christ and the saints, mingling Heaven and earth that we may shatter this greedy world to bits'.[29] Noel's flying of the Red Flag and the Tricolour of Sinn Féin side by side with the Flag of St George did not go down well with patriotic (or Tory) undergraduates in neighbouring Cambridge who thus began the 'Battle of the Flags', only terminated by the intervention of Noel's bishop.

Noel was a patron of the Arts and Crafts movement, festooning his church in tapestries and banners, and stocking his vestry with admirably crafted vestments. The composer Gustav Holst (1874–1934) who lived nearby was his organist, with Ralph Vaughan Williams (1872–1958) as an occasional substitute, and among the congregants drawn by sympathy was Joseph Needham (1900–95), the world expert on Chinese science and medicine and a practitioner of gymnosophy, the naked exercising favoured by some Hindu philosophers which, however, does not seem to have been included in the rich mixture that was Thaxted Anglo-Catholicism.[30] Worship at Thaxted, and in parish churches influenced by the Catholic Crusade, and its offspring, the Trotskyite) Order of the Church Militant, was seen as the 'People's Mass', an event in which the 'Sacrament of Fellowship' was, for Sacramental Socialists, incompatible with pious individualism. It was not the time for private prayers.[31] That would be fertile soil for ploughing by the emerging champions of the 'Parish Communion', defined over against a combination of an early Communion service and Sunday Mattins, or the former along with attendance at a non-communicating Solemn High Mass.[32]

The turn to 'Christendom' thinking

A series of private conferences at an early Tudor mansion, Paycocke's House in Coggeshall, Essex (near to, if not within the bounds of, Percy Widdrington's parish at Great Dunmow, and owned by close relatives of Noel), led to the publication in 1922 of *Return to Christendom*, crucial background to which was the revival of the 'guild' idea through the National Guilds, for these, wrote Widdrington, 'turned our minds to the mediaeval achievement and its significance'.[33] This, of course, was exactly what Noel had been doing—but the 'excesses' of Thaxted made that a trifle impolitic to admit.

The resultant book was a call to recover the social traditions of the Church, and to make the idea of the divine Kingdom a 'regulative principle of theology'—and therefore *the* regulative principle of social theology.[34] Reckitt himself, writing in the Introduction to *Prospect for Christendom*, had said of the forerunner volume, 'It sought rather in Christian doctrine and tradition than in the ethical idealism of the age the sanction and the clue for the recovery of a Christian sociology.'[35] After *Return to Christendom* in the course of 1922 and 1923 the Church Socialist League turned itself into the League of the Kingdom of God and abandoned its institutional connexions to the Socialist movement which itself was becoming, remarks Widdrington, ever more secular in outlook.

The radically reformed League's guiding maxim was the need for the 'Catholic idea' to manifest itself in the political order. It was a 'retreat to the mountains' with the consequent risk of becoming a purely academic affair, without contact with working people, or even the common run of the parochial clergy. Widdrington does not mention, though it must have been in his mind, the founding of the Summer School of Sociology and the quarterly journal begun in 1931. The word 'sociology' was itself still a neologism in the 1920s, and the enticing proposal of a distinctively Anglo-Catholic school of sociology the fruit of brainstorming by a diverse body of delegates—from the Anglo-Catholic Congresses Committee, the Federation of Catholic Priests, the English Church Union and the League of the Kingdom of God itself. For once a committee had not produced a camel when seeking to design a horse. Appropriately enough, the Warden of Keble (then Beresford James Kidd, 1864–1948) was to be its president, and its first conference, in 1926, had taken as its theme the social teaching embedded in the Church's sacraments.

Distinctive it may have been, sectarian it was not. It played its part in the Christian Social Council, a delayed outcome of William Temple's ecumenically conceived 1924 'Conference on Politics, Economics and Citizenship', which, astonishingly for the period, had Roman Catholic participation from the Catholic Workers College (then in Oxford's Walton Well Road). Reckitt family money paid for V. A. Demant (on whom more anon) to be the Council's robustly Anglo-Catholic director of research.[36] In 1941 a conference organized by Archbishop Temple at Malvern had included Reckitt on its planning committee though the conclusions from its bewilderingly multitudinous academic papers were only rescued from utter incoherence by Temple's last minute editing.[37]

The failure of the Malvern Conference to send a clear enough message was what lay behind *Prospect for Christendom*. Resources were to hand inasmuch as the English Church Union (later, 'Church Union') Summer School in Sociology lasted from 1925 to 1970, and brought together a galaxy of figures, some from abroad, such as Nicolas Berdyaev (1874–1948) and Jacques Maritain (1882–1973), and others from home, including not only Eliot but the 'Third Inkling' Charles Williams, the doctrinal theologians E. L. Mascall and A. M. Ramsey, and the unplaceable George Every (1909–2003) of Kelham, as well as—*aves rarae* in these circles—English Roman Catholics in the shape of the cultural historian Christopher Dawson (1889–1970) and the philosopher of culture E. I. Watkin (1888–1981). In this way the 'Christendom Group' had become more eclectic, with Barthian and Scholastic input, by the time of the Second World War.

By 1945 much had changed from the heady days of the early Christian Socialists, both in terms of living standards and in the way the working-class movement, at least in Widdrington's eyes, had lost its idealism, becoming either 'an integral part of the whole social set-up [via the Attlee Government, inaugurated that year] or the instrument of an unreal class struggle [through continuing Communist penetration among trades unionists]'.[38] The War had generated no widespread conviction that all sheerly human and secularist programmes must end in like fiascos—Widdrington's omnium-gatherum dismissal of Liberalism, Fascism, and Communism. Widdrington's fear that, with the expansion of the State in wartime, State education had become the new substitute for Religion, echoed Newman's critique of Sir Robert Peel's trust in the former in *The Tamworth Reading Room*. Widdrington cited a prophecy by the Community of the Resurrection's John Neville Figgis (1866–1919), historian and political thinker, to the effect that the future task of the Church will not be narrowly humanitarian. Its call will be to awaken the 'vision of God in a world rationally cultivated and enjoying moderate but not excessive comfort'.[39] Widdrington recognized that *Prospect for Christendom*, while not equating Europe with the faith, or Western civilization with the faith, had nothing to say about Asia, Africa, or Polynesia, where prospective comfort might, one supposes, be less readily forthcoming. But they were not forgotten. In the inter-War period, missionary conferences at Jerusalem (1928) and Madras (1938) had shown, he said, the strength of the will to expand Christendom beyond Europe and its outliers in the Americas. But the 'awakening peoples', once saved from exploitation and illiteracy, still need to build up a Christian civilization—with the implication that *Prospect* has something for them as well. There was certainly no abandonment of the 'Great Commission' in the Anglicanism of the inter-war years, any more than there was in the Roman Catholicism of the pontificate of Pius XI (pope, 1922–39).

Major figures

But what effectively was the manifesto, the substance of the 'Prospect' the contributing authors held out? The common view of a series of major figures was concisely spelt out in the book's introduction by Reckitt.

Maurice Reckitt (1888–1980), sometime editor of *The Church Socialist*, and subsequently author of *Faith and Society*, and *Religion in Social Action*, as well as an autobiography detailing his further reflections and activities, was an old hand at orchestrating the players at this concert.[40] An independently wealthy man (his father, a Yorkshire manufacturer had seen to that), Reckitt had been able to devote his life to the conjugation of Anglo-Catholicism and Christian Socialism—though he was also the president of the Croquet Association, which perhaps gives a glimpse of his social life in a more restricted sense of that word. The lodestar for a brighter future will be a 'natural order relying for its preservation on supernatural convictions, standards and means of grace'. Obedience to the laws of God will produce a healthier society, with the ancient Christendom furnishing 'clues' for a new Christendom to come.[41]

That was the consensus. But needless to say, the essayists had differences of angle. I consider here five such contributors: F. N. Davey, V. A. Demant, E. L. Mascall, T. S. Eliot, and Philip Mairet, before returning in conclusion to Reckitt himself—and adding, as a notable absence who should have been a presence, the redoubtable figure of Dorothy Sayers.

Francis Noel Davey (1904–73), Vicar of St Benet's, Cambridge, and a Fellow of the adjacent Corpus Christi College which owned the living, was best known as the collaborator with Sir Edwyn Hoskyns (1884–1937) in a version of New Testament studies that combined Barthianism with modern exegesis.[42] In 1944 he became director of the Society for Promoting Christian Knowledge, with its highly active publishing arm. In line with Widdrington and Reckitt, Davey affirmed, 'We... keep the idea of Christendom before us as our immediate goal, not in the naive illusion that God will enable us to build a society perfect in structure, but in the deep-founded faith that it is God's will that we should try to build such a society, and His will also to crown our obedient—albeit unsuccessful—attempts by using them for His own final purpose'.[43] A Christendom society cries out for the perfection no human achievement can give, only divine agency—note the Barthian emphasis. Indeed, 'To draw men into a spiritual, intellectual and social order informed by the Gospel will itself secure neither wholesale conversion nor universal perfection; yet it may help to clarify the fundamental issues of men's present existence, and to leave those outside the Church in no doubt but that there are some men for whom the world of sense and experience fulfils its original function of being witness to God, and of offering, under His promise, the material of His eternal Kingdom'.[44] This was eschatological thinking in line with Barth's celebrated second edition of his Commentary on Romans. Yet, avoiding any spectral Manicheanism that might be lurking behind the Barth of that date, Davey had also spoken respectfully of the God-given 'natural order', a characteristically Roman Catholic or more generally Christian-Scholastic concern.

It was left to Vigo August Demant (1893–1983) to unpack that key phrase which he did with considerable sophistication, conscious of the objections to natural law thinking from both secular Liberals and Protestants in a Lutheran succession.[45] Demant was born in Newcastle in 1893 and had the unusual academic formation—for an Anglo-Catholic clergyman—of Engineering Science at Armstrong College (founded as the Durham College of Science, it became the University of Newcastle in 1963), followed by a theology degree at Manchester College, a Unitarian establishment in Oxford. The explanation is, Demant only became Anglican in 1918 (he was received into the Church by Gore),[46] after which he attended Ely Theological College, whose Anglo-Catholicism he evidently drank in deep draughts since his first curacy was at Chamberlain's church, St Thomas the Martyr, Oxford, prior to becoming assistant priest at St Silas, Kentish Town, where Eliot was wont to make his Confession.

In the 1930s Demant had published, to critical acclaim, *God, Man, and Society. An Introduction to Christian Sociology* — the last a term he had some claim to have invented.[47] His book *Christian Polity* followed. Unlike its predecessor, it had emerged from the prestigious publishing house of Faber and Faber for which T. S. Eliot was a reader, hardly an accidental coincidence.[48] In 1940 Demant became a canon of St Paul's, the cathedral chapter of which could boast an historic Tractarian element in its lineage since the time of Liddon and Church. In 1949 he reached the top of the tree, becoming Regius Professor of Moral and Pastoral Theology at Oxford, with a canonry of Christ Church attached. For an advanced Anglo-Catholic it was a remarkable breakthrough, if well deserved.

In his contribution to *Prospect for Christendom* Demant begins from two requirements of a Christendom society. First, there must be a 'strong nucleus of people' who, through sharing in the worshipping life of the Church, are fully aware that the Kingdom is 'not a name for a better earth' but comes from 'beyond this world'. That said, the same nucleus will be conscious that their 'experience of the Kingdom now will give them an insight into the essential nature of man', an insight capable of serving as a 'criterion for judging the human validity of social activities and their organization'.[49] The 'essential nature' thus exhibited *is* the 'natural order', and its coherent and adequate exhibition *is* the 'natural law'.

Eliot had already described the 'idea of a Christian society' in the book of that name. It was a 'society in which the natural end of man — virtue and well-being in community — is acknowledged for all, and the super-natural end — beatitude — for those who have eyes to see it'.[50] Demant did not call such a society *inevitably* more virtuous than the current arrangements. Yet in the society Eliot had described the pursuit of virtue would at least be less ensnared in intellectual confusion. The current 'we' does not know which are the permanent elements of human 'morphology' worthy of inclusion in a genuinely 'civilized' life. Historic destiny — 'progress' — is co-opted in service of a gigantic attack on basic truths about humanity, truths that in consequence are losing their hold on culture. It was a theme Demant had explored in his own study *The Religious Prospect*.[51] 'Both the eviscerated liberal societies and the violent dictatorial ones represent conflicting movements' in a phase of history defined by virtual disbelief that 'man is a real kind'.[52]

Such recognition of the reality of species did not of course signify metaphysical naturalism. 'All forms of naturalism and immanentism', wrote Demant, 'are in contradiction to the Gospel of Grace and to rationally apprehended law, both of which tell of man as standing somewhat outside and above the flux of events: the one [the Gospel] by its declaration of the particularity of each man in God, the other [the law] by its general truths which ignore the particularity of each.'[53] And here it will not do, when seeking an antidote, to appeal solely to the role of values, in deliberate disprizing of dogma and organized culture. 'Moral aims for society cannot be effective if they stand alone as objects of the social will. Such aims require support in metaphysical certainty or dogma, in emotional and cultural bent largely induced by the habits of a community, and in the organization of the social activities.'[54]

In his discussion, Demant steers his way carefully between the Scylla of rationalism and the Charybdis of historicism. Under the impact of pure rationalism, when reason exalts the common truths it knows about man into the central constitutive principle of anthropology, the bearers of the Gospel 'may well make cause with non-Christian forces which oppose *idées générales* in the name of historical and natural process'.[55] Yet when, contrastingly, it is 'historical or natural dogmas' that confuse their 'notions of man's concrete existence' with what Demant terms the 'central spiritual concreteness which Christianity upholds', the Church sorely needs natural law theory.[56]

Demant draws German Idealism into service when he remarks that the 'spirit-centred structure of man' at once permeates all his activities and yet, precisely because it is spirit and not nature, can deny its own centrality and reconstitute itself in some activity which it makes the new *centrum hominis*, the 'centre of man'. In an elegant formulation, spirit is the 'ground both of the proper place of each activity and of the misplacement of one or more of them'.[57] An ensuing 'spiritual' fixation on politics, technology, trade, class, race, exemplify false egocentricity in the living out of human existence.

So what is to be done? At the *individual level*, the opening inwards of spirit toward God always enables it to recover its proper centrality, albeit not simply through its own willing (Christendom thinkers are not to be Pelagians), for man 'must lose his self in the Divine Action operating upon and through him, a process begun and carried through by the spiritual culture we call the practice of religion'.[58] At the *social level* the 'centrality of the spirit in its sociological force cannot be recovered by moral desire alone, but requires that this desire be sustained and that real will be formed out of it, by a social order that provides a habitat for the soul'.[59] For the natural order is more than source of a moral norm. It is a 'noumenal reality which tugs at [man] all the time and that he suffers in the alienation because it is never a compete alienation'.[60]

In his subsequent essay, *Religion and the Decline of Capitalism*, Demant gave a new twist to the 1926 classic of social history *Religion and the Rise of Capitalism* by R. H. Tawney (1880–1962).[61] For Demant, social cohesion can survive the triumph of capitalism only owing to a residue of religious culture. When religious loyalty corrodes, the strains internal to capitalism become unbearable—until (that is) capitalism discovers a way to retain its own unity by asserting the hegemony of State power over all sectional interests—with the consequent victory of the more-or-less idolatrous view of State agency such an assertion entails.[62]

It followed from Demant's account in *Prospect for Christendom* that a 'particular layer of man's social activity is only kept true to its proper place in the social order, when it is recognized that the loyalty for which it calls stands *under* man's super-temporal loyalty to God'.[63] Within this overall context, cultural activities ('arts, knowledge and ceremonies— all that qualifies life and does not merely preserve it') rightly enjoy a metaphysical priority over political and economic, since in the former the 'spirit of man operates most centrally from within outwards, less conditioned by the determinisms which of necessity belong to political and economic activities'.[64]

Demant's intellectual sophistication was obvious. The essay was a *tour de force* (an appetizer for his *Theology of Society* of two years later),[65] and the remaining contributions to *Prospect for Christendom* somewhat paled in comparison. Yet, however original Demant's way of laying the foundations, it was notable that the concrete content of the subsequent essays corresponded remarkably closely to the social teachings developed from Leo XIII's pontificate onwards (he was Bishop of Rome from 1878 to 1903) by the Roman popes.

In *Prospect for Christendom*, the redoubtable Eric Lionel Mascall of the Oratory of the Good Shepherd, then teaching at Lincoln Theological College (there will be more on him in Chapter 7), praised the family as a 'school for the rearing of human beings as persons', which for its role in this regard should have the respectful acknowledgement of the State.[66] Mascall was drawing on Jacques Maritain's distinction between persons and individuals as adumbrated in *Scholasticism and Politics*, lectures given in English at the University of Chicago in 1938.[67] On the topic of the education of the poor, and here the teacher, he insisted, is *in loco parentium* not *in loco civitatis*, Mascall was explicitly indebted to the 1929 Low Week Declaration on that topic of the Roman Catholic Bishops of England and Wales. Mascall was one of comparatively few Anglo-Catholics happy to cite as authoritative not only papal documents but texts of the 'intruded' Roman hierarchy as gathered round the Archbishop of Westminster. That hierarchy studiously ignored the Anglo-Catholics, and the 'compliment' was repaid—part of the justification for my writing the present book. Mascall would write a full, if condensed, social philosophy in his *Man: His Origin and Destiny*,[68] where man is for God, things for man, and money for things, an order inverted in modern society where 'Things are for the production of Money, Man is for the production and consumption of Things, and a very hypothetical God is for the convenience of Man'.[69]

The essay by T. S. Eliot (a figure dealt with more fully in Chapter 9 on Anglo-Catholics and the arts) was chiefly analytic rather than prescriptive. That is no shock since its title, 'Cultural Forces in the Human Order',[70] anticipates his 1948 *Notes towards the Definition of Culture*.[71] There is, however, a turn toward the close, where Eliot affirms that the culture of a people is not its religion, no, and yet it *is* the incarnation of its religion—from which there issues the need for a lay elite, 'men and women whose intellect and sensibility qualify them for a higher religious education than is at present, for the laity, obtainable'.[72]

Philip Mairet (1886–1975) son of a Swiss watchmaker, was not an academic but a craftsman-cum-thinker. Trained in the design of stained glass at the Hornsey School, editor of the avant-garde journal *New English Weekly*,[73] his combination of gifts singled him out to be the dedicatee of Eliot's *Notes towards the Definition of Culture*. In *Prospect for Christendom* he wrote on the drawbacks of a civilisation of 'technics'—not a coining of his own but something of a contemporary vogue word at the time. Not only as producers (in machine work) but also as consumers (of machine-made goods) people take less pride in human sub-creation—to anticipate a Tolkienesque term.[74] The essay by Mairet, who stood at the crossing-point of Christian Socialism, the Arts and Crafts movement, organic farming, and the 'Social Credit' thinking of Major C. H. Douglas (1879–1952), was a recall to a theocentric, and more especially a doxological view of life. That fitted well enough the Anglo-Catholic template.

A civilisation of technics does not know what to do with its amazing abilities. 'For in the first and last analysis there is nothing to do with them, except to dedicate them to the Source whence they came.'[75] Mairet predicted that when a society 'succumbs to the fascination and the power and pride of technics, it loses not only its sense of the supernatural order, but also its foothold upon natural life.'[76] In communion with the see of Rome, Eric Gill (1882–1940) was saying much the same thing (Mairet had farmed on land belonging to the Ditchling 'Guild of St Joseph and St Dominic', scene of Gill's early labours), and it is surprising that Fiona MacCarthy has not yet written a scintillating vignette.[77]

Prospect for Christendom's own editor, Maurice Reckitt, wrote on 'Catholic Sociology and the English Situation'.[78] A Catholic Sociology, argued Reckitt, will be deducible from Christian dogma, with a reference to *Catholicisme* by the French Jesuit Henri de Lubac (1896–1991) which itself took that very view.[79] Reckitt also aimed to draw on the 'Catholic philosophers', the 'consecrated intelligence of Christendom', since they were possessed of a fresh outlook on the 'significance of order' as well as the 'meaning of life'. And finally, after dogma and the Schoolmen, the 'social theories and institutions of that period of history which was explicitly dominated by Christian ethics' will be grist to his mill.[80] That turned out to include Morris, Ruskin, and Arthur Penty (1875–1937, a Guild Socialist thinker, as well as architect), and not just John Keats (1795–1821), the Pre-Raphaelites, and the 'Mass and Maypole' school.

Reckitt offered clues for social recovery. It will require a proper hierarchization of society whereby agriculture, industry, commerce, and finance are rated *in that order*. It will entail the operation of the 'Just Price' (Demant had written a study of this element in mediaeval but also [Roman] Catholic social teaching in 1930).[81] It will mean restraining usury, for money is to be treated as a medium of distribution, not as a commodity to be dealt in. There must be due preservation of vocational values and professional standards, which will best be achieved through guilds. Rather by way of afterthought, Reckitt added that a 'widespread if unequal distribution of property [is] a necessary support for the realization of personality',[82] and 'though we have seen reason to doubt whether a "pre-national" Christendom can suggest to us an all-sufficing solution for our international difficulties, yet it is certainly true that the modern "omni-competent " state, fighting for its own hand in a world of "foreign power", is utterly at variance with the Christian doctrine of the law of nations'.[83]

The essays that round off *Prospect for Christendom*, Reckitt reports, suggest or imply that the achievement of a Christian realm will require the rescue of the rural community in defiance of "the City" and the heresies of a predominantly export economy, for the peasant tradition has been almost lost and agricultural skills have decayed. The (Roman) Catholic 'Back to the Land Movement in England was saying just the same.[84] Small-holding of productive property must be defended by legislation directed to restrain monopoly—that was the Distributist economics of the 'Chesterbelloc', G. K. Chesterton and Hilaire Belloc (1870–1953) combined. Steps must be taken to guarantee to all some form of unconditional income such as alone can underpin the family in a world of forces threatening to disintegrate it (the 'family wage' advocated by Rome).

Reckitt proposed a technique for the assessment of cost which would result in the extrusion of bank-created debts from prices and their calculation on a basis of objective realities; the establishment of social control over finances on such truly scientific principles as will enable a community to buy what it cam make and exchange; and the re-alignment of industry on a basis of 'democratic corporatism', combining cooperation for many matters of common interest with flexibility for the units within the producing associations or guilds, and competition in respect of methods of production'.[85] These proposals reflected his own shifting intellectual history: apart from his role in the National Guilds League he had been a member of the 'Chandos Group', defined by support for Douglas's Social Credit theory of the economy.[86]

Reckitt was trusting all the while in the existence of a still widely 'diffused Christianity' which would respond with intuitive favour to these appeals.[87] And yet he could not deny that '[v]ast heresies have seized upon and devoured the body politic'.[88] His analyses in *Prospect* evidence his mastery of the material, to be shown in a different format in 1947 with the publication of his *Maurice to Temple: A History of the Social Movement in the Church of England*.[89]

Finally, one major figure who did not put in an appearance in *Prospect for Christendom*, though she had participated in the Malvern Conference, was Dorothy L. Sayers (1893–1957). Sayers, the daughter of a headmaster of Christ Church Cathedral School and chaplain to the 'House', had been brought in in the Fens, near Earith, a singularly isolated corner of England.[90] At Somerville College, Oxford, she specialized in mediaeval French. After a varied business career (at one point she found herself devising advertisements for Guinness), she established her name as a writer of detective fiction. In the golden age of the genre, the 1920s and '30s she became an acknowledged 'queen'. Her aspirations, however, soared higher than that. Her knowledge of literature in the Romance languages of the mediaeval period stood her in good stead when she embarked on a translation of Dante. Despite its oddities (the exact replication of Dante's metre in the *Commedia* does not work well in a language relatively poor in rhymes, and the use of a southern Scottish dialect in the *Purgatorio*—on the grounds that Dante sometimes had recourse there to Provençal—seems bizarre) brought the text, for the most part in colloquial English, before a wider audience for the first time.[91] T. S. Eliot had already argued for giving the *Divine Comedy* pride of place in the entire European literary canon.[92] Between them these two Anglo-Catholic writers did more to present Dante to a Protestant, or post-Protestant, society than any others.

So far, this may not seem a likely *curriculum vitae* for a contributor to the Anglo-Catholic social movement. But in line with her explicitly Christian plays, performed in Anglican cathedrals and on the national broadcasting service, Sayers' theological essays, with their generous admixture of ethics and culture criticism, were largely motivated by the need for social and cultural reconstruction. *Begin Here: A War-time Essay Collection, Creed or Chaos*, both from 1940, and *The Other Six Deadly Sins*, from 1943, express her conviction that only through return to the doctrinal building blocks of Christian belief (creation, Trinity, and the Incarnation, as well as sin and the Atonement)—which is as much as to say the truth about man and God, would people be likely to live out more justly their corporate co-existence in the 'City', meaning thereby post-War Britain.[93] The all too brief renaissance of Church of England, not least Anglo-Catholic, life and thought that accompanied the end of the 1940s and the first half of the 1950s, seemed to augur well for that 'prospect' of a future recreated Christendom.

7

The Theologians

PUSEY WAS PRIMARILY A BIBLICAL EXEGETE and a patrologist, so the first considerable Anglo-Catholic dogmatician must be accounted his biographer, Henry Parry Liddon, an accomplished theologian in his own right. With Liddon there may be coupled, as 'Late Tractarians', the name of Charles Gore—though at one major crisis, already noted in Chapter 2, they were distinctly at loggerheads. In this chapter are considered, further, three theologians who emerged from the new Religious Brotherhoods: Gabriel Hebert of Kelham, Lionel Spencer Thornton of Mirfield, and Gregory Dix of Nashdom. Two academic clergy, Austin Farrer and Eric Mascall, will stand for survivors of the period when Anglo-Catholic theology was so predominant in the Church of England as to enjoy if not a hegemony than a distinct predominance. Mark Chapman, looking at Anglican theology between the reign of Edward VII and the start of the new millennium, gives his section on the interwar years, together with the 1940s and 50s, the overall sub-title 'The Triumph of Anglo-Catholic Theology.'[1] Lastly, justice must be done to two bishop-theologians, Kenneth Kirk of Oxford and Michael Ramsey of Canterbury. That produces, in the aftermath of World War One, a trio of categories—monastic, academical, episcopal. But first I must deal with the figures already well-established (Gore) or even deceased (Liddon) before the War began, those afore-mentioned 'Late' Tractarians.

The Late Tractarians

Henry Parry Liddon (1829–90) carried the torch of Dr Pusey with a firm wrist, when Pusey's Oxonian successor, Charles Gore, seemed to be stumbling, and causing a flickering of the flame. Liddon was the son of a naval captain, born in the Hampshire Basin, and educated at King's College School and Christ Church, Oxford.[2] In 1859, the newly ordained Liddon was removed from the vice-principalship of Cuddesdon Theological College through the anti-Tractarian agitation of Charles Portales Golightly (1807–85): Golightly was still to be found fulminating against nefarious teachings at Cuddesdon as late as 1878.[3] Liddon was rescued from his resultant Limbo by Kerr Hamilton of Salisbury, Lord Aberdeen's lonely Tractarian pelican in an otherwise episcopal wilderness, who conferred on him a prebend. A happy chance gave Liddon the opportunity to show his mettle as Bampton Lecturer at Oxford, whence derives his magnum opus, *The Divinity of Our Lord and Saviour Jesus Christ.*

Though Liddon published a series of wide-ranging *Essays and Addresses*,[4] and two posthumous commentaries on Pauline epistles,[5] his fame rests essentially on one book, an exceedingly well-organized and carefully thought out book, whose pious title could lead the unwary to underestimate the substantial theology of its contents. Added to which, Liddon's objections to Gore's—by later standards, modest—use of the 'Higher Criticism' has gained for him the unwarranted reputation of an obscurantist. But as he himself wrote to Gore: 'We are not opposed in *this* sense, that I hold all Criticism to be mischievous, while you hold it to be generally illuminating and useful. For Criticism is an equivocal term, and is applied to very different kinds of Textual or Exegetical work ... All Criticism, I suppose, *really* proceeds on certain principles, preliminary assumptions for the critic to go upon. The question is, Whence do the preliminary assumptions come? A Catholic critic would say, "From the general sense of the Church". But a modern "psychological" critic (if that is the right word) would say, "From his own notion of the fitness of things, or from the outcome of literature [including, presumably, philosophy] at large".'[6]

When commending the Old Catholics to Anglicans in his Preface to the Report on the 1874 Conference of Anglican, Old Catholic, and Orthodox theologians (to be visited in Chapter 10), Liddon himself had praised them for 'sympathizing with all that is thorough and honest in the critical methods of Protestant Germany'—though he was quick to add 'yet holding on firmly and strenuously to the faith of antiquity'.[7]

The qualities of *The Divinity of Our Lord and Saviour Jesus Christ* were, in fact, rapidly acknowledged, and a canonry at St Paul's followed, on which basis Liddon soon established his reputation as perhaps the most successful preacher of the Victorian era, typically drawing an audience of several thousand to hear his pulpit oratory which was supposedly modelled on that of the France of *le Roi-Soleil*. In the same year as he acquired his canonry he was made Dean Ireland Professor of the Exegesis of Holy Scripture at Oxford.

The Divinity, to abbreviate the title, answers the question put by the Jesus of the Synoptic Gospels at Caesarea Philippi, 'Who do men say the Son of Man is?' (Matthew 16:13). In his first lecture, Liddon identified three possible answers: the humanistic, the Arian, and the Catholic, but the second, as he explains, is an implausible compromise between the first and third. Followers of F. D. E. Schleiermacher (1768–1834 — Liddon regards the 'Father of Liberal Protestant Theology' as essentially a 'Humanitarian') may affirm the 'ethical glory' of Christ's person but a Christ who, while the 'perfect Revelation of God', is not 'personally God' does not 'really differ from the altogether human Christ of Socinus' (Fausto Sozzini, 1539–1604, a Sienese Unitarian especially influential in Eastern Europe).[8] The Arian Christ who is not merely a man, but is nevertheless a created being, also belongs, whatever his peculiarities, to the realm of naturalistic thinking. The Catholic answer, expressed in the Nicene Creed, has the advantage of protecting the truth of Jesus's manhood while at the same time securing the full force of the idea of Godhead in his regard, and in this way it reflects the Gospel narrative. For the latter 'exhibits Jesus as the Son of Man, while yet it draws us on by an irresistible attraction to contemplate that Higher Nature which was the seat of His Eternal Personality'.[9]

Liddon discussed, and refuted, three sorts of objection to a mono-personal but dual nature Christology: from the viewpoints of what he termed 'Historical Aestheticism' — an approach which, to retain the 'poetry' of the Gospel repudiates Scholastic-type enquiry and distinctions; an anti-doctrinal morality — an approach which considers the dogmatic temper ('intellectual ritualism') a distraction from the real human task that is moral effort, and, lastly, subjective pietism — an approach which would create a chasm between the 'simple Gospel' and 'metaphysics'. But the Gospel claims are already metaphysical, and Liddon warns against an 'earnest but shortsighted piety which imagines that it can dare actively to exercise thought on the Christian Revelation, and withal to ignore those ripe decisions which we owe to the illuminated mind of Primitive Christendom'.[10]

In lecture two he put forward the principle of the organic unity of Scripture. Here he goes beyond what in later twentieth century biblical studies would be called 'canonical criticism' to the latter's ontological depths. '[B]eneath the differences of style, of language, and of method, which are undeniably prominent in the Sacred Books, and which appear so entirely to absorb the attention of a merely literary observer, a deeper insight will discover in Scripture such manifest unity of drift and purpose, both moral and intellectual, as to imply the continuous action of a Single Mind. To this unity Scripture itself bears witness'.[11] On that principle, the Hebrew Bible with its proto-Trinitarianism, theophanies in angelo-human form, divine yet creation-indwelling 'Wisdom' with its quasi-hypostatic character, transformed by the Alexandrian Jew Philo into the language of 'Logos', using Platonist terminology as its vehicle: all these foreshadow the 'Catholic answer', which has, accordingly, its proper predictions and announcements throughout biblical history. It was owing to a debased version of Messianism, disregarding the 'Superhuman Personality' of the promised King to come, that the majority of the Jews rejected Emmanuel when at last he came. 'When the destructive critics have done their worst, we are still confronted by the fact of a considerable literature, indisputably anterior to the age of Christianity, and foretelling in explicit terms the coming of a Divine and Human Saviour.'[12]

Lecture three shows how the Lord's work is a witness to his divinity. He 'proclaimed Himself the Founder of a world-wide and imperishable Society', which was 'not to be a school of thinkers, or a self-associated company of enterprising fellow-workers', but the 'kingdom of God', a society invisible and visible together.[13] His plan is unaccountable except in terms of his origin as well as his mission. Liddon cannily notes that the 'idea of an indefinite progress of humanity, to whatever perversions that idea may have been subjected, is really a creation of the Chrisian faith'.[14] But note well that the 'Christian life springs from and is sustained by the apprehension of Christ present in His Church, present in and with His members as a *pneuma zôopoioun* [quickening Spirit]'.[15]

Lecture four chose a tricky topic: the witness to his divinity provided by his consciousness. The Christ of history, declared Liddon, is none other than the Christ of dogma. The miracles Jesus worked 'manifest forth His Mediatorial Glory',[16] while 'those of which Our Lord's Manhood is Itself the subject', as he enters this world by one miracle (the Virginal Conception), and leaves it by another (the Bodily Resurrection), 'especially point to the Catholic doctrine as their justification'.[17] Because he himself claimed to work miracles his 'moral character' cannot be divorced from the issue of their historicity, which leads Liddon to discuss his self-awareness. At an initial stage, the manifestation of his mind is chiefly ethical, yes. He preaches a Gospel of repentance. But increasingly the habit of that mind becomes self-assertion, since transparency—full disclosure—whatever its risks in a jealously monotheistic culture, is essential to his mission. Liddon looks to Jesus's awareness of absolute sinlessness, his willingness to abrogate not only the 'traditional doctrines of the Jewish schools, but the Mosaic law itself',[18] and his persistent assertion of the 'real character of His position relatively to God and man',[19] which, if in its explicit form is Johannine is nevertheless implicitly given in the Synoptic Gospels through the 'public assumption of such titles and functions as those of King, Teacher, and Judge'.[20] 'If He is not God, He is not a humble or an unselfish man.'[21]

Lecture five considered St John's Gospel which Liddon described as the battlefield of New Testament studies. Its distinctive features are to be explained by its supplementary character vis-à-vis the Synoptics as well as by its polemical and dogmatic concerns. The Fourth Gospel is in a dogmatic and moral unity with the Epistles of John and the Apocalypse, and in an 'essential' unity with the Synoptics. 'If St. John could be blotted out from the pages of the New Testament, St. John's central doctrine would still live on in the earlier Evangelists as implicitly contained within a history otherwise inexplicable, if not as the illuminating truth of a heavenly gnosis'.[22] And if someone concedes that the four Gospels are not incompatible with each other, yet maintains that the doctrine taught by John is incredible ('How can Godhead and Manhood thus coalesce without forfeiture of that unity which is a condition of personality?',[23] Liddon defends its rationality. 'Christ's Manhood is not of Itself an individual being; It is not a seat and centre of personality; It has no conceivable existence apart from the act of Self-incarnation whereby the Eternal Word called It into being and made It His own.'[24]

Lecture six looks at the back-up provided by the other apostolic letters, notably James, Peter, and Paul, conceding that the 'writers of the apostolic epistles represent different attitudes of the human soul towards the one evangelical truth',[25] but arguing, with some exegetical care, against the claim that this constitutes a 'supposed division of the Apostolical Church into schools of thought holding antagonistic beliefs', the specialty view of the Protestant Tübingen school.[26]

The seventh lecture, which considers ante-Nicene readings of the scriptural record, culminates in that key word of all later patristic witness to the biblical rule of faith: *homoousia*, the 'consubstantiality' of the Son with the Father. 'In the *Homoousion*... the Church felt that she had lighted upon a symbol which was practically adequate to an expression of the truth which she had from the first possessed, and capable of resisting the intellectual solvents which had seemed to threaten that truth with extinction. The *Homoousion* did not change, it protected the doctrine. It clothed the doctrine in a vesture of language which rendered it intelligible to a new world of thought while preserving its strict unchanging identity.'[27]

And the final lecture draws out the consequences of belief in the divinity of Jesus. Theology for Liddon must be, within limits, a furnisher of appropriate inferences, and here we can say that the doctrine of Christ's divinity has the merit of protecting the idea of God in human thought, for while deism cannot destroy pantheism orthodox Christology, for Liddon, can achieve this goal. God incarnate in Jesus Christ is no mere cosmic principle. Confession of the Lord's divinity also secures the true dignity of man: God was willing to conjoin divine substance with human. Liddon brings together these two claims under the heading of the 'conservative force' of this article of the Nicene Creed. That same article, he goes on to explain, has 'illuminative force', too, for such matters as Christ's infallibility as teacher. The limitation of knowledge in his soul (which does not, argues Liddon, entail Nestorianism or 'Agnoetism'), is consistent with the practical immensity of that knowledge. Belief in the divinity of the Saviour explains the atoning virtue of his death and the supernatural power of the sacraments, and indicates the meaning of his kingly office. Finally, it brings with it ethical fruitfulness. It might be objected that a divine Christ is ethically inimitable, but there can be approximate imitation via the reality of his manhood, owing not least to the grace flowing from the God-man. Belief in his Godhead propagates virtues unattainable by paganism and naturalism, notably purity, humility, and charity as the history of sanctity attests.

In 1882 Liddon began a series of travels, in the Levant, Germany, Russia, making contact with the Orthodox and Old Catholics. His death left his massive four volume life of Pusey to be finished by John Octavius Johnston (1852–1923), Principal of St Stephen's House in Oxford, and later of Cuddesdon, and Robert Wilson (1840–97), the second Warden of Keble. Johnston would serve in turn as Liddon's own biographer.

Charles Gore (1853–1932) has already appeared twice in these pages: first, in Chapter 2 as a disturber—later, somewhat repentant—of settled Anglo-Catholic convictions in the narrative of post-1845 events (the *Lux Mundi* affair), and then, in Chapter 5 in his role as a founder-figure for the Community of the Resurrection. Gore had aristocratic background in the peerage of Ireland. A great-uncle on his father's side was Earl of Arran, and his mother was the Countess of Kerry. The family house in Wimbledon where he grew up was set in an estate of forty acres. At Harrow School the influence of the future Bishop Westcott taught him the value of scholarship, which remained with him through life as the hallmark of a priest in a 'learned Church'. It also oiled his effortless rise via a Double First in Greats at Balliol to a Fellowship at Trinity College, Oxford, Newman's original *alma mater*.

Made Vice-Principal of Cuddesdon (once the uneasy seat of the ejected Liddon) at the age of 28, he became within two years the first Principal of Pusey House, the setting for his founding of the Community of the Resurrection from whose corporate life, as already noted, he rapidly became an absentee. If Gore's Pusey period saw the delivery and publication of his Bampton Lectures, *The Incarnation of the Son of God*, in 1891,[28] with a second edition in 1892, it was during his time as a canon of Westminster Abbey (1894–1901) that he published major follow-up works: *Dissertations on Subjects connected with the Incarnation* in 1895,[29] with a second edition in 1896, and in 1901 his manifesto in Eucharistic theology, *The Body of Christ*.[30] He continued to write throughout his episcopate and beyond: landmarks in the life of the writing bishop include *The New Theology and the Old Religion*,[31] and from the time after his resignation, *The Reconstruction of Belief*, a trilogy,[32] and his Gifford lectures *The Philosophy of the Good Life*.[33] Gore's appointment as Bishop of Worcester showed Lord Salisbury resuming the prime-ministerial favour to Tractarians once showed by Gladstone. It was clamorously greeted, 'some opponents regarding him as a destructive radical, others as a treacherous Romanizer'.[34] That was because the name of *Lux Mundi* stank in some nostrils, the name of Pusey in others. It was also because insufficient attention had been paid to the overall tenor of his theological work.

Though the alliance of Anglo-Catholicism with a form of Hegelianism in *Lux Mundi* was unexpected, it was presented in a peculiarly English form which drew what might otherwise have been its venom. '[F]or Gore and others, traditional Christian doctrine simply *was* the most compelling and yet progressive framework through which the growth of modern knowledge could be interpreted.'[35] That sounded well, but—depending on the construction placed on 'modern knowledge' in its 'growth'—it could also be the sprinkling with holy water of a fashionable philosophical idealism or evolutionary optimism or both of those together. The role of philosophical idealism was the more worrying, insofar as its persistent tendency was to collapse completely the distinction between divine and non-divine. Reality was, to borrow a term from Indian philosophy, 'non-dual' (*advaita*), with man as not only part of a world which expresses the agency of 'spirit', i. e. self-conscious being, but sharer, in incremental fashion, in that unique consciousness as it both expresses itself in the world and distinguishes itself from it. Gore embraced the holism especially in regard to divine presence in the development of the moral life, but he drew back from the fashionable denial of duality.

Both in *The Incarnation of the Son of God* and in *The New Theology and the Old Religion*, with its attack on the (then) Congregationalist R. J. Campbell's talk of God as the 'deeper Self' or the 'Self of the world', Gore claims that the Christian concept of God does justice to the elements of truth in both pantheism and deism, and is, accordingly, more satisfactory than either.[36] In these matters, English 'restraint' in the use of Hegel was not enough. After all, T. H. Green was English,

Marriage of the modern and the traditional at the level of elevated theological theory eased the way for the late nineteenth century commitment of Anglo-Catholics to social progressivism in welfare matters where old convictions were coupled with new strategies for the amelioration of the *polis*. In Gore's case—he supported the cautious Henry Scott Holland's Christian Social Union, that fell considerably short of advocacy of Socialism in the dictionary sense: the corporate ownership of the means of production, distribution, and exchange. In the making of this Leftward movement an equal role must be allotted to the role of slum parish clergy, often from upper class backgrounds comparable to Gore's own, and to University men who took part in 'Settlement' work in some of London's most deprived areas. Both reacted with outrage to the state of English cities. When Bishop of Oxford Gore would have added, 'not only cities but villages as well'.

As Chapter 2 has shown, Gore himself became a robust, not to say ferocious, opponent of doctrinal Modernism, above all in *The Basis of Anglican Fellowship*,[37] while also making space for the exercise of the scholar's critical acumen in the reading of Scripture, and here his willingness, in old age, to serve as editor of *A New Commentary in Holy Scripture* was eloquent (C. S. Lewis considered it the best such commentary in the English language).[38] On one reading, that might be considered a retrieval of Reformation principles from the Limbo in which Keble and the later Pusey had left them. But 'sound' learning in relation to Scripture was not a purely Protestant preoccupation. In Christopher Dawson's words, 'In the religious sphere, which was its proper territory, the Oxford Movement stood for spiritual freedom against Erastianism and for scientific theology against the emotionalism of popular Protestantism.'[39]

Roman opposition to methods of 'higher criticism' devised in the German Universities could easily give papally inclined Anglo-Catholics, especially in the pontificates of Pius X (pope 1903–14) and Benedict XV (pope 1914–22), a wrong impression. The question in biblical studies is not *whether* to study through exact scholarship but *how* to study, meaning by *which* methods employed on *what* wider theological (and philosophical) basis: precisely Liddon's point to Gore. A false turn on that road—not, then, the road itself—could lead Anglo-Catholics into full-scale Modernism, by the 'intrusion of an intellectual element that is entirely incongruous with [Tractarianism's] original spirit'.[40] There is such a thing as using the wrong tool.

To place the Liddon-Gore clash in suitable perspective, it should not be forgotten that, while such Late Tractarians as Liddon and Gore were making a splash, the solid translating or editing work pioneered by the Oxford Fathers was continuing apace behind the scenes. *The Library of the Fathers of the Holy Catholic Church before the division of East and West* was completed in 1885 with forty-eight volumes. *The Library of Anglo-Catholic Theology* carried on until 1863, an early point of cut-off for the projected programme was never completed. And yet the total of eighty-eight volumes published was hardly a bagatelle.

Monastic theologians

Lionel Spencer Thornton (1884–1960) came from a family Evangelical on his father's side, Anglo-Catholic on his mother's—especially in the person of his uncle, Frederick William Puller, SSJE (1843–1938), who, curiously enough, was, among other things, a theologian of the sacrament of Confirmation, one of Thornton's own areas.[41] After secondary school at Malvern, Thornton attended Emmanuel College, Cambridge, where he came under the influence of Figgis. He would dedicate his first work, *Conduct and the Supernatural*, to that thinker whose 'pluralist' view of the good *polis* returns recurrently in fashion in English discussion. It is, in effect, an Anglo-Catholic version of the language of 'subsidiarity' and 'solidarity' which came to dominate the papal social tradition, emphasizing in so doing the distinction between civil society and the State.

In 1913 Thornton followed Figgis in a further sense. He entered Mirfield, where he would teach until 1944, when he transferred to the Community's London house instead.[42] Figgis' influence may account for Thornton's combined concern with Incarnation and Atonement, and not least, in the latter respect, theodicy—the 'problem of evil' to which the social strains of Edwardian England, followed by the horrors of the 'Four Year War', brought to the attention of both these writers.

Thornton shared with all the twentieth century Anglo-Catholic theologians, Hebert, Ramsey, Dix, Kirk, Mascall, and Farrer a strong emphasis on supernaturality, a word which, in its adjectival form entered into his first slim book, *Conduct and the Supernatural*. There the youthful Thornton (the work had started life as the Norrisian Prize Essay from his undergraduate years) took on Friedrich Nietzsche (1844–1900), George Bernard Shaw (1856–1950), and the racial theorist Housten Stewart Chamberlain (1855–1927), while making its claim that the problems of natural ethics can only be resolved by moving to a higher level—with an attendant defence of Christian asceticism as both intensifying a sense of the spiritual world and also protecting a broadly sacramental view of natural reality.

Thornton would look to such Anglican predecessors as Richard Hooker, Robert Sanderson (1587–1663), and Joseph Butler, all of whom were important for moral theology, as well as the 'Three Great "A"'s' of the Western tradition—Augustine, Anselm, and Aquinas, as his masters in dogmatics. But more especially, in his mature work, he engaged closely with the Ante-Nicene fathers, notably St Irenaeus. He realized that Protestant theology, whether Lutheran in the manner of Albrecht Ritschl (1822–89) or Calvinist, in the manner of contemporary Anglophone Evangelicalism, was leaving out of count the order of creation, so different in this from the practice of the Fathers of the first three centuries. Thornton made it his business to reinstate due theological consideration of that order in the name of Catholic tradition.

Thornton's contribution to *Essays Catholic and Critical* recommended analogical predication in language about God, doing so within an account of reality as a series of graded levels leading up to man and to Christ—though never actually reaching the latter who is unthinkable without the personal Incarnation of the eternal Logos.[43] Looking back, he saw that essay collection as the swansong of an experimental modern Catholicism which had hoped to find a suitable philosophical interlocutor in Green's Idealism. For Green, over against British Empiricism, the proper or ideal content of the human mind is a spiritual cosmos of thought-relations in which, through a metaphysical if also historical development, the divine has become manifest. In between the two world wars, Thornton grew increasingly dissatisfied with such thinking, partly from the contrast provided by his reading of Aquinas (not that he was especially attracted by what he knew of Neo-Thomism).[44]

His first great book, *The Incarnate Lord*, 1928, drew on the early 'emergentist' metaphysics of Alfred North Whitehead (1861–1947), seeing them as a restatement of a Platonism—much preferable to Idealism as a philosophical handmaid of Christianity—now re-crafted for an evolutionary world-view.[45] Whitehead, after all, had famously declared all philosophy to be footnotes to Plato. Whitehead seemed to have reinstated formal and final causality in the universe in a way reminiscent of the best thinking of Hellenism. He was plainly opposed to any reductive materialism. His version of emergentism was, moreover, akin to what was right about Idealism in its relative openness to a spiritual explanation of the world. (At the Chicago Divinity School, a stronghold of theological liberalism, it was feared that Whitehead could be interpreted in a way that would serve orthodoxy.)

Thornton abandoned Whitehead after the latter, in *Process and Reality*,[46] his Gifford Lectures, showed himself to be a Monist for whom all reality, from an atom to the 'consequent nature' of God is ultimately the same kind of thing. Whitehead denied creation from nothing and saw personality as an epiphenomenon, while to Thornton's mind his theodicy was less satisfying than that provided by Scripture. Whitehead's Monism collapsed the distinctions between matter and life, body and soul, individual and society, and ultimately between the cosmos and God. Platonic Realism would have preserved all these qualitative distinctions.

Thornton's chief commitment, in fact, was to a Christian Platonism for which the immaterial, intelligible reality of an ultimate explanatory principle has ontological priority over the sensuous world, over against an account whose conclusions are finally nominalist and materialist in character—the two errors being sides of the same coin.

The book had shown a fine systematic sense, exploring not only the cosmic site of the Incarnation but its implications at both the personal and corporate levels—something to which Thornton would return. In the 1920s and '30s he was involved in the discussions between Modernist and non-Modernist theologians that eventually (after fifteen years of gestation!) produced the 1938 report, *Doctrine in the Church of England*.⁴⁷ He thus came to write his short study of the Atonement, which, unlike the corresponding work by Gustaf Aulèn (1879–1977), as translated by another of my trio of monastic theologians, Gabriel Hebert, took together all the New Testament images for the Saving Work, seeing them as complementary facets of a single mystery.⁴⁸ In that way it announces a turn towards not simply Scripture in general but a biblical 'figural realism', relating Scriptural images to the creation and to each other as the twin 'books' of God.

After that he retreated for a while into a world of reading—except when the annual conferences of the Fellowship of SS Alban and Sergius could draw him forth. Like the Mirfield Community at large he was hostile to the mixed Anglican/Free Church union in the Church of South India, fearing it would call into question the Catholic credentials of the Church of England not least in the eyes of the Orthodox.

For his writing during and after the Second World War, his *Revelation and the Modern World* proved to be the first part of a trilogy under the overall title *The Form of a Servant*, describing revelation as mastering its own environment in the way in which it submitted itself thereto—and in this reflecting the servant-form of the Incarnate One. Thornton insisted over against Liberalism—and to a degree, over against the Newman of the 'Essay' on doctrinal development—that the creaturely forms taken by revelation constitute integral parts of revelation itself even as they are changed in being assumed or taken up. His revival of figuralism in interpreting Scripture took further the Tractarian love of the exegetical approach of the Alexandrian school. The second volume, *The Dominion of Christ*, in 1952, was dedicated to the members of the Fellowship of St Alban and St Sergius, even though it was the third and final part, *Christ and the Church*, in 1956, which, by its stress on female imagery for the Church, reminded the Fellowship of his contribution to its Anglo-Russian symposium on Mariology, 'The Mother of God in Holy Scripture', edited by Mascall in 1949. People said it was the kind of thing Henri de Lubac and Jean Daniélou (1905–74), great historians of typological exegesis, should have written but did not.

In 1950 *The Common Life in the Body of Christ* expanded on the ecclesial corollaries of *The Incarnate Lord*. Reaching a fourth edition in 1963 it meshed well with the Mystical Body ecclesiology so dominant in Latin Catholicism in the inter-war years and till the eve of the Second Vatican Council (1962–5). In this work, Thornton maintained his overall view of the relation between divine revelation and the rest—divine revelation and culture, one might say now. 'The contents of the revelation are mysteriously inseparable from the form in which they are conveyed, and this is true notwithstanding the fact that within the New Testament itself the forms are already partially transfigured by their content.'[49]

Gabriel Hebert (1886–1963) was no stranger to the notion of the distinctiveness of the historic revelation in its supernatural character. Hebert was a Cumbrian, born at Silloth into a clerical household. From Harrow School he moved on to New College, Oxford, where he took Firsts in both Greats and Theology. He was priested in 1912 and served his title at St Peter's, Horbury, a strongly Anglo-Catholic parish. The young Hebert met Herbert Kelly—that major founder of Anglo-Catholic Religious life described in Chapter 5—at a Student Christian Movement camp and was moved to offer himself to the Society for the Sacred Mission. After a six-year noviciate (there appear to have been some doubts about his toughness or resilience), he made profession with the Society, spending some time on its mission in South Africa before his outstanding intellectual gifts began to be used more obviously at Kelham itself.

Hebert's earliest published work consisted in a trilogy of translations from the Swedish: *Eucharistic Faith and Practice* by Yngve Brilioth (1891–1959), Gustaf Aulèn's *Christus Victor*, and *Eros and Agape* by Anders Nygren (1890–1978).[50] Contacts between English Anglicans and Swedish Lutherans were in the air at the time Hebert was ordained. The Lambeth Conference of 1908 had taken its time over replying to a suggestion of a comprehensive 'alliance', originally made in 1888. But in 1909 Randall Davidson of Canterbury appointed a commission which undertook serious study at an extended meeting at Uppsala in September of that year. Its 1911 Report recommended viewing the Augsburg Confession, interpreted with a little latitude, as a satisfactory sort of doctrinal instrument, and acknowledging the maintenance of a succession of bishops in the apostolic succession in the Church of Sweden (even if the 'tactile' succession was not usually rated there as of any more than historical interest). Not everything in the report could have gladdened Anglo-Catholic hearts: the diaconate had been set aside in Sweden, the laying on of hands at Confirmation was omitted, the Eucharistic presence associated with the distribution and consumption of the elements, rather than their consecration. In the upshot, all that was decided, for now, was to allow Swedish Lutherans access to the Anglican sacraments.

But in the twenty years that separated the Report from Hebert's trio of translations, a 'high church' movement, concerned with theological orthodoxy, an ecclesiology independent of either 'State-Church' or 'Folk-Church' notions, and an enriched liturgical practice gained ground in the countries of the former 'Swedish Empire'—Finland, Estonia and Latvia, as well as in Sweden itself. (Much on the Baltic was intact from the mediaeval tradition, at least when compared with the more German-influenced Denmark, Norway, Iceland.) That advance was both

The Theologians

signalled and further prompted by Gunner Rosendal's (1897–1988) founding of the movement *Kyrklig Förnyelse* in 1935.[51] Hebert was evidently enthused by the thought of a growing Swedish 'Oxford Movement', and its possible convergence with Tractarian and Post-Tractarian theology at home.[52] Swedes of the kind Anglo-Catholics might cultivate were inclined to think they already had more of the pre-Reformation liturgical inheritance than was contained in the English Prayer Book, while the Lutheran adherence to 'confessional' documents had made their Church life more doctrinally conscious than that of Anglicanism. Be that as it may, the historical, biblical, and sacramental learning of the Swedish writers stood Hebert in good stead when he moved onto work in his own right.

What was that work? Any account must begin with the books for which he is now most famed: *Liturgy and Society*, and (under his editorship) *The Parish Communion*, themselves inspired in part by the admirable liturgical life of the Kelham Priory.[53] Only in part, however, since at Kelham the by now traditional Anglo-Catholic Eucharist, looking like a Roman Solemn High Mass but with the Prayer Book as its basic libretto (and without sermon), remained the norm, its ceremonial perfection winning for it the accolade, 'High Mass at Wellington Barracks'.[54] In fact, Hebert never taught liturgiology in his college. His *Liturgy and Society* and *The Parish Communion* were of more interest to the Central Society for Sacred Study, or to European Catholics (and others, especially the Swedes) caught up in the movement of liturgical *ressourcement* in the Inter-War years.

For Hebert, liberalism was the enemy of the Liturgy but it must be fought not by going back, in the manner of the Gothic Revival, but by going forward. Hebert's aim was to show 'how Christian dogma finds its typical expression in worship, and how Christian religion is not merely a way of piety for the individual soul, but is in the first place a participation in a common life'.[55] Those words contain a hint of a rather less contemplative-cum-ritual liturgical style. The book's sub-title, 'The Function of the Church in the Modern World' is not to be overlooked either. Like Maurice (shades of Herbert Kelly's teaching), Hebert saw the Church as an 'empirical sign of the Kingdom of Christ', set in the midst of the world of culture, of politics, and of economics—in a social order, then, that in his own day, was, to his mind, 'on the verge of disintegration'.[56] Like the contributors to *Prospect for Christendom* he proposed that only the common life offered by Christianity could restore social cohesion and purpose. Not surprisingly, it 'has been said of [Hebert's] *Liturgy and Society* that the "liturgy" was Hebert and the "society" was Eliot.'[57] The book was often seen chiefly as advocacy for the 'Parish Communion' movement. It *was* such advocacy, but it was also more than that, presenting the Liturgy in its bearing on the social process while constituting at the same time a 'perpetual point of contact with the eternal world'.[58]

A Liturgy which is to form parish life requires a formative use of Scripture, so the transition is easy to Hebert's works of biblical theology which, unlike his liturgical writings, stem from his Kelham teaching. They seek to show the inter-relation of the Testaments, and the way their climax in Christ, with the opening of the new Aeon, both dwarfs the stature of literal exegesis of a Fundamentalist kind and, in the process, furnishes for the Catholic reader the very form of the Church. So *The Throne of David*, in 1941, with its Christocentric and therefore typological view of the Bible as a whole, was followed by *The Authority of the Old Testament* in 1947, and, towards the end of Hebert's life *The Old Testament from Within*, in 1961.[59] If *Fundamentalism and the Church of God* exemplified the approach to Scripture read in Church Hebert wished to avoid—what he called 'scriptural Monophysitism' where the two 'natures' of the Bible, the Word of God in the words of men', were overlooked in favour of a 'verbal' theory of inspiration, *The Christ of Faith and the Jesus of History*, dating from the year before his death, indicated the Christological approach he favoured with, as its ecclesiological 'a priori', *The Form of the Church*, published a generation earlier in 1944.[60] Hebert sought to show the overall pattern of revelation, which, in a biblical perspective, meant a comparison of two diptychs: promise—the Messianic hope, broadly conceived, and fulfilment—Christ and the Church.[61]

Gregory Dix (1901–52, born George Eglinton Alston Dix) was the son of an Anglo-Catholic clergyman and his Methodist wife. Educated at Westminster School and Merton College, Oxford, his brilliance was early noted: he became a lecturer in history at Keble while still finishing ordination studies at the theological college at Wells. Priested in 1925, he entered Pershore, shortly to be Nashdom, the following year, and in pursuit of a madcap scheme of Abbot Prideaux was sent to the Gold Coast (present-day Ghana) to complete his novitiate. His health broke down and on return to the Abbey in 1929 he remained (perhaps for this reason) an oblate until 1940 when he made his Religious vows.[62]

There were further absences: regular visits to the British Museum (now British Library); a spell as parish priest of Beaconsfield during World War Two, when he stood in for the Vicar, his brother, who had gone to be a military chaplain; lectures in Uppsala, and American lecture tours to raise money for Nashdom's fledgling daughter monastery, Three Rivers, in Michigan. Yet right up to his early death in 1952 Dix's life was essentially that of a Benedictine monk following the round of the liturgical Hours. Observance was, however, never without the accompaniment of reading and reflection that lies behind his writings, to the benefit of patristic scholars and students of the Liturgy. That was sometimes at the expense of certain exalted victims of his incisive and witty interventions, as a confirmed Anglo-Papalist, in the politics of the Church of England, to which his election to Convocation for Oxford in 1945 gave him ready access. (The sign of a bishop, he sardonically noted, is a crook, and that of an archbishop is a double cross.) 'In every case his concern was to ensure that the Church reached catholic conclusions—or if she could not be helped to do that, that no decision at all was made.'[63]

The issue of the Church of South India tested this maxim to the full. An 'Open Letter' from the superiors of Anglican Religious Orders raised the spectre of schism; Dix is reportedly its author.[64] When Temple said the hand was that of the Superiors but the voice was somehow familiar, Dix replied, 'Jacob speaking, your Grace'.[65] He could not stomach the thought of a pan-Protestant alliance.

Geoffrey Fisher of Canterbury (1887–1972) sought to buy off the rebels by inviting them to author a report on 'Catholicity' in preparation for the 1948 Lambeth Conference.[66] Emphasizing the unity of creation and salvation, and the irreplaceable role of the Church as Body of Christ in the latter, it acknowledged distortions in the Western Middle Ages but thought the Reformation had added to them, notably by intensifying individualism. Dix, like Hebert, was a co-author while Ramsey chaired the committee. The 1950 declaration of 'impaired communion' between South India and the rest was just about acceptable to him, and his talk of a 'continuing Church' or a new non-Jurors' church came to nothing.

Among his writings one should signal *The Apostolic Tradition of St Hippolytus*,[67] where Dix's willingness to make decisive judgments was shown not only in his confident dating and ascription of authorship but in his insistence that the *epiklêsis*, or appeal to the Holy Spirit for consecration, was an adventitious late addition to the text. This irritated the Eastern Orthodox, and those Anglo-Catholics who instinctively looked towards Constantinople in preference to Rome. *The Idea of the Church in Primitive Liturgies* included the 'Canon of Hippolytus' which would go on to exercise a perhaps unjustified dominance in Western liturgical revision.[68] Looking for ideas of the Church unwittingly embodied in the language and forms of ancient worship prepared Dix for the subtle approach of a trio of articles in Nashdom's journal *Laudate* later brought together as *Jurisdiction in the Early Church*. The Achilles' heel of Anglo-Papalism was the paucity of evidence for a universal 'Petrine' office in antiquity. Dix had written an apologia for not only episcopal but papal authority as a genuinely homogeneous development from apostolic roots.[69] *A Detection of Aumbries* defended Eucharistic Reservation, that rallying-cry of Anglo-Catholics,[70] while in *The Question of Anglican Orders: Letters to a Layman* Dix argued that Thomas Cranmer's (1489–1556) undoubtedly erroneous opinions on the apostolic ministry should be deemed a personal quirk and thus essentially irrelevant to the issue of validity.[71] *The Theology of Confirmation in Relation to Baptism* took a Catholic view of the distinct sacramental reality of the former and stressed, over against Nonconformity, the necessary connexion between the two rites.[72]

So Dix's *magnum opus*, *The Shape of the Liturgy*, does not stand alone, even though it is with this 'fat green book', as he called it, that his name is permanently linked.[73] The passion he brought to Eucharistic devotion has its head in the amazing peroration, 'Was ever another command so obeyed', rightly selected for special mention in a recent anthology of Dix highlights by Simon Jones.[74] It was a 'serious contribution to scholarship' that 'reads like a novel'.[75] The four-fold 'shape' (taking or presentation, blessing or offering, breaking, sharing), the identification of Eucharistic *anamnêsis*, with that word's biblical pedigree, with the Eucharistic sacrifice anathema to the Reformers, the eschatology theme so crucial for the earliest Christianity but overlooked by much writing on the sacraments: these pervasive motifs were orchestrated with uncommon brilliance.

The posthumous *Jew and Greek* juxtaposes Greek and 'Syrian'.[76] In these Uppsala lectures Dix recognised the importance of cultural contrasts in history, a lesson learnt, possibly, from Eliot and Demant. Such contrasts could be over-stated. In the Nashdom journal *Laudate* he had already subjected to hilarious dissection the hypothesis proposed by N. P. Williams (1883–1943), Lady Margaret Professor and canon of Christ Church, according to which a pure and unsuperstitious 'Northern Catholicism' had been typical of Cisalpine Europe and was now gloriously reborn in the Church of England. 'Even at that early date [the collection *Northern Catholicism* appeared in 1933] he was impressed by the conservatism of Rome and the religious ebullience of Scandinavia.'[77] When writing *Jew and Greek* Dix had not grown in enthusiasm for an Anglo-Nordic Catholic church. 'England lies somewhere in between…, closer to the North but affected by the South.'[78] The principal cultural contrast that engaged him, as his title indicates, did not in any case bear on Williams' hobbyhorse. It concerned the tension—shades of the second century North African apologist Tertullian!—between Athens and Jerusalem. Greece was the temple of beauty, her thinkers moved from the cosmos to the concept of an organized world. Israel—the 'Syriac' culture—was the temple of worship whose prophets began, rather, from the living God. The 'Hellenization' of the Gospel, he told Swedish Lutherans under the influence of Adolf von Harnack (1851–1930), had enriched its forms while leaving intact the divine message from Israel's Messiah. In the Orthodox world, Georges Florovsky (1893–1979) had been persistent in making the same point.

Academic theologians

Austin Farrer (1904–68) was born in Hampstead, the son of a Baptist minister.[79] He was educated at London's St Paul's School and then at Balliol College, Oxford where he became an Anglican, worshipping at St Barnabas, Jericho, later immortalised by an Anglo-Catholic poet-laureate, John Betjeman ('Byzantine St Barnabas, be mine abode!'). After theological training at Wilberforce's Cuddesdon, where Farrer was a contemporary of Michael Ramsey, he became, following a short curacy, an academic priest who spent his entire life teaching, if also, 'pastoring' Oxford students at, successively, St Edmund Hall, Trinity, and Keble, of which College he was Warden from 1960 to 1968. He would be its last, and intellectual most masterful, Anglo-Catholic Warden.

Farrer combined a metaphysician's mind with a poet's imagination, bringing the two into conjunction in his theology and New Testament exegesis. Chiefly inspired as a philosophical theologian by Aquinas, he defined God as 'Intelligent Act'. The relation between man and God consists for Farrer in the interplay of divine and human agency. In his early metaphysical masterpiece *Finite and Infinite* he described that interaction as a double agency, where the 'wills' in question, Uncreated and created, are not to be thought of as lying side by side but 'ranged in depth', with the 'causal joint' eluding further analysis.[80] Farrer's later writings, coming under the rubric of 'revealed' rather than 'natural' theology, are not so systematic, but those sources—which include his sermons—attest a highly coherent thinking that lends itself to systematic presentation by others.[81]

In *Faith and Speculation*, lectures given at New York University, Farrer described the effect of grace—supernatural as distinct from natural divine acting—as the Creator bringing the 'creature's mental and voluntary life... into his own'.[82] *Mental*, as well as *voluntary*, since, like Aquinas, when Farrer thinks of will he is not excluding intellectuality (compare God as 'Intellectual Act'): 'action', he writes, can be a 'movement of thought' as well as, say, an 'employment of the hand'.[83] From the human side, grace appears as active faith—indeed, 'saving belief',[84] enabling man, as the image of God, not simply to echo God impressionistically as in a 'sketch', but, as he put it in *A Science of God?*, to act as a 'pencil' with which God can write in the world,[85] though the deficiencies of sinful humankind require of the divine Agent an 'infinite patience of improvisation'.[86] Farrer was much concerned with theodicy, as in *Love Almighty and Ills Unlimited*, where, though embracing a Platonist understanding of evil as non-being, he considers the multiple 'privations' involved to be an inevitable consequence of the way the cosmos is a system of systems, where advantages of some of the constituent systems mean disadvantages for others.[87] While God does not create evil, he can use it for positive purposes, notably in the enhanced humanization which follows from resisting evil, or simply responding to it by compassion. Divine revelatory action does not furnish explanations for evil (even of this kind), but, instead, culminates in the redemptive Incarnation: God does not give us explanations, he gives us his Son, who himself gives us a life.[88]

In his interpretation of the New Testament texts, which met with incredulity by the majority of historical-critical scholars but has since been vindicated by the rise of 'narrative' criticism focused on the 'rhetorical art' of the Gospels and other New Testament texts, Farrer sought to show how the principal Church dogmas — the doctrines of Incarnation, Atonement, and the Holy Trinity — are already embodied in the imagistic schemes of the evangelists, and, to say the least, not contradicted by biblical authors using other literary genres, whether exhortatory or historical. The general case was proposed in *The Glass of Vision*, his Bampton Lectures at Oxford,[89] and then exhibited in detail in his studies of St Matthew, St Mark, and the Revelation of St John the Divine. The New Testament constitutes a 'rebirth of images' whereby the divine-human Messiah transformed the foundational images of faith in Judaism, 'clothing himself in them and dying in the armour'.[90]

Farrer was careful to explain that the 'images' he was speaking of were not simply the product of human imagination. They were specifically divinely given images without which it would be impossible to know divine supernatural act. The congruent discerning of what such images signify is faith. Still, behind Farrer's thinking lies a wider concept of figural imagination which was shared with a variety of Oxonian or Oxford-connected Christians of the period, including Dorothy L. Sayers, C. S. Lewis, Charles Williams and his editor, the poet Anne Ridler, 1912–2001.

The Johannine Apocalypse, the richest source of insight into that process, is at the same time the key to the entire if covert methodology employed in the apostolic witness, and should, accordingly, inform the reading of the Gospels at large — including the Synoptics. On Farrer's proposed solution of the Synoptic Problem: whereas, over against a modern and still more or less intact consensus, Luke read Matthew's Gospel, Mark was (as the same quasi-consensus claimed) the aboriginal Gospel, the first to be written. His unhesitating application of this 'Johannine' method to what was apparently the least theological — the most naif — of the four, was the exegetical equivalent of hurling a Molotov cocktail through the windows of the Senior Common Room. His case entails an elaborate use of typology — with master images, secondary images, 'imagery laws' of attraction, comparable in its sophistication, not to say over-sophistication, with Lionel Thornton's.

The Theologians

Farrer was a highly God-centred man, who never lost sight of the telos of human life: heaven as the proper pattern of relations between humans and above all with God.[91] More's the pity that he held an unsound view of the status of mentally handicapped people, wondering whether they could be called human in the full sense at all. Similar blindspots were occasional hazards of Anglo-Catholicism which, unless it had read Kenneth Kirk, did not have the fluency in moral theology that immersion in the 'Second Part' of Thomas's *Summa theologiae*, and the practice of Confessional case studies, of the sort which made Alphonsus Liguori a master of moral thinking, gave, or should have given, the Roman clergy.

Eric Lionel Mascall (1905–95), already encountered in Chapter 5 as an 'Oratorian' and in Chapter 6 for his social thought, was a Londoner by birth though Brighton, hallowed fane of Anglo-Catholicism, was his real spiritual home. After Latymer School in Hammersmith he went to Pembroke College, Cambridge, to study mathematics—it would give him the logical caste of mind that characterizes the theological writing of the only (more or less) systematically Thomist theologian the Church of England has produced. On leaving Ely Theological College he served curacies at St Andrew's, Stockwell, south of the Thames, and then across the river at St Matthew's, Westminster, a parish that, as the following chapter will describe, played so crucial a role in the first great Anglo-Catholic Congress. Teaching posts followed at Lincoln Theological College and Christ Church, Oxford, before his appointment to the chair of historical theology at King's, London. By that time he was a dedicated celibate of the Oratory of the Good Shepherd.

Mascall's early writings suggest he might have been more at home among French Dominicans of the stripe of Reginald Garrigou-Lagrange (1877–1964) than in an English vicarage, both in regard to his interests and the way he handled them. *He Who Is*, and *Existence and Analogy*, are exercises in Thomist metaphysics,[92] while *A Guide to Mount Carmel* (these are all works from the 1940s) faithfully follows Garrigou in treating the mystical theology of St John of the Cross (1542–91) with its background in Salamanca Scholasticism, as the perfect spiritual complement to the philosophy and theology of the Thomist school.[93] But the metaphysical studies show an informed awareness of what was happening on the English intellectual scene—something which can also be said of his slightly later *Words and Images*, reflecting the linguistic turn of 'ordinary language' philosophy at Oxford and the later Ludwig Wittgenstein (1889–1951) at Cambridge, and the interest in symbolic modes of knowledge evident in, say, Dorothy Emmet (1904–2000), the first women to occupy a chair of philosophy in the British Isles.[94]

Nevertheless, the ropes that tied him to Anglo-Catholic moorings still held: *Christ, the Christian, and the Church* announces, by way of its sub-title 'A Study of the Incarnation and its Consequences', a perch in a genealogical tree stretching from Liddon and Gore to Lionel Thornton and beyond.[95] Along with Gore,[96] Mascall's own Anglo-Catholic contemporaries Gregory Dix and Gabriel Hebert, are the Anglican theologians most likely to be cited in a body of writing where source-material gratefully received comes overwhelmingly from French Catholic and Russian Orthodox writers, and other Church of England writers (including his fellow 'Oratorian' Alec Vidler) enter the picture chiefly into order to be rapped over the knuckles for this or that dereliction of theological duty.[97]

Mascall was at once synthesizer and sophisticated polemicist. Sophisticated polemicist (he used the term 'systematic apologist') inasmuch as he took on a range of intellectual challenges to orthodox Christianity, from those posed by physics and biology in *Theology and Natural Science*, from 1956,[98] to a whole series of texts taking issue with the radical theologies of the 1960s and '70s.[99] 'I hope to show that the affirmations about God, man and Christ which the Christian Church has taught throughout its history, and the manner of living which those affirmations imply, are more satisfying to the intellect, more enriching to our imagination, and more fulfilling to our whole personality than either the secularist humanism which is so widespread today or the etiolated substitutes for orthodox Christianity which are frequently offered for our consumption.'[100]

Polemicist, then, but also synthesizer as in the audaciously entitled *Via Media*, which by its title seemed to risk comparison with Newman,[101] Mascall's 'via media', it should be said, was not, as was Newman's, between popular Protestantism and Rome.[102] It consisted in showing how, in matters of divine revelation, whether the topic be the God-world relationship, or Trinitarian theology, or Christological doctrine, or the understanding of grace (Mascall's four key examples), the orthodox view typically lies midway between two extreme positions, such that it is at once more 'medial' but also more comprehensive than either. In discovering that is how things stand, argued Mascall, 'orthodoxy finds itself enriched and strengthened',[103] which is of course an improvement on simply being, in the manner of theological apologetics, defended and re-affirmed.

The many-sidedness of his theological persona showed itself in profound but accessible dogmatic meditations, such as *Corpus Christi*, from 1953, *Grace and Glory*, from 1961, and *The Triune God*, from 1986,[104] while his Gifford Lectures, *The Openness of Being*, published in 1971, continued the trajectory of his early studies in metaphysics. In his 'Giffords' he took only the most hesitant of steps toward the revisionist Thomism of the post-War German 'Transcendental' school, discovering, in reaction to its barely concealed Kantianism, the counter-attractions of the mediaeval

The Theologians

Franciscan St Bonaventure's 'contuition' of the divine.[105] His priorities were exactly those of the best Roman Catholic theology of years just before and after the Second Vatican Council, not least in the way he maintained an equal regard for philosophical theology, and dogmatic reflection of an inspirational kind.

Perhaps unsurprisingly, his memoirs give the impression of one who was less at home in the official world of Anglican theology than he was in lecturing at Roman Catholic institutes in North America or visiting Romanian Orthodox monasteries (from 1929 to 1936 he had been chairman of the executive committee of the Fellowship of St Alban and St Sergius, and from 1937 to 1946 editor of its journal).[106] In Mascall's own explanation, the 'suspicion of Thomism was as much of a disqualification in official eyes as was that of Communism or homosexuality'.[107] His 'perpetual curacy' at St Mary's Bourne Street placed him at the centre of the Anglo-Catholic world of Martin Travers (1886–1948), architect of the church and house illustrator for the Society of SS Peter and Paul, and the only honour he received from his Church was the stall of a canon-theologian at Truro, the gift of Graham Leonard (1921–2010), who as emeritus Bishop of London would 'swim the Tiber' in the year of Mascall's death.

Bishop-theologians

Kenneth Escop Kirk (1886–1954) was born in Sheffield, the grandson of a Methodist minister. He was educated at the city's Royal Grammar School and St John's College, Oxford, where he gained a Double First in Greats. Accepted for graduate study at Keble he preferred a move to London where the Student Christian Movement had launched a mission to students arriving from the Indian Raj. While in their employ he became an assistant lecturer in the philosophy department at University College London—rather a coup since it was a self-consciously secular foundation. Kenneth Kirk was barely ordained deacon before the Great War took him as an army chaplain to France, but after the return of peace he went back to Keble where as a theology tutor he published his *Some Principles of Moral Theology*, inspired by the distinctive approach to the subject of the Caroline divine Jeremy Taylor (1613–67).[108]

Taylor had been chaplain to Charles I, and as such highly suspect to the Parliamentary party in the Civil War (he was several times imprisoned under the Commonwealth but survived to fight another day, becoming a bishop in the Irish Church at the Restoration and vice-chancellor of Trinity College, Dublin).[109] Taylor's theology was based not only on Scripture and Fathers but on Aristotle and mediaeval moral theology as well, and helped to ensure that applied morals, in the form of casuistry, despite its association with the Church of Rome, became central to Anglican pastoral theology in the seventeenth century.[110] This was the tradition Kirk revived.

In 1922 he became Fellow and Chaplain of Trinity College, Oxford, and in 1927 University Reader in Moral Theology. That was in good time for the publication of his *Conscience and its Problems* in 1928,[111] which was also the date of his Bampton Lectures, to be published in 1931 as *The Vision of God*.[112] The book, which remains in print, has a Tractarian hallmark in its concern with the centrality of worship (compare Mr Keble) and the importance of asceticism (compare Dr Pusey). That was less noticed than its Thomist character, which was much remarked on, but apparently did not worry University or Crown since in 1933 Kirk was made Regius Professor of Moral and Pastoral Theology — the predecessor, in fact, of V. A. Demant. In that year Kirk also brought out *The Threshold of Ethics*,[113] and a contribution to the multi-authored *Marriage and Divorce* where his strong line on indissolubility drew the notice of the editor of his 'Life and Letters', his son-in-law Eric Kemp (1915–2009).[114] Evidently, he was not to be one of those bishops whom Gregory Dix had called 'Edwardian': Edward VI in theology, Edward VII in mental equipment, Edward VIII in attitude to marriage.

For in 1937 Kenneth Kirk became bishop of Oxford, re-organizing the huge largely rural diocese (counties of Berkshire and Buckinghamshire as well as Oxfordshire) yet finding time to edit *The Study of Theology* in 1939. His Anglo-Catholicism was hardly a secret. 'At Christ Church Kirk celebrated High Mass in full pontificals, down to the gauntlets, and elsewhere was often to be seen in the *cappa magna* with purple biretta, dripping in Brussels lace.'[115] After World War Two, as a leading Anglo-Catholic on the Bench of Bishops, he was much exercised by the problem of the Church of South India. Warning against any attempt to introduce full Communion with that body (as we have noted, it would fatally damage Tractarian ecclesiology), he was mollified by a compromise scheme for limited intercommunion, though his death intervened before it could be introduced in 1955.

Arthur Michael Ramsey (1904–88) was the most distinguished theologian to become archbishop of Canterbury before Rowan Williams (born 1950), and the first who could be called an Anglo-Catholic as distinct from a high churchman (of the stamp of, say, earlier in the twentieth century, Cosmo Gordon Lang, 1864–1945). He was born in Cambridge to an academic family, his father, Arthur Ramsey (1867–1954), a Congregationalist, was president (that is, deputy Master) of Magdalene College where Michael Ramsey would go as undergraduate after early education at King's College School and Repton.[116] Influenced by Edwyn Hoskyns, he took Milner-White's counsel before enrolling at Cuddesdon College,

The Theologians

Oxford, for Ordination training. There he became friendly with Farrer and was exposed to Greek Orthodox ideas by Derwas Chitty (1901–71), later an authority on ancient monasticism in the Christian East.[117] After a curacy at Liverpool Ramsey began teaching at Lincoln Theological College where Eric Mascall would succeed him as Sub-Warden.

It was during this time that *The Gospel and the Catholic Church* was published.[118] Few books written a century after 1833, symbolic date of the Oxford Movement's inception, are more Tractarian in spirit for it ties together Gospel and Church in an unbreakable unity, even while warning against treating the age of the Fathers as the supreme template. The latter can only be found in the matrix of the Church in the Pasch of the Lord.[119] The death and resurrection of Christ, claimed Ramsey in the foreword to the first edition, is at once the central theme of the Gospel and the model for the Church's existence as his 'Body'. '[I]n this dying and rising again the very meaning of the Church is found … the Church's outward order expresses its inward meaning by representing the dependence of the members upon the one Body, wherein they die to self.'[120] The 'main structure of Catholicism' issues directly from the 'Messianic Gospel'.[121] The Church is called 'apostolic' because sent by the one Redeemer and 'catholic' because living a single universal life, both of which traits are crucial to its nature as expressive of the Lord's death and resurrection in which the Church's 'holiness' consists.[122] Ramsey made good use of the brilliant Scottish Congregationalist Peter Taylor Forsyth (1848–1921): 'The Great Church is not the agglutination of the churches but their *prius*…. The local church was not a church but *the* Church … the totality of all Christians glowing to a certain spot and emerging there'.[123]

In examining the structure of the Church-Body, as the bulk of Ramsey's book proceeds to do, we find not only the canonical Scriptures which attest the Pasch of the Lord as the climax of its story, and the Creed which subsumes Scripture into confession, and the two great sacraments of dying and rising (Baptism and Eucharist), but also episcopacy—bishops, succeeding to the apostles, as the organs of its unity and continuity. The entire organism thus articulates the Gospel and can be belittled only at the Gospel's expense.

It was an apologia for Church order of a kind intended to beguile, and enthuse, Evangelical Christians, including Nonconformists. 'The Bishop by his place in the one Body bears that essential relation to the Gospel that the Apostle bore before him.'[124] The mediaeval Latin church failed to uphold the original vision through an exaggerated Papalism, acting via canon law. The Reformers grasped the need to return to a view of the Church as born from the Word of the Gospel—but the return was defective. In genuflection before the shade of Maurice, Ramsey hoped to see Catholic, Evangelical, and Liberal 'parties' in the national Church not merely comprehended by the fact of Establishment but brought to see how, abandoning 'isms', they could unite around the 'great facts of the Gospel and the Church and the Spirit of Truth before and behind all partial theories about them'.[125]

This, then, was the manifesto whereby this loveably eccentric man first came to the notice of the wider Church. It was a sign of his eccentricity that he was reputed, in the labours of composition, to have scrawled most of the text as jottings on his study's wallpaper.

Returning to Cambridge as curate at St Benet's church (a Corpus living later bestowed on members of the Society of St Francis), he brought out two scintillating short studies, combining detailed exegesis with doctrine: *The Resurrection of Christ* and the *Glory of God and the Transfiguration of Christ*, the latter his favoured child among his writings and the text that best shows the influence of Byzantine and Russian Orthodoxy on his mind.[126] By this time he occupied a canonry and chair at Durham, at the start of a meteoric rise in the worlds of academe and the episcopate: Van Mildert professor at Durham in 1940, then Regius Professor at Cambridge in 1950 before becoming in 1952 bishop of Durham, archbishop of York in 1956, and in 1962 archbishop of Canterbury.

He did not satisfy Anglo-Catholic hopes. He brought almost to successful completion a reunion with Methodism, a prospect that renewed their anxieties about the South India scheme. And while he encouraged warm relations with the Rome of Paul VI (pope 1963–78) and the Second Vatican Council (1962–5), he took positions on moral issues, notably artificial contraception and the legalization of abortion, incompatible with the moral ethos of, say, Gore and Kirk. His reaction to radical 'South Bank' theology was vacillating. Most dramatically of all for an Anglo-Catholic in the Tractarian mould, as Primate of the global Communion he found no theological difficulty, if some personal discomfort, with the idea of women priests. Opening Orders to women in the Anglican Communion (not yet in the Church of England) was simultaneously to open a breach in the classic high church appeal to solidarity with Orthodoxy and Rome in the succession of ministers on whom the apostolicity of the Church as a sacramental community necessarily depends.

So a question mark hung over his Catholic credentials in a way that now began to overshadow the Anglo-Catholic movement as a whole.[127] Mark Chapman, no slouch in matters of the history of Anglican theology, considers Ramsey fundamentally unplaceable. 'Ramsey represented a form of Anglo-Catholicism that was both open to the Reformation and to the challenge of the Bible. His overall theological system, however, is difficult to pin down: he was influenced by the Platonizing tendencies of F. D. Maurice, the Protestant Congregationalism of his upbringing, as well as some strands from the Orthodox tradition.'[128] To Chapman's mind, Ramsey is really an Anglo-Catholic only 'in appearance and [as] holding a high view of the ministry'. He was 'neither socially nor theologically conservative', his ecumenical ventures pointing in conflicting directions.[129]

Ramsey's writings in the 1950s, the decade of that precipitous shooting to leadership, bear witness to a strenuous effort to (re)situate himself in the wider story of Anglican theology: thus *F. D. Maurice and the Conflicts of Modern Theology* in 1951 and *From Gore to Temple*, in 1960.[130] A convert from Nonconformity to the 'party' (in later terminology 'constituency') that was Anglo-Catholicism not unnaturally wished to find a way to steer a larger ship. And in regard to the radical theologies combated during his primacy by Mascall, his criticisms were more nuanced than pointed, if, on balance, on the side of the angels.[131] His legacy was therefore an ambiguous one yet irradiated by the memory of personal holiness shaped by perception of divine glory, in no way unworthy of the Oxford Fathers.[132]

— 8 —

The Inner-Church Struggle

THE DEVELOPMENT OF SOCIETIES, and, for a time, the holding of Congresses (to which those Societies were closely relevant) were among the chief features of the distinctive Anglo-Catholic culture as it emerged from out of the Oxford Movement. They belonged with a burgeoning institutional life which also included newspaper media, guilds, and schools. 'During the same years that the distinctive culture of Anglo-Catholicism was being elaborated and clarified, a number of organizational developments were transforming the movement from an inchoate, decentralized, and largely clerical enterprise into an organized and articulated social movement, comprising laity as well as clergy and operating on a national scale as a force within the National Church. A complex, interlocking network of associations, guilds, newspapers, suppliers, publishers, and the like began to take shape, providing channels for communications and the mobilization of resources, focusing nation-wide attention on particular trouble spots, co-ordinating campaigns of various sorts.'[1]

Some—obviously not all—of these organizations followed Evangelical models. For example: the Simeon Society had been buying up advowsons for Evangelicals since 1817 in order to acquire livings for low church clergy (not for nothing were they were sometimes called 'Church Methodists'). The Anglo-Catholic Society for the Maintenance of the Faith would set itself a like aim. In 1836 the Church Pastoral Aid Society was created for supplying and supporting Evangelical curates and lay workers—the latter suspect to the old high churchmen—in neglected parishes. By counter-reaction there popped up the Additional Curates Society, founded to address the problem of adequate remuneration for curates when those acting for non-resident incumbents (and therefore living in their houses) ceased to be commonplace. But mimesis of Evangelicals was involved as well, and the timing, 1837, suited the Tractarians, if only they could gain entry. In 1846 the Evangelical Alliance—shades of the future Anglo-Catholic 'English Church Union'—came into being. But it was really a persuader to an international reformed Protestantism rather than a confessionally Anglican body, and its anti-Establishmentarianism alienated Anglican Evangelicals who approved of an established Church as a better boat from which to fish, and, more especially, to preserve Christian influence in the education of the nation's children. The Evangelical Movement had its newspapers, the *Christian Observer* and *The Record*, and this surely gave the Tractarians and their Anglo-Catholic successors a nudge in that direction.

The boot could also be on the other foot. In 1840 the Parker Society was founded to reprint the classics of the English Reformation, a deliberate challenge to the Tractarian efforts that went into the making of the *Library of Anglo-Catholic Theology*, with its recovery of the texts of Caroline, Restoration, and later high church divines.

The Societies

Among Societies proper the English Church Union was not the first but it was by far the largest. [2] It had begun life during the riots at St George's-in-the-East as 'The Church of England Protection Society' — in the context, wisely named. Its speakers' bureau recommended suitable preachers and lecturers. The English Church Union also provided legal advice and, where necessary, funds for legal expenses incurred by Anglo-Catholic clergy or laity. Its leadership bombarded Convocations and Parliament with argued statements of the Movement's viewpoint. By 1890 it claimed 4000 clerical members and 15, 000 lay members, ranging from old-fashioned Tractarians to the most up-to-date extreme Ritualists. Moderate high churchmen could sometimes be persuaded to lend it their sanction as well. A list of its committees in 1920 indicates the formidable organizational structure the Union had formed by that date. They included: Theological and Liturgical, Legal, Finance, Organization and Efficiency, Library and Publications, Foreign Missions, Religious Education, Women's Work in the Church, Church and State, and Prayer Book Revision.[3] A monthly *Gazette* was published, to keep readers informed of this whirlwind of bureaucratically controlled action. In the years 1933 to 1934, the centenary of the movement, the English Church Union amalgamated with the Anglo-Catholic Congresses to form the 'Church Union'. 'English' was of course presupposed.

The Society of the Holy Cross (post-nominal letters for members read 'SSC', reflecting the Latinity of its official name), created in 1855 by Charles Lowder, assisted by five other London priests, was a priestly society with a Rule formulated, as Chapter 1 had occasion to note, by Pusey himself.[4] The Rule proposed the making of the Sign of the Cross on rising and retiring; the regular celebration of Mass with appropriate preparation and thanksgiving; daily self-examination and frequent

The Inner-Church Struggle

Confession, and an annual Retreat of at least three days. These practices, in a Roman Catholic perspective, were so common as to be anodyne. Things looked rather different in Blighty. Attracted by the combination of the slightly exotic and the spiritually serious, clerical membership rose in spectacular fashion so that by the mid-1870s the *Societas Sanctae Crucis* could count around 400 adherents.

The Society's efforts could sometimes be counterproductive, as with the 1873 appeal to the bishops in Convocation to provide for the training and licencing of priests for sacramental Confessions. That led the bishops to condemn, four years later, any doctrine of Confession that might be thought to make sacramental absolution a necessity.

There had already been a furore over the production—anonymous but the editor was John Chambers, SSC (died 1874)—of *The Priest in Absolution. A Manual for Such as are Called unto the Higher Ministries of the English Church*.[5] This was a 'handbook' for confessors closely based on Roman models, notably the Jesuit Johann Reuter's *Neo-Confessarius* (Reuter's dates were 1680–1761) and the Abbé Jean Gaune's *Manuel des Confesseurs* (he lived from 1802 to 1879).[6] Ordinary members of the SSC might have thought, with friends like this, who needs enemies? Yet some kind of experience-based instruction was obviously helpful. And the Society provided much needed social support for Anglo-Catholic clergy in the slum parishes. Even if the strong disapproval of the bishops encouraged an atmosphere of secrecy about the membership list, its utility guaranteed its continued life.

Not all the Society's productions were controversial. On the eve of the Second World War, Geoffrey Arundell Chatfield Whatton (1898–1977) authored a standard anthology of spiritual texts for members—and other sympathetic clergy, plus women in the Sisterhoods.[7] In its opening sections *The Priest's Companion. A Manual of Instructions and Prayers for Priests and Religious* reflected the Puseyan 'Rule'. But essentially it was a selection of prayers and litanies, or what it termed 'common forms of prayer'. The Foreword admitted it was largely drawn from Roman sources but went on to add: 'The peculiar feature of this book, in which it differs both from all such Latin manuals and also from most Anglican books of devotion, is that it contains a high proportion of prayers drawn from the various Eastern Liturgies and other Rites. If Catholic be defined, as most Anglicans would define it, as the common teaching of the Western and Eastern Churches both before and since the Great Schism with a leaning to Western Theologoumena where there are differences, it is right and proper that we should make use not only of Western but also of Eastern prayers so far as we can'. This was an exact replication of Pusey's own views. The complier went on to add that such inclusiveness should show Evangelicals that what they call

After Newman

'Modern Romanism' is really the common heritage of the 'whole Catholic Church' from the 'very early centuries of Christianity'.

Between the World Wars, except in times of acute Church disputes as over Prayer Book Revision or the Church of South India crisis, the Society's 'work' was whatever transpired on the humdrum daily round of its members, overwhelmingly engaged as these were in pastoral ministry. 'The brethren were hardworking parish priests at a time when the Anglo-Catholic parish was understood to be the most effective missionary organization in the Church of England.'[8] In 1930 they were discussing inter alia 'The Child's Confession', 'The Child at Communion', 'The Child at Benediction'.[9] No doubt in Roman Catholic 'Deanery Meetings' a comparable range of topics was tabled for the 'business' element in what were otherwise fraternal gatherings for mutual support.

Other Anglo-Catholic Societies were usually either lay or mixed in character, and less conspiratorial, or at any rate less invisible, in their operations. The Ecclesiological Society (the old pre-Tractarian 'Cambridge Camden Society', under a new name) advised on church buildings and decoration. When in 1868 its journal *The Ecclesiologist* ceased production the Society seemed to be on the way out. But it was soon re-constituted, with a new series of 'Transactions', beginning in 1879, and still exists. Its seal, appropriate enough, was designed by Pugin with a scroll added some decades later by Ninian Comper — figures who will reappear in this book in Chapter 9. The Society's *Hierurgia Anglicana* constituted a kind of programme of the enhancements it wished to see made in the conduct of the Liturgy — and was an early plea for the restoration of Eucharistic vestments: 'nowhere', so its authors lamented, 'have we witnessed one instance of compliance with the Rubrick as to the vestments'.[10]

At the Liturgy the Gregorian Society (1870) could provide help with the introduction of the Chant. Here the great name was G. H. Palmer (1846–1926), later assisted by Francis Burgess (1879–1948). In 1900 Palmer and Burgess became choirmaster and organist, respectively, of St Mary the Virgin, Primrose Hill, whose standard music until the 1960s was English chant sung by a choir of men and boys. The importance of dignified serving of the Liturgy, whether sung or said, was, naturally, not neglected. The 1898 Guild (it might equally have been termed 'Society') of the Servants of the Sanctuary, organized in local chapters, also aimed to beautify the Liturgy by the provision of reverent and ceremonially well-trained servers, each wearing a medallion inscribed *Introibo ad altare Dei*, a psalm-verse used in the opening 'Prayers at the Foot of the Altar' in the traditional Roman Liturgy.

The 1864 Society of St Alphege could be of service in the paraphernalia of worship. It supported needleworkers in church embroidery — a skill which attained dizzy heights at Anglo-Catholic hands, rivalling the *opus anglicanum* of the Middle Ages.

A more ambitious project, which combined the provision of church furnishing with a publishing arm was the 1905 Society of the Faith, founded by two-priest brothers, Charles Edward Douglas (1870–1955) and his better-known sibling John Albert Douglas, a figure to be discussed at greater length in Chapter 10, in the context of Anglo-Catholic ecumenical activity.[11] The Society of the Faith described itself as an 'Association of Christians in communion with the See of Canterbury for mutual assistance in the work of Christ's Church and for the furtherance of such charitable undertakings as may from time to time be decided upon, more especially for the popularization of the Catholic faith'. In 1907 the Douglas brothers acquired a cowshed in the small Bedfordshire market town of Leighton Buzzard which they converted into a printing shop. As work increased, with the publication of books, periodicals, and, after 1917, church music, they exchanged it for a derelict brewery. 'The Faith Press was, in its early days, unique in industrial history for every Saint's Day its employees attended Mass in the parish church, and on Ascension Day they went on an excursion into the countryside, where Mass was said in some village church before spending the rest of the day in a more leisurely way'.[12] Such were the humble beginnings of Faith Press, in time a major Anglo-Catholic publishing business run from Faith House, Westminster, close to the heart of the English (and Anglican) Establishment. Faith House, the lease of which was acquired in 1935, also had workspaces for 'Faith-Craft', the other aspects of the Society's work. In 1916 the Society began to accept commissions for vestments, to which it added in 1938 a workshop for joinery and the making of statuary, based eventually at St Alban's. The high point of the Society's contribution to the liturgical arts was the restoration and refurnishing, after the Blitz, of St Mary-le-Bow in Cheapside, for which it undertook work in every relevant medium, including stained glass.

The Society of the Faith is not to be confused with the similarly named Society for the Maintenance of the Faith, an especially crucial body since its remit from the time of its foundation in 1873 was the delicate matter of patronage. Its founder, Edmund Gough de Salis Wood (1841–1932) Vicar of St Clement's, Cambridge, was a rare example of Anglican learning turned to the topic of canon law. (De Salis Wood's *The Regal Power of the Church or the Fundamentals of Canon Law*, originally published in 1888, would be reprinted in 1948 with an introduction by Eric Kemp, the premier historian of canon law in the Church of England.[13]) In situations where the 'absence of Catholic privileges' proved irremediable, or the suppression of Catholic observances unavoidable, the Society for the Maintenance of the Faith helped to establish chapels and oratories that were not dependent on the State connexion. Over time, bit by persistent bit, it acquired advowsons of its own, allowing its officers to present incumbents to established livings. That usually came about through gifts, perhaps especially through bequests. By 1876, all its council members belonged to the English Church Union and a majority to the Society of the Holy Cross.

The Catholic League, created in 1913, was a specifically Anglo-Papalist organization, with a limited but also a notably zealous following.[14] The *dëroulement* of its inaugural service, in the parish church of Corringham in Essex (Clifton Kelway, a co-founder, had been licensed there as a lay reader), was witnessed with increasing horror by John Alfred Kensit, the secretary of the Protestant Truth Society. The report he sent to the Bishop of St Albans led eventually to a threat of prosecution before the Court of Arches of the League's superior, Richard Llewellyn Langford James and its assistant general, Henry Fynes Clinton.[15]

In 1915 at St Cuthbert's, Philbeach Gardens, on the feast of the Sacred Heart, the League founded an Apostleship of Prayer, modelled on the Jesuit organization of the same name, and, as in its Roman paradigm, monthly changing intentions. One such ran, 'That the Church of England may be delivered from State appointed Bishops and dignitaries'.[16]

The Catholic League's periodical, *The Messenger*, set out its aims at the end of the Great War: '1, The provision of fellowship among Catholics, and the reunion of Christendom; 2, The conversion of the world to the Catholic religion; 3, the sanctification of our members'.[17] In 1920 it adopted as its own the Creed of the Council of Trent on the ground that this document 'aptly summarises the Faith of the Pre-Reformation Church of England'.[18] The *Church Times* had previously supported the League, but its leader-writer found the adoption of a Post-Reformation Creed, in preference to the ancient credal formulae offered in the Prayer Book, somewhat bizarre. 'The Catholic laity is English. It respects order and authority. It resents freakish religion.'[19] But the League stuck to its guns. Thirty years later, in *The Creed of the Council of Trent with Explanations*, its spokesmen were still defending the choice, pointing out that, after the Eastern Schism, the 'authority which is the guarantee of truth must belong to some party'—unless such truth-affirming power has disappeared altogether from the Church of the New Covenant, that is. The church of the City of Rome should be recognized as 'mother' of all churches—not, it was explained, because she gave birth to all local churches (obviously 'she' did not), but because 'she possesses and bestows upon all local churches precisely that family status which guarantees their mutual relationship both with her and with one another'.[20]

The explanation was intelligent enough and seems to bear the mark of a study by Spencer John Jones (1856–1943), *England and the Holy See. An*

The Inner-Church Struggle

Essay towards Reunion.[21] The rector of Batsford with Moreton-in-Marsh in Gloucestershire's Evenlode Valley (could any location be more quintessentially English?), Jones's work had been favoured with an Introduction by the irrepressible Viscount Halifax. Correspondence with Paul Wattson (1863–1940), founder of the Order of the Atonement (later 'Franciscan Friars of the Atonement'), initiated by Jones's book, led to the creation in 1908 of the Octave of Prayer for Christian Unity, an observance embraced officially in due time by both Canterbury and Rome.[22]

The Catholic League's reunionism was consistent and not infrequently audacious. At a London commemoration in the 1960s of the Protestant martyrs of Queen Mary Tudor's reign (they had been burnt in Smithfield market where the memorial event took place), members of the League held a silent protest in reparation for the persecution of (Roman) Catholics under monarchs from Henry VIII (reigned 1509–47) onwards.[23] Associated with the League was the Sodality of the Precious Blood, exclusively for celibate clergy, the Anglo-Papalist ideal. Among membership requirements was the ability to recite the Breviary (intelligently) in Latin.

The Federation of Catholic Priests, also Anglo-Papalist, was born in the diocese of Lichfield in 1917 and took as its first president the admirably learned Darwell Stone of Pusey House. Its members met (and meet) to support each other in the work of Catholic teaching, for which they were soon needed to maintain a 'Catholic voice' in the new context of the National Church Assembly, brought into being as that was in 1919, forerunner of the disastrous 'General Synod'.

Schools, guilds, newspapers

Schools, guilds, and newspapers were the other chief weapons in the hands of Anglo-Catholics in the 'Inner-Church Struggle'—though the equivalent in their armoury of massed cavalry took the form of the Anglo-Catholic Congresses which are also to be discussed below.

Parochial schools naturally took their colour from the churchmanship of Anglo-Catholic parishes. In the nature of the beast these were elementary schools—foundational, but none the worse for that. They formed a small fraction of the church schools, which numbered some 13,000 in 1831 on the eve of the Oxford Movement's beginnings, and from 1833, the date of the Movement's inception, received annual Treasury grants.[24] By the First World War about a quarter of all English children attended Church of England schools.

At the other extreme from Anglo-Catholic efforts in the primary education for the poor lay Radley College. The 'College of St Peter' was a public school in the Oxfordshire countryside, founded in 1847 by a critically minded Tractarian, William Sewell (1804–74), Fellow of Exeter College, Oxford. Sewell's resources did not extend to an adequate endowment, so it had to be rescued by a group of Anglo-Catholic laity, pre-eminent among them John Hubbard, first Baron Addington (1805–89) who had built and endowed St Alban's, Holborn.[25] Schools like Radley were essentially for the landed classes: that is, the aristocracy and gentry.

Among the secondary schools founded privately to further the Anglo-Catholic cause, Nathaniel Woodard's schools, the earliest of which were founded in the early 1850s, were of first importance. That was because, well-provided as the landed elite was with suitable schools, there remained a major lacuna in middle class education. The historic grammar schools, to which townsmen of the middling sort might have been attracted, had typically confined their teaching to the 'learned languages', Latin and Greek. The Woodard Schools provided a boarding school education of a wider kind for the children of the middle classes, and they did so on firmly Anglo-Catholic lines. Nathaniel Woodard (1811–91), relieved of his curacy at Bethnal Green for a sermon on auricular Confession which displeased his bishop, and finding himself re-located to the more sympathetic setting of the Chichester diocese, saw both a gap in the market and an apostolic opportunity.[26]

Beginning in the late 1840s from the unlikely starting-point of an ill-paid curacy at Shoreham (and there was no inherited money, for his father's procreative success—there were twelve surviving children—had pauperised his family), Woodard began to create, first in Sussex itself (as with Hurstpierpoint and Lancing, for boys, and Bognor, for girls) and then further afield, a series of single sex schools dotted across the length and breadth of England, together with one in North Wales. His begging campaigns were stupendously effective as was especially shown in the dimensions of Lancing College, the magnificent chapel of which dominates the surrounding landscape for miles around.

Woodard lacked Newman's ability to think through the principles of a philosophy of education. But he was a paramount practical administrator of the funds he gathered. And he ensured the churchmanship of his schools by placing their governance in the hands of a Corporation open only to those willing to make a 'solemn affirmation of belief in the three creeds contained in the Book of Common Prayer of the Church of England, and in "the other mysteries of our holy religion, as set out in the several offices of the Church of England"', a coded reference to the full gamut of Tractarian commitment: so-called 'Prayer Book Catholicism'.[27] Woodard's ideal of education was almost entirely couched in religious terms (another contrast with Newman), an observation which may remind the chronicler not to forget the existence of the Church's Sunday schools, attended at their height by some two million children, though

The Inner-Church Struggle

that number more than halved by the start of the Second World War.

Anglo-Catholic Guilds operated with a more restricted than the movement's Societies. Typically, they gave information about Catholic rites and set forth devotions not to be found in the Prayer Book. (Obviously enough, they have nothing in common, except a conceptual affinity, with the National Guilds discussed in Chapter 6, which were civil units of a socio-economic kind.) These ecclesiastical guilds encouraged fasting, auricular Confession, and frequent church attendance, often by incorporating all of these into a Rule of life. Like the schools, they were usually parochial in character. But they could also be professional. New associations were aimed at doctors, the Guild of St Luke; nurses, the Guild of St Barnabas; soldiers, the Guild of the Holy Standard; railway workers, the Guild of the Holy Cross. St Martin's League for postmen had a relatively short life, between 1877–1902. It existed to provide houses where postboys carrying mail on foot across London could rest, enjoy a pot of tea, and thumb through edifying Anglo-Catholic literature. It lost its rationale when motorized vehicles made their appearance instead.

Many such bodies were later consolidated into the Church of England Working Men's Society, which may therefore be considered under this heading, though much of its membership will have been drawn not from the guilds but from parish clubs like 'St Saviour's Working Men's Club' at St Peter's, London Docks. The national organization was founded in 1876. By 1888 it listed 285 branches, based in Ritualist strongholds, and with some ten thousand members.[28] One of its tasks was to provide bodyguards for threatened clergy, and protection for Liturgies or other gatherings where there might be disruption. Two thousand members turned out to protest at Arthur Tooth's imprisonment in 1877. The authorities' alarm may have played a part in his unexpectedly early release. Perhaps the 'Anglican Crusade', created in the 1880s for Boy Scouts, could be considered its junior branch.

Guilds were sometimes offshoots of, or auxiliaries to, wider, usually clerical, bodies. The 1862 Confraternity of the Blessed Sacrament originated in the troubles of the 1850s. The original adverse decision, given in 1858 at Bath, in the Denison case, had led Pusey, Keble, and others to sign a declaration of traditional doctrine on the Holy Eucharist. Among the signatories was Thomas T. Carter, the Rector of Clewer and founder of the Community of St John the Baptist there. Subsequently, Carter began to plan a brotherhood specifically dedicated to spread the word about Jesus in the Blessed Sacrament. At St Mary's, Crown Street, Soho, where the vicar was John Chambers of *The Priest in Absolution* fame, a number of clergy came together in 1857 to found just such a body, originally under the title 'Society of the Blessed Sacrament', with Thomas Carter as its first superior general. It took on its new name in 1862, at

All Saints, Margaret Street, Frederick Oakeley's church. Five years later it could boast over two hundred priests in its membership, and some twelve thousand laity. Five years after that the number of laity had more than quadrupled, the number of priests more than doubled, and a trio of Scottish or colonial bishops came along for the ride.[29]

A substantial Fund, presided over by a Clewer Sister, offered grants to poor parishes to acquire objects for the Eucharistic cultus, and still furnishes largesse for, among other things, aumbries and tabernacles, lest the Species, as the Confraternity's current website has it, be kept in mouldy masonry, or even cocoa tins. William Bright, Regius Professor of Ecclesiastical History at Oxford from 1868 till his death in 1901 (as mentioned in Chapter 5, he was Father Ignatius's tutor), did not think it beneath his dignity to be a member. The Confraternity was unique in having its 'own' community of Sisters, founded in 1869, the Community of Reparation to Jesus in the Blessed Sacrament, with a 'Convent of Reparation' at Rushworth Street, Southwark, designed by Sir Walter Tapper (1861–1935), the architect of the Community of the Resurrection's house at Mirfield.[30] Its aims were stated as threefold: to make reparation, insofar as it might be possible, to dishonour caused to Jesus in the Sacrament of the Altar; to pray for those who do not know him under the sacramental veils of bread and wine; to carry out missionary work in large towns—in practice, that amounted to in the mission district of St Alphege, Southwark. The Eucharistic ethos paralleled that of two French Congregations, *Adoration Réparatrice* and *Marie Réparatrice*, dating from 1848 and 1857 respectively, even if actual institutional links are missing. Traditional Roman Catholics will be further encouraged to know that the motto of the entire Confraternity ran, 'Let us Adore for Ever the Most Holy Sacrament' (in Latin).

Some research would suggest that even when such Guild life was well organized parochially, in a project of making the whole body of congregants a 'Eucharistic community', the results could be disappointing. Often enough only a fraction, if a substantial fraction, of those attending church, at any rate in old-established parishes, became actual communicants. 'Anglo-Catholic clergy must have felt like Sisyphus', wrote Jeremy Morris, 'heaving up a hill the great boulder of their parishioners' reluctance to change the ingrained devotional habits of generation.'[31] It was not a problem their Roman Catholic contemporaries had to face. Communion taken fasting from midnight was probably a disincentive, as was the recommendation of prior Confession. Yet for many people the message got across, as John Betjeman's poem *A Lincolnshire church*', written in the 1940s, movingly attests. 'There where the white light flickers/ Our Creator is with us yet,/ To be worshipped by you and the woman/ Of the slacks and the cigarette./ The great door shuts and lessens/ The roar of churchyard trees/ And the presence of God Incarnate/ Has brought me to my knees.'[32] Post-Conciliar Catholics in the West, where in the wake of liturgical change a degree of Zwinglianism has entered in, must envy such strength of Eucharistic conviction.

As its name suggests, the 1873 Guild of All Souls promoted prayer for the dead, with, in particular, the introduction as a matter of course of Requiem Masses for the souls of the departed. It could appeal for its Anglican credentials to the language of the commendation of a dying person in the Prayer Book's Order for the Visitation of the Sick, which spoke of sins being purged and done away with—seeming to imply some kind of post-mortem 'intermediate state'.

During and after the Great War, with its colossal casualties, such prayers were ordered anyway by episcopal authority in some Anglican Provinces. Approved high church hymnals, notably *The English Hymnal* and *Hymns Ancient and Modern*, already had metrical English-language versions of the *De profundis*, the traditional psalm for the dead in the Latin Church. This enabled the Guild's spokesmen to argue that such prayer was implicitly taking place anyway in 'Cathedrals and Churches throughout the length and breadth of the land'.[33] Originally, the 'Guild Burial Society', with Arthur Tooth of Ritual Riots fame as its president, it had sought to 'provide furniture for Burial according to the use of the Catholic Church to set forth the two great doctrines of the Communion of Saints and the Resurrection of the Body; and Intercessory prayer for the Dying and the repose of the soul of the deceased members and all the faithful departed'.

At least one guild was a lay confraternity which only allowed clerics to enter as associates—the reverse of a more customary structure. This was the Guild of St Alban, founded by Shirley Fielding Palmer (died 1901), a Fellow of the Royal College of Surgeons, in Birmingham in 1851. The Guild's aim was to organize laymen in densely populated areas where the reach of clergy was short. They were to assist in maintaining and extending the Catholic faith, defend that faith against attacks by error or unbelief, and to protect the independence of the English Church against the claim to jurisdiction of the Church of Rome—rather a superfluous undertaking in Victorian England (probably what was meant was offering dissuaders to secession). A decade later it claimed branches in a dozen English cities and towns, and its members included the publishers Alfred Richard Mowbray (1824–75) and J. T. Hayes, the second of whom published in a series of biennial volumes collected issues of the Guild's monthly, *Church Work*. The Guild of St Alban's papers, which cover the period 1873 to 1961, were deposited in the London Archives in 1961 and 1962, indicating likely cessation of activity at that time.

After Newman

The Confraternity of our Lady (1880) and The League of our Lady (1904), founded by Viscount Halifax, and, even more audaciously, the Union of the Holy Rosary (1886), encouraged the ancient devotional attitude of tender piety towards the Mother of God—though that particular title of the Virgin, sanctioned though it was by the Third Ecumenical Council (Ephesus, in 431), made many broad church (never mind low church) Anglicans wince. These sundry bodies came together in 1931 as the Society of Mary, whose members keep a Rule of life that includes such traditional Latin Catholic Marian devotions as the Angelus and the Rosary, 'dedicated to the Glory of God and the holy Incarnation of Christ under the invocation of Our Lady, Help of Christians'.[34]

With the re-founding of the Shrine of Our Lady of Walsingham in north Norfolk, Anglo-Catholic Marian devotionalism really took off, so much so that, for many, an annual pilgrimage to the Shrine was an indispensable badge of adherence to the Movement.[35] Charlotte Boyd (1838–1906), a *dirigée* of John Mason Neale, used her considerable inherited wealth, and the co-opted service of the three Religious of the Society of St John the Evangelist, to plan an ambitious scheme for restoring the ruins of monastic houses destroyed at the Henrician Dissolution and returning them to their original purpose. In 1893 she approached the owners of the former house of Augustinian canons at Walsingham, the guardian of England's premier Marian shrine, though all she was offered was a farmer's cottage said to have been the 'Slipper Chapel' where the shrine's pilgrims removed their footwear. In 1894, on a sudden impulse, she became a Roman Catholic at Bruges.

But despite her removal from the scene a seed had been sown. A decade later an Anglo-Catholic Vicar of Walsingham, Edgar Reeves (1861–1940), received through His Majesty's postal service a small alabaster statue of the Mother of the Lord, produced by the League of Our Lady. Reeves' successor, Alfred Hope-Patten (1885–1958) brought up as a youth in the Wagner churches of Brighton, always described this as Mary of Nazareth 'going before him' to Walsingham.[36]

Taking over from Reeves, Hope Patten lost no time in resuming Charlotte Boyd's unfinished work. On the basis of the Shrine's mediaeval seal, discovered in an archaeological dig in the 1850s, he commissioned a Carmelite nun to carve a replica of the original image, burnt, according to most historians, at Chelsea Manor, in the presence of the Lord Privy Seal, Thomas Cromwell (c. 1485–1540), no less. In July 1922, a procession of parishioners, carrying the image, initiated the 'Shrine Prayers', with daily Rosary and Intercessions, and these have continued ever since. That was shortly followed by the first organized pilgrimage. It proved a minuscule affair but after that came a regular growth in visitors, chiefly (at first) from London. As difficulties with the Bishop of Norwich were beginning to show themselves, Hope Patten acted decisively. He bought a piece of land as near to the original site as makes no difference, commissioned a chapel of the same dimensions as the building of 1061 to 1538, providentially discovered an underground spring, which he had incorporated it into the new edifice as the perpetually running source of 'Walsingham Water'. In 1931 the carved image was translated to the new site and supplied with a crown of silver—the 'Oxford Crown' since the gift of the priest and people at St Paul's, Walton Street, Oxford (subsequently the Café Freud).[37] The Holy House, eventually refurbished by Comper in exquisite style, was set within an increasingly elaborate church whose fifteen altars are said to be based on those of the Rosary basilica at Lourdes. The Shrine grew in other senses too as Hope Patten began to acquire dilapidated properties in a village that had never properly recovered from the 'Great Depression' of English agriculture (1873–96), and these enabled an ever-expanding set of Shrine facilities, including a convent for Sisters, an anchorhold for a hermit, a home for orphans, and, at least for a while, a 'college' of Augustinian canons, a choir school, and a retirement home for priests.

The life of devotion remained the clear focus of Anglican Walsingham in consequence of which it acquired serious devotees. In 1925 Hope Patten created the Society of Our Lady of Walsingham, with a Rule of life for its members, along with a companion body, the Association of Priest Associates of the Holy House. In 1960 his successor as Shrine Warden, Colin Stephenson (died 1973), instituted an 'Order of Our Lady of Walsingham' (or, more fully, 'Order of the Living Rosary of Our Lady of Walsingham'), with a rather complex remit. Each of the fifteen Rosary altars in the Shrine church was to have assigned to it a Dame, a Clerk, and a Lay Clerk, each class to have ingeniously devised insignia.[38] This innovation had a comparatively short shelf life prior to radical simplification. One feels he would have made an excellent companion to Miss Sellon, whose pictorial imagination, when thinking up her elaborately ramified Society, ran on similar tracks.

Walsingham had no real competitors though the Shrine of Our Lady of Egmanton, near Newark-on-Trent, went back earlier, to 1897 when Comper redesigned St Mary's, Egmanton, a living belonging to the Dukes of Newcastle. It was the seventh Duke, Henry Pelham-Clinton (1864–1928), who had thought up the whole thing. Along with an imagined version of the mediaeval cult-image, Comper created a remarkable east window showing the Virgin and Child with scenes not only of the Annunciation but also of the Assumption, together with an enormous thurible.

Not that, among the guilds, Christological (as distinct from Mariological) piety was wanting. The Guild of the Sacred Heart of Jesus (quite distinct from the Roman Catholic 'Guild of the *Most* Sacred Heart of Jesus) made space for devotion to the Saviour under that title. And it might be argued that the (1926) Glastonbury (or 'West of England') Pilgrimage Association had a focus on the Christ who, according to traditions assiduously cultivated there, came as an infant with Joseph of Arimathea. After the events of Passion and Resurrection, Joseph is said to have returned to Somerset with the Holy Grail, the Cup of the Last Supper. The 'traditions' concerned might be said to bring together quite neatly the Incarnation (as in Blake's *Jerusalem*) and the Paschal Mystery (as in the Arthurian cycle), though their historical value is more than doubtful. Alas, the modern 'pop' Glastonbury Festival has, if not swept away, then at any rate thoroughly dowsed the Christian legendarium in a New Age flood.

The Pilgrimage Association had achieved a definitely Anglo-Catholic character by the beginning of the 1930s when Lord Halifax was president of the Association. In 1931 the Abbot of Nashdom celebrated Mass at St Patrick's Chapel amid the Abbey ruins—anticipating his Roman Catholic counterparts among the English Benedictines.

What was read by church workers, and the most susceptible of their clients, in such schools and guilds? Among the newspapers, the *Church Times*, from 1863, has already been mentioned. Founded by George Josiah Palmer (1828–92), Anglo-Catholic scion of an Evangelical publishing family, its 1880 total of some 20, 000 subscribers, won partly by the polemical brilliance and mordant Irish wit of Richard Frederick Littledale (1833–90), struck fear into the hearts of Evangelicals. Littledale's reputation as a confessor and his association with Neale, whose *Commentary on the Psalms* he finished after Neale's death, will have added to their alarm. Eric Mascall would recall of his undergraduate days in the 1920s that '[I] got my thrills from the *Church Times*, which was not then, as it has become since, all things to all men, but was the defiant organ of a movement which rejoiced in being persecuted and was confident of victory'.[39]

Not irrelevantly for its commercial success, the paper was much less restrained than the *Christian Remembrancer*, begun by William Scott (1813–72), Vicar of Christ Church, Hoxton, in 1841 and relaunched as a quarterly in 1843, with a sober Tractarian piety, especially when edited by James Bowling Mozley (1813–78) who from 1871 was Regius Professor of Divinity at Oxford. There was also the immoderately moderate *Guardian*, begun in 1846 and associated with Richard William Church and Sir Frederick Rogers (1811–79), later Lord Blachford. Rogers was a friend of both Newman and Gladstone, and an archetypal Whitehall civil servant, which probably explains the tone of the paper.

Both the *Guardian* and the *Christian Remembrancer* had succeeded the *British Critic* when the latter succumbed to high-and-dry disapproval of

Oakeley and Ward. One of the complainants at the change of management, commenting on the time when the periodical was edited, in the cause of Newman's advanced thinking, by his brother-in-law, Thomas Mozley (1806–93), compared the *British Critic* to the 'Athenian sacred ship, a thing that sails under the same colours, while scarcely a plank of the old timbers is left'.[40] Newman's takeover, for the sake of the Tractarian cause, of an old-established high church organ had shown him at his most Machiavellian and thus in an unaccustomed light.

For highbrows there was the *Church Quarterly Review* which continued the scholarly emphasis of the Oxford Fathers. Lowbrows would prefer *The Surplice*, a weekly sixpenny review. Monthlies included the *Churchman's Companion*, *The Penny Post*, and *The Monthly Packet*. The *Saturday Review* was also Tractarian, though not especially ecclesiastical in its interests. Notable among its contributors was Lord Robert Cecil, later the third Marquess of Salisbury and Prime Minister (he it was who added to Gladstone's score of promotions of Anglo-Catholic clergy to high office).[41]

But nothing among these various media could compare in pungency with the *Church Times* or, for that matter, compete in the perpetuity stakes. Its uncompromising tone, and popular style—its copious advertisements catered for every conceivable orthodox taste—went down well with the rank and file in the parishes, as did its low cost (a penny).[42] The *Church Times* not only guaranteed its own longevity. Its mass mobilization of opinion did much to prepare the way for the highly successful Anglo-Catholic Congresses of the 1920s and 30s.

The Congresses

The efforts of Anglo-Catholics in the Societies (with one partial exception), in education, guild-activity, and the print media came to a peak in the 'Congress Movement' of the years 1920 to 1933. The Anglo-Catholic Congresses were the Movement's most ebullient expression, its 'high noon'.[43] In the opinion of one commentator: more than that, they were its 'high-water mark'.[44]

The idea had begun modestly enough as a pooling of clerical minds on how best to respond to the world that followed the Armistice of 1918. The incumbents of All Saints, Margaret Street, and St Augustine's, Kilburn, thought up the idea of a comprehensive Anglo-Catholic Congress, and outsourcing the practicalities hit upon an organizer of brilliance in Marcus Ethelbert Atlay (died 1934), Vicar of St Matthew's, Westminster. Atlay was fortunate in being able to draw on the varied talents of a highly successful central London parish with an extraordinary social mix, ranging from 'high-ranking military officers, Members of Parliament and judges, to the owner of a fish barrow and working men from nearby Old Pye Street and Perkins' Rents'.[45] Some of the former, at least, were key to the professionalism of the Appeal, but, as all organizers know, the quality of the advertising is nothing worth without the always unpredictable consumer-reaction, which in this case was favourable. 'As interest and response moved from hundreds of people to thousands, so ambitions rose. A nerve in Anglo-Catholicism had been touched.'[46]

As applications poured in, the choice of venue was changed more than once. In the end, the only London auditorium able to accommodate the numbers involved was South Kensington's Royal Albert Hall. That process re-set the date of the first Congress until, by fortunate accident for lovers of publicity, it immediately preceded the 1920 Lambeth Conference. A letter by Atlay to the *Church Times* set out the exceedingly ambitious aims: 'to make plain and evident that the Catholic position in the English Church is the true mind of the Church of England', while putting before the 'English-speaking world what English Catholics really hold with regard to such great questions as modern philosophy, modern criticism, the Roman Church, Nonconformists, and social and industrial problems'.[47] Atlay added the wry comment that the bishops of the Church of England, taken as a body, were among the primary intended targets of such enlightenment. In fact, three diocesans attended, Gore (predictably) among them. Otherwise, any bishops present came from overseas where Crown prerogative did not exclude advanced Anglo-Catholics.

As Atlay had predicted, the lectures gravitated round intellectual and cultural issues: the 'effects of contemporary biblical criticism and theological speculation on Faith and the Gospel in the light of the challenge from modernism and the dislocation of the old order of thought and values wrought by the War'.[48] A parallel set of addresses provided catechesis on distinctively Catholic beliefs and practices. Other speakers dealt with the economic problems of the post-War era. Booklets on social issues had been commissioned, edited by Percy Widdrington and Reginald Tribe (1893–1945), Director of the Society of the Sacred Mission and Warden of the College at Kelham from 1925 to 1943. Among the Catholic Societies, the Society of the Holy Cross stood apart, seemingly owing to the organizers' recognition that a degree of pluralism was only to be expected (thus, not the towing of a Roman line), though individual members came along. The Society of SS Peter and Paul undertook to publish all the Congress Reports—true for the successor events of 1923, 1927, 1930, and 1933, though the Reports from the first Congress were published by 'SPCK'—the Society for Promoting Christian Knowledge.

In the wake of this dizzy success, the Congress organization acquired a building in London's Hanover Square as its centre of operations, along with the services of a General Secretary. That clearly implied a pattern had now been set for the future. Between 1922 and 1934 the Congress Secretariat generated local congresses in over a score of English cities, towns, or, in one case—Walsingham, inevitably—villages, with a 'Congress van' providing a travelling platform for speakers at outdoor meetings.[49] Priests had their own follow-up conference at Oxford in 1921 (almost twelve hundred attending), with high quality lecture-material from speakers who included two holders of chairs at King's College, London, sundry Fellows of Oxford and Cambridge colleges, and two principals of theological colleges as well as incumbents of well-known London parishes (All Saints, Margaret Street; St Barnabas, Pimlico; The Ascension, Lavender Hill) and other parish clergy from extra-metropolitan settings. Lecturers includes figures from the Oratory of the Good Shepherd and the Society of the Sacred Mission, as well as the then Principal of Pusey House, the hymn writer V. S. S. ('Stuckey') Coles. Advice given ranged from the theoretically highfalutin'—an appeal from N. P. Williams to 'evangelize the intellect of the country' ('in a fully developed Catholicism the spirit of St Francis, who spent himself in the service of the poor and degraded, needs to be complemented by the spirit of St Dominic, who made his appeal to the learned and cultured[50]), to the down-to-earthly practical such as how best to counsel folk in the Confessional.

The combined effect of Congress and conference was galvanizing. 'The change in the ecclesiastical climate inspired the revival of an evangelistic campaign and opened opportunities to enthuse Anglo-Catholics with missionary endeavour both at home and abroad.'[51] That set its seal on the second Congress, 1923, notable for confirming the emergence of Frank Weston, bishop of Zanzibar, as Anglo-Catholic leader.[52] He was already celebrated (or, to some, notorious) for calling out Anglican bishops in mainland East Africa for the crimes of schism and heresy when they had participated in joint Nonconformist-Anglican rites.[53] Now, as chairman of the Congress (the sympathetic bishop of London, Arthur Winnington-Ingram, who turned a blind eye to many Anglo-Catholic illegalities, was patron),[54] Weston, who had already made his mark at the first Congress, encouraged parish priests to 'fight for the right of adoring Jesus in his Blessed Sacrament', as well as urging his hearers to make what, in the papal Communion, would later be termed an 'option for the poor': the poor who were already, of course, for well over half a century the preferred choice of the slum clergy. 'You cannot claim to worship Jesus in the Tabernacle if you do not pity Jesus in the slum.'[55]

A sign of the times was the opening Mass at St Paul's—a privilege denied participants in 1920, though the Dean and chapter might have demurred had the contents of Weston's speech been known in advance.

'I am not asking for obedience to a Bishop. I ask for obedience to the Bishop in far as they themselves obey the Catholic Church.'[56] His sudden and premature death in November 1924 deprived the Movement, some would say, of its (potentially) greatest leader since Newman.[57]

The third Congress, 1926, was overshadowed by the onset of the Prayer Book controversy, more prominently so in as much as the Congress organizers had chosen for the event a Eucharistic theme. The fourth Congress, 1930, was a disturbed affair, owing to the State-and-Church crisis of 1927 to 1929, with the successive rejections of two proposed schemes for Prayer Book revision, and the beginning of the further slow-burning crisis over the Church of South India. Ironically, the topic chosen this time was ecclesiology, 'The Doctrine of the Church'. Attacks from Kensitites were especially virulent, uncomfortably for the more easily intimidated, who were less than fully compensated by a show of support from the two archbishops, Cosmo Gordon Lang of York and William Temple of Canterbury. Crowds came nonetheless to an opening Mass in Stamford Bridge football ground and other events at the Wembley Arena and, as with the first Congress, the Royal Albert Hall.

The 1933 Congress was the 'Centenary Congress' since the organizers (and more importantly the Church Union, with which they were now fused) accepted Keble's 'National Apostasy' sermon as the Movement's true beginning. Indeed, they invited the appropriately christened Keble Talbot, CR (1877–1949), to preach from the pulpit where that historic sermon had been delivered, St Mary the Virgin, Oxford's University Church. Numerically the Centenary Congress proved the all-time winner, its final Mass attracting up to 50, 000 of the faithful.

The Congress Movement, in William Davage's words, 'appeared to be about to capture the commanding heights of the Church of England but never quite made it'.[58] In the view of its chief chronicler, John Gunstone, from one point of view it deterred conversions to Rome by assuring participants of the strength of support for the Church's 'Catholic' claims, but in another perspective it unwittingly encouraged such conversions through raising expectations that, in the event, could not be fulfilled.[59] That was apparent in 1948, the date of the final Congress (and the present writer's birth). Numbers were not what they were, though what they were was not nugatory, either. Perhaps Davage's summing-up is too coloured by knowledge of what came next—the era after 1965. 'By accepting a tolerated place within a comprehensive economy, falling into an establishment embrace, the Anglo-Catholic missionary edge to recover the whole of the Church of England to its right mind was blunted; its aims were watered down, practices and disciplines became increasingly compromised'.[60] The experience of the 1950s and early 60s was nevertheless that the show was still on the road.

— 9 —

Anglo-Catholics and the Arts

THE ANGLO-CATHOLIC MOVEMENT brought with it efflorescence in the arts. That compendious term includes architecture, glass, and painting, novels and poetry, hymnography and music.

Architecture, glass, and painting

The revival of church architecture and decoration under Anglo-Catholic auspices must not be considered in non-theological terms. The architecture meant sacrality, just as the decoration meant the iconic dimension. Here for once Cambridge weighed more with Anglo-Catholics than did Oxford. For the *afficionados* of the Cambridge Camden Society, later the Ecclesiological Society, the 'science of church building as the ecclesiologists understood it was not architectural science: it was the unveiling of the inner mystical meaning of old churches and the infusion of the same meaning into new churches. Its relation to the science of church-building in the most obvious sense was almost that of astrology to astronomy. Astronomy is the serious scientific study of the stars; astrology attempts to find a mystic significance in them'.[1] And the architectural historian Basil Clarke continued by admitting: 'This is not made clear in the statement of the objects of the Society. Anyone could study architectural remains or make rubbings of brasses—even heretics or schismatics. But it is clear from the Society's writings that only a good Churchman could appreciate the inwardness of it all, or build new churches as they should be built. Only a good Churchman could be an ecclesiologist.'[2]

Like the Oxford Movement's movers and shakers, the members of the Society produced 'Tracts',[3] and then from 1841 onwards a monthly magazine, *The Ecclesiologist*, already touched on in Chapter 8. John Mason Neale was probably its foremost contributor, especially on matters of hymnology, liturgiology, symbolism, and ritual.

The practical challenge of providing appropriate vestments and other church furnishings was taken up by needleworkers, workers in wood and metal, painters, and other craftsmen (and women).[4] In *Church Enlargement and Church Arrangement* Neale had written: 'A church is not as it should be, till every window is filled with stained glass, till every inch of floor is covered with encaustic tiles, till there is a Roodscreen glowing with the brightest tints and with gold, nay, if we would arrive at perfection, the roof and walls must be painted and frescoed. For it may safely be asserted that ancient churches were so adorned.'[5] In 1843 Neale and his collaborator Benjamin Webb (1819–95) translated the *Rationale* of 'Durandus', otherwise Guillaume Durand, a thirteenth century bishop of Mende, bringing sunken Western treasure to light just as Neale had done, and was still doing, solo for the Orientals. Not that these efforts were everywhere appreciated. Francis Close (1797–1882), later Dean of Carlisle, appended to the title of his *Restoration of Church is a Restoration of Popery* the words 'Proved and Illustrated from the Publications of the Cambridge Camden Society'. For Close, Romanism was taught analytically at Oxford, artistically at Cambridge. His campaign led to a temporary closure of the Society, and its reopening under a different name if not management.

But the great Anglo-Catholic architects were not deterred. The Big Six were George Gilbert Scott, William Butterfield, George Frederick Bodley, George Edmund Street, John Loughborough Pearson, and John Ninian Comper, though in reality all were dependent ultimately on Augustus Welby Pugin (1812–52), who became a Roman Catholic but discovered to his dismay that his ideals were often shared more enthusiastically by Anglo-Catholics than by the members of the Communion he had made his own.[6] That was not only because some English Roman Catholics preferred other styles, notably the Neo-Classical.[7] It was also because Pugin, who was what the eighteenth century would have called a 'Cisalpine' (the opposite, then, of an 'Ultramontane'),[8] wished to see an indigenous style used everywhere in an ultra-English Catholic Church—albeit in communion with Rome.

Cisalpines who wanted to emphasize their English patriotism would sometimes refer to Ultramontanes as 'Ultramarines', thereby making a point: the problem as they viewed it began not in Italy but at Calais. And granted the plethora of pre-Reformation cathedral, churches, and chapels in the towns and countryside of England who could doubt that Gothic was the native taste? Pugin was able, through Newman's Littlemore curate, John Rouse Bloxam, to become acquainted with the 'Oxford men', and they with him. Pugin's influence, combined with that of the Cambridge Camden Society, accounts for the emergence of these Neo-Gothic masters.

The first to rally to architectural Tractarianism was William Butterfield (1814–1900) who, travelling far from his Nonconformist origins, built a missionary college for Anglican colonial clergy within the ruins of St Augustine's Abbey, Canterbury. Sympathetic with such monastic remains as survived, it now forms part of the King's School. That was prior to designing three flagship Anglo-Catholic buildings: All Saints, Margaret Street (with its adjoining clergy house and school the Butterfield church was hailed by the Cambridge Camden Society as a perfect model for future work), St Alban's, Holborn, and Keble College, Oxford. These were the best known items in a long catalogue of commissions, though the Holborn church was burnt out in the London Blitz, and ended up with an interior by Scott's grandson, Adrian Gilbert Scott (1882–1963).[9] St Alban's was not, then, an example of the phenomenon described by Michael Yelton, whereby the 'war destroyed many strongholds of the Catholic Movement in cities', though that did not prevent it exemplifying his equally important claim that 'afterwards there was a dispersal of population from the inner cities where those churches had stood'.[10]

Butterfield's idiosyncratic use of colour, heralded at Margaret Street by contrasts of black and red brick on the exterior, and marbles and tile marquetry within, is somewhat controversial. Yet it never detracts from the noble proportions of his churches. Polychromy had been recommended by Ruskin, enthused in *The Stones of Venice* by what remained in his day of the Italian Gothic. That could have been a problem for Puginesque Anglo-centricity, and the issue—English Gothic models or European?—was to recur.[11]

John Loughborough Pearson (1817–97) was the son of a topographical artist. Perhaps owing to William Pearson's professional itinerancy, it is disputed whether his gifted offspring was born in Brussels or Durham. Within the 'utterly conservative framework of the Gothic Revival' Pearson burst forth with a medley of novel architectural ideas, producing 'spatial intricacies' without loss of unity, furnishing contrasts sometimes as bold as that between classical and Baroque, and proportioning his churches by reference to the 'Golden Section'.[12]

In London and environs three churches in particular—St Augustine's, Kilburn, with its amazing illusion of great length on a comparatively small site; St John's, Red Lion Square (destroyed in World War Two), and the graciously elegant St Michael's, Croydon, all built for Tractarian patrons—prepared the way for Pearson's Cornish masterpiece, Truro Cathedral, with inspiration drawn from Normandy and Lincoln.[13] Geometric design, elegance, and refined detail, were his constant hallmarks, though his source of inspiration shifted from a once exclusive interest in Early English Gothic to the most severe early French Gothic style, and, in the last building he completed, St John's Cathedral, Brisbane (in Australia), the Spanish Gothic of the cathedral of Barcelona.[14] Some three hundred of Pearson's British churches are listed buildings.

One of his more remote projects, Christchurch, Appleton-le-Moors, in the North Riding of Yorkshire, was described by the Victorian architectural historian Charles Locke Eastlake (1836–1906), author of *A History of the Gothic Revival*, as almost Byzantine in the details of its interior.[15] If so, there is a touch here, as elsewhere in Pearson's work, of the 'unity by inclusion' to be associated with the last of the sextet of great names, and the only one whose work falls well within the twentieth century, Ninian Comper.

George Edmund Street and George Frederick Bodley both came out of the office of George Gilbert Scott (1811–78) who rather blotted any Tractarian credentials he might have claimed by designing the *Nikolaikirche*, a Lutheran church in Hamburg, and defending Lutheranism—albeit only for its resistance to Iconoclasm—when criticized for his lapse. His 'Martyrs' Memorial' in Oxford, erected to honour the three principal Protestant martyrs of Mary Tudor's reign, was also controversial in as much as it divided Tractarians, depending on whether they saw benefit in the English Reformation taken overall. (Unlike the Vicar of Littlemore, Pusey did not dismiss financial contribution out of hand.) Yet Scott's *Plea for the Faithful Restoration of our Ancient Churches* was pure Cambridge Camden Society incarnate.[16]

Scott was a pious man with an Evangelical background; his grandfather was the biblical scholar Thomas Scott (1747–1821), whose *Commentary on the Whole Bible* went through numerous editions and influenced the young John Henry Newman. But until he encountered Pugin and the ecclesiologists Scott found no way to link his religious devotion to his professional practice. St Giles, Camberwell, was his first major Neo-Gothic creation along these approved Tractarian lines—though inclusion of wooden galleries, typical of eighteenth centuries churches, departed from Ecclesiological Society prototypes.

Scott's cathedrals for the Scottish Episcopal Church in Edinburgh and Glasgow were to be his most prestigious ecclesiastical buildings, along with the Cathedral Church of Christ in Christchurch, New Zealand (the primatial see of 'Aotearoa' and Polynesia). The building was completed by the immigrant architect Benjamin Woolfield Mountfort (1825–88), son of a Birmingham *parfumier*, but it suffered terribly from the earthquake of 2011.

Scott's progeny began a veritable architectural dynasty including Adrian Gilbert Scott, the grandson who took in hand Butterfield's Holborn church, set amid the London jewellers and lawyers, after the Third Reich had done its worst.

George Edmund Street (1824–81), the son of an Essex solicitor, was converted to Anglo-Catholicism by Butler of Wantage, with whose encouragement he designed the conventual buildings of the Community of St Mary the Virgin and became an active member of the Ecclesiological Society.[17] A highly gifted draughtsman, Street's Continental tours produced two copiously illustrated works which encapsulated quite a revolt against the national style: *Brick and Marble in the Middle Ages. Notes of a Tour in the North of Italy*, in 1855, and, ten years later, *Some Account of Gothic Architecture in Spain*.[18] (So now we know where Pearson found his information.) Street was sufficiently successful, from a financial standpoint, as an architect not only of churches — he was made diocesan architect for York, Winchester, Oxford, and Ripon — but also of such secular buildings as the Strand Law Courts, better known as the Royal Courts of Justice, that he refused remuneration for his work on the East Grinstead motherhouse of the Society of Saint Margaret. He also built at his own expense St Mary the Virgin, Holmbury, in Surrey, in memory of his second wife who died of cholera while on their honeymoon. Other churches of his, such as All Saints, Clifton, destroyed by an incendiary bomb in the Second World War, and St Mary Magdalene, Paddington, generally seen as his London masterpiece, became well known as places of distinctively Anglo-Catholic worship.

Street took the (ecclesiological) war into the enemy's camp by his two Roman churches, All Saints, in the Via del Babuino (the 'English church') and St Paul's Outside the Walls, on the Via Nazionale (the 'American church'), with mosaics designed by the Pre-Raphaelite artist Edward Burne-Jones (1833–98). In a paper read to the Ecclesiological Society 'On the Future of Art in England', Street had gone so far as to declare that the 'Pre-Raphaelite movement is identical with our own and ... the success of the one aids immensely the success of the other', namely, Tractarian architects.[19] Colour and natural form were back, and in the service of Anglo-Catholic religion.

George Frederick Bodley (1827–1907), a doctor's son from Brighton (in his youth he was churchwarden at St Paul's, one of the Wagner churches described in Chapter 4), also had links to the Pre-Raphaelites. Bodley's early commissions for stained glass and church decoration did much to establish William Morris in business. His relationship by marriage to the family of George Gilbert Scott helped not only to guarantee economic security but, once established in Scott's office, access to a 'liberating environment, both artistically and intellectually' since Scott's 'essential mildness' restraining him from 'imposing an aesthetic vision' on those who worked with him.[20] That gave the younger man *carte blanche* in the choice of both collaborators and sources of influence.

Bodley's interest in the late mediaeval Northern European Gothic distinguished him from other Revivalists. Here the Flemish enthusiasms of Dante Gabriel Rossetti (1828–82), Philip Webb (1831–1915), and Burne-Jones influenced his style, as did his very focussed concern not only with glass, where his later collaboration with Charles Eamer Kempe was crucial, but also with the accoutrements of worship in fabrics of every kind. That was a Puginesque trait in his conception of the church architect. Wherever possible, the latter should be the church furnisher as well. Not for nothing was Bodley one of the founders of Watts and Company, the premier ecclesiastical designer in Britain, situated in Tufton Street, off Dean's Yard, in the precincts of Westminster Abbey.[21]

In terms of scale, his most ambitious buildings are abroad: St David's Cathedral, Hobart, in Tasmania, and the National Cathedral in Washington, DC.[22] (There could have been a hat-trick had the prize competition for the Anglican cathedral in Liverpool not been won by George Gilbert Scott, Jr, 1839–97.) Yet the huge mass of St Augustine's Pendlebury, on the river Irwell in south Lancashire, runs these buildings a close race. The artist L. S. Lowry who lived in Pendlebury from 1912 to 1948 captures in his drawings and paintings St Augustine's 'haunting fusion of monumentality with a sense of fragility'.[23]

England also has a multitude of smaller Bodley masterpieces, such as the richly stoned carved Holy Angels, Hoar Cross, in Staffordshire, hailed by John Betjeman as a 'perfect association of splendour and intimacy architecturally expressed',[24] or his Cambridge gem, All Saints, Jesus Lane, alias 'The Painted Church', now, alas, under the care of the Churches Conservation Trust, a sign of its current redundancy. The early Gloucestershire venture that is St John the Baptist, France Lynch, combines sculpture and polychromy. Bodley's gifts, remarks the architectural historian Michael Hall, included 'creating effects that lend a small-scale cheap church an air of heroic sublimity'.[25] In that Gloucestershire example, a contemporary described the overall result as 'unique and very handsome, entirely suitable for a Roman Catholic Chapel, but extremely objectionable for the Reformed Church of England'.[26] The youthful churchwarden from St Paul's, Brighton, would not have been displeased by the comment.

John Ninian Comper (1864–1960) was, in this company, untimely born, surviving until almost the end of the period studied in this book.[27] The son of an English priest settled in Aberdeen (a non-graduate, the elder Comper could only be a candidate for Orders north of the Border), Comper was educated at Glenalmond (Ignatius Leycester Lyne's old stomping ground), and the Ruskin School of Drawing in Oxford. He was articled first to the stained-glass artist Charles Eamer Kempe, and then in 1883 to the architects' office of Bodley and Thomas Garner (1839–1906) where he discovered his *métier*.

Comper's first new building was the exquisite St Cyprian's, Clarence Gate, designed according to the Alcuin Club principles he supported. As with so much of Bodley's work (and he followed Bodley in wanting to design everything in a church, and not just the four walls), Comper was inspired by late mediaeval English Gothic. In its purity of recreation St Cyprian's has been called an example of 'unity by exclusion'. That phrase was meant to contrast with the 'unity by inclusion' apparent in Comper's greatest church, St Mary the Virgin, Wellingborough, where he ranged widely among the successive styles of Western Christendom to produce a masterpiece of synthesis. Other notable spaces included the Lady Chapels of St Matthew's, Westminster, All Saints, Margaret Street and — a rare Roman Catholic commission — Downside Abbey, near Bath.

Comper placed great emphasis on the altar, as the central building of the church — literally so at St Philip's, Cosham, Hampshire, a commission from the later 1930s when he had come under the influence of the twentieth century Liturgical Movement associated among Anglo-Catholics with Gabriel Hebert of 'Parish Communion' fame. More of Comper's altars, however, follow the 'English' (really Northern European) model where the rear altar screen, the reredos, takes its cue from the elaborate painted or carved work of late mediaeval Flanders, where frontals and curtained riddell posts become opportunities for gloriously beautiful textile design.

Of all the Catholic Revival architects, Comper was the one who did most to promote the amazing recreation of the *opus anglicanum* work which was mediaeval England's main contribution to the art of Catholic Europe. Pugin, designing Eucharistic vestments for St George's Cathedral, Southwark, had been obliged to turn to the theatrical embroiderers of the Royal Opera House — even if, later, John Hardman's (1827–95) Birmingham workshop 'Mediaeval Manufactures' provided him with substitutes.[28] Comper was fortunate in chancing on the Society of Sisters of Bethany, Lloyd Square, in Clerkenwell. That came about through the accident of taking lodgings as a young man with their chaplain, a Cowley Father. The Sisters' apostolate, touched on in Chapter 4, was really Retreat and parish work, but he persuaded them to open first a workroom and then a school for embroidery the excellence of which reached a level hardly surpassed by their pre-Reformation predecessors.

Here Comper was both building on and shaping an expectation shared among the Anglican architects of the Gothic Revival. Surely nuns would be especially good at such activity. After all, Victorian gentlewomen generally had some training in its basics. It was an expectation richly rewarded.[29] By 1900 the Bethany school had a worldwide reputation, and commissions to match. The Sisters' work can be found from Philadelphia to Paris. Comper insisted on only the best material — silk-damask and tapestry, and that combination was characteristic too of his younger contemporaries Frederick Charles Eden (1864–1944) and

Geoffrey Webb (1879–1954) who brought English church furnishing, by the 1930s, to an unparalleled height.[30]

But Comper looked beyond textiles to church furniture, to metalwork, statuary and painted glass, all with a view to making the church building a *Gesamtkunstwerk*, or total work of art, to borrow a Wagnerian expression. Designers of twentieth century aniconic church buildings of the International Modernist school, please note. Anyone who has anything to do with building, restoring, re-ordering or re-furbishing a church in the Latin West should read Comper's seminal essay 'On the Atmosphere of a Church', now conveniently available by reprinting in the standard study cum Gazetteer of his work.[31]

The Catholic Revival, with no shortage of pious benefactors at its disposal, did not baulk at painting entire ceilings in the churches 'Revivalists' had an opportunity to restore as well as those they built from the ground up.[32] Thomas Gambier Parry (1816–88) finished the painted ceiling of Ely Cathedral left incomplete by Henry Styleman L'Estrange (1815–62), an amateur artist who doubled up as a Norfolk squire. Parry also painted frescoes at Tewkesbury Abbey and in Gloucester cathedral.

The son and grandson of directors of the East India Company, he had been brought up in the opulent surroundings of Highnam Court, just west of Gloucester, and after Eton and Trinity, Cambridge, devoted himself to art collecting, notably of Italian Primitives, as well as perfecting his own method of fresco painting derived from the latter. Parry applied those techniques not least to the interior of Holy Innocents, Highnam, a church he built as a memorial to infants lost in childbirth by his wife.[33] His Anglo-Catholicism had been sealed by his marriage to the daughter of Henry Fynes Clinton, a leading Anglo-Papalist cleric, described by his biographer as issued from a 'typical clerical dynasty with close connections to the aristocracy'.[34]

William Dyce (1806–64) did much the same for All Saints, Margaret Street, where his frescoes are said to be reminiscent of Pinturrichio and Perugino, painters of the fifteenth century 'Perugian Renaissance'. An Aberdonian, educated at Marischal College and the Royal Academy schools in Edinburgh and London, Dyce's outlook was informed by lengthy excursions to Italy where he met, among others, the Nazarene painter Johann Friedrich Overbeck (1789–1869, the 'Nazarenes' were the likely archetype of the Pre-Raphaelite Brotherhood). He settled in Edinburgh, beginning to paint religious subjects as well as portraits.

In 1838 Dyce was made head of the newly founded Government School of design, later the Royal College of Art, and in 1844 Professor of Fine Art at King's College, London, positions that gave him great influence in art education in Britain. His later painting is described as Pre-Raphaelite in its spirituality — in effect, a sobriquet for Anglo-Catholicism. His services to the latter include his founding of the Motett Society with a view to rescuing and putting to liturgical use polyphonic music of the pre-Reformation era in Britain.

Painting in church can be, of course, on glass as well as on wood or canvas, though the techniques of painting and staining glass differ.[35] Charles Eamer Kempe (1837–1907) was indisputably the greatest mastermind in the art of stained glass thrown up by Tractarianism, and arguably the finest in the post-Reformation history of the arts in England.[36] Kempe was born in Brighton into an Evangelical family whose money had been made through wool-stapling and, subsequently, land. His father, childless by his first marriage, had taken *en secondes noces* the daughter of a Lord Mayor of London who bore him six children. Charles Eamer was the last, his father being almost eighty years old at his birth. On the death of Nathaniel Kemp (1759–1843, the final 'e' had not yet been added to the name), his house, Ovingdean Hall, was first leased and then sold to make possible the trust funds created for the children, whereupon his widow moved into lodgings. But money was found to pay for Charles's education at Rugby and Pembroke College, Oxford.

Kempe's aesthetic appreciation of glass appears to have been aroused by installation of new glass at Rugby chapel. It soon intensified once he came into contact with the Oxford Society for the Promotion of Gothic Art. That was at a time when Oxford city contained not only Street (as diocesan architect, he was currently planning SS Philip and James, on the Woodstock Road) but also Morris, Burne-Jones, and Rossetti, who were working together on their murals for the Oxford Union. Concurrently, Butterfield was building Balliol chapel, and the University Museum was under construction in the style of Venetian Gothic, supervised appropriately enough, if not always from close at hand, by the author of *The Stones of Venice*.

Kempe was especially drawn to the late mediaeval English glass in All Souls chapel and the east window of Merton, but most of all to St Mary's, Fairford, in the nearby Cotswolds, where he encountered the most complete cycle of mediaeval glass surviving in England. (It is ascribed to the court glazier of the early Tudors, Barnard Flower, died 1517). Coincidentally, but not ineffectually, Fairford was Keble's birthplace, where the same glass 'stamped on his mind the significance of symbol and imagery as channels of religious truth'.[37] In the opinion of Kempe's biographer, '[t]hese extramural expeditions were his real education at Oxford.'[38] He could not have known that one day he would be asked to oversee the entire redecoration of his own collegiate chapel at Pembroke. Based on a scheme of glass and statuary illustrative of the Incarnation and its reception, he would turn what was 'once as unadorned as a Welsh Calvinistic tabernacle into the most Catholic Chapel in Oxford'.[39]

After Newman

After Oxford, divine Providence threw him together with Bodley. Both had come to Anglo-Catholicism from families with low church backgrounds (though Bodley's brother William passed through Anglo-Catholicism to the Church of Rome, ending as a lecturer at Wiseman's seminary and school at Oscott). Both had problems with a stammer (it kept Kempe from Ordination). And both gravitated towards the last pre-Reformation phase of the history of glass.

What has been called Bodley's 'Anglo-Aestheticism' was attraction to the most refined of the Gothic forms, in various media. Kempe 'never troubled himself with labels, but found Bodley's colours, his use of natural forms, and his designs for fabrics and furnishings (whether incorporated into stained glass or executed in silks and damasks) entirely in accordance with his own.'[40] The painted ceilings and wall paintings Kempe created for Bodley's churches gained him a national reputation by his mid-thirties.

Establishing a London base for drawing offices on the Marylebone Road and also a glassworks (the site is now Mornington Crescent Underground station) he set out to form a circle of draughtsmen and artists trained in what would become the instantly recognizable 'Kempe style', enriching figural design in glass by adding architectural features or details of natural landscape but not in such a way as to detract from the centrality of the holy figures depicted. Techniques of silver-staining and the use of enamels gave a delicate clarity of line and extraordinary chromatic intensity. The antique white backgrounds for which he was also celebrated came later.

A number of Kempe's commissions were Yorkshire based, most ambitiously All Saints, Wakefield (now Wakefield cathedral), and the chapel at Castle Howard), probably reflecting the influence of Halifax, who as President of the English Church Union, was largely responsible for making the Kempe Studio the frescoists and glaziers *par excellence* of the Catholic Movement.[41] (On Kempe's death Halifax would be a pall-bearer at his Requiem Mass at St Mary Magdalene, Munster Square.) But Kempe was in demand more widely. In a single year, 1895 his craftsmen produced three south windows for the south transepts of three cathedrals: Southwark, Lichfield, and Hereford. Thanks to a Dean of Lichfield, Herbert Luckcock (1833–1909), who had been Vicar of All Saints, Cambridge, when the young Kempe worked there with Bodley, Morris, Burne-Jones, and others, Lichfield cathedral was particularly indebted to Kempe. That means not only for glass but for sculpted figures, stone and wooden reredoses, alabaster altar-rails, copes, frontals, and stoles. Lichfield also shows the beginning of early Renaissance influence on his work—a pointer to the future Kempe inheritance of Ninian Comper, though paradoxically Comper claimed to like only

Kempe's early work, rejecting as dreary his later preference for muted greens and greys.

Kempe's church contacts were catholic in the sense of the lower case 'c', a business requirement. But his Tractarian allegiance was shown in his own parish church at Old Place, Lindfield, in Sussex. Pushing through a reform to abolish pew rents and install free seating throughout was resented by locals, and, though, by the late 1880s, something of a local grandee, he was speedily ejected from his elected role as churchwarden.[42]

It has to be said, however, that the Arts and Crafts Movement had a point when they claimed about Kempe that an 'inceptor' was hardly the same as an artist. The cohort of artists who worked on his schemes were reduced in the Kempe Studio vision to mere 'artisans'.[43] Morris (and even more Burne-Jones) had more radical ideas of what to do with the mediaeval tradition than had Kempe, though Morris's company was, in its business structure, closer to Kempe's than Morris's admirers might have cared to admit. Yet the religious and not just financial motivation of Kempe's work speaks for itself in the theological and church-historical knowledge apparent in his designs and is summed up in a saying of George Herbert (1593–1633) that he loved to quote, 'Nothing lasts but the Church'.[44]

Literary arts

It was not necessary to wait for the 1927 conversion of T. S. Eliot to find the literary offspring of Anglo-Catholicism though Eliot's famous self-description in his *For Lancelot Andrewes* (a 'classicist in literature, royalist in politics, anglo-catholic in religion') has a lapidary character of straightforward self-identification it might not be easy to parallel elsewhere.[45] Novelists at least were a-plenty. One historian has listed no less than one hundred and twenty-eight Tractarian novels.[46] As the example of Keble would suggest, poets would not be in short supply, either. In what follows I consider five figures, all of whom have left behind a literary corpus of some stature. By way of compensation for the lack of ladies among the architects and designers, women predominate. Three women writers—Charlotte Yonge, Christina Rossetti, Rose Macaulay, stand over against two men: Eliot, and Charles Williams.

Tractarian novelists may have been ten-a-penny, but the case of Charlotte Yonge (1823–1901), whose work is currently undergoing a revival, was exceptional. From an old High Church, even non-Juror family, and thus highly susceptible to Tractarian solicitations,[47] she became Keble's principal *aide de camp* in his Hursley parish.[48] From her home in nearby Otterbourne Yonge used her imaginative writing, admired by an unlikely combination of Charles Kingsley (1819–75), George Eliot, the Pre-Raphaelites, and Alfred Lord Tennyson (1809–92), to communicate the 'Church principles' of which Keble approved. The role models she presented, through richly orchestrated dialogue carried on via a series of inter-linked novels in the Trollopian manner, were missionaries and slum priests, together with a select few heroically self-sacrificing women, from Joan of Arc (c. 1412–31) to Florence Nightingale (1820–1910). Both for women and for men she advocated the primacy of sacrifice within a context of family loyalty in an increasingly competitive society. As a 'handmaid of the Church' she encouraged docility to the Church and its pastors, not a trigger of enthusiasm for early twenty-first century readers but nevertheless when the pastors know their stuff theologically sound.

Her 'theo-political' ideal, like that of the Tractarians generally, was a welfare Church where processes of social improvement were ecclesiastical, not civil in character—except insofar as a beneficent Anglican Crown (not a religiously mixed Parliament) presided over their unfolding. The godless education provided by Board Schools was to be avoided at all costs. And why not when there were Church schools that could do the moral and spiritual task so much better?[49] But Yonge kept her theology in the background in her novels, following the Tractarian 'principle of reserve', though it emerged in its full force in such non-fiction works as *Musings over The Christian Year and Lyra Innocentium*, where her own reflections were mingled with *obiter dicta* from Keble's teaching. [50]

She was influential, not least through her bestseller, *The Heir of Redclyffe*. 'William Morris and Edward Burne-Jones, when undergraduates at Oxford, read the novel aloud to each other, chose Guy [its hero] as the object of their emulation, and took his medieval tastes and chivalric ideals as presiding elements in the formation of the Pre-Raphaelite Brotherhood.'[51] Knighthood helping the weak was often transposed by Anglo-Catholics into terms of priestly mission in urban slums. And lest this be thought impossibly esoteric, it can be added that the novel was reported to be the favoured reading of hospitalized junior officers in the Crimean War. Despite her agnosticism George Eliot (Mary Ann Evans, 1819–80) read aloud another of Yonge's novels to George Henry Lewes (1817–78), her partner, at Florence. The chaplain to Bishop Patteson, the martyred or at least murdered bishop of Melanesia, while on board the ship carrying the bishop's body away from the scene of the crime, consoled himself by reading her Tractarian-shaped fictions,[52]—not inappropriately since Yonge's chronicle of the death would become the high point of her two-volume biography of the man enriched, in the fashion of Victorian biographies, by complete reproductions of documents.[53]

As Keble's single most effective disciple, Yonge's central concern was the study of the formation of character through the disturbances of life, whether large or (especially) small. A connexion with Tractarian 'ethos' is unmistakable, including the persuasive portrayal of such virtues as truthfulness, self-sacrifice, humility, and filial piety—though her veneration of not only fathers but husbands and even brothers carried anti-Feminism to Olympian heights. She made virtuous people interestingly attractive, to more sophisticated readers' surprise. Despite her economy of style, she was not afraid of symbols: another feature learned from the theological style of the Oxford Fathers.

Charlotte Yonge's Anglo-Catholicism was the motivation of her writing. She had no financial incentive. Well to do and without a family to support, she gave much of her royalties to building church schools, restoring church buildings, supporting new Sisterhoods, or funding Anglo-Catholic missionary activity through the Universities' Mission to Central Africa, the Melanesian Mission to the Pacific, and the pre-Tractarian but high church 'SPG', the 'Society for the Propagation of the Gospel in Foreign Parts'.[54] '[S]he was fortunate in believing that her highest enjoyment was also her God-given duty, that she was called to testify *Pro Ecclesia Dei*, which she understood as the Church of England in its Tractarian aspect.'[55]

For Christina Rossetti (1830–94)—so opined William Holden Hutton, Archdeacon of Northampton and Reader in Indian History at Oxford (1860–1930), author of the chapter on the Oxford Movement and its literati in the *Cambridge History of English Literature*—the 'Catholic theology of the English Church was the very breath of life'.[56] No English poet, Hutton declared, had synthesized the aspirations of religion with such exquisite expressiveness. A. M. Allchin, introducing the 1963 reprinting of Ollard's *A Short History of the Oxford Movement* (from 1913, but with a revised edition of 1932 in time for the Movement's centenary), feared that such praise of Rossetti—cited approvingly by Ollard—would strike the modern reader as one of the most dated features of the latter's book. Allchin did not reckon with the rise of the Feminist criticism which has shot women poets of various times and places to dizzy heights.[57] And, like others, he may have confused the deliberate modesty of Rossetti's persona, actual and literary, with a failure in audacity.[58]

Christina Rossetti was born in London to a political exile from Bourbon Naples, better known for his son, the Pre-Raphaelite artist Dante Gabriel Rossetti, and, like Christina and Dante Gabriel, a poet. Gabriele Rossetti (1783–1854) held the chair of Italian at King's College, London, and was known as a Dante scholar, though his major work, 'The Mystery of Platonic Love in the Middle Ages', a study of mediaeval esotericism in several volumes, was only posthumously published (in Italian). Gabriele's wife, Frances Polidori (1800–86), could be considered a suitable match. Her father had been secretary to the dramatist Vittorio

Alfieri (1749–1803), the founder of the tragic theatre in Italy, while her mother, Anna Maria Pierce, an Englishwoman (which explains Christina Rossetti's Anglicanism), was the daughter of a successful writing-teacher. Lord Byron's friend and physician John William Polidori (1795–1821), an early product of Ampleforth College, and author of the first known English vampire story, was one of Frances Polidori's brothers. Though her Byronic uncle was dead before Christina Rossetti entered the world, with a family background like that it would probably have been difficult not to become a writer.[59]

From 1843, the year after she began to record and date her poems, Christina Rossetti was a regular attender, with her sister and mother, at a church opened just a few years previously. Situated in the then borough of St Pancras, this was Christ Church, Albany Street, a Tractarian stronghold, with William Dodsworth as Vicar and Pusey as an occasional preacher. When she reached adulthood Christina's confessor, discovered through the Pre-Raphaelite artist William Bell Scott (1811–90), was a figure already encountered in these pages: Richard Frederick Littledale, the robustly Ritualist curate of St Mary the Virgin, Crown Street, Soho, and contributor of fiery articles to the *Church Times*. Littledale was also, perhaps more interestingly to a pious girl with aesthetic sensibilities, the author of *Catholic Ritual in the Church of England: Scriptural, Reasonable, Lawful*.[60] Published in 1865, it may possibly have influenced her writings as it certainly did the settings of her worship.

Her first book of devotional verse, the 1874 *Annus Domini*, sub-titled 'A prayer for each day of the year, founded on Holy Scripture',[61] received a stamp of approval from Henry William Burrows (died 1898), Perpetual Curate at Albany Street, another London Tractarian of the second generation and the historian of that parish.[62] But Burrows warned Rossetti that, since all her poems were addressed exclusively to the second Trinitarian Person, it might be better if they were treated as supplementary to other devotional sources. That did not prevent several of her poems appearing in Anglo-Catholic anthologies such as the collections by Orby Shipley (1832–1916), *Lyra Mystica*,[63] and *Lyra Eucharistica*.[64]

The background of Rossetti's writing was undoubtedly Tractarian, though her devotional poetry is often under-represented in secular-minded anthologies from more recent years. 'Hers is a poetry that grows out of the act of worship, poetry that is frequently tied to established forms of worship and liturgical observance.'[65] *Annus Domini*, linking devotional life to the cycle of seasons and feasts, had been dependent on Keble's steady conviction of the close nexus between poetry and religion. Keble's 'bedrock principle that poetry is the expression of intense religious longing finds no more complete exemplification than in the poetry of Christina Rossetti'.[66] A 'Christian Year' could indeed be put together from her verse, so prominent in it is the sequence of the annual liturgical round, centred as the latter is on the Flesh-taking, Paschal Mystery, and expected Parousia of God the Word.

Rossetti's passionate Christological focus replicated the 'intense Incarnationalism' of Keble and Isaac Williams (1802–65), the early Tractarian who should have been—had *odium theologicum* not intervened—Keble's successor as Professor of Poetry at Oxford.[67] And that distinctive Tractarian 'ethos' whereby moral and intellectual faculties enter into mutual relations permeates her 1892 verse sequence *The Face of the Deep. A Devotional Commentary on the Apocalypse*,[68] where 'Rossetti's Tractarian-informed suggestion is that a right apprehension of God enables believers to shape themselves into vehicles "trembling of love" and enlarge their hearts as they "worship Thee"'.[69] Her prose, typically interspersed with poems and laid out in a Missal-like typographical form, echoes 'Kebelianism' inasmuch as the prosaic strains after the condition not only of poetry but of Liturgy.

In the 1860s Rossetti became more identified with another Tractarian center: All Saints, Margaret Street. Her sister Maria had entered the All Saints Sisterhood as an 'Associate' in that decade's opening year. In 'Divers Worlds: Time and Eternity', included in her final (1893) edition of *Verses*,[70] she aims to inter-relate inward and outward worship in a characteristically Tractarian manner. Coming as 'Divers Worlds' does from her Margaret Street period (after 1876 she would more commonly be found at another 'Christ Church', this time in Bloomsbury's Woburn Square), the attractive suggestion has been made that its two stanzas are intended to mirror William Dyce's chancel frescoes and the celestial blue and stellar gold of the chancel vaulting in the newly rebuilt Butterfield church of All Saints. 'Just as the frescoes depict the saints looking up to an enthroned Christ, Rossetti's lyric envisions the upward longing for those called to be saints... Enabling recognition of the "deep pause" within which glimpses of eternity are realized, the sounds of the church are imbued with transcendental significance. The "dimness where the anthems are" invokes the haze of incense accompanying the service and suggests that the sight and sound of the church represent a "dim" analogical shadow of the eternal.'[71] It was the 'Alexandrian' symbolism of Newman, Keble, Pusey in another form, and a testimony to the lasting influence of Neale and the Cambridge Camden Society.

But Rossetti is also a cosmic poet so much so that she has been regarded as a prototype ecologist. This too can be called Tractarian. 'As a movement that saw nature as a codified revelation of the Trinity, Tractarianism directed the believer to the things of the world, floral, animal, mineral, as part of a network in which every being was connected with the divine.'[72] It was a religious inspiration combined with other factors: the Pre-Raphaelite aesthetic, Platonic philosophy, her inherited Italian culture, and, a featured shared with Manning, the anti-vivisection movement.[73]

The First World War was a watershed for writers as for English society at large. Thomas Stearns Eliot (1888–1965) in his principal poems *The Waste Land* and *Four Quartets* can be regarded as offering a diagnosis of the sickness of Western culture long detached from its Christian roots — thus the *Waste Land*, from 1922, and a prescription for recovery — in *Four Quartets*, from 1936 to 1942.[74]

A hard going Eliot had of it, to move to Anglo-Catholicism from Unitarian roots, already half pulled up by sophisticated scepticism: a journey comparable in its own fashion to that memorably described in his 1927 *The Journey of the Magi*, written in the year of his entry into the Church.[75] Through a tortuous process of intellectual enquiry, accompanied in its latter phase by a traumatic process of personal suffering bound up with his marriage, Eliot reached the moment when, to the astonishment of the Bloomsbury set, leaders with him in literary Modernism, he could ask for Baptism and Confirmation, and began the diligent round of devout attendance at his South Kensington parish which made him, by way of his professional work as editor at Faber's publishing house, his literary criticism, authorship of Church plays, and contributions to Anglo-Catholic social thinking of the 'Christendom' variety, something of a hero of the Catholic movement, albeit a self-effacing one.

Whereas Eliot's paternal grandfather had moved to St Louis, Missouri, becoming, as minister and academic, a noted figure in the advocacy of social reform, Eliot himself was drawn back to the family's New England origins. Enrolled at Harvard, he learned to despise Romanticism for its anarchic individualism and became a convert to literary classicism instead. (In his maturity he would turn to the Neo-Thomism of Maritain to find a basis for such classicism in both aesthetic and metaphysical terms.[76]) After a stay in Paris where he heard the vitalist thinker Henri Bergson (1859–1941) whose metaphysic was at least a cosmology of sorts, and occasionally attended High Mass at the Madeleine (an Irish nursemaid had taken him as a child to Catholic churches), Eliot made his return to a Harvard no longer, as at its foundation, a stronghold of theological Puritanism but still a religiously interested academic institution.

At this juncture, William James (1842–1910) of *The Varieties of Religious Experience* fame was prominent in the philosophy school.[77] Pursuing one possible 'variety', Eliot took up the study of Sanskrit and the religions of South Asia. He was seeking an absolute point outside the flow of historical time, having rejected pragmatism, materialism, and even the Idealism which, in the shape of Bradley's 'Absolute Idealism' he would go on to study, from 1914 onwards, at Merton College, Oxford.

The lodestar was the right juxtaposition of the eternal and temporal orders and not (*pace* the Eastern religions and Idealism) the ultimate abolition of the distinction between them. Eliot had read Evelyn Underhill's *Mysticism* shortly after it appeared in 1911, and noted not just her definition of her topic, the 'expression of the innate tendency of the human spirit towards complete harmony with the transcendental order', but also her companion assertion that the 'dogmas of Christianity are necessary to an adequate description of mystical experience'.[78] Thus alerted, he found the dogma he was looking for in the Incarnation, where created and Uncreated are united without either separation or confusion.

The dogma was taught by an authority-bearing community, the Church, which claimed for its sacramental life an ongoing extension of the Incarnation moment. Now, after World War One, settled in England, that meant for Eliot an Anglo-Catholic, not a Roman Catholic, commitment. In his view, a religion needs an historic culture to inhabit, and the historic religious culture of the post-Reformation English was essentially Anglican. That did not prevent him from gravitating towards the Anglo-Papalist end of the Anglo-Catholic spectrum as is shown by his seemingly perfectly serious proposal to enter the monastic community at Nashdom Abbey. But there his second marriage intervened.[79] He had not intended to go so far when, in circumstances of some secrecy, he was baptized at Holy Trinity, Finstock, by William Force Stead (1884–1967), the chaplain of Worcester College, Oxford, on the feast, in the Church of England's calendar, of St Peter the Apostle and driven the next day to the Bishop of Oxford's private chapel to be confirmed.

How to chart the relation between the Eternal and the temporal, guided by the Incarnation, itself not just an historical event but an invitation to continuing personal and corporate transformation: this would be the nerve of Eliot's post-conversion writing. '[M]ost of his writing—and, we can imagine, his spiritual life, is about the difficulty of attaining to worthiness for the beatific vision and, more positively, about the celebration of the rare intersections of the spiritual and the temporal, here and now, in an incarnational interpretation of creation and of human life in its midst.'[80] In this matter he had, in his own words in the journal *Christendom*, 'absolute ideals' but 'moderate expectations'.[81] So it is not surprising that even his most confessional poetry, such as the 1930 *Ash-Wednesday*,[82] is as much about the difficulty of faith as it is about either faith's own act or faith's intrinsic content: what Thomism would call the *fides qua* and the *fides quae*. Eliot would consider that only appropriate for those *in via*, on the troublesome way to becoming, hopefully, saints. That did not prevent his saying that the 'division between those who accept, and those why deny, the Christian revelation I take to be the most profound division between human beings'.[83]

The Eliot scholar Barry Spurr was warned by Dame Helen Gardner (1908–86), *doyenne* of Eliot studies in her day, against assuming Eliot's Christianity was full faith Anglo-Catholicism. His research disabused her. Eliot was punctilious in his attendance at Mass (in the Roman rite, according to the *English Missal* and *Ritual Notes*), whether on Sundays and holydays in a service enacted by celebrant, deacon, and sub-deacon, with much Latin polyphony, or more simply in the form of Low Mass on weekdays. He was rigorous about fasting before Communion and, on Fridays, careful to abstain from meat. He made his Confession regularly if infrequently, first to Francis Underhill (1878–1943, he was cousin to the author of *Mysticism* and a future Bishop of Bath and Wells), then to a clergyman-baronet, Sir Percy Maryon-Wilson (1898–1965), Vicar of St Mary's, Somers Town (Sir Percy was a 'Guardian' of the Marian Shrine at Walsingham) before transferring care of his conscience to the priests at St Silas the Martyr, Kentish Town. Retreats in monastic settings played a significant part in his life, whether at Cowley, Kelham, or Nashdom. It was a prayerful life in which the Rosary figured prominently: he was given a chaplet by Pius XII (pope 1939–58) at an audience in early January 1948. His advanced Mariology (not for him Austin Farrer's 1960 rejection—at a sermon at Pusey House—of Mary's Assumption into glory[84]) appears in *Ash-Wednesday*, where the Virgin as Mediatrix accompanies the self in its search for redemption. 'The single Rose/ Is now the Garden/ Where all loves end.' The figure of the Lord's Mother is presented subtly, her identity semi-occluded, for Eliot's poetry works by intimations, not declamations.

Eliot's Church drama is a partial exception to this rule, as the Archbishop's Christmas morning sermon in the 1935 play *Murder in the Cathedral* demonstrates.[85] Audaciously, it was a sermon where Eliot adapted Cranmer's language to place on the lips of another Thomas, St Thomas of Canterbury, a robustly Catholic doctrine of Eucharistic sacrifice, familiar to Anglo-Catholics in the audience. They knew about the 'Sacrifice of the altar'. The reduction of the saint of Canterbury, Chaucer's 'holy blissful martyr', to the status of 'Becket' and the order to destroy all evidence of his cult—owing to the theo-political implications of a martyrdom for the liberties of the Church and notably the freedom to communicate with the Church at Rome—had been, a defining moment in the Henrician Reformation, as Eliot was hardly unaware. If it suggests Eliot's looking beyond the English Channel to Latin Christendom that would not be misleading. The debt he owed philosophically to the Neo-Thomism conventionally defined by Leo XIII's encyclical *Aeterni Patris* of 1879 is widely recognised.[86]

Charles Williams (1886–1945) was a Londoner whose historical—and mystical—imagination was stimulated by a move to St Albans, then a market town, mediaeval in appearance and dominated by its massive Abbey.[87] His father ran a shop there, selling artists' equipment on what had been the site of the Roman *Verulamium*. Williams was more than conventionally devout and when on marriage he moved back to London regularly attended St Silas the Martyr, Kentish Town, taking up responsibilities as a sidesman in the church where Eliot, on his conversion to Christianity in its Anglo-Catholic incarnation, was wont, after a certain stage in life, to make his sacramental Confession.

Williams' attendance at University College, London, had been cut short by the inability of his parents to pay the fees, so he was fortunate in getting a post at Oxford University Press's London headquarters, Amen House, near St Paul's cathedral—an ideal environment for the poet, dramatist, novelist and theological writer that he became. He rose with remarkable smoothness from proofreader to editor, selecting and commissioning books for the Press which saw itself as the highest quality publisher in the world.

Meanwhile, owing to his love for the ceremoniousness of ritual activity, presumably triggered at St Silas, and a fascination with advanced states of mystical, or at any rate para-normal, consciousness, he had become initiated into two of the esoteric societies rampant in the period around the First World War. Participation in the 'Fellowship of the Rosy Cross', substantially Christian, despite its Rosicrucian-derived name, was a regular feature of his week all the time he was to live in London. His association with the distinctly neo-pagan Order of the Golden Dawn, a body both occultist and Masonic in character, was at once more informal and a carefully guarded secret.

The 'Rosy Cross' connexion assured a continuing concern with the mystical dimension of Christianity to which he gave a theological turn all his own via the inter-related concepts of 'co-inherence' and 'substitution'. 'Co-inherence' was extended from its historical rooting in Trinitarian theology and Christology to anthropology, for human beings are, or can be, 'in' each other by an intimate mutual identification. 'Substitution' was likewise extended, from use in the theology of the Atonement (the 'vicarious substitution' of the God-man for sinners), to the domain of human relations. Williams applied St Paul's advice to 'carry one another's burdens' (Galatians 6:2) beyond practical considerations to mental states of suffering or joy.

William's poetic output was encouraged by Alice Meynell (1847–1922), a Hampstead poet once considered for the post of poet laureate (she would have been its first female holder). With her husband she had recognized, and rescued from drug-induced destitution, the Roman Catholic religious poet Francis Thompson (1859–1907). Williams' early poetry might well be compared stylistically to Thompson's writing. Its principal theme, the analogy between erotic love and mystical union with God or what he came to call his 'Romantic Theology', was drawn, however, so far as literary influences go, from Thompson's co-religionist Coventry Patmore (1823–96), where its expression was rather more muted, or perhaps coded. Not until he broke free of Meynell's influence could he abandon the style of his strictly metrical poems, over-rich (like Thompson's) in archaic diction, and strike out on the free verse which, in writing inspired by the Arthurian cycle as well as his mystical and theological ideas, made him a leading Modernist poet of the stature of Eliot, Ezra Pound (1885–1972), or David Jones (1895–1964). His fellow poet W. H. Auden (1907–73) wrote to him 'You're the only one since Dante who has found out how to make poetry of theology and history'.[88]

Williams' plays, almost always on religious themes, formed part of the revival of Christian drama to which Dorothy L. Sayers also belonged, but were far more formally experimental, notably in *Seed of Adam*, a Nativity play like no other, but reminiscent in its allegorical figures of the mummers' plays of the Middle Ages.[89] His novels, described as 'spiritual shockers', orchestrate the theme of metaphysical good and evil and their combat, and combine conventional settings in London or the southern English countryside with exotic explorations of unusual states of consciousness and the possibilities and limits of magical power. Their common theme is order, its disintegration, and possible reconstitution.[90] The influence of the Jewish Kabbala on Williams' outlook is apparent, as is that of the fourteenth century mystic Julian of Norwich whose book, *Revelations of Divine Love*, was continuing its rise to devotional popularity in Anglican as well as Roman Catholic circles of the time. Despite his idiosyncrasies and a series of passionate, if non-consummated, relationships with young women at the Press (he thought sexual energy could be transmuted into spiritual), William's orthodoxy was not impugned by the 'Inklings'—above all, C. S. Lewis and J. R. Tolkien (1892–1973)—when the London branch of Oxford University Press was evacuated to Southfield House, a mansion on the north-east side of Oxford, in expectation of German bombing of the capital.[91] Williams became a welcome member of that now celebrated circle of scholars, writers, talkers. Indeed, he became the 'Third Inkling', in due hierarchical ordering after those two household names.[92]

Williams' theological works, notably *He Came Down from Heaven*, an exposition of the Apostles' Creed,[93] *The Descent of the Dove*, subtitled, 'A History of the Holy Spirit in the Church',[94] and *The Forgiveness of Sins*,[95] are a mine of original insight, or at least expression, and integrate into a theology of the Communion of Saints the notions of co-inherence and substitution he made so intensely his own. Their immediate success contrasts with the fate of his incisive studies of English poetry, too methodologically sophisticated to find a ready readership at the time but praised half a century later by an exigent judge, Geoffrey Hill (1932–2016, Professor of Poetry at Oxford from 2010 to 2015).⁹⁶ Still in the line of literary criticism, Williams' Dante study, *The Figure of Beatrice*,⁹⁷ was shaped by his notion of two 'ways' to God, the Way of Affirmation and the Way of Negation: discovering God in and through the finite, or apart from the finite. It followed from his elegant if antinomic maxim for the God-world relationship, 'This also is Thou; neither is this Thou'.

Coming now to the last of this quintet of figures: on both sides of her descent Rose Macaulay (1881–1958) came from Anglican clerical families though her father, George Campbell Macaulay (1852–1915) who was briefly a Fellow of Trinity, Cambridge, before becoming a professor of English language and literature at Aberysywth (he edited a late mediaeval author, John Gower), described himself as an 'Anglo-agnostic'.⁹⁸ It was left to her high church mother (daughter of the Vicar of Barington, a Cambridgeshire village) to instil in her the rudiments of the faith. In Rose's blissful Mediterranean childhood on the Ligurian Riviera (a warmer climate was needed for her mother's health), she became more familiar, if uncomprehendingly so, with Latin-language Roman services than with Anglican. (The Macaulays made a habit of avoiding expatriates.) From her father she inherited her sceptical temperament, useful for the many discordant voices to be heard in her novels, which spin together personalities and ideas.

When George Macaulay was appointed to a Cambridge lectureship and the family left Wales they acquired a house at Great Shelford where the local incumbent was Anglo-Catholic, though Rose also attended St Giles', Cambridge, then under Catholic Revival management. She became actively involved in church life as Sunday school teacher, parish visitor, and participant in a scheme to identify and re-house orphans. From 1912 to 1922 she made frequent visits to the Cowley Fathers' London base, St Edward's House, seeking from her confessor, Lucius Cary (1866–1950), clear answers to ethical conundrums.

In 1922 there came a change. Her successfully concealed love affair with a married man led to a temporary withdrawal from Anglo-Catholic life. Gerald O'Donovan (1871–1942) was a civil servant and writer who had suppressed his previous identity. He had been Jeremiah O'Donovan, priest of the diocese of Clonfert, responsible for the Arts and Crafts decoration of St Brendan's cathedral, Loughrea, and for many initiatives favouring the development of the somewhat moribund Irish Catholic Church and civil society of the late nineteenth century. The entanglement gave her a lasting sense of guilt over the injustice she had done to Beryl, O'Donovan's wife, much younger than her husband and a delicate flower of the Anglo-Irish ascendancy.

Rose Macaulay's 1950 novel *The World is my Wilderness*, where the ruins of bombed-out London becomes a metaphor of her central character's own interior desert, presaged her return to the Church after Gerald's death.[99] Resuming a long broken off conversation with a Cowley Father, John Hamilton Cowper Thompson (1877–1960), by then transferred to the Society's New England house in Boston, Massachusetts, she returned to sacramental practice and became a regular communicant at Mayfair's Grosvenor Chapel, South Audley Street (where she knelt in a pew behind John Betjeman's) as well as at St Paul's, Knightsbridge, the mother church of St Barnabas, Pimlico.

Macaulay's masterpiece *The Towers of Trebizond* attests her continuing struggle between faith and doubt, locating that struggle in a decidedly Anglo-Catholic environment.[100] She somehow combined a degree of doctrinal apophaticism with Revival fervour. The 'towers' of her title symbolize the Church as what she called 'that strange bright city on the hill... barred from all but those who desire it more than anything in the world'.[101] Her irritation with Roman Catholic dismissal of the Anglican patrimony, in papistical apologetics prosecuted with much vigour in the pre-ecumenical 1950s, is rather tediously obsessive in her letters to Johnson. She was of course posthumously vindicated by Benedict XVI (pope 2005–13) who in his Apostolic Constitution *Anglicanorum coetibus* established a corporate life for Anglo-Catholics in union with the Holy See.[102] But there is nothing tedious about the wit and wisdom of her last novel—though, to be sure, humour and compassion, or at least pity, had been the principal features of her imaginative writing throughout.

Her eye for the many eccentricities of Anglo-Catholic clergymen in an England which still appreciated eccentricity comes over in her portrait of the 'Rev. the Hon. Hugh Chantry-Pigg, an ancient bigot, who had run a London church several feet higher than St Mary's Bourne Street [Halifax's church when in London] and some inches above even St Magnus the Martyr [its decoration by Fynes-Clinton was the only radiant note in Eliot's *The Waste Land*], and, being now just retired, devoted his life to conducting very High retreats and hunting for relics of saints, which he collected for the private oratory in his Oxford manor house.'[103]

Hymnography and music

Hymns were not, historically, a feature of the Church of England's Liturgy, unlike in the Divine Office of the Latin Church. The *Book of Common Prayer* makes no provision for them. They had entered the Anglican mainstream through Methodism—which makes it the more surprising that the Tractarian Revival should possess not the least of its glories in the hymns it produced.

When licence for ministry was refused John Mason Neale by that doughty Evangelical, Bishop Charles Sumner of Winchester (later Archbishop of Canterbury), obliging him to abandon his diaconal curacy at St Nicholas, Guildford, where the rector was allowing him a free hand, the future archbishop of Canterbury unwittingly released Neale for a life of founding Sisterhoods, introducing advanced liturgical practices in chapels and oratories, and writing studies of the Eastern Churches to sustain a Catholic view of Church history, together with historical novels serving the same end. Last but certainly by no means least in that *catena* of achievements came Neale's copious work in the translation of the hymns of the Latin, Byzantine and Syrian Christian traditions.[104]

Neale's periodic ill-health necessitated lengthy stays on various sunny and relaxed 'riviera' locations from Cornwall to Madeira. That was the context in which he began to write both the hymns and the novels and planned his *A History of the Holy Eastern Church*. To serve as a priest—and without a liturgical life, his hymnody had no context—he needed a charge. In 1846 one was found through aristocratic connexions, and he became Warden of Sackville College—not an educational institution but a group of almshouses with a couple of dozen inmates. Suspicious of his Anglo-Catholicism, even in this miniscule pastoral setting, Neale's bishop, now Ashurst Turner Gilbert of Chichester (1786–1870), a turncoat former Tractarian, inhibited him from ministerial practice between the years 1847 and 1863. Gilbert had been shocked at Neale's iconographic improvements, the 'frippery with which Mr Neale had transformed the simplicity of the chapel at Sackville College into an imitation of the degraded superstitions of an erroneous Church'.[105] So in future Neale would celebrate the Eucharist privately for his almsmen. Notice, though, how in 1850 the high church Alexander Penrose Forbes (1817–75), Bishop of Brechin—who himself got into hot water, this time with other Scottish bishops, for his Catholicizing views—thought so highly of John Mason Neale as to offer him the Deanery of Perth with its brand-new cathedral, the first to be built in Scotland since the Reformation.

A major twentieth century monograph on Neale interprets his hymn-writing as, above all, his personal reaction to the Gorham Judgment (see Chapter 2 above). If the Thirty-Nine Articles are ambiguous and the clergy unreliable, then teach the people true doctrine by another route. Teach them hymns stuffed full of orthodox doctrine from beginning to end. And it is indeed the case that Neale's essay on the history of hymnography appeared in the immediate wake of that 'Judgment', in 1851. Where the church jurisprudence of modern Canterbury has failed, let the hymnody of ancient Salisbury succeed!

But in the upshot Neale did not really adhere to the strict Sarum-oriented line he laid out in that text. 'When the attention of the Ecclesiological Society was first turned to the subject of Hymnology', he had written, 'we could only act on the same principle as we have endeavoured to carry out in all things: that is, if we were Catholics in the first place we were English Catholics in the second. We felt that we could look for our hymns to only one source, the offices or rather, to use the proper old, as well as modern word, the *services* of the older English Church, and of the uses of that Church the ritual of Sarum had so incomparably the most authority that its hymns, we felt, were to be regarded as our special inheritance.'[106]

On the hymnic road Neale explored in over four hundred hymns, 'Sequences', and carols, the great majority are translations not only from Latin but also from Greek and Syriac, with some carols versions of home-spun vernacular material. In 1856, accordingly, he was invited to help Keble compile a hymnal under the aegis of Bishop Hamilton of Salisbury—until Gladstone's first premiership the only reliable supporter of Tractarians on the Bench, and thus (in Neale's eyes) a worthy successor to the mediaeval bishops of that see.

He began work by collecting together the Latin sources as in the 1851 *Hymni Ecclesiae*, the sub-title of which told the Latinate reader that its contents were 'drawn from some French, German, Spanish and Portuguese Missals and Breviaries,[107] to which he added in 1852 his *Sequentiae*,[108] an anthology of liturgical poems used in some abundance prior to the liturgical reading of the Gospel until the reforming efforts of the Council of Trent reduced their number to a handful. This time they were advertised as 'collected from German, English, French and some other mediaeval Missals'. Neale realised that what was needed were English hymns to complement the reviving Liturgy, so from these collections he offered to the public his own masterly translations, initially under the title *Mediaeval Hymns and Sequences*.[109] They include translations in regular use today, in Roman as well as Anglican practice. 'Blessed city heavenly Salem', 'Christ is made the sure foundation', 'All glory, laud and honour', 'The royal banners forward go'.

Then came a cooperative effort by the Ecclesiological Society—the successor to the Cambridge Camden Society after the latter ceased to be an all-round if antiquarian Anglican enterprise and reconceived itself under Anglo-Catholic auspices for a new age. The result was *The Hymnal Noted*, all its contents taken from Latin,[110] and set to plainchant by Thomas Helmore (1811–90), one of the compilers of *Hymns Ancient and Modern*. It took its name from Helmore's earlier *The Psalter Noted*.[111] Neale was guided in his choice of texts by indications provided in the Sarum service books. His 1853 *Carols for Christmastide* and 1854 *Carols for Eastertide* were drawn from traditional sources though 'Good King Wenceslas' was, as pavement artists say, all his own work.

The fruits of Neale's Greek-language research were offered to the church public in the 1862 *Hymns of the Eastern Church*. That again includes classics: 'The Day of Resurrection', 'O Happy Band of Pilgrims', 'The Day is Past and Over'.[112] The background to these hymns in Greek patristics, and the Byzantine theologians, as reflected in Eastern Orthodox liturgical books was not so familiar to Westerners. So Neale added helpful notes and a substantial introduction. He was appealing to the what the twentieth century Roman pontiff John Paul II (pope 1978–2005) would call Christendom's 'other lung'. 'The eighteen quarto volumes of Greek Church-poetry can only at present be known to the English reader by my little book. Yet surely, if in the future Hymnal of the English Church we are to build an eclectic superstructure on the foundation of the Sarum book, the East ought to yield its full share of compositions.'[113]

Neale's ulterior motive was even more far-seeing. He 'wanted to use Greek hymns as a model of what he considered religion untainted by the Liberal Protestant theology of his day'.[114] It was in this noble cause that he ransacked Damascene, Cosmas the Melodist, Andrew of Crete, Theodore of Studios and his brother Joseph of Thessaloniki, and the Italo-Hellenes of Syracuse. The sheer length and complexity of the material, unlike the terse Latin hymns, made his versions adaptations rather than translations in the proper sense of the word. They were the better for it in terms of their effect.

A survey of Victorian hymnography summed up, appropriating Neale's own perspective: '[H]is work created a solid foundation for Anglican hymnody that was Orthodox, Catholic, objective and doctrinally sound as well as deeply devotional… Thanks to Neale, hymn singing now became an Anglo-Catholic as well as an evangelical passion within the Church of England.'[115] Ian Bradley was a Scots Presbyterian author looking in from outside. An Anglican author looking from within put it differently, 'He explodes out of the landscapes of Victorian Anglo-Catholicism and shows us a marvellous sense of expansion, rich in fascination, imagination, generosity and intellectual ambition.'[116] For J. R. Watson, who has revolutionized the study of hymnography by bringing to it the specific methods of literary critical close reading, Neale was unconditionally the 'most important Anglican hymn writer'—granted, that is, the ambivalent position of Charles Wesley in the Church's regard.[117] Neale was 'engaged in a massive and innovative project, an attempt to swing the writing and appreciation of hymns away from a post-Reformation individualism into a matter of deeper impersonality'.[118]

Neale's hymns, especially when combined with the impact of Keble's *The Christian Year* (some favoured items of which entered the huge number of hymnals produced between 1821 and 1850—Watson calculated two per year!),[119] inspired an entire generation of Victorian hymn writers and in the process put paid to the notion that the English hymn was the 'badge of Dissent', or, at best, the hallmark of Anglican Evangelicalism.[120]

So far as the wider church public was concerned these anthologies were distinctly transient selections until the appearance of the first edition of *Hymns Ancient and Modern* in 1861. Over sixty entries were Neale's work, far more than any other author or translator. Hymns of Latin origin were almost a majority—but not quite. So the hymnal, while lambasted as a 'Tractarian manifesto', escaped a general tarring with a partisan brush.[121] It did indeed have a Tractarian editor, Henry Williams Baker (1821–77), baronet, and Vicar of Monkland in Herefordshire. Among his contributions was 'Shall we not love thee, Mother dear', worthy competitor to Faber's over-the-top compositions where exalted Mariological feeling is concerned. But Baker also wrote the more sober Christological hymn, 'The King of love my Shepherd is'. Described as structured in the spirit of the English Prayer Book, *Hymns Ancient and Modern* was a huge success. Drawing on the flowering of hymnody in the 1870s and 80s, it was able to expand without loss of quality, adding an 'Appendix' in 1868, while a 'Revised and Enlarged Edition' appeared in 1875, and a 'Supplement' in 1889. A further supplement in 1916 was edited by Sydney Nicholson (1875–1947), the founder of the School of English Church Music (now the Royal School of Church Music), whose own setting of the Mass, the 'Communion Service in G major', was chiefly used in Anglo-Catholic churches though his anthems soon entered the repertoire of the mainstream cathedrals.

The new hymn writers—'modern' rather than 'ancient'—were themselves often Anglo-Catholics, as with William Chatterton Dix (1837–98) whose 1867 *Altar Songs* takes for a sub-title, 'Verses on the Holy Eucharist intended for the use of those who believe in, revere and love the Doctrine of the Real Presence'.[122] Dix's 1871 follow-up, *A Vision of All Saints*, reflected the liturgical seasons, Epiphany-tide in 'As with gladness men of old', and Ascensiontide in 'Alleluia, sing to Jesus', both now equally familiar to Roman Catholic congregations.[123] William Bright, Ignatius Leycester Lyne's old teacher, contributed the great vernacular hymn on the Eucharistic Sacrifice, 'And now, O Father, mindful of the love'. John Bacchus Dykes (1823–76), Vicar of St Oswald's, Durham, a former Evangelical who suffered for his Tractarian conversion, offered the editor a choice of several hundred hymn tunes, criticized by later musicologists for their extreme chromaticism. One such, Dykes' *Gerontius*, written as a setting for Newman's 'Praise to the Holiest', was used at Gladstone's funeral. Thus *Hymns Ancient and Modern* had many beauties. But in the early twentieth century the book met for the first time a serious rival.

Anglo-Catholics and the Arts

The *English Hymnal*, edited by Percy Dearmer and published in 1906 by Oxford University Press, included the most modern Anglo-Catholic writers, such as Henry Scott Holland, who provided 'Judge eternal, throned in splendour', and G. K. Chesterton, represented by 'O God of earth and altar'. Both reflected the social concerns of the two writers, along the lines of the Anglo-Catholic social movement at large, as described in Chapter 6 above. The principal difference was owed, however, to the musical genius of Vaughan Williams. Neale's hymns, when drawn from the English vernacular, had already favoured anything that might suggest the oral culture of the English Middle Ages. But between Neale and Dearmer there had intervened the English folk song revival. In his highly successful collaboration with Vaughan Williams, Dearmer wanted to revive not only the Latin hymnody, vernacularized, of the pre-Reformation *Ecclesia Anglicana* (Neale had already attempted that) but also the musical traditions of English folklore, which, at a pinch, could be regarded as survivors of a Catholic 'Merrie England'. The traditional carols and other musical items, often orally transmitted, were certainly innocent of the teachings of the Magisterial Reformers—even if some English nursery rhymes are said to carry traces of Reformation propaganda. But where Protestant sensibilities were concerned the editors sailed close to the wind. Invocations of the Mother of God or the saints in some of the hymnody meant that, on publication, the *English Hymnal* was banned in various Church of England dioceses. The four hymns deemed most objectionable were later dropped from an 'abridged' edition—euphemistic term!—in 1907.

In this connexion it is impossible to omit mention of Sabine Baring-Gould (1834–1924), best known to Victorians as a prolific novelist, but also a writer of hymns. Offspring of a 'county' family in Devonshire, he was privately tutored while travelling abroad with his parents, gentlefolk of leisure, before studies at Clare College (then Clare Hall), in Cambridge. Prior to Ordination he taught at the choir school of St Barnabas, Pimlico where he came under Lowder's influence and in the Woodard schools at Lancing and Hurstpierpoint where he painted the library with scenes from Chaucer's *Canterbury Tales* and Spencer's *The Faerie Queene*.

Both the range and the quantity of Baring-Gould's writing were formidable: almost two thousand books and articles on a bewildering variety of topics. His literary production was matched by his progenitive activity. His marriage produced fifteen children, starting at Dalton, in the North Riding of Yorkshire, and then moving on to the salt-flats of Essex at East Mersea, the setting of his best novel, *Mehelah*, which Algernon Charles Swinburne (1837–1909) compared favourably to *Wuthering Heights*, sole novelistic offspring of Emily Brontë (1818–48).[124]

In 1881, on his father's death, Baring-Gould was able to present himself to the living of Lew Trenchard, near Exeter. As squire, he proved an exceedingly good landlord to his tenants, while as parson he recast the parish along Tractarian lines, making the Holy Eucharist the centre of its worship and refurbishing the parish church with fine artefacts brought out of Germany, Switzerland, France, and Belgium, as well as commissioned work from local craftsmen, acting as carvers and painters of screen and pulpit.

Baring-Gould's concern for hymnography has to be seen in that overall context, though in fact his four best-known compositions, 'On the Resurrection morning', 'Through the night of doubt and sorrow', 'Onward Christian soldiers', and 'Now the day is over', date from his first curacy at Horbury Brig, near Wakefield, where he built a school for the illiterate poor and taught them personally.

Sabine-Gould forms a link between *Hymns Ancient and Modern* and Dearmer's *English Hymnal*. As the earliest major collector of folk song material in England, he was quite appropriately the dedicatee of its first substantial literary study: *English Folk Song: Some Conclusions*, by that colossus among scholarly folklorists Cecil Sharp (1859–1924).[125] Accompanied on his folk-song collecting expeditions by Bussell, whom we encountered as the author of an early work on social theology in Chapter 6 (Bussell's mother and sister rented a house on the Lew Trenchard estate), Baring-Gould was assisted in transcribing melodies by one of the plainsong revivalists, Henry Fleetwood Sheppard (1824–1901). It was a pleasing example of two musicological traditions converging.[126] Whether directly or indirectly, Sabine-Gould was the inspiration for much of Vaughan Williams' provision of music in the *English Hymnal*.

A tremendous collector of carol material from not only English but also Continental sources must not be overlooked. George Ratcliffe Woodward (1848–1934) was born at Birkenhead and educated at Harrow School and Gonville and Caius College, Cambridge, after which he followed a perfect Anglo-Catholic trajectory from curacy at St Barnabas, Pimlico, where he took a wife from among the parishioners, to his burial with her at Little Walsingham.[127] Woodward's *Carols for Christmastide* and *Carols for Easter and Ascensiontide* were brought together in a combined edition in 1901.[128] *Songs of Syon*, originally from 1904 but enlarged in succeeding editions until 1923,[129] and a mine of material from the languages Neale had favoured, was so highly regarded by the Northern Irish composer and teacher Charles Wood (1866–1926) that the latter agreed to collaborate in a second series of *Carols for Christmas, Easter and Ascensiontide* in 1919,[130] and then brought out with Woodward the classic *A Cambridge Carol Book* in 1924.[131]

Woodward's one original carol, 'This joyful Eastertide', remains a favourite of the Paschal season—including when the modern Latin Church in England worships in the vernacular. Woodward straddled the gap between the folklorists and the Gregorianists. His *Piae Cantiones* was the result of research carried out on behalf of the Plainsong and Mediaeval Music Society.[132]

These efforts of Dearmer, Vaughan Williams, Woodward, and Wood left English hymnody, and allied music, in an excellent state by the early 1920s. Anglophone Roman Catholics in the Latin church should stand amazed at how much of the vernacular repertoire of carols and hymns they became familiar with, notably after the Second Vatican Council, is owed to the work of creative, or scholarly, Anglo-Catholics.

It was a pity that Dearmer did not stop there. His later efforts, the 1925 *Songs of Praise* and its revised version in 1931,[133] rowed back Neale's foundational achievement by taking as the model reader the 'normal Englishman' for whom Nealean impersonality meant nothing. Extracted verses of poems by Percy Bysshe Shelley (1792–1822) and Swinburne, both of whom were apostates and self-proclaimed atheists, did nothing to promote the orthodoxy of the original volume, while the revised version, by including such nature ditties as Eleanor Farjeon's (1881–1965) *Morning has Broken*, weakened the link between Liturgy and doctrine for which Neale had laboured so hard. And it did so without any compensating indebtedness to any genuine folk song tradition.

Church music does not, however, consist wholly in hymns, and their extension to carols could even be called peripheral. The wider reform of music in the nineteenth century Church of England precedes the Catholic Revival. As early as 1811 a parishioner of St Paul's Cathedral took the matter in hand with a letter to the Bishop of London on the deplorable state of chorister education.[134] To the high church mindset, cathedrals (and collegiate churches) were key since they were the models for parish churches to emulate on their more modest scale. A surpliced choir, voluntary or professional, singing from the chancel, not a gallery, became in this way the Tractarian ideal—even if the classic plea for, not just weekly but even daily, choral services of this kind was uttered by a pre-Tractarian, Walter John Jebb (1805–86).[135]

The Oxford Movement assisted Jebb's programme by insisting on a repertoire attuned to the Church's feasts and seasons, on the proper dignity to be given to everything connected with the Eucharistic sacrifice, and by prioritizing the recovery of ancient resources in plainsong and early polyphony. The basic principles of Tractarian musicology were laid out in 1845 in Robert Druitt's *A Popular Tract on Church Music*.[136] Druitt (1814–83) proved an effective organizer and not just an author, founding the Society for Promoting Church Music and its official journal, *The Parish Choir*.

The plainsong revival could easily fit into this context, not least because the sixteenth century composer John Merbecke (c. 1510-c, 1585) had already set the Anglican service to a form of monophony derived from the ancient chant.[137] William Dyce brought out a modified version in 1843, an initiative rapidly taken up by others. The Cambridge Camden Society was especially enthusiastic for 'Gregorian', and antipathetic to its organ accompaniment.[138] That might have suggested a rather specialized rendition by a schola, but the Tractarians (unlike Jebb) were keen on congregational participation in sung music. In 1850 Pugin had published his own *Earnest Appeal for the Revival of Ancient Plain Song* which, according to Peter Anson, 'received a far better reception from Anglican readers than from Roman Catholics'.[139] It was the approach taken up among English Roman Catholics by the Society of St Gregory, created as late as 1929—though the twentieth century Society was more ambitious than its Victorian predecessors when it took the teaching of congregational plainsong into schools.[140]

Early champions of the chant revival were Walter Kerr Hamilton, when Vicar of St Peter's-in-the-East in Oxford, and Frederick Oakeley who introduced it at the Margaret Street Chapel. At St Mark's College, Chelsea under a Tractarian Vice-Principal, Thomas Helmore, a choir of boys and men sang daily services which included 'plainsong, Anglican chants (from Boyce's *Cathedral Music*) and Tallis's litany and responses combined with English (and Italian) sixteenth and seventeenth century anthems and service music'.[141] Helmore's adaptation of plainsong into English has already been mentioned: from *The Psalter Noted* it grew experimentally into *A Manual of Plainsong*, revised in 1902. St Barnabas, Pimlico; All Saints, Margaret Street; St Alban's, Holborn; St Mary Magdalene, Paddington: all these Anglo-Catholic churches followed the Helmore model.[142] In 1870 the London Gregorian Association was founded though the chant revival could not win the day everywhere.[143]

The two streams—hymnody, with or without carols, and chant—could of course come together. John Rouse Bloxham, Newman's curate at Littlemore, when responsible, along with the choirmaster and composer John Stainer (1840–1901) for the chapel of Magdalen College, Oxford, introduced a mixed repertoire of chant, anthems, and carols. Once expanded by the publication of *Hymns Ancient and Modern* (and, later, the *English Hymnal*), that became the regular staple of Anglo-Catholic parishes. The Tractarian trio of Liddon, Robert Gregory (1891–1911), and Richard William Church had their hands on the levers of power at St Paul's Cathedral, and they rapidly made it, on this kind of musical basis, the model not only for other English cathedrals but for parishes as well, and to excellent effect.[144]

Anglo-Catholics and the Arts

Its combination of vernacular hymns, plainsong or some analogous chanted setting of the Ordinary, together with occasional more ambitious anthem-like pieces wherever a choir exists that is worthy of the name, will surely strike the modern worshipper in the *Novus Ordo* Liturgy of Pope St Paul VI (pope 1963–78) as somehow rather familiar. The archetype—for the hymn and the motet have no historic place in the Roman Mass—comes from the Tractarian Revival.

── 10 ──

Ecumenism and Mission

To make use of an anachronism, the 'ecumenism' practised by the followers of the Oxford Movement was directed to the three bodies with whom they shared, in the Christian universe, the greatest common ground—the Orthodox, the Old Catholics, and, most difficult of these relations, the Church of Rome.

With the Orthodox

Dr Pusey was a forerunner of Anglo-Catholic interest in Eastern Orthodoxy as appears from Liddon's multi-volume biography.[1] That he was looking to the East was plain well before Newman's departure, and specifically in 1841, in his Open Letter to Richard William Jelf (1798–1871), a Fellow of Oriel and canon of Christ Church who later became Principal of King's College, London. Pusey's 'letter', *The Articles Treated on in Tract 90 Reconsidered and their Interpretation Vindicated*, was, presumably, not well received by Jelf, who was shortly to be one of the doctors responsible for suspending Pusey from preaching before the University.[2] The following year Pusey wrote to Archbishop William Howley of Canterbury (1766–1848) to the same pro-Oriental effect, encouraging what a successor of Howley's would term 'looking East in winter'.[3]

A Letter to His Grace the Archbishop of Canterbury, on some Circumstances Connected with the Present Crisis in the English Church, arrived at what was for Howley an awkward moment.[4] He had not approved of William Palmer of Magdalen's union-seeking visit to Russia in 1840–1, not least because Palmer proposed, on the basis of his Baptismal initiation and Orders, that he should be admitted to the Orthodox sacraments there. Newman, editing Palmer's *Notes of a Visit to the Russian Church*, explained the 'Branch Theory' on which Palmer based his request.[5] It is customarily considered distinctively Tractarian but historians have wondered whether it may go back as far as Lancelot Andrewes' (1555–1626) *Preces Privatae*, a text where Andrewes is overheard praying for the 'good estate of the Ecclesia: *Orientalia, Occidentali, Brittanica*'.[6] (Andrewes had given a copy to Archbishop Laud who, according to report, had himself been offered a cardinal's hat in Rome.) Although the Tsardom had been allied with Great Britain against Napoleon, fear of Russian advance into the Eastern Mediterranean rendered Anglo-Russian relations tricky waters for the primate of an Established Church to navigate.

When in 1853 to 1856 the two powers went to war over the 'Eastern Question', meaning by that the fate of Ottoman Turkey, John Mason Neale, a great lover of Byzantium, and thereby of Orthodoxy, spoke out against a covenant with the Turk and especially an alliance targeted on the protector of Eastern Christians in the Ottoman lands. Neale appreciated the Russian notion of a global Christian mission, linked though it was to the interests of the Romanov dynasty.

In the years 1843–5 Neale turned increasingly away from Rome and towards the East. The learned historian Charles de Montalembert (1810–70) is usually deemed a Liberal Roman Catholic. But encountering him at Funchal, on Madeira, Neale was put off by what he considered Montalembert's Ultramontanism and responded by writing in 1847 a foreword to the English translation of a highly anti-Ultramontane work by the Portuguese theologian Antonio Pereira (1725–97) — in Neale's judgment, the 'last great Cismontane Divine whom Europe has produced'.[7] The see of Rome, remarks Neale in his 'Introduction', undoubtedly enjoyed a primacy in the first millennium but she herself came to reject it: 'She will have the Supremacy, or she will have nothing'.[8] According to Neale's preface, the Uniate patriarchs were no better than the 'pope's slaves',[9] a thought that came to him because 1847 was also the year of publication of the first part of his uneven, but highly readable, *History of the Holy Eastern Church*. In his philo-Byzantinism, Neale was moved by the struggles of the Iconodules, which, in his estimation, parallelled his own concern for the restoration of iconographic symbolism in architecture, over against churches conceived as audience-halls. The topic of Image-worship also confirmed his loathing for Ultramontanism: that ghastly fascination with Italianate style in buildings! (How thoroughly Pugin would have agreed, the Pugin who thought St Peter's Basilica would make an excellent ballroom only unfortunately it was too large.) Neale was instrumental in the founding of the Eastern Church Association in 1863. Pusey was happy to join it.

For his part, Henry Parry Liddon echoed Neale in regarding the sheer existence of the separated Eastern Churches as a serious objection to the Roman Catholic standpoint in ecclesiology. 'If the East did not run out like a jetty, breaking up the advancing wave of the Roman argument, our position, I admit, would be a much less defensible one.'[10] Neale drew close enough to Orthodoxy to want the *Filioque* clause removed from the Creed, a move much discouraged by Pusey who considered it would undermine the coherence of Western Trinitarian theology.[11]

After Neale's death in 1866, those who stressed the 'Anglo' in 'Anglo-Catholicism' increasingly followed him in looking to the East. In 1867, two straws blew in the wind. Liddon, accompanied by Charles Dodgson (1832–98, canon of Christ Church and the author of the *Alice* stories) went to Russia and was bowled over.[12] After the Liturgy in St Isaac's Cathedral in Petersburg he wrote home excitedly to William Bright, 'There was an aroma of the fourth century about the whole which was quite marvellous... Right or wrong, it is a vast, energetic, and most powerful body, with an evident hold upon the heart of the largest of European empires.'[13] At Moscow they were presented to Metropolitan Filaret (Drozdov, 1782–1867), a venerable figure responsible for the Russian Catechism and the (then) modern Russian Bible and were pleased to discover that one of his assistant bishops was conversant with Anglican affairs. Coincidentally, it was in the same year, 1867, that the first Lambeth Conference made a point of translating into Greek its closing encyclical letter and sending it round to various Orthodox hierarchs.[14]

The definition of the supreme jurisdiction and magisterial infallibility of the pope at the First Vatican Council inevitably encouraged this *Tendenz*. Where did Vatican I leave national churches? Nowhere. In 1879 Littledale, the well-known controversialist (and Christina Rossetti's confessor) opined that as a national Church the 'Church of England bore more resemblance to Eastern Orthodoxy than to Roman Catholicism'.[15]

Hopes of Anglo-Catholics for reunion with the East got nowhere in Victoria's reign, nor in that of her son. Having a Church of England bishop in Jerusalem (the joint Anglo-Prussian bishopric which had so disturbed early Tractarians collapsed in 1881 and was replaced by a purely Anglican version in 1886) had produced a few friendly contacts. But the 1908 Lambeth Conference, the only meeting of Anglican Communion bishops in Edward VII's short reign (1901–10), had little of substance to say on the topic. Most members of the English Church held a poor opinion of Orthodoxy, especially if it was Russian. A successor to Dean Church at St Paul's Cathedral, William Ralph Inge (1860–1954), saw no point in 'associating with the State Church of a semi-barbarous autocracy, sunk in intellectual torpor and gross superstition'.[16]

Such rhetoric could not continue in wartime once England and Russia became allies again, this time against the Central Powers. In 1915 the clergy of the Canterbury Convocation observed that the 'alliance with Russia... affords a unique opportunity for deepening and extending the friendly relations which already exist between ourselves and the Orthodox Eastern Church'.[17]

That was largely a misdescription of a rather chilly and distant relationship, though, in the wake of Liddon's journey, Walter Frere, on a variety of pretexts, had paid four visits to pre-Revolutionary Russia, two of which (in 1912 and 1914) entailed lecturing on Anglicanism.[18] William John Birkbeck (1859–1916), a wealthy layman and private scholar, settled in Norfolk, had also been assiduous in cultivating contacts in the Russian Empire. He attended the ninth centenary celebration of the Kievan church in 1888. In 1896 he even managed to secure an invitation to the coronation of Nicholas II. Little did it avail.[19]

But after the War, a thaw began in earnest. Both Anglicans and the Orthodox were faced with the increasingly obvious civilizational disintegration that followed on the global hostilities and the collapse of the great monarchies of Continental Europe and the Levant. In 1920 a new Lambeth Conference issued an 'Appeal to All Peoples', recommending Christian reunion while setting out in broad brush terms the basis on which Anglicans might consider union with others.

Then in 1921 the Ecumenical Patriarch Meletios IV Metaxakis (1871–1935), in the midst of a Greco-Turkish War which would leave his successors increasingly exposed in a Hellenophobe and anti-religious Turkey, wrote an encyclical letter to 'all the churches' proposing a programme of mutual contact and (hopefully) increased understanding. The coincidence of these two initiatives changed the scenery. 'Mindful of the British role in protecting the patriarchate of Constantinople after the Great War, many Orthodox saw Britain as their only hope as they faced the political and economic challenges that lay before them. They hoped for money, and they craved the political muscle they believed the archbishop of Canterbury could flex. Russian exiles from the Bolshevik Revolution flooded into Western Europe and England, hungry and impoverished, and they looked to the generous efforts of the English-organized Russian Clergy ad Church Aid Fund for assistance'.[20] It was a state of mind that would continue throughout the inter-War years.

In response to Patriarch Meletios' encyclical, a number of Anglo-Catholics, headed by Bishop Gore, had sent the Phanar a Declaration of Faith. In glowing language it portrayed a Church of England committed to the adorable Presence and the unbloody Sacrifice in the Eucharist, to sacramental absolution of the penitent and, more widely, a ministry ruled by the ancient faith and practice of the undivided Church.[21]

Starting with Constantinople, various autocephalous Orthodox churches began to issue documents favourable to the apostolicity of Anglican ministerial Orders—a defining concern of the Oxford Movement since the first of the *Tracts for the Times* (the title of *Tract 1*, after all, had been *Thoughts on the Ministerial Commission*). Yet immediately the Declaration's contents were published, Arthur Cayley Headlam

Ecumenism and Mission

(1862–1947), Regius Professor of Theology at Oxford—whose Bampton Lectures, *The Doctrine of the Church and Christian Reunion*, would ease his path to becoming Bishop of Gloucester in 1923,[22] and, in the fulness of time chair of Canterbury's Committee on Relations with Episcopal Churches—complained vociferously that the Declaration was incompatible with the official formularies of the Church of England and more especially with an agreement just outlined, on the basis of the Lambeth Appeal, with the Free Churches (the 'Mansfield Statement').

Four thousand Church of England clergy had added their signatures to a petition which accompanied the Gore Declaration. That showed the contemporary strength of Anglo-Catholicism, even if, owing to the doctrine of *oikonomia*, the acceptance of Anglican Orders by the various Orthodox autocephalies was, in effect, a promise that, in the event of individual priests becoming Orthodox, their Ordinations would not be repeated. That would be, presumably, through what Latin theology, when thinking of Baptism, would call a 'reviviscence' of an otherwise dormant grace. In 1931 a Joint Doctrinal Commission appointed by the Ecumenical Patriarch Photios II Maniatis (1874–1935) and Archbishop Cosmo Gordon Lang of Canterbury recognized that only on the attaining of full dogmatic agreement would sacramental Communion be established.[23] Anglo-Catholic efforts were inhibited, not so say stymied, by their co-existence with the other 'parties' in the bosom of the national Church.

A love affair of Anglo-Catholicism with Orthodoxy would continue to run. Its flagship was the journal *The Christian East*, founded by Canon John Albert Douglas (1868–1956), Vicar of St Luke's, Camberwell, and the 'Church of England's chief advocate for Anglo-Orthodox rapprochement'.[24] Douglas, already encountered in Chapter 8 as co-founder of the Society of the Faith, was instrumental in bringing together Anglo-Catholics with the Orthodox in the early twentieth century Ecumenical Movement. The 1910 World Missionary Conference at Edinburgh had thrown up the idea of a conference on 'Faith and Order' in the hope of a consensus among divided Christians about the content of the faith and the character of the Church structure which carries it down the ages. In 1927 that came to birth in the elegant lakeside city of Lausanne, a stronghold, since the sixteenth century, of the Swiss Reformed religion. Anglo-Catholics felt uncomfortable and anxious in the overwhelmingly Protestant assembly and it was with relief that they discovered allies from the East. At Lausanne, the '*Church Times* wrote warmly of Professor Glubokowskii's insistence that Scripture alone could not provide a sufficient basis for reunion, of Archbishop Chrysostom's and Metropolitan Stefan's emphasis on apostolic succession, and of Bishop Nikolai of Okhrida's defence of the seven sacraments', while in a personal summation of the proceedings, Douglas portrayed the Orthodox declaration as a useful dam that impeded a conference "swept towards disaster by its unconscious Protestant impulse'".[25]

Douglas was admirably placed to facilitate this exchange. In 1906 he had founded the Anglican and Eastern Orthodox Churches Union which in 1914 merged with Neale's Eastern Churches Union to form the Anglican and Eastern Churches Association. His efforts also extended to Old Catholics (Society of St Willibrord in 1908[26]), and the general ecumenical outreach of successive archbishops of Canterbury (via the 'Nikaian Club', whose finances he arranged through the Society of the Faith, co-founded by him in 1905). This whirl of behind-the-scenes activity which gained him the post of first General Secretary of the Church of England Council on Foreign Relations (later, 'Council for Christian Unity') in 1933 was principally for the benefit of the Anglo-Catholic party.[27] 'Shortly after Lausanne Metropolitan Germanos suggested that it might be possible to unite Orthodoxy with the Church of England if [Douglas's] Anglo-Catholic colleagues could reform their church in their own image'.[28] And there of course was the rub. 'If all Anglicans were Anglo-Catholics, Douglas mused, "agreement would be easy". But they are not.'[29]

Not entirely coincidentally, in the following year the Fellowship of St Alban and St Sergius emerged, a joint project of Russian emigrés from the Bolshevik Revolution and their English sympathizers.[30] The papers of its annual conference at High Leigh in Buckinghamshire, and the other material to be found in the Fellowship's journal, *Sobornost*, became a rich vein of both Orthodox and Anglo-Catholic theology and spirituality, which well repay inspection.[31] But hopes of actual reunion, never truly realistic—and not only because of Anglican diversity for there was much hostility toward the Ecumenical Movement in substantial sections of Orthodoxy—gradually faded away. Not till sometime after 1965 did they wholly disappear. It was, ironically, at the Annual Nicaean Club Dinner at Lambeth Palace in September 2010 that Metropolitan Hilarion Alfeyev (born 1966), then 'foreign secretary' of the Moscow Patriarchate, would deliver what appeared to be a definitive *non possumus* over the issue of women priests. By that date the heirs of the Oxford Movement found themselves in considerable disarray.

With the Old Catholics

Old Catholicism as now known is a product of the First Vatican Council.[32] All that could count under that name in the Tractarian springtime was what Neale himself called the 'Jansenist Church of Utrecht'.[33] By the nineteenth century the—from the Roman standpoint—schismatic Utrecht archdiocese was only 'Jansenist' in as much it was radically Cismontane. The soteriology typical of classical Jansenism had largely disappeared. But the negative response of many Latin Catholics in central Europe to the 1870 definition of the pope's universal jurisdiction and infallibility had, by century's end, changed all that.[34]

The Old Catholics, reconstituted in 1889 as a small-scale yet international communion of churches, fitted perfectly into one kind of Anglican paradigm: the non-Roman Catholicism which led Charlotte Yonge to write her confession of faith, *Reasons why I am a Catholic but not a Roman Catholic*.[35] 'These new national Old Catholic churches looked like attractive dialogue partners in building a catholic alliance of independent churches pitted against Rome.'[36] Two Church of England bishops, Christopher Wordsworth of Lincoln (1807–85) and Harold Browne of Ely, then Winchester (1811–91), were particularly engaged. In the case of Wordsworth, the poet's nephew, this was against the backcloth of an inflamed anti-Romanism, as in his *Babylon, or the Question Examined, Is the Church of the Rome the Babylon of the Apocalypse?*[37] Wordsworth was especially incensed about the definition of universal ('ordinary and immediate') papal jurisdiction which had just deprived the French bishops of their ancient privileges—a response that testifies, accurately enough, to his instinctive if also historically informed sympathy with 'Gallicanism'. Wordsworth persuaded his diocesan synod to send a letter of support to the German Old Catholics. In 1872 he and Browne attended together an Old Catholic Congress in Cologne.[38]

Anglican theologians met with their Old Catholic, as well as Orthodox, counterparts at two further gatherings at Bonn in 1874 and 1875. Wordsworth had been warned in advance that the Swiss and French Old Catholics were decidedly Liberal, not to say rationalist, in their theology, and there were also anxieties that the role of divines representing 'extreme' positions, whether Liberal, Evangelical or Anglo-Catholic, would subvert proceedings. So, as Mark Chapman explains, a kind of shadow official working party emerged, under the umbrella of the Anglo-Continental Society, to keep the dialogue with Old Catholicism on a course acceptable to moderate high churchmen. The Anglo-Continental Society's activities had been galvanized by the 'Vatican Decrees', which triggered an appeal to Roman Catholics to 'return from the novelties of modern doctrine and mediaeval discipline to the Scriptural Faith and Apostolic Order of the Primitive Church'.[39]

The Bonn Conferences, facilitated not least by Gladstone, who was out of office and had time on his hands, were working towards a reunited Christendom based on 'temporal catholicity'—that is, a shared continuing adhesion in a variety of religious bodies to the faith of the apostolic age. Classical Anglo-Catholics, despite Wordsworth and Browne, were not deprived of a voice. Liddon, who attended the 1874 gathering as the Anglo-Catholic spokesman, was by no means entirely happy with the anti-Roman tone, intervening on behalf of the *Filioque* (its truth, but not necessarily the legitimacy of its insertion into the Creed) and disagreeing with the condemnation of belief in the Immaculate Conception which he thought a perfectly legitimate pious opinion. He was relieved that an acceptable, if much qualified, formula was found to affirm the Eucharistic Sacrifice. When other Anglican participants were silent, he spoke up on behalf of prayer for the dead. But what of prayer to the glorified dead in the Body of Christ? Anglicans found that the Orthodox were unwilling to concede that invoking the intercession of the *Theotokos* and the saints is not something necessary for salvation. The Council of Trent, when justifying the veneration of those holy figures, had not gone so far. It was an example of how the Orthodox could be remoter from Anglicans than were Roman Catholics.

Before the 1875 assembly, the anti-Roman (or, better, anti-Vaticanist) temperature was raised by Gladstone's publication of his critique of the First Vatican Council's document on the Petrine prerogatives in their civil, rather than strictly ecclesial, bearing.[40] Ignaz von Döllinger (1790–1890), the German Catholic church historian excommunicated for his rejection of the definition of papal infallibility, gave a five hour lecture on the iniquities committed by the Papacy during its history.[41] The meeting saw the Evangelical Anglican John Saul Howson (1816–85), Dean of Chester, retract his agreement to the 1874 resolution on Eucharistic Sacrifice, a diplomatic setback which exposed Anglican disunity. And there was also the uncomfortable discovery that appeal for recognition of the 'Icon Council'—to Old Catholics as well as the Orthodox this was the Seventh Ecumenical Council (787)—exposed divisions about what should count as the age of the undivided Church.

The Anglo-Continental Society was nevertheless content with progress made toward full communion with Old Catholicism. Pusey, however, was unreconcilable. The legitimacy of the *Filioque* was in his eyes a non-negotiable item of faith. Probably to his relief, there would be no more Bonn assemblies. The difficulty over the Seventh Council, combined with the Balkan Crisis—when many Conservative-leaning Anglicans supported the Ottoman Porte against Russia, the leading Orthodox power—made sure of that. In Gladstone's eyes, 'Disraeli's Eastern policy had served to ensure the end of ecumenical negotiations in much the same way as had Pius IX's declaration of infallibility'.[42] That did not, however, prevent the 1878 Lambeth Conference noting with satisfaction, in regard to Old Catholicism, the 'solemn protest' it had raised against the 'usurpations of the See of Rome and against the novel doctrines promulgated by its authority'.[43]

But Romanophobe Anglicans of every hue noted with sorrow that the new Old Catholic churches did not grow much, while Anglo-Catholics in particular could note with satisfaction that, by entering in 1889 into union with the (original) Old Catholics of Utrecht, those churches had been brought into a Communion which was, in the words of the chairman of the Anglo-Continental Society, 'all but Roman Catholic'.[44]

The friendly relations the Bonn Conferences fostered with Old Catholics were subsequently disturbed by a blip. Arnold Harris Mathew (1852–1919), a colourful character (self-styled fourth Earl of Llandaff and Conte Povoleri di Vicenza in the Marquisate of the Papal States) who throughout his lifetime had oscillated between the Churches of England and Rome, was consecrated an Old Catholic bishop for England in 1908, with a view to gathering together disaffected Roman Catholics and Anglo-Catholics who, in the light of the 1904 Royal Commission on Ecclesiastical Discipline, feared a crackdown on ritual practices that never came.[45] Once Utrecht had eaten humble pie (the authorities there declared Mathew had obtained consecration 'in bad faith', and that, as a consequence, his Orders were null and void), relations could happily resume.

At a 1931 meeting, again in Bonn, a joint doctrinal commission advised that inter-communion be established on the basis of a common holding of 'essential' (not necessarily, then, 'all') dogmas of the faith. That same year the Old Catholics ratified the decision in Vienna and the Convocations of Canterbury and York did likewise at home.[46] But in these negotiations, thanks to Headlam's adroit chairmanship, issues opposing Anglo-Catholics to Evangelicals had been sedulously avoided. So the former could only experience modified rapture.

Perhaps surprisingly, with the exception of mutual participation in episcopal consecrations, the Bonn Agreement produced remarkably little in terms of concrete results for either Church. An archbishop of Canterbury, looking back in its centenary year, remarked that 'being in communion' had not in fact turned into an 'intimate sharing in both faith and witness'. He was inclined to blame the way the Agreement had stressed so strongly the independence of the Old Catholic Union and the Anglican Communion—and this in despite of its foundational ecclesiology which took as its model the 'eucharistic communion of local churches'.[47] But of course Old Catholics were few and far between, and not likely to make much impact should some of them be domiciled, whether temporarily or permanently, in either England or other countries with significant Anglican populations. Likewise, Anglicans in European countries with Old Catholic minorities might prefer to look for the equivalent of what were once 'Embassy chapels' or the churches built for expatriates in cities such as Florence or Cannes—or indeed, if they had strong 'party' attachments and were at home in foreign languages, they could readily gravitate to the parishes of the Reformed or of Roman Catholics.

With the Church of Rome

Anglo-Catholic relations with Roman Catholics were historically fractious, despite a good start with the 1857 Association for the Promotion of the Unity of Christendom, a joint Anglo- and Roman Catholic affair.[48] The Leicestershire squire Ambrose Phillips de Lisle (1809–78), a pre-Tractarian convert,[49] and Frederick George G. Lee (1832–1902), 'Dr Lee of Lambeth',[50] were the principal movers, through among Anglo-Catholics sympathetic to the Association's aims Alexander Forbes, Bishop of Brechin, was a more prominent, and, while controversial, a less conspiratorial figure—at any rate in comparison with Lee.[51] Newman, by now an Oratorian, and in the process of finishing up his singularly unsatisfactory affairs at the Catholic University in Dublin, was characteristically nuanced in his attitude. He wrote to Phillips who had sent him his pamphlet *The Future Unity of Christendom*:[52] 'I think it is for the interest of Catholicism that individuals should not join us, but should remain to leaven the mass. I mean that they will do more for us by remaining where they are than by coming over, but then they have individual souls, and with what heart can I do anything to induce them to preach to others, if they themselves become castaways'.[53] The Association, while assuming the correctness of a branch theory in ecclesiology (Anglicans, 'Greeks', Roman Catholics), was highly pro-papal in its orientation, to the extent that notable Tractarians protested, including three already encountered in these pages: Neale, R. M. Benson, and Thomas Chamberlain.

No doubt the latter were relieved when in 1864 the Association was condemned by Rome. The Curial rescript declared the Association's aims to be subversive of the divine constitution of the Church. The Association lingered on, seeking to promote union chiefly through publishing sermons and items of scholarly interest until in 1921 Athelstan Riley, its Master at that time, closed it down on the ground of the absence of English Roman Catholics in its membership.

On the eve of the First Vatican Council, Pusey had made his own overtures, stating the case for the English Church to several French bishops, including Georges Darboy of Paris (1813–71), martyred during the Commune, and Félix Dupanloup of Orleans (1802–78). To concentrate efforts on Francophone Europe was a wise move, as later events would prove. Olive-branches were offered at this time in the shape of two Philo-Catholic presentations of Anglican belief: a *Commentary on the Thirty-Nine Articles* by Alexander Forbes,[54] and *The Kiss of Peace, or England and Rome at one on the Doctrine of the Holy Eucharist* by Gerard Francis Cobb (1838–1904), an Anglican layman, composer and Reunionist.[55] Pusey's 1864 *Eirenikon* had already produced from Newman's side the sharp, if in part concessive reply, described in Chapter 1.[56] But matters did not end there.[57] In 1867 Pusey produced a second 'Eirenicon' devoted more exclusively to the recently defined dogma of the Immaculate Conception, discussed by Newman in the Mariological section of his original reply, but now re-appearing as a test case for the limits of development in doctrine.[58] In Newman's view, whereas the 1854 dogma had to be considered a *fait accompli*, it might nonetheless be useful for Pusey to go in person to Rome to put his case about the foundations of dogma before the Vatican Council opened. Pusey himself thought his time would be better spent writing his third 'Eirenicon'. Entitled *Is Healthful Reunion Impossible?*,[59] it appeared shortly after the Council began. Lord Acton distributed some copies to the bishops present in Rome, telling Gladstone it might do some good if anybody could be persuaded to read it.[60]

In the third 'Eirenicon', Pusey did not rule out totally the notion of new definitions, so long (of course) as they were grounded in Christian antiquity. The trouble was that in a divided Church no single ecclesial body was able to carry out the act. He had a more specific objection in regard to the matter to hand: the proposed definition of the pope's teaching office, and one which held good even on (Roman) Catholic premises as to where the true Church could be found. 'It would need an infallible authority to declare what Popes heretofore have infallibly declared.'[61] The objection raises a difficulty that is still not adequately dealt with in Catholic theology. How many *ex cathedra* definitions are there? The disparity of opinion, unless authoritatively adjudicated, somewhat undermines the point of the exercise.

Unsurprisingly, Pusey's anxieties were not met. After the decree *Pastor aeternus* was promulgated, Pusey brought out a new edition of his third 'Eirenicon' under the title *Healthful Reunion, as conceived possible before the Vatican Council*. For Pusey had given up hope. In that perspective, the private correspondence during these years between Pusey and Newman on the topic of Transubstantiation, in which by late 1867 they had 'reached a common mind on the Interpretation of the Tridentine formulae on the Eucharist in a way that Pusey believed to be compatible with Anglican teaching', can hardly fail to seem something of a bagatelle.[62] .

After the Council, it became clear that the scenery had shifted. Dr Lee, co-founder of the ill-fated Association for the Promotion of the Unity of Christendom, now came to concentrate on a new venture, the Order of Corporate Reunion, founded in 1877. The *sub rosa* character of the organization was not confined to its foundation. Lee, who appears to have received episcopal Ordination in the 'Vilatte Succession' made confidential agreements to 'supply'—in other words, to validate by a supplementary Ordination—the sacramental status of Anglican clergy concerned for the authenticity of their priesthood.[63] It was a descent into an ecclesiastical underworld based on the confounding of Reunionist hopes. Bernard Vaughan (1847–1922), Manning's successor at Westminster, would have told them not to bother. 'Tarry not for Corporate Reunion. It is a dream, and a snare of the Evil One... The individual may no more wait for Corporate Reunion, than he may wait for Corporate Conversion'.[64]

Yet on that very topic of Anglican Orders, Charles Lindley Wood, Viscount Halifax, indomitable Anglo-Catholic layman, had been putting out feelers to sympathetic Frenchmen about the possibility of some future Roman recognition of Anglican Orders. A chance encounter on Madeira with the Abbé Fernard Portal (1855–1926), a seminary lecturer sent abroad for his health, triggered a wider consultation. The great historian of the early Church, Louis Duchesne (1843–1922), from 1895 director of the *Ecole française* at Rome, thought it not inconceivable. A new periodical, *La Revue Anglo-Romaine* (1893–6), encouraged friendly contacts between Roman Catholic and Anglo-Catholic clergy, with the same ultimate aim in mind. Mr Gladstone took an interest, as did William Maclagan (1826–1910), the Archbishop of York. (This was the same Primate of the Northern Province who had turned a blind eye to the affairs of the Abbot of Painsthorpe, as described in Chapter 5.[65]) Halifax pulled down the house on himself when the expected answer was not forthcoming. That was good for business at the Order of Corporate Union, and Lee is thought to have amassed a hundred or more clients in its wake.[66]

Yet it was Halifax who tried again, and this time with something more like success—or what could reasonably pass for success in an age before Roman Catholic ecumenism officially existed. The Malines Conversations would hardly have been thinkable without Anglo-Catholics—meaning thereby not only the existence of the latter but the impression they were able to give in the 1920s that the 'conquest' of the Church of England by the Catholic movement was only a matter of time. Between 1921 and 1925 a series of private (yet, in elevated ecclesiastical circles, well-known) 'conversations' took place in the Flemish city of Mechelen, the historic primatial see of Belgium.[67] The prime movers were once again Halifax, and Portal. The meetings were made possible by the Belgian primate, Cardinal Désiré Mercier (1851–1926), to whom Halifax was commended by Archbishop Davidson of Canterbury in a diplomatically worded letter. Knowledge of the dialogue alarmed Anglican Evangelicals, but Davidson insisted that fear of Rome should not disable talking—and was sure Anglicans would stand by the principles of the Reformation. Davidson's confidence was not entirely well-founded.

Ecumenism and Mission

The original Anglican participants (rounds one and two) were Halifax himself, the liturgical scholar Walter Frere of the Community of the Resurrection, who was made Bishop of Truro during the Conversations, in 1923, and the patristic scholar Armitage Robinson, Dean of Wells (1858–1933). This trio was not unduly attached to the Magisterial Reformers. Later (in the Conversations' third and subsequent session) they were joined by the historian Beresford Kidd, Warden of Keble, and by Gore, who was sharply critical of the concessions already made on matter of the 1854 and 1870 dogmas. Gore had long been a critic of Roman authoritarianism and its insouciance in regard to historical science, the defining issues in the sudden expansion, well beyond Utrecht, of Dutch Old Catholicism.

Though Gore considered union with either Protestants or the Orthodox more feasible than union with Rome, 'Gore's involvement hardly compensated for the absence of Evangelicals at Malines.'[68] Where Gore was, however, clearer than the original trio was in his root-and-branch rejection of anything resembling the universal primacy in the form put forward at the Vatican Council. 'We are bound to disregard as untrue the theory that holds that the Bishop of Rome holds *jure Divino* in the Church of Christ a position of distinct and unique authority, operative everywhere, and perhaps even… that, directly or indirectly, it is through that channel alone (at all events in the West) that the Ministerial Commission can be rightly or validly exercised.'[69] Armitage Robinson thought possible recognition of a 'general superintendence' by Rome; Gore would not go beyond the phrase a 'spiritual responsibility'.[70]

The fifth and final Malines meeting was rather nominal, but the fourth proved productive. Mercier read a paper commissioned from Dom Lambert Bauduin (1873–1960) proposing a Canterbury patriarchate with a married clergy, its own Liturgy and a distinctive canon law, along with the right to present names of episcopal candidates to the pope. That would entail, Bauduin supposed, the suppression of the post-1850 Roman hierarchy in England. The paper was the birth-moment of the formula of a Church united but not absorbed: *l'Eglise Anglicane unie mais non absorbée*. Had its contents been known back at Westminster Cathedral more than a slight *frisson* would doubtless have ensued.

Gore's paper was also a decisive moment: a plea for the broadest tolerance compatible with agreement on the 'necessary articles' of Catholic communion—with all the difficulties that phrase carries. The difference between essential and non-essential doctrines would soon surface in discussions with Old Catholics but Gore had a long-standing preoccupation with the distinction between fundamental and non-fundamental articles. No one who had read his *Roman Catholic Claims* would have expected him to be as positive as he now turned out to be. 'I write as an Anglican who has not the slightest desire to submit himself as an individual to the Roman authority, but with all his heart would desire to see his own Anglican communion, and the communion of the Orthodox Churches, reunited to the Holy See of Rome.'[71] Gore's message ran, Diversity within unity.

Shortly after the fourth meeting Mercier died and soon Portal was dead too. Pius XI, previously favourably, got cold feet, and by means of the encyclical *Mortalium animos*, 1928, effectively put an end to the whole affair. It was a failure but, at least in Walter Frere's judgment, a magnificent failure: an eirenic gathering which showed a surprising depth to the desire for unity. Anglo-Catholics continued to revere the joint memory of Halifax and Mercier.[72]

The Centenary of the Oxford Movement showed that Anglo-Papalists at least were not willing to abandon this baby, as could be seen from such publications as *The Church of England and the Holy See: What are We to Say?*, by Henry Joy Fynes-Clinton (1875–1959), Vicar of St Magnus the Martyr, London Bridge, and William Robert Corbould (1880–1957), Vicar of All Saints, Carshalton,[73] or *Catholic Reunion. An Anglican Plea for a Uniate Patriarchate of Canterbury and for an Anglican Ultramontanism* by the barrister turned clergyman James Tait Plowden-Wardlaw (1873–1963) writing under the pseudonym 'Father Clement'.[74] *Clementia* was of course the ancient Roman version of 'mercy', while *Clemens*, an early Bishop of Rome, was the *titulus* of Plowden-Laidlaw's Cambridge parish.[75] In the hope of a merciful adjustment of Anglican-Catholic relations he made some practical preparation for the liturgical life of a future Uniate patriarchate, publishing the 'Oxford Movement Centenary (Supplementary) Missal' with its *memoriae* for Anglo-Catholic *beati*, starting with John Keble.[76]

The 'Tractate' by Fynes-Clinton and Corbould was the culmination of a series of eight, following a broadly historical outline—for example, the first was entitled *What do the Celtic Churches Say?* In 1933 Fynes-Clinton led a Holy Year pilgrimage to Rome where these tractates were presented, in handsomely bound form, to Pope Pius XI at a private audience. [77]

Plowden-Laidlaw (perfect name for a lawyer—Edmund Plowden had been the leading legal theorist of the Late Tudor period) pleaded for a decisive break with the notion that, owing to the Tractarian 'Branch Theory', the Roman Catholic hierarchy, as restored in 1850, was not only unwelcome in England but actually schismatic there. That peculiar theory had been reiterated only four years earlier by an historian of the Society of the Holy Cross.[78] '[W]e must abandon wholly and utterly the High Church denial of the continuity of the present Latin Church in England with the pre-Reformation Church of England. With the facts before us it is astounding impertinence to look upon the Roman Church in England as schismatic.'[79] And as to Fynes-Clinton, it was noted how he 'hoped and worked and prayed for the day when the Church of England would be clothed again with the fulness of Catholic unity, upright and in its right mind... The various ecclesiastical crises of his time never shook Fynes-Clinton's devotion to the reunion of his beloved Church of England with the See of Rome, and, indeed with Constantinople'.[80]

Such Anglo-Papalists naturally considered official Anglican dalliance with Old Catholicism to be chasing after hares—putting Anglo-Catholics at variance with the official national hierarchies of the Church of Rome while pursuing the chimera of a non-papal Catholicism.[81]

Mission in the Global South

In its first two generations insofar as Anglo-Catholicism was a missionary Christianity it was domestic mission that it practiced. Missionary enterprise overseas took place principally in three regions: India, the eastern and central regions of Africa, and the Pacific, including both New Zealand and 'Polynesia'—a term used in the period for all the archipelagos of the South Pacific, whether Melanesian, Micronesian, or Polynesian in the more limited sense of that word.

The first Anglo-Catholic missions abroad were the pioneering efforts of the Society of St John the Evangelist in India. In 1874 the Society sent out two missionaries. One, Robert Lay Page (died 1912), went to Bombay and subsequently Poona, where the governing classes retired for the monsoon season (this was the mission supported by St Bartholomew's, Brighton, as described in Chapter 4). Helped by Wantage Sisters at Poona and All Saints Sisters at Bombay, Page created a formidable array of primary and technical schools, an industrial workshop, hostels, and a fruit farm. The church he built, St Peter's, Bombay, with architecture ill-chosen for a monsoon climate, is described as a miniature replica of London's St Paul's cathedral. Functioning not only as a school chapel and a parish church for Europeans and Indians, it formed a notable 'centre of Catholic teaching and practice'.[82] At Poona he created a church of the Holy Name in neo-classical style: the 'altarpiece, which would not have looked out of place in a renaissance basilica at Rome, was made from dozens of different marbles and dominated by an enormous tabernacle'.[83] Certainly more Roman than Sarum, at any rate.

On ending his term of office as Superior General, Page returned to India where he would die at Poona in 1912. Page's 1907 return coincided with the arrival in Bombay of a strongly Evangelical bishop determined to stamp out Ritual offences, notably Eucharistic Reservation—which was incompatible with his own 'Receptionist' theory of the sacrament.

The Cowley Fathers, determined to resist, were under real threat of expulsion until Reginald Copleston (1845–1925), bishop of Calcutta, who was the pertinent Metropolitan, gave judgment in their favour.[84]

The other principal Cowley missionary, Simeon Wilberforce O'Neill (1837–82), was an early exponent of 'inculturation', adopting a lifestyle specifically designed to attract Indians accustomed to ascetic religion.[85] (He was quite possibly egged on by Benson himself who, while a member of the Brotherhood of the Holy Trinity, had thought of going to India himself, with similar ideas of living as a Christian *saddhu*.) O'Neill made his base at Indore, then capital of a Princely State, now in the province of Madhya Pradesh, and with the help of a converted Brahmin created an 'ashram' on the Indian model, outside the European cantonment, with preaching in the bazaars and public chanting of the Litany in Hindi. His early death from cholera in 1882 brought this highly distinctive mission to an end.[86]

The ancient Universities made their contribution. In 1877 an Anglo-Catholic brotherhood revitalized the Cambridge Mission to Delhi which the (high church but not Anglo-Catholic) Society for the Propagation of the Gospel in Foreign Parts (SPG) had initiated in 1859. In 1880 an Oxford Mission to Calcutta followed suit. In each case the missionaries were celibate priests who were, respectively, Cambridge and Oxford graduates. In the circumstances of the Indian Raj it was difficult to escape entanglement with the Establishment. Whereas many British missionaries in India were responsible to the Societies that had sent them, that was not the case with these two brotherhoods which were directly responsible to local bishops, so much so that '[b]oth brotherhoods contributed bishops to the Indian establishment in the nineteenth century, and their mission houses in the respective city centres became frequent visiting destinations of Raj administrators'.[87]

One breakthrough in north-east India was in the mission of higher education for Bengali students. The Cambridge mission had been influenced by Bishop Brooke Foss Westcott's theology of fulfilment (meaning: the fulfilment not only of Judaism but of the non-Judaeo-Christian religions) and had some hope that the writings of Rabindranath Tagore (1861–1941), with his monotheistic mysticism, might serve as a conduit to Christian belief.[88]

From 'India's coral strand' the focus shifts, following the motion of Reginald Heber's (1783–1826) missionary hymn, to 'Afric's sunny fountains': a reference to a river system which in practice was not always so benign. The Universities' Mission to Central Africa began with the ill-fated expedition of Charles Frederick Mackenzie (1925–1862), a journey inspired by the national speaking tour of David Livingstone (1813–73), missionary and opponent of (indigenous) slavery.[89] A gifted mathematician, Fellow of Gonville and Caius College, Cambridge, Mackenzie was Archdeacon of Natal when consecrated in Cape Town in 1862 as missionary bishop for central Africa. (The consecration took place in South Africa owing to doubts as to whether a bishop could be appointed by licence of the Crown—and thus, in England, legally—for territory outside the British dominions.) Mackenzie set out with Livingstone along the Zambezi Valley with a view to making his headquarters in Nyasaland, but, just over a year later, and still in his thirties, he died of Blackwater fever when his medical supplies were lost on the Shiré river.[90]

A successor, William George Tozer (1829–99), was quickly appointed and prudently established his see on the island of Zanzibar in 1863. The choice was wise not only because Zanzibar was a crossroads, a vast entrepot of trade. The Sultanate of Zanzibar, with which British consular officials had good relations, extended in effect not just to neighbouring islands and the coast of the mainland opposite, but deep into the interior of East Africa. So the original objective, the tribes in the region of Lake Nyasa (now 'Lake Malawi'), remained steadily in view. In 1873 the British succeeded in persuading the Sultan of Zanzibar to abolish the slave trade.

In a striking gesture, Tozer's successor, Edward Steere (1828–82), chose to build his cathedral on the site of the former slave market. After Steere's resignation in 1881, the mission, which had been backed by both old high churchmen and Tractarians, and was readily able to draw on the Colonial Bishoprics Fund (created in 1841, Gladstone was one of its three treasurers), became more specifically Anglo-Catholic. Its support base now lay in southern English parishes where Anglo-Catholic strength was concentrated rather than with the original Universities orientation of Oxford, Cambridge, Durham, and Trinity College, Dublin.

The third Bishop, Charles Alan Smythies (1844–94) had been Vicar of St Margaret of Antioch, Roath, a poor suburb of Cardiff, in which post he had succeeded Frederick William Puller—theological writer and uncle of Lionel Thornton (see Chapter 6)—when Puller decided to enter the Cowley Fathers and leave the parochial ministry. During Smythies' ten-year episcopate the mission advanced into the Usumbara mountains and the Ruvuma country—both in present-day Tanzania, with Ruvuma bordering Lake Nyasa.[91] In 1892 the missionary bishopric was divided, accordingly, into two ecclesiastical circumscriptions, Zanzibar and Nyasaland, with the latter centred on Likoma, an island in the lake.

In 1910 a third mission diocese was set up in what is now Zambia (then Northern Rhodesia). Such geographical expansion was welcome not least because, through a combination of ill-understood treatises made with local chiefs and gunboat diplomacy aimed at the Sultanate, it was the case that by 1886 almost all the original area of the Tanganyika missions had come under the German flag—with difficulties which may be imagined when war broke out between Britain and Imperial Germany in 1914.

Throughout the dioceses run by the Universities' Mission a single model prevailed. What should be sought was the conversion of an entire village, where communal life could be shaped by the liturgical customs and discipline of the patristic Church. 'UMCA' was hostile to urbanisation, an attitude probably inherited from the cultural prophets of nineteenth century England, including Pugin and Morris. That came into a certain tension with African economic aspirations later on.[92] By the time (1965) the Mission entered into amalgamation with the much older Society for the Propagation of the Gospel, it was criticized for the way it 'largely cleaved to its vision of an unchanged, unchanging Africa'.[93] 'It was in Africa... that Anglo-Catholic unease and anxiety about western civilization found deepest expression.'[94]

The best-known figure thrown up by the Universities' Mission to Central Africa was undoubtedly Frank Weston (1871–1924), son of a London tea-merchant, educated at Dulwich College and Trinity College, Oxford where he heard Smythies preach at St Barnabas, Jericho, and was moved to read the life of Smythies' own predecessor, Edward Steere.[95] From the townships of Magila and Masasi,[96] missions had fanned out with a characteristic cluster of school, chapel, and homes for boys or girls for there were many famine orphans. Hearing of these developments amid the Neo-Byzantine splendour of St Barnabas and fostering recollection by subsequent reading, seeds were sown. They started to germinate during Weston's first curacy which he served at St Matthew's, Westminster. Volunteering for the Universities' Mission, he was invited to train teachers for Ordination on the exotic island.

Soon after arrival in Zanzibar in 1898 he began raising money for a theological college (a project remotely mooted by Smythies). It duly opened with a modest total of eight students: a deacon, six readers and a reader in training. Weston saw its possibilities for a thoroughly African church. Adopting a severely ascetical lifestyle, he was quick to learn Swahili, a necessary precondition of missionary success.

Made Bishop of Zanzibar in 1907, Weston's *bêtes noires* were the urban economy and Islam. 'Two great dangers are threatening tropical Africa at this moment, the advance of commerce without religion from the South, and the still more determined advance of Mohammedanism from the North for the conversion of Central Africa to the obedience of the Prophet.'[97] He analyzed the reasons Islam could not solve the moral problems of Zanzibar society. Yet moral weaknesses on the part of European Christians, with their poor sense of fraternity with other

Ecumenism and Mission

races (let us call it by its name, 'racialism'), was no good argument for the superiority of their inherited faith. So Weston appealed instead to the fervent Christocentrism learnt in his Evangelical childhood and strengthened by his Anglo-Catholic doctrinal convictions as a mature man. The reason for mission was, Jesus, the Logos incarnate, wanted Abdullah to love him.

In the post-War world, Frank Weston was a thorn in the side both of British colonial servants in the newly acquired Tanganyika Protectorate and of Anglican Modernists back home. In his 1919 rocket 'The Serfs of Great Britain' he excoriated the authorities for continuing the German Empire's scheme of forced labour for work on roads and railways in the mainland region of his diocese.[98] On preaching tours in England he pleaded, 'Save our converts in Africa from reading in books by Christians at home all those things that are calculated to make them doubt whether there be a God at all, and such a thing as the Catholic revelation'.[99] He did not spare high ecclesiastics from this censure, in *The Christ and His Critics* branding Hensley Henson, the newly appointed Bishop of Hereford, an out-and-out Christological heretic.[100]

In characteristic late Tractarian style, he founded the Community of the Passion for Religious women, bringing Sisters on loan from the Community of the Holy Name at Malvern Link and the Society of Saint Margaret in Aberdeen to give his new foundation a promising start.[101] His efforts for East Africans were more successful than in dispelling Anglican Modernism at home. In 1921 when Winston Churchill (1874–1965) became Colonial Secretary he agreed with the Governors of Kenya and Uganda that the practice of forcibly dividing families in the name of cheap (or free) labour had to stop.

The last principal area of Anglo-Catholic missionary enterprise was in the Western Pacific. The career of George Augustus Selwyn, a missionary bishop in the Tractarian mould, but a moderate who was happy to work with old high churchmen of the Society for the Propagation of the Gospel, is inextricably bound up with that of the martyr bishop John Coleridge Patteson of Melanesia.

Selwyn (1809–78) was born in Hampstead, the son of the barrister who had initiated Prince Albert into the mysteries of English constitutional law.[102] After attending Ealing School, where he was a contemporary of Newman, he went on to Eton and St John's College, Cambridge, where he held a Fellowship from 1833 to 1840. A curacy at Windsor, 1837 to 1841, gave him access to high circles of Church and State where he came to the notice of Bishop Charles Blomfield of London. Following up the new possibilities opened by the Colonial Bishops Fund, Blomfield proposed him as first Bishop of New Zealand—a territory deemed to include Melanesia, possibly owing to a drafting mistake in the royal charter. Such was the scope of Selwyn's missionary ambitions that he looked even further afield, envisaging the 'conversion to Anglican Christianity of a vast region stretching from New Caledonia to Papua and New Guinea'.[103] He had to be content with a narrower canvas on which to draw: the northern New Hebrides (now Vanuatu) and the eastern and central Solomon islands—this was the 'Melanesia' of his prospective mission.

Selwyn travelled from England on a boat fitted out as a Noah's Ark of potentially useful animals, along with beehives. En route, he studied Maori and learned enough seamanship to be his own sailing master in the Pacific (he had a good start, as a member of the Cambridge crew in the first Oxford and Cambridge Boat Race held at Henley in 1829). Selwyn's Tractarian credentials are somewhat mysterious—in part, an inference from his difficult relations in New Zealand with (Evangelical) Church Missionary Society clergy, though in the twentieth century the College he created for ordinands was shunned by two dioceses on the grounds of its undesirably definite Anglo-Catholic ethos.[104] This was the College of St John the Evangelist, originally located at the Bay of Islands on the northernmost tip of North Island until Selwyn moved it to Auckland which he made his missionary base.

He was a vigorous bishop, setting up in 1844 a system of synods of local clergy (without reference to the Crown, and that four years after New Zealand became a Crown colony), and developing the home diocese sufficiently to justify its partition into four, with himself as metropolitan. In 1847 he made a series of voyages among the myriad island chains to the north of New Zealand, in consequence of which he realized the need for a suffragan to coordinate such insular missions. Selwyn's formation of the Australasian Board of Missions in 1850 led in turn to the foundation of the Melanesian Mission in the Western Pacific for which work he recruited John Coleridge Patteson in 1864.

Patterson (1837–71) was the nephew on his mother's side of Samuel Taylor Coleridge, growing up in the poet's birthplace, Ottery St Mary, in Devon, before schooling at Eton, followed by Balliol.[105] As an Oxford undergraduate he did not cover himself with glory, but on the strength of outstanding linguistic gifts (he would learn over twenty of the thousand and more Melanesian languages, producing grammars and dictionaries), he became in 1852 a Fellow of Merton College, Oxford, from whose cloistered calm Selwyn rudely uprooted him two years later. Selwyn was plainly his model since Patteson's first act on arrival was to set up an ordinand's training establishment, St Barnabas College on Norfolk Island.

In 1861 Patteson was consecrated the first Bishop of Melanesia. An episcopate of ten years was tragically ended by his murder at Nuhapu in the Solomon Islands in 1861. He had apparently been mistaken for a 'blackbirder', one of the piratical slave-merchants who captured men for labour in the plantations of Fiji and Australia. An alternative theory about his death was put forward by Norwegian ethnologists in 2010. He may have upset native elites by giving gifts that disrupted precedence and through seeking support among women.[106] In a period that preceded social-anthropological awakening, the circumstances did not worry Charlotte Yonge, whose own Tractarian eulogy, a two volume life of Patteson, assured Anglo-Catholics that they too, and not Evangelicals alone, had obeyed the 'Great Commission' given at the end of St Matthew's Gospel.[107]

The ambiguity which attended John Coleridge Patteson's death—whatever his enemies thought of him, his remains were reverently treated, his body placed in a canoe with a palm leaf on his chest, and pushed out to sea—foreshadowed, oddly enough, a comparable ambivalence attaching to George Augustus Selwyn's memory in New Zealand at the end of his mission there. His role as military chaplain-general in the suppression of the Kingitanga Movement—a protest against the alienation of Maori tribal land and the fiercest of the New Zealand wars of the nineteenth century—soured his memory among the indigenous population before he took leave of Auckland to return to England as Bishop of Lichfield. That was despite his enlightened attitudes to the Maori language and culture at large. In 1928 growing Maori pressure extracted the reluctant concessions of an all-Maori bishopric within the territory of the diocese of Waiapu which had been the scene of most of the fighting.[108]

Patteson's efforts, like Selwyn's, were long-lasting. By 1918 some fourteen thousand communicants were scattered across more than thirty islands. In 1926 the foundation of the Melanesian Brotherhood by indigenous islanders created a stock of native missionaries.[109] Its founder, Ini Kupuria (died 1945), a colonial policeman educated at St Barnabas College, underwent a visionary experience which led him to embrace a vocation inspired partly by Franciscanism but also by what he knew of ancient monasticism. In the Brotherhood, the practice was to take Religious vows but to do so only a year at a time. Its existence was invaluable not least in withstanding the shock of the Japanese invasion during World War Two and the difficulties of subsequent reconstruction. But by 1947 Melanesia had over eighty indigenous priests and deacons in place.

Aside from Melanesia, Oceania consists of Polynesia (Hawai'i, Fiji, Tonga, Samoa), Papua and New Guinea, and Micronesia. Anglo-Catholicism was no more influential in Polynesia than Anglicanism generally, for these islands had been largely evangelized by Methodists and

Congregationalists. In a strange interlude, a Tractarian priest, Alfred Willis (1836–1920), was brought out from London after the State visit of King Kamehameha IV of Hawai'i (1834–63) to Queen Victoria in 1849. A short-lived 'Reformed Catholic Church', supported by the king and his queen, had Willis as its bishop from 1872. After the American annexation of the islands in 1892–3 the Protestant Episcopal Church of the United States of America absorbed this fledgling body, with Willis becoming 'PECUSA' bishop of Honolulu. A missionary diocese for the remainder of Polynesia was created in 1908.

British New Guinea became the Australian colony of Papua in 1906. Missionary activity from Australia had already started, but not so long previously, in 1891.[110] 'Imbued by Anglo-Catholic reverence for both Catholic liturgical traditions and the sacramental functions of episcopate and the priesthood', missionaries typified by 'muscular Christian vigour and semi-monastic self-abnegation' envisaged for their converts 'absorption into the visible Church's fabric, disturbing only those traditional customs (namely, infanticide, sorcery, tribal warfare, and cannibalism) that explicitly contradicted the Christian teachings'.[111] They garnered a reputation that led Cosmo Gordon Lang, as archbishop of Canterbury, to put forward these missioners as evidence that the Church of England could still produce saints.[112] Active in translation work, ethnography, botany, they encouraged Papuan vocations through St Aidan's College, Dogura, where, as of 1937, a bishop had his chair in a Neo-Romanesque cathedral made entirely of local coral. At the time of the Japanese invasion, the Papuan church would count its losses: over three hundred martyrs. In 1960 the first Papuan bishop, George Ambo (1922–2008), was consecrated, descendant of a line of cannibal warrior chiefs. (He remembered his grandfather commenting on the peculiar succulence of the palm of the human hand.)

The further organization of Anglican life in the 'global communion' was not always kind to these missions. As a general rule, when dioceses were grouped together into Provinces there was a danger that those of Anglo-Catholic tradition would be swamped by others, whether Evangelical or broad church.[113] This proved especially to be so in east and central Africa where the Universities' Mission to Central Africa dioceses in Nyasaland, Zanzibar, Northern Rhodesia, the Masai and south-west Tanganyika found themselves dispersed across three Provinces (Central Africa, 1955, East Africa, 1960, Uganda, 1960). In the former German East Africa, together with Zanzibar, Evangelical growth considerably outstripped the successors of the Tractarians.[114] Anglo-Catholic efforts in India disappeared into the inter-Protestant melting pot of the 'Church of North India' in 1970. A glowing exception was the Church of Papua New Guinea, with its five homogeneously Anglo-Catholic dioceses.

Ecumenism and Mission

The future Archbishop Tait, Newman's nemesis, had argued in Convocation in 1860 against the 'plan of appointing Bishops at the head of merely inchoate churches', or entrusting bodies of Christians to their care. Might not a provincial synod adopt 'so completely... a mediaeval view of the Church as to make it very different from that wide and tolerant system which we have inherited from our forefathers'.[115] What he feared, and he was not alone, was a totally Tractarianised Church. But then that is the historic quandary of Anglo-Catholicism.

11

Conclusion

IN A LETTER DATED 26 November, 1844, John Mason Neale wrote from his place of convalescence in Madeira, 'I hope and believe that Newman will not leave us, but I should not despair if he did. My sheet anchor of hope for the English Church is that you cannot point out a single instance of an heretical or schismatic body which after apparent death awoke to life'.[1] The statement presupposes that the pre-Tractarian Church of England was more moribund than historians are now likely to admit. But Neale's touching words express both his wonderment at the amazing fruits of the Catholic Revival and also an argument that is not without merit. In matters of theology and spirituality, the liturgical life and the consecrated life, in social criticism and the realm of the arts, telltale signs of the agency of grace were there for all to see. At any rate, that was so if they were perceiving the phenomena with an orthodox mind and heart: with right *ethos* (favoured word of the Oxford Fathers) functioning as it should.

But the *content* of the Anglo-Catholic revival had to contend with an inherited ecclesial *form* which was not a good fit, or so its difficulties not only with primates but with Victoria suggest. For the form took its character from 'Anglicanism's historical origins [which lie] in anti-papal national royalism.'[2] The Anglo-Saxon kings had summoned synods and applied their rulings. When the link with Rome was snapped, corporate memory allowed the monarchy to enter the resultant jurisdictional void. The English Reformation might even be regarded, as the early Gladstone and Pusey were apt to do, as the Crown's recovery of its papally usurped role. The Cambridge mediaevalist Zachary Nugent Brooke (1883–1946), came to the sources with the antecedent view that this was correct, but *The English Church and the Papacy* shows he was quickly disabused.[3] The *Ecclesia anglicana* of the Middle Ages, whatever the particularities of its profile, had accepted the spiritual authority of the pope in the same terms as the rest of Western Christendom. An incoherence in the narrative is unavoidable. In the words of an Irish commentator, contemporary with Brooke, the 'reason why in the Church of England a pro-Roman party repeatedly arises is that the Church of England has no satisfying doctrine of the Church'.[4] In 2017 Colin Podmore (born 1960), Clerk to the General Synod of the Church of England, would comment on the disparity between 'episcopal' and 'mixed' forms of Church governance: those who 'saw the primates as the natural international representatives of their churches; and those who were 'uncomfortable with ceding authority to any forum in which the clergy and laity were not represented by members of their own "Orders"'. The 'difficulty in agreeing where ultimate responsibility should lie reflected differences in the understanding of the role of bishops in Church government that stemmed from the formation in 1867 of an Anglican Communion that brought together churches with very different ecclesiologies.'[5]

Disparity between content and form created the need for supplementation from without. 'Though we make full use of the Book of Common Prayer, insofar as we are able, and the canons and formulae of the Church of England, in order to support Catholic teaching, we do not believe these sources to be our only ones in matters of faith and practice.'[6] And again, 'Because we have been "initiated" into the Church of God in this particular country by the sacraments which the English Church gives us, we have an inherent sense of loyalty to her, and an affection for her which it is difficult to deny. Her Tudor formulations have at times proved a temporary inconvenience to us, and often a positive embarrassment, and we have treated the Church of England in consequence as an authority in matters of faith and discipline only insofar as she had echoed in her teaching and practice the doctrinal and liturgical heritage of that which is far greater than herself, in the Universal Church, and especially that "Western" part from which she sprang'.[7] Erastianism and doctrinal vagary were the Church of England's twofold Achilles' heel.

Dealt, in this sense, a weak hand, it was nevertheless remarkable what the Oxford Fathers made of it. William Stubbs told his clergy and churchwardens, the 'influences that wrought [the Oxford Movement] were more intellectual and more spiritual than those which effected the Reformation'.[8] Those 'influences' sowed seeds in all the areas scanned in this short book, and the seeds sprouted. And the fruit—herein described—is undeniable. In consequence, Roman Catholics, who, historically, were not their friends, must now, out of justice as well as by generosity of spirit, become their admirers. And more than admirers, their allies.

SELECT BIBLIOGRAPHY

General

Brown, Stewart J., and Peter B. Nockles (eds.), *The Oxford Movement: Europe and the Wider World, 1830–1930* (Cambridge: Cambridge University Press, 2014)

Brown, Stewart J., Peter B. Nockles and James Pereiro (eds.), *The Oxford Handbook of the Oxford Movement* (Oxford: Oxford University Press, 2012)

Chadwick, Owen, *The Victorian Church*, two volumes, 2nd edn (London: Adam & Charles Black, 1972)

Chapman, Mark D., Sathianathan Clark and Martyn Percy (eds.), *The Oxford Handbook of Anglican Studies* (Oxford: Oxford University Press, 2015)

Herring, George, *What was the Oxford Movement?* (London and New York: Continuum, 2002)

Hylson-Smith, Kenneth, *High Churchmanship in the Church of England. From the Sixteenth Century to the Late Twentieth Century* (Edinburgh: T. & T. Clark, 1993)

Lloyd, Roger, *The Church of England, 1900–1965* (London: Student Christian Movement, 1966)

Morris, Jeremy, *The High Church Revival in the Church of England. Arguments and Identities* (Leiden: Brill, 2016)

Morris, Jeremy (ed.), *The Oxford History of Anglicanism, Volume IV. Global Anglicanism, 1910–Present* (Oxford: Oxford University Press, 2017)

Nockles, Peter Benedict, *The Oxford Movement in Context. Anglican High Churchmanship, 1760–1857* (Cambridge: Cambridge University Press, 1994)

Ollard, S. L., *A Short History of the Oxford Movement* (London: Faith Press, 1963 [1932])

Sparrow-Simpson, W. J., *The History of the Anglo-Catholic Revival from 1845* (London: George Allen and Unwin, 1924)

Leslie Stewart, Herbert, *A Century of Anglo-Catholicism* (London: J. M. Dent, 1929)

Strong, Rowan (ed.), *The Oxford History of Anglicanism, Volume III. Partisan Anglicanism and its Global Expansion, 1829-c. 1914* (Oxford: Oxford University Press, 2019)

Vaiss, Paul (ed.), *From Oxford to the People. Reconsidering Newman and the Oxford Movement* (Leominster: Gracewing, 1996)

Williams, N. P., and C. Harris (eds.), *Northern Catholicism. Centenary Studies in the Oxford and Parallel Movements* (London: Society for Promoting Christian Knowledge, 1933)

Chapters 1 and 2

Battescombe, Georgina, *John Keble. A Study in Limitations* (London: Constable, 1963)

Blair, Kirstie (ed.), *John Keble in Context* (London: Anthem Books, 2004)

Butler, Perry, *Gladstone. Church, State, and Tractarianism: A Study of his Religious Ideals and Attitudes* (Oxford: Clarendon, 1982)

Butler, Perry (ed.), *Pusey Rediscovered* (London: Society for Promoting Christian Knowledge, 1983)

Coombs, Joyce, *George Anthony Denison: The Firebrand, 1805–1896* (London: Church Literature Association, 1984)

Cross, F. L., *Darwell Stone, Churchman and Counsellor* (London: Dacre Press, 1943)

Douglas, Brian, *The Eucharistic Theology of Edward Bouverie Pusey. Sources, Context, and Doctrine within the Oxford Movement and Beyond* (Leiden: Brill, 2015)

Galloway, Peter, *A Passionate Humility. Frederick Oakeley and the Oxford Movement* (Leominster: Gracewing, 1999)

Herring, George, *The Oxford Movement in Practice. The Tractarian Parochial World from the 1830s to the 1870s* (Oxford: Oxford University Press, 2006)

Hughes, Anselm, *The Rivers of the Flood. A Personal Account of the Catholic Movement in the Twentieth Century* (London: Faith Press, 1961)

Liddon, Henry Parry, *The Life of Edward Bouverie Pusey*, four volumes (London: Longmans Green, 1894–8)

Martin, Brian, *John Keble, Priest, Professor and Poet* (London: Croom Helm, 1976)

Morse-Boycott, Desmond, *Lead Kindly Light. Studies of the Saints and Heroes of the Oxford Movement* (London: Centenary Press, 1932; Macmillan 1933)

Moyse-Boycott, Desmond, *They Shine like Stars. The Story of the Great Church Revival* (London: Skeffington, 1947)

Newton, John, *Search for a Saint: Edward King* (London: Church Literature Association, 1983)

Select Bibliography

Ollard, S. L., *The Anglo-Catholic Revival. Some Persons and Principles* (London: Mowbray, 1925)
Prestige, Leonard, *Pusey* (London: Mowbray, 1982 [1933])
Rowell, Geoffrey, *The Vision Glorious. Themes and Personalities of the Catholic Revival in Anglicanism* (Oxford: Oxford University Press, 1982)
Smith, B. A., *Dean Church. The Anglican Response to Newman* (London: Oxford University Press, 1958)
Strong, Rowan, and Carol Engelhardt Herringer (eds.), *Edward Bouverie Pusey and the Oxford Movement* (London: Anthem Press, 2013)
Ward, Wilfrid, *William George Ward and the Oxford Movement* (London: Macmillan, 1889)
Wheeler, Robin, *Palmer's Pilgrimage. The Life of William Palmer of Magdalen* (Berne: Peter Lang, 2006)
Yelton, Michael, *Anglican Papalism. An Illustrated History, 1900–1960* (Norwich: Canterbury Press, 2005)

Chapters 3 and 4

Crouch, William, *Bryan King and the Riots at St George's-in-the-East* (London: Methuen, 1904)
Cuming, G. J., *A History of Anglican Liturgy* (London: Macmillan, 1969)
Ellsworth, L. E., *Charles Lowder and the Ritualist Movement* (London: Darton, Longman & Todd, 1982)
Gordon-Taylor, Benjamin, and Nicholas Stebbing (eds.), *Walter Frere: Scholar, Monk, Bishop* (Norwich: Canterbury Press, 2011)
Gray, Donald, *Earth and Altar. The Evolution of the Parish Communion in the Church of England to 1945* (London: Alcuin Club, 1986)
Gray, Donald, *Percy Dearmer. A Parson's Pilgrimage.* (Norwich: Canterbury Press, 2012)
Hawes, John, *Ritual and Riot* (Lewes: East Sussex County Library, 1995)
Kelway, A. Clifton, *George Rundle Prynne. A Chapter in the Early History of the Catholic Revival* (London: Longmans, Green and Company, 1905)
Macfarlane, Elizabeth, *Gilbert Hunter Doble. Cornish Anglo-Catholicism in a Celtic Context* (London: Anglo-Catholic History Society, 2015)
Maiden, John, *National Religion and the Prayer Book Controversy, 1927–1928* (Woodbridge: Boydell and Brewer, 2009)
Palmer, Bernard, *Five Victorian Clerics and their Fight against Authority* (London: Darton, Longman & Todd, 1993)
Reynolds, Michael, *Martyr of Ritualism, Father Mackonochie of St Alban's Holborn* (London: Faber and Faber, 1965)
Wagner, Anthony, and Antony Dale, *The Wagners of Brighton* (Cheltenham: The History Press, 1983)

Yates, Nigel, *Anglican Ritualism in Victorian Britain, 1839–1910* (Oxford: Oxford University Press, 1999)

Chapter 5

Allchin, Arthur Macdonald, *The Silent Rebellion. Anglican Religious Communities, 1845–1900* (London: Student Christian Movement, 1958)

Anson, Peter F., *The Call of the Cloister: Religious Communities and Kindred Bodies in the Anglican Communion* (London: Society for Promoting Christian Knowledge, 1956)

Brandreth, Henry R. T., OGS, *The Oratory of the Good Shepherd. An Historical Sketch* (Cambridge: Oratory of the Good Shepherd, 1958)

Dunstan, Petà, *The Labour of Obedience. The Benedicines of Pershore, Nashdom and Elmore: A History* (Norwich: Canterbury Press, 2009)

Dunstan, Petà, *This Poor Sort. History of the European Province of the Society of St Francis* (London: Darton, Longman & Todd, 2011)

Hill, Michael, *The Religious Order. A Study of Virtuoso Religion and its Legitimation in the Nineteenth Century Church of England* (London: Heinemann, 1973)

James, Serenhedd, *The Cowley Fathers: A History of the English Congregation of the Society of St John the Evangelist* (Norwich: Canterbury Press, 2019)

Kollar, René, *Abbot Aelred Carlyle, Caldey Island, and the Anglo-Catholic Revival in England* (New York: Peter Lang, 1995)

Mason, Alistair, *History of the Society of the Sacred Mission* (Norwich: Canterbury Press, 1993)

Mumm, Susan, *All Saints Sisters of the Poor. An Anglican Sisterhood in the Nineteenth Century* (London: Church of England Record Society, 2001)

Smith, Martin L., SSJE (ed.), *Benson of Cowley* (Oxford: Oxford University Press, 1980)

Tibbatts, George, OGS, *The Oratory of the Good Shepherd. The First Seventy-five Years* (Windsor: The Almoner, 1988)

Wilkinson, Alan, *The Community of the Resurrection. A Centenary History* (London: Student Christian Movement, 2011)

Williams, Barrie, *The Franciscan Revival in the Church of England* (London: Darton, Longman & Todd, 1982)

Williams, Thomas Jay, *Priscilla Lydia Sellon, the Restorer after Three Centuries of Religious Life in the English Church* (London: Society for Promoting Christian Knowledge, 1950)

Williams, Thomas Jay, and Allan Walter Campbell, *The Park Village Sisterhood* (London: Society for Promoting Christian Knowledge, 1965)

Chapter 6

Bettany, E. G., *Stewart Headlam. A Biography* (London: John Murray, 1926)
Chapman, Mark D., *Liturgy, Socialism and Life. The Legacy of Conrad Noel* (London: Darton, Longman & Todd, 2001)
Eliot, T. S., *The Idea of a Christian Society* (London: Faber and Faber, 1939)
Gloyn, Cyril K., *The Church in the Social Order: A Study of Anglican Social Theory from Coleridge to Maurice* (Forest Grove, OR: Pacific University, 1942)
Lyttelton, Edward, *The Mind and Character of Henry Scott Holland* (London: Mowbray, 1926)
Norman, Edward R., *The Victorian Christian Socialists* (Cambridge: Cambridge University Press, 2002)
Peart-Binns, John S., *Maurice B. Reckitt: A Life* (London: Marshall Pickering, 1988)
Reckitt, Maurice, *Maurice to Temple: A History of the Social Movement in the Church of England* (London: Faber and Faber, 1947)
Reckitt, Maurice, *P. E. T. Widdrington. A Study in Vocation and Versatility* (London: Society for Promoting Christian Knowledge, 1961)
Reckitt, Maurice (ed.), *Prospect for Christendom. Essays in Catholic Social Reconstruction* (London: Faber and Faber, 1947 [1945])
Rowlands, J. H. L., *Church, State and Society. The Attitudes of John Keble, Richard Hurrell Froude and John Henry Newman, 1827–1845* (Worthing: Churchman, 1989)
Skinner, S. A., *Tractarians and the 'Condition of England': The Social and Political Thought of the Oxford Movement* (Oxford: Oxford University Press, 2004)
Wakefield, Gordon, *Francis Noel Davey. A Memoir* (London: Society for Promoting Christian Knowledge, 1981)

Chapter 7

Bailey, Simon, *A Tactful God. Gregory Dix, Priest, Monk and Scholar* (Leominster: Gracewing, 2002)
Bockmuehl, Markus, and Stephen Platten (eds.), *Austin Farrer. Oxford Warden, Scholar, Preacher* (London: Student Christian Movement, 2000)
Chadwick, Owen, *Michael Ramsey. A Life* (Oxford: Clarendon Press, 1990)
Curtis, Philip, *A Hawk among Sparrows: A Biography of Austin Farrer* (London: Society for Promoting Christian Knowledge, 1985)
Hefling, Charles, *Jacob's Ladder: Theology and Spirituality in the Thought of Austin Farrer* (Cambridge, MA: Cowley Publications, 1979)
Irvine, Christopher, *Worship, Church and Society: The Work of Arthur Gabriel Hebert* (Norwich: Canterbury Press, 1993)

Johnson, John Octavius, *Life and Letters of H. P. Liddon* (London: Longmans, Green and Co., 1904)
Jones, Simon (ed.), *The Sacramental Life. Gregory Dix and his Writings* (Norwich: Canterbury Press, 2007)
Kemp, E. W., *The Life and Letters of Kenneth Escott Kirk, Bishop of Oxford, 1937–1954* (London: Hodder and Stoughton, 1959)
Mascall, E. L., *Saraband. The Memoirs of E. L. Mascall* (Leominster: Gracewing, 1992)
Ramsey, Arthur Michael, *From Gore to Temple. The Development of Anglican Theology from 'Lux Mundi' to the Second World War, 1889–1939* (London: Longmans, 1960)
Slocum, Robert Boak, *Light in a Burning-Glass. A Systematic Presentation of Austin Farrer's Theology* (Columbia, SC: University of South Carolina Press, 2007)
Waddell, Peter, *Charles Gore, Radical Anglican* (Norwich: Canterbury Press, 2019)

Chapter 8

Bayfield-Roberts, George, *The History of the English Church Union, 1859–1894* (London: Church Printing, 1895)
Gunstone, John, *Lift High the Cross: Anglo-Catholics and the Congress Movement* (Norwich: Canterbury Press, 2010)
Higgs, Owen, David Houlding, Anthony Howe, Trevor Jones, Robert Mackley, Kenneth Macnab, Luke Miller and Geoffrey Rowell, *In This Sign Conquer: A History of the Society of the Holy Cross (Societas Sanctae Crucis) 1855–2005* (London: Continuum, 2006)
Kirk, Kenneth E., *The Story of the Woodard Schools* (London: Hodder and Stoughton, 1937)
Walsh, Michael, *Look to the Rock. The Catholic League and the Anglican Papalist Quest for Reunion* (Norwich: Canterbury Press, 2019)

Chapter 9

Baker, Joseph Ellis, *The Novel and the Oxford Movement* (Princeton, NJ: Princeton University Press, 1932)
Barlow, Adrian, *The Life and Legacy of Charles Eamer Kempe* (Cambridge: Lutterworth Press, 2018)
Barnes, John E., *George Ratcliffe Woodward, 1848–1934, Priest, Poet, Musician* (Norwich: Canterbury Press, 2012)
Bremner, G. A., *Imperial Gothic. Religious Architecture and High Anglican Culture in the British Empire, 1840–1870* (New Haven, CT: Yale University Press, 2013)

Select Bibliography

Brandwood, Geoff, *George Edmund Street*, ed. P. Howell and P. C. W. Taylor (Liverpool: Liverpool University Press, 2024)

Cavaliero, Glen, *Charles Williams, Poet of Theology* (Grand Rapids, Eerdmans, 1983)

Chandler, Michael, *The Life and Work of John Mason Neale, 1818–1866* (Leominster: Gracewing, 1995)

Chapman, Raymond, *Faith and Revolt. Studies in the Literary Influence of the Oxford Movement* (London: Weidenfeld and Nicolson, 1970)

Dennis, Barbara, *Charlotte Yonge (1823–1901), Novelist of the Oxford Movement: A Literature of Victorian Customs and Society* (Lewiston, NY: Edwin Mellen Press, 1992)

Dickinson, B. H. C., *Sabine Baring-Gould: Squarson, Writer, and Folklorist, 1834–1924* (Newton Abbot: David and Charles, 1970)

Emery, Jane, *Rose Macaulay. A Writer's Life* (London: John Murray, 1991)

Hall, Michael, *George Frederick Bodley and the Later Gothic Revival in Britain and America* (New Haven, CT: Yale University Press, 2014)

Hayter, Alethea, *Charlotte Yonge* (London: Northcote House, 1996)

Howard, Thomas, *The Novels of Charles Williams* (New York and London: Oxford University Press, 1983)

Jones, Kathleen, *Learning Not to be First. A Biography of Christina Rossetti* (Oxford: Oxford University Press, 1991)

Lindop, Grevel, *Charles Williams. The Third Inkling* (Oxford: Oxford University Press, 2015)

Litvack, Leon, *John Mason Neale and the Quest for Sobornost* (Oxford: Clarendon, 1994)

Lockerd, Benjamin G. (ed.), *T. S. Eliot and Christian Tradition* (Lanham, MD: Fairham Dickinson University Press, 2014)

Mason, Emma, *Christina Rossetti. Poetry, Ecology, Faith* (Oxford: Oxford University Press, 2017)

Olsberg, Nicholas, *The Master Builder: William Butterfield and his Times* (London; Lund Humphries, 2021)

Quiney, Anthony, *John Loughborough Pearson* (New Haven, CT: Yale University Press, 1979)

Rainbow, Bernard, *The Choral Revival in the Anglican Church, 1839–1872* (New York: Oxford University Press, 1970)

Spurr, Barry, *Anglo-Catholic in Religion. T. S. Eliot and Christianity* (Cambridge: Lutterworth Press, 2010)

Symondson, Anthony, and S. A. Bucknall, *Sir Ninian Comper. An Introduction to his Life and Work* (Reading: Spire Books, 2006)

Tennyson, G. B., *Victorian Devotional Poetry: The Tractarian Mode* (Cambridge, MA: Harvard University Press, 1981)

White, James F., *The Cambridge Movement. The Ecclesiologists and the Gothic Revival* (Cambridge, 1962)

Chapter 10

Denaux, Adelbert, and John A. Dick (eds.), *From Malines to ARCIC: The Malines Conversations Commemorated* (Leuven: Peeters, 1997)

Etherington, Norman (ed.), *Missions and Empire* (Oxford: Oxford University Press, 2005)

Evans, J. H., *Churchman Militant: George Augustus Selwyn, Bishop of New Zealand and Lichfield* (London: Allen and Unwin, 1964)

Good, James, *The Church of England and the Ecumenical Movement. A Catholic Appreciation* (Cork: Cork University Press, and London: Burns and Oates, 1961)

Greenacre, Roger, *Lord Halifax* (London: Church Historical Association, 1983)

Huelin, Gordon (ed.), *Old Catholics and Anglicans, 1931–1981* (Oxford: Oxford University Press, 1983)

Maynard Smith, H., *Frank, Bishop of Zanzibar* (London: Society for Promoting Christian Knowledge, 1926)

Wilson, G. H., *The History of the Universities' Mission to Central Africa* (London: Universities' Mission to Central Africa, 1936)

Yonge, Charlotte, *Life of John Coleridge Patteson, Missionary Bishop of the Melanesian Islands*, two volumes (London: Macmillan, 1875)

NOTES

Preface

1 Aidan Nichols, OP, *The Panther and the Hind. A Theological History of Anglicanism* (Edinburgh: T. & T. Clark, 1992), pp. 177–80.
2 Francis Penhale, *Catholics in Crisis* (London: Mowbray, 1986).
3 Aidan Nichols, OP, *Catholics of the Anglican Patrimony. The Personal Ordinariate of Our Lady of Walsingham* (Leominster: Gracewing, 2013).
4 Geoffrey Rowell, *The Vision Glorious. Themes and Personalities of the Catholic Revival in Anglicanism* (Oxford: Oxford University Press, 1982).
5 For a personal view, see Aidan Nichols, OP, *Apologia: A Memoir* (Leominster: Gracewing, 2023).

Chapter 1

1 John Shelton Reed, *Glorious Battle. The Cultural Politics of Victorian Anglo-Catholicism* (Chapel Hill, NC: Bozart Books, 2017 [1996]), p. 12.
2 Owen Chadwick, *The Victorian Church*, 2nd edn (London: Adam & Charles Black, 1970), two volumes, i, p. 168.
3 Peter Benedict Nockles, *The Oxford Movement in Context. Anglican High Churchmanship, 1760–1857* (Cambridge: Cambridge University Press, 1994). Insofar as a more Catholic understanding of doctrine, including ecclesiology and sacramental theology, survived the advent of the House of Hanover, it was best evidenced in the non-Jurors: thus Richard Sharp, '"The Communion of the Primitive Church"? High Churchmen in England, c.1710–1760', in Stewart J. Brown, Peter B. Nockles and James Pereiro (eds.), *The Oxford Handbook of the Oxford Movement* (Oxford: Oxford University Press, 2012), pp. 23–37. Yet a modest but not insignificant pre-Tractarian high church recovery took place under George III. Compare Nigel Aston, 'High Church Presence and Persistence: in the Reign of George III, 1760–1811', *ibid.*, pp. 51–66.
4 Chadwick, *The Victorian Church*, i, p. 181.
5 For Keble's life, see Georgina Battescombe, *John Keble. A Study in Limitations* (London: Constable, 1963); Brian Martin, *John Keble, Priest, Professor and Poet* (London: Croom Helm, 1976).
6 S. L. Ollard, *A Short History of the Oxford Movement* (London and Oxford: Mowbray, 1963 [1932], 2nd edition), p. 39.
7 John Keble, *Sermons Academical and Occasional* (Oxford: Parker, and London: Rivington, 1847)

8 See notably John Keble, *On the Mysticism attributed to the Early Fathers of the Church* (*Tracts for the Times*, 89) (London: Rivington, 1841).

9 John Keble, *Lectures on Poetry* (Oxford: Clarendon Press, 1912, 2nd edition [Latin original, 1844]).

10 John Keble, *The Christian Year. Thoughts in Verse for the Sundays and Holydays throughout the Year* (New York: Appleton, 1975 [1827]). There were ninety-five editions by the date of Keble's death. Keble's view of poetry was not, however, vatic: the Romantics for him were not oracles but by piling up imaginative associations these poets had awakened moral, religious, even mystical feelings which prepared the way for *real* religious revival when it came.

11 James Pereiro, 'John Keble and the Ethos of the Oxford Movement', in Kirstie Blair (ed.), *John Keble in Context* (London: Anthem Press, 2004), pp. 59–72, and especially pp. 60–5.

12 For an attempt to characterize it, see F. L. Cross, *Preaching in the Anglo-Catholic Revival* (London: Society for Promoting Christian Knowledge, 1933).

13 Jeremy Morris, *The High Church Revival in the Church of England. Arguments and Identities* (Leiden: Brill, 2016), p. 186.

14 For a full discussion of 'Tractarian poetics', based primarily on Keble, and, in dependence on Keble, Newman, see G. B. Tennyson, *Victorian Devotional Poetry. The Tractarian Mode* (Cambridge, MA: Harvard University Press, 1981), pp. 12–71.

15 For the influence of the Lake Poets, see Stephen Prickett, *Romanticism and Religion. The Tradition of Coleridge and Wordsworth in the Victorian Church* (Cambridge: Cambridge University Press, 1976).

16 Rowell, *The Vision Glorious*, p. 10.

17 H. L. Stewart, *A Century of Anglo-Catholicism* (London and Toronto: Dent, 1929), p. 69.

18 John Keble, *National Apostasy: Considered in a Sermon Preached in St Mary's, Oxford before His Majesty's Judges of Assize on Sunday, July 14th, 1833* (London: Mowbray, 1931 [1833]). For a detailed study of the Tracts through their various nineteenth century editions see Rune Imberg, *In Quest of Authority: The 'Tracts for the Times' and the Development of the Tractarian Leaders, 1833–1841* (Lund: Lund University Press, 1987).

19 George Herring, *What was the Oxford Movement?* (London and New York: Continuum, 2002), pp. 46–7.

20 Robert Harvie Greenfield, SSJE, 'Such a Friend to the Pope', in Perry Butler (ed.), *Pusey Rediscovered* (London: Society for Promoting Christian Knowledge, 1983), pp. 162–84, and here at p. 166.

21 John Keble, *Occasional Papers and Reviews* (Oxford and London: James Parker, 1877).

22 On one view, Pusey was consistent in his 'Germanist' period, as later, in seeking a scriptural warrant for doctrine. But in his Tractarian maturity he found the Fathers superior to the moderns in their 'insight and spirituality' as exegetes. On a rather jaundiced account, which fails to see the need for adjudication of the mind of the Fathers, a later turn to ecclesiastical 'authoritarianism' was a regrettable falling away from both: thus Leighton Frappell, '"Science" in the service of orthodoxy: the early intellectual development of E. B. Pusey', in Butler, *Pusey Rediscovered*, pp. 1–33.

Notes

²³ E. B. Pusey, *The Holy Eucharist a Comfort to the Penitent. A sermon preached before the University in the cathedral church of Christ in Oxford on the fourth Sunday after Easter, 1843* (Oxford: Parker, and London: Rivington, 1843).

²⁴ Ruth Teale, 'Dr Pusey and the Church Overseas', in Butler, *Pusey Rediscovered*, pp. 183–209, and here at p. 205.

²⁵ E. B. Pusey, *Entire Absolution of the Penitent. A sermon preached before the University in the cathedral church of Christ in Oxford on the first Sunday in Advent, 1846* (Oxford: Parker, and London: Rivington, 1846).

²⁶ The Tractarian 'ethos' might be called a synthesis of old high churchmanship with Evangelicalism, despite the major differences over *sola scriptura* and justification: compare Robert Wilberforce, *The Evangelical and Tractarian Movements* (London: John Murray, 1851).

²⁷ Cited in Keith Denison, 'Dr Pusey as Confessor and Spiritual Director', in Butler, *Pusey Rediscovered*, pp. 210–30, and here at p. 216.

²⁸ Quoted in Reed, *Glorious Battle*, p 117,

²⁹ Cited in Denison, 'Dr Pusey as Confessor and Spiritual Director', p. 226.

³⁰ E. B. Pusey, *The Doctrine of the Real Presence as contained in the Fathers from the Death of St John the Evangelist to the Fourth General Council vindicated by notes on a sermon 'The Presence of Christ in the Holy Eucharist' presented before the University of Oxford* (Oxford: Parker, and London: Rivington, 1855); see also Brian Douglas, *The Eucharistic Theology of Edward Bouverie Pusey. Sources, Context, and Doctrine within the Oxford Movement and Beyond* (Leiden: Brill, 2015).

³¹ Rowell, *The Vision Glorious*, p. 35.

³² Chadwick, *The Victorian Church*, ii, p. 189.

³³ See for instance the skilful 'Introduction' added to Ollard, *A Short History of the Oxford Movement*, at pp. 7–14. Allchin wrote the Introduction in 1963 and revised it in 1983.

³⁴ Ollard, *A Short History of the Oxford Movement*, pp. 105–6. Despite an initial show of sympathy Evangelicals remained unconvinced by early Tractarianism, as in Peter Toon, *Evangelical Theology, 1833–1856: A Response to Tractarianism* (London: Marshall, Morgan and Scott, 1979).

³⁵ A. M. Allchin, 'Pusey: The Servant of God', in Butler, *Pusey Rediscovered*, pp. 366–90, and here at p. 371.

³⁶ Peter G. Cobb, 'Leader of the Anglo-Catholics?', in Butler, *Pusey Rediscovered*, pp. 349–65, and here at p. 349.

³⁷ Cited from George Anthony Denison, Archdeacon of Taunton, *ibid.*, p. 359.

³⁸ Roderick Strange, 'Reflections on a Controversy: Newman and Pusey's *Eirenicon*', in Butler, *Pusey Rediscovered*, pp. 332–48.

³⁹ Cited in Greenfield, 'Such a Friend to the Pope', p. 173.

⁴⁰ John Henry Newman, *A Letter Addressed to His Grace the Duke of Norfolk on Occasion of Mr Gladstone's Recent Expostulation* (London: Pickering, 1875).

⁴¹ H. E. Manning, *The Workings of the Holy Spirit in the Church of England A Letter to the Rev. E. B. Pusey, D. D.* (London: Longmans, 1864).

⁴² E. B. Pusey, *The Church of England a Portion of Christ's One Holy Catholic Church and a Means of Restoring Visible Unity. An Eirenicon in a Letter to the Author of 'The*

Christian Year' (Oxford: John Henry and James Parker, 1865).

43 Greenfield, 'Such a Friend to the Pope', p. 173.

44 E. B. Pusey, 'Introduction', in Frederick George Lee (ed.), *Essays on Reunion* (London: Gilbert and Rivington, 1867), p. xxvi.

45 R. W. Church, *The Oxford Movement: Twelve Years, 1833–1845* (London: Macmillan, 1889), Chapter XIX, 'The Catastrophe'.

46 William Palmer, *Harmony of Anglican Doctrine with the Doctrine of the Eastern Church* (Aberdeen: A. Brown, 1846).

47 Robin Wheeler, *Palmer's Pilgrimage. The Life of William Palmer of Magdalen* (Berne: Peter Lang, 2006).

48 William Palmer, *Notes of a Visit to the Russian Church in the Years 1840, 1841*, selected and arranged by Cardinal Newman (London: Kegan Paul Trench & Co., 1882).

49 Frederick Oakeley, *Sermons Preached Chiefly in the Royal Chapel at Whitehall* (Oxford: Parker, 1839).

50 Chadwick, *The Victorian Church*, i, p. 212.

51 Ollard, *A Short History of the Oxford Movement*, p. 119.

52 Chadwick, *The Victorian Church*, i, p. 221.

53 Oakeley left accounts of his own side of the story: *Personal Reminiscences of the Oxford Movement* (London: Teulon, 1855), and *Historical Notes on the Tractarian Movement* (London: Longmans, 1865). See also Peter Galloway, *A Passionate Humility. Frederick Oakeley and the Oxford Movement* (Leominster: Gracewing, 1999).

54 William George Ward, *Ideal of the Christian Church in Comparison with Existing Practice* (London: James Toovey, 1844).

55 Wilfrid Ward, *William George Ward and the Oxford Movement* (London: Macmillan, 1889).

56 Despite its name, the *Review* was edited and published in London. Co-founded by Daniel O'Connell, 'The Liberator', along with Nicholas Wiseman, the head of the restored hierarchy, it represented at once Irish Emancipationism and a renascent Romanism: the two chief political bugbears of those who regretted the effective end of the Tory union of Throne and Altar in the old Post-Restoration 'Church-State'. See Wilfrid Ward, *William George Ward and the Catholic Revival* (London: Macmillan, 1895).

57 Theodore K. Hoppen, 'William George Ward and Liberal Catholicism', *Journal of Ecclesiastical History* 23 (1972), pp. 327–44; Theodore K. Hoppen, 'Church, State, and Ultramontanism in Mid-Victorian England: The Case of William George Ward', *The Journal of Church and State* 18. 2 (1976), pp. 289–309.

58 Michael Yelton, *Anglican Papalism. An Illustrated History, 1900–1960* (Norwich: Canterbury Press, 2005).

59 Cited in A. T. John Salter, *The Anglican Papalist: A Personal Portrait of Heny Joy Fynes-Clinton* (London: Anglo-Catholic History Society, 2012), p. 136.

60 B. A. Smith, *Dean Church. The Anglican Response to Newman* (London: Oxford University Press, 1958).

Notes

Chapter 2

[1] J. C. D. Clark, *English Society, 1760–1832. Religion, Ideology and Politics during the Ancien Regime* (Cambridge: Cambridge University Press, 2000), 2nd edition.

[2] O. J. Brose, *Church and Parliament, The Reshaping of the Church of England, 1825–1860* (London: Oxford University Press, 1959).

[3] Chadwick, *The Victorian Church*, i, p. 296.

[4] See E. R. Norman, *Anti-Catholicism in Victorian England* (London: George Allen & Unwin, 1968).

[5] Chadwick, *The Victorian Church*, i, p. 303.

[6] *Ibid.*, p. 263.

[7] *Ibid.*, p. 318.

[8] *Ibid.*, p. 270.

[9] Reed, *Glorious Battle*, p. 64.

[10] Ollard, *A Short History of the Oxford Movement*, p. 90.

[11] Cited *ibid.*, p. 102.

[12] Roy Nash, *Scandal in Madeira. The Story of Richard Thomas Lowe* (Lewes: Book Guild Publishing, 1990), pp. 34–87.

[13] Peter B. Nockles, 'Pusey on Church and State', in Butler, *Pusey Rediscovered*, pp. 255–97, and here at p. 282.

[14] Cited *ibid.*

[15] For these differentiated attitudes, see J. H. L. Rowlands, *Church, State and Society. The Attitudes of John Keble, Richard Hurrell Froude and John Henry Newman, 1827–1845* (Worthing: Churchman, 1989).

[16] E. B. Pusey, *The Royal Supremacy not an Arbitrary Authority, but Limited by the Laws of the Church of which Kings are Members* (Oxford: Parker, 1850).

[17] Charles's star, however, continued to rise. A decade or so after Pusey's death, Anglo-Catholics would create, in 1894, a 'Society of King Charles the Martyr', seeking to advance knowledge of his life and the worthy celebration of his 'feast' day — more like a day of national penitence — 30 January (in fact the day been removed from the Prayer Book Kalendar in 1859 by Royal Warrant — had they not noticed?). In 1911 a 'Memorial of Merit of King Charles the Martyr' would be instituted for services to the Anglo-Catholic cause.

[18] Nockles, 'Pusey on Church and State', pp. 284, 285.

[19] The 'Catholic' movement in the United States had a different lineage, owing to the origins of the Episcopal Church in Scottish Episcopalianism, from that elsewhere. For the intersection, see Peter Nockles, *The Oxford Movement and the United States of America* (London: Anglo-Catholic History Society, 2012), who, however, stresses, over against earlier writers, the Latitudinarian component in American Episcopal polity and policy, *ibid.*, p. 1. Though Tractarianism found a ready hearing in some quarters, 'Native and long-standing fears of episcopal despotism and "priestcraft", dating back to the Colonial era, resurfaced', such that '[s]ignificantly, the number of high church clerics raised to the American episcopate declined after the 1840s', *ibid.*, p. 16.

[20] Teale, 'Dr Pusey and the Church Overseas', p. 199.

21 Cited *ibid.*, pp. 199–200. In the twentieth century, the theological quality of discussion in successive forms of a 'house of laity' was notably lower, observers agreed, than in Convocations. And by the time a 'General Synod' was instituted in 1970, such a house had a veto on all legislation.

22 Perry Butler, *Gladstone. Church, State, and Tractarianism: A Study of his Religious Ideals and Attitudes* (Oxford: Clarendon, 1982), p. 36.

23 Butler, *Gladstone*, pp. 59, 52.

24 W. E. Gladstone, *The State in its Relations with the Church* (London: John Murray, 1838), p. 80.

25 Butler, *Gladstone*, p. 89.

26 W. E. Gladstone, *The State in its Relations with the Church* (London: John Murray, 4th edn, 1841).

27 For the problems involved in a 'colonial Church', see Joseph Hardwick, *An Anglican British World, The Church of England and the Expansion of the Settler Empire, c. 1790–1860* (Manchester: Manchester University Press, 2014).

28 Butler, *Gladstone*, p. 112.

29 Cited *ibid.*, p. 127.

30 *Ibid.*, p. 204.

31 'Edward King's "Bishopric of Love"' was the title given to the chapter on King in Rowell, *The Vision Glorious*, pp. 144–57.

32 Chadwick, *The Victorian Church*, ii, pp. 337–8.

33 William Whitla and Victor Shea (eds.), *Essays and Reviews: The 1860 Text and its Reading* (Charlottesville: University Press of Virginia, 2000).

34 H. J. Stewart, *A Century of Anglo-Catholicism*, p. 181.

35 Ieuan Ellis, *Seven against Christ. A Study of 'Essays and Reviews'* (Leiden: Brill, 1980).

36 Cited in Stewart, *A Century of Anglo-Catholicism*, pp. 182, 181.

37 Charles Gore (ed.), *Lux Mundi. A Series of Studies in the Religion of the Incarnation* (London: John Murray, 1889).

38 *Ibid.*, p. 360.

39 Chadwick, *The Victorian Church*, ii, p. 101.

40 Cited in Stewart, *A Century of Anglo-Catholicism*, p. 189.

41 For this figure see Gwendolin Stephenson, *Edward Stuart Talbot, 1844–1934* (London: Society for Promoting Christian Knowledge, 1936).

42 Charles Gore, *The Incarnation of the Son of God* (London: John Murray, 1895).

43 Charles Gore, *The Basis of Anglican Fellowship in Faith and Organisation* (London: Mowbray, 1914). This was not a change in consequence of preferment, as some have alleged. He held the same position in *The Clergy and the Creeds* (London: Rivington, 1887).

44 There was less question with the Orthodox of appeal to magisterium, the 'authority of the Church rendered peremptory and absolute' in appeal to revelation: Charles Gore, 'The Bible in the Church', in Charles Gore, Henry Leighton Goudge and Alfred Guillaume, *A New Commentary on Holy Scripture. Including the Apocrypha* (London: Society for Promoting Christian Knowledge, 1929), pp. 1–18, and here at p. 17.

Notes

45 Charles Gore, *Lambeth on Contraceptives* (London: Mowbray, 1930). For Gore's theology overall, see P. D. L. Avis, *Gore: Construction and Conflict* (Worthing: Churchman, 1988), and more recently Peter Waddell, *Charles Gore, Radical Anglican* (Norwich: Canterbury Press, 2019).

46 Robert Ottley, *The Doctrine of the Incarnation* (London: Methuen, 1896).

47 Richard Watson Dixon, *History of the Church of England from the Abolition of the Roman Jurisdiction* (London: G. Routledge & Sons, 1877–90. A second edition appeared from Oxford University Press, a sign of academic recognition, in 1895 to 1902.

48 Diarmaid MacCulloch, 'The Myth of the English Reformation', *Journal of British Studies* 30 (1991), pp. 1–4; see also Alec Ryrie, 'The Reformation in Anglicanism', in Mark D. Chapman, Sathianathan Clark, and Martyn Percy (ed.), *The Oxford Handbook of Anglican Studies* (Oxford, Oxford University Press, 2015), pp. 34–45.

49 Cited in Reed, *Glorious Battle*, p. 63. Among the historians Nicholas Pocock came closest to this in his *The Recovery from the Principles of the Reformation* (London: English Church Union, 1877).

50 James Kirby, *Historians and the Church of England. Religion and Historical Scholarship, 1870–1920* (Oxford: Oxford University Press, 2016), p. 11.

51 J. R. Green, *A Short History of the English People* (London: Macmillan, 1874).

52 John Hungerford Pollen, *Narrative of Five Years at St Saviour's, Leeds* (Oxford: J. Vincent, 1851). Pollen himself left over the Gorham Judgment, the year after the book's publication. A member of the Pre-Raphaelite circle, he designed the Catholic University of Ireland Church in Dublin, where he also became Professor of Fine Arts—on Newman's recommendation in both cases.

53 George Herring, 'The Parishes', in Stewart, Brown, Nockles and Pereiro, *The Oxford Handbook of the Oxford Movement*, pp. 349–60, and here at p. 350. See more widely the same author's *The Oxford Movement in Practice: The Tractarian Parochial World from the 1830s to the 1870s* (Oxford: Oxford University Press, 2018).

54 Herring, *What was the Oxford Movement?*, pp. 67–9.

55 Morris, *The High Church Revival in the Church of England*, p. 12. See Frances Knight, 'The Influence of the Oxford Movement in the Parishes: A Reassessment', in Paul Vaiss (ed.), *From Oxford to the People. Reconsidering Newman and the Oxford Movement* (Leominster: Gracewing, 1996), pp. 127–40; Jeremy Morris, 'The Regional Growth of Tractarianism', *ibid.*, pp. 141–59.

56 Morris, *The High Church Revival in the Church of England*, p. 6.

57 That reflected the increasingly sophisticated organizational structure of dioceses: see Arthur Burns, *The Diocesan Revival in the Church of England, c. 1800–1870* (Oxford: Oxford University Press, 1999).

58 John Gunstone, *Lift High the Cross: Anglo-Catholics and the Congress Movement* (Norwich: Canterbury Press, 2010), p. 83.

59 T. S. Eliot, *Reunion by Destruction: Reflections on a Scheme for Church Union in South India* (Westminster: Pax House, 1943).

60 Serenhedd James, *The Cowley Fathers: A History of the English Congregation of the Society of St John the Evangelist* (Norwich: Canterbury Press, 2019), p. 299. The view that the Church of South India scheme was a 'stalking horse' for a Pan-Protestant federation in England was vindicated when it became the prototype of the later scheme for Anglican-Methodist union, see Yelton, *Anglican Papalism*, pp. 54–5.

61 Michael Yelton, *The South India Controversy and the Converts of 1955–1956: An Episode in Recent Anglo-Catholic History* (London: Anglo-Catholic History Society, 2011). The best known of the presumably relatively small number were two priests: Hugh Ross Williamson (1901–78), an utterly unplaceable figure, *ibid.*, pp. 46–59, and Walton Hannah (1912–66), a spirited critic of Freemasonry, not least in the Church, *ibid.*, pp. 26–45. For other seceders, see *ibid.*, pp. 60–75. In his account of Hannah, Yelton reports that George VI, Archbishop Fisher, and at the start of the reign of Elizabeth II, an estimated dozen or so other Anglican bishops were members of Lodges, and that Fisher instructed the Society for Promoting Christian Knowledge not to stock Hannah's book on the incompatibility of Christianity with Freemasonry, namely: *Darkness Invisible: A Revelation and Interpretation of Freemasonry* (London: Augustine Press, 1952).

62 Henry St John, OP, 'Anglicanism and the Church of South India', *New Blackfriars* 36. 426 (1955), pp. 321–7.

63 Edward Loane, *William Temple and Church Unity. The Politics and Practice of Ecumenical Theology* (London: Macmillan, 2016), pp. 123–52.

64 Yelton, *The South India Controversy*, pp. 23–4.

Chapter 3

1 For the (distinctly limited) precedents of Ritualism in British Anglicanism before the trio of antiquarianism, mediaevalism and Romanticism was set to work in the context of the Oxford Movement see Nigel Yates, *Anglican Ritualism in Victorian Britain, 1839–1910* (Oxford: Oxford University Press, 1999), pp. 10–39.

2 James Pereiro, 'The Oxford Movement and Anglo-Catholicism', in Rowan Strong (ed.), *The Oxford History of Anglicanism. III. Partisan Anglicanism and its Global Expansion, 1829–c. 1914* (Oxford: Oxford University Press, 2017), pp. 187–211, and here at p. 202.

3 *Ibid.*

4 On his life see Joyce Coombs, *George Anthony Denison: The Firebrand, 1805–1896* (London: Church Literature Association, 1984).

5 Robert Wilberforce, *The Doctrine of the Holy Eucharist* (London: John and Charles Mozley, 1853).

6 E. B. Pusey, *The Doctrine of the Real Presence as contained in the Fathers and set forth by the Divines and Others of the English Church since the Reformation* (Oxford: John Henry Parker, and London: Rivington, 1855).

7 John Keble, *On Eucharistical Adoration* (Oxford and London: John Henry and James Parker, 1859).For a composite picture see Alf Härdelin, *The Tractarian Understanding of the Eucharist*, Acta Universitatis Upsaliensis, Studia Historico-Ecclesiastica Upsaliensia, 8 (Uppsala: University of Uppsala, 1965).

8 Chadwick, *The Victorian Church*, i, p. 495.

9 G. A. Denison, *Ritualism and the Real Presence* (London, Oxford, and Cambridge: Rivington, 1866), p. 2.

10 William Palmer, *Origines Liturgicae, or Antiquities of the English Ritual, with a Dissertation on Primitive Liturgies* (Oxford: Oxford University Press, 1832), two volumes.

11 Cited in Reed, *Glorious Battle*, p. 17.

Notes

¹² See W. J. Sparrow-Simpson, *The History of the Anglo-Catholic Revival from 1845* (London: George Allen & Unwin, 1932, pp. 59–65. The Bishop of Bath and Wells (Bennett's bishop) at once denounced the ruling as facilitating the imposition of popery.

¹³ Reed, *Glorious Battle*, p. 42.

¹⁴ Chadwick, *The Victorian Church*, i, p. 500.

¹⁵ William Crouch, *Bryan King and the Riots at St George's-in-the-East* (London: Methuen, 1904).

¹⁶ Cited in Reed, *Glorious Battle*, p 88.

¹⁷ Cited *ibid.*, p. 71. A Student (i.e. Fellow) of Christ Church, Wynell-Mayow was the author of *Eight Sermons on the Priesthood, Altar and Sacrifice* (Oxford: James Parker, 1867).

¹⁸ L. E. Ellsworth, *Charles Lowder and the Ritualist Movement* (London: Darton, Longman & Todd, 1982).

¹⁹ *Ibid.*, pp. 162–3.

²⁰ *Ibid.*, p. 172.

²¹ Reed, *Glorious Battle*, p. 165.

²² Ollard, *A Short History of the Oxford Movement*, p. 69.

²³ Michael Reynolds, *Martyr of Ritualism, Father Mackonochie of St Alban's Holborn* (London: Faber & Faber, 1965).

²⁴ Chadwick, *The Victorian Church*, i, p. 501.

²⁵ *The Day Hours of the Church of England* (London: Joseph Masters, 1858).

²⁶ *The Day Hours of the Church* (London: Longmans, Green & Co., 1950).

²⁷ *The Day Office of the Church. According to the Kalendar of the Church of England* (London: Walker, 1870). Peter Anson thinks the editors were two priests of the Society of the Holy Cross, T. I. Bell and H. A. Walker: Peter F. Anson, *The Call of the Cloister: Religious Communities and Kindred Bodies in the Anglican Communion* (London: Society for Promoting Christian Knowledge, 1956), p. 96, fn 2.

²⁸ Reed, *Glorious Battle*, p. 55.

²⁹ Anson, *The Call of the Cloister*, p. 346.

³⁰ *The Diurnal, from the Salisbury Use*, translated into English and adapted to the original Musick-Note by the Revered G. H. Palmer (Wantage: Community of St Mary the Virgin, 1921). Anson, disclaiming any completeness in his bibliography, lists over fifty 'Anglican Office Books', *The Call of the Cloister*, pp. 606–9, rightly commenting on the serious and widespread character of this desire for a fuller recovery of the Divine Office.

³¹ Chadwick, *The Victorian Church*, ii, p. 320.

³² Cited in Ellsworth, *Charles Lowder*, pp. 130–1.

³³ Chadwick, *The Victorian Church*, ii, pp. 322–3.

³⁴ Ellsworth, *Charles Lowder and the Ritualist Movement*, p. 1.

³⁵ *The Life and Letters of Thomas Pelham Dale, sometime rector of St Vedast's, Foster Lane* (London: George Allen, 1894), two volumes.

³⁶ Miles Platting was bracketed with London Docks as a high point of 'hideous and odoriferous squalor', in Maurice B. Reckitt, *Maurice to Temple. A Century of the Social Movement in the Church of England* (London: Faber & Faber, 1947), p. 113.

After Newman

37 Statistics in Chadwick, *The Victorian Church*, ii, p. 350.

38 On the distinctive qualities of the 'First Prayer Book', see G. J. Cuming, *A History of Anglican Liturgy* (London: Macmillan, 1969), pp. 66–95.

39 Cited in Ellsworth, *Charles Lowder and the Ritualist Movement*, p. 119.

40 Cited *ibid*.

41 Chadwick, *The Victorian Church*, ii, p. 348.

42 A. Clifton Kelway, *George Rundle Prynne. A Chapter in the Early History of the Catholic Revival* (London: Longmans, Green & Co., 1905).

43 G. R. Prynne, *Truth and Reality of the Eucharistic Sacrifice, Proved from Holy Scripture, the Teaching of the Primitive Church and the Book of Common Prayer* (London and New York: Longmans, Green & Co., 1894); idem, *Devotional Instructions on the Eucharistic Office of the English Church* (London and Oxford: Mowbray, 1903).

44 Reed, *Glorious Battle*, p. 69.

45 Chadwick, *The Victorian Church*, ii, p. 352.

46 G. W. E. Russell, *Edward King, Sixtieth Bishop of Lincoln* (London: Smith, Elder, 1912).

47 See the account in Chadwick, *The Victorian Church*, ii, p. 354. For King's life, see John Newton, *Search for a Saint: Edward King* (London: Church Literature Association, 1983); more fully, Michael Marshall, *Edward King, Teacher, Pastor, Bishop, Saint* (Leominster: Gracewing, 2021).

48 Wearing a cope, he attended the Moscow coronation of Nicholas II and found no way of removing it before the State banquet. For more on this figure, see Louise Creighton, *Life and Letters of Mandell Creighton*, 2 vols (London: Longmans, 1904–5).

49 Chadwick, *The Victorian Church*, ii, p. 355. Walter Walsh, *The Secret History of the Oxford Movement* (London: Swan Sonnenschien, 1897) was a best-seller, and remains in print in a variety of modern editions.

50 For this highly influential figure, see Roger Greenacre, *Lord Halifax* (London: Church Historical Association, 1983).

51 G. I. T. Machin, 'The Last Victorian Anti-Ritualist Campaign, 1895–1906', *Victorian Studies* 25 (1982), pp. 277–302.

52 Ollard, *A Short History of the Oxford Movement*, p. 139. For an account of the subsequent discussions in the Convocations, an auxiliary 'Committee of Experts' and, finally, the new Church Assembly, which led up to the production of the 1927 revised Prayer Book, see Donald Gray, *Earth and Altar. The Evolution of the Parish Communion in the Church of England to 1945* (London: Alcuin Club, 1986), pp. 29–35, 50–8.

Chapter 4

1 Anthony Wagner and Antony Dale, *The Wagners of Brighton* (Cheltenham: The History Press, 1983).

2 [John Purchas], *Directorium Anglicanum: being a Manual of Directions for the Right Celebration of the Holy Communion, for the Saying of Matins and Evensong, and for the Performance of the other Rites and Ceremonies of the Church, according to ancient uses of the Church of England* (London: Joseph Masters, 1858). Later editions were edited by Frederick George Lee.

Notes

3   Anonymous, *Ritual Notes on the Order of Divine Service* (London: Mowbray, 1890). It was many times reprinted.

4   John Hawes, *Ritual and Riot* (Lewes: East Sussex County Library, 1995), p. 19.

5   For the Sisters of Bethany, see Anson, *The Call of the Cloister*, pp. 405–12.

6   I am grateful to Father Benjamin Eadon of the Anglican Shrine in Walsingham for sending me an electronic copy of this booklet.

7   *St Bartholomew's, Brighton. A Short History of the Last Fifty Years on the Occasion of the Jubilee* (Brighton: no publisher, 1924), p. 34.

8   On this see Martin Wellings, *Exploring the Protestant Underworld: John Kensit, the Protestant Truth Society, and Anglo-Catholicism* (London: Anglo-Catholic History Society, 2018). Under the leadership of Kensit's son, John Alfred Kensit (1881–1957) violence continued well into the twentieth century: for a Cornish example, Bernard Walke, *Twenty Years at St Hilary* (London: Methuen, 1935), pp. 292–300, whose story is given fuller context in Yelton, *Anglican Papalism*, pp. 174–91.

9   Reed, *Glorious Battle*, p. 36.

10   See for instance Kenneth Ingram, *The Changing Order. How a new parson came to the village, disquieted it with strange practices, and how the meaning of Anglo-Catholicism was expounded to the squire* (London: Philip Allen & Co., 1925). For the incursion of advanced Ritualism in a small market town, and the consequences thereof, see David Yandle, *The Clash of Churchmanship in Nineteenth Century St Ives. The Coming of Anglo-Catholicism* (London: Anglo-Catholic History Society, 2021).

11   Reed, *Glorious Battle*, p. 185.

12   Chadwick, *The Victorian Church*, ii, p. 317.

13   Charles E. Osborne, *The Life of Father Dolling* (London: Edward Arnold, 1903), which naturally drew on Dolling's own memoir, *Ten Years in a Portsmouth Slum* (London: Swan Sonnenschein, 1896).

14   Percy Dearmer, *The Parson's Handbook* (London: Grant Richards, 1899).

15   Percy Dearmer, *The Prayer Book and How We Should Use It* (London: Mowbray, 1910). That entailed re-thinking attitudes to the contemporary Roman Catholic Church as in Percy Dearmer, *Reunion and Rome* (London: Mowbray, 1911).

16   Eamon Duffy, *The Stripping of the Altars. Traditional Religion in England, 1400–1580* (New Haven, CT and London: Yale University Press, 1992).

17   Dearmer, *The Parson's Handbook*, p. 2.

18   *Ibid.*, pp. 5–6.

19   Percy Dearmer, *The Server's Handbook* (London: Oxford University Press, 1932, 3rd edition).

20   It appeared in *New Lights for Old Chancels. Verses Topographical and Amatory* (London: John Murray, 1940).

21   Percy Dearmer, *The Parson's Handbook*, revised and rewritten by Cyril E. Pocknee (London: Oxford University Press, 1965, 13th edition).

22   Michael Yelton, *Martin Travers and the Society of SS Peter and Paul* (London: Anglo-Catholic History Society, 2024), p. 11.

23   *Ibid.*, p. 13.

24   Ollard, *A Short History of the Oxford Movement*, pp. 126–7.

25 Dearmer, *The Parson's Handbook* [1st edition], p. 30.

26 Alban Baverstock, *Benediction and the Bishops* (London: Cope and Fenwick, 1919).

27 The case was put more diplomatically, so far as episcopal sensitivities were concerned, by Darwell Stone, *The Reserved Sacrament* (London: Robert Scott, 1917).

28 See Michael Yelton, *The 21. An Anglo-Catholic Rebellion, London, 1929* (London: Anglo-Catholic History Society, 2009).

29 One might compare the Tractarian series, *Lives of the English Saints*, with the Oratorian Richard Stanton's *A Menology of England and Wales, with brief memorials of ancient British and English saints, arranged according to the calendar, together with the martyrs of the sixteenth and seventeenth centuries* (London: Burns & Oates, 1892).

30 Derek R. Williams (ed.), *Henry and Katherine Jenner: A Celebration of Cornwall's Culture, Language and Identity* (London: Francis Boutle, 2004). As Librarian of the British Museum (now the British Library), he could hardly have avoided Percy Dearmer who, however, would have regretted his conversion to Rome in 1933.

31 Peter W. Thomas and Derek R. Williams (eds.), *Setting Cornwall on its Feet: Robert Morton Nance, 1873–1959* (London: Francis Boutle, 2007).

32 Elizabeth Macfarlane, *Gilbert Hunter Doble. Cornish Anglo-Catholicism in a Celtic Context* (London: Anglo-Catholic History Society, 2015), p. 13.

33 G. H. Doble, *John Wesley and his Work in Cornwall* (Liskeard: , 1935).

34 Elizabeth Macfarlane, *Gilbert Hunter Doble*, p. 22.

35 Reed, *Battle Glorious*, p. 14.

36 'Proposals for an Alternative Canon', in G. J. Cuming, *A History of Anglican Liturgy*, pp. 396–8.

37 Cited in John Maiden, 'The Prayer Book Controversy', in Brown, Nockles and Pereiro (eds.), *The Oxford Handbook of the Oxford Movement*, pp. 530–41, and here at p. 530, and, more fully, John Maiden, *National Religion and the Prayer Book Controversy, 1927–1928* (Woodbridge: Boydell and Brewer, 2009).

38 Gregory Dix, *The Shape of the Liturgy* (London: Dacre Press, 1945), pp. 707–8.

39 John Maiden, 'The Prayer Book Controversy', p. 538.

40 Walter Frere, *Some Principles of Liturgical Reform. A Contribution towards the Revision of the Book of Common Prayer* (London: John Murray, 1911).

41 Percy Dearmer, *The Prayer Book Measure and Parliament* (London: no publisher, 1927).

Chapter 5

1 Chadwick, *The Victorian Church*, i, p. 505.

2 Michael Hill, *The Religious Order: A Study of Virtuoso Religion and its Legitimation in the Nineteenth Century Church of England* (London: Heinemann, 1973), p. 276.

3 Reed, *Glorious Battle*, p. 209.

4 R. Warner Townsend, *Marian Rebecca Hughes, Foundress of the Society of the Holy and Undivided Trinity* (Oxford: Oxford University Press, 1933).

5 Peter G. Cobb, 'Thomas Chamberlain—a Forgotten Tractarian', in Derek Baker (ed.), *The Church in Town and Countryside*, Studies in Church History 16 (Cambridge:

Notes

Cambridge University Press, 1979), pp. 373–87.

6   Anson, *The Call of the Cloister*, pp. 288–97.

7   Cited *ibid.*, p. 292.

8   *Ibid.*, pp. 26–7.

9   Stephen Young, *William Dodsworth: Pioneer of Tractarianism in London* (London: Anglo-Catholic History Society, 2023). In 1851 Dodsworth left the Church of England, scandalized by the Gorham Judgment: he had been strongly influenced by 'Irvingite' theology, which in Pauline fashion linked the life of the Resurrection to the sacramental life inaugurated by Baptism.

10 Thomas Jay Williams and Allan Walter Campbell, *The Park Village Sisterhood* (London: Society for Promoting Christian Knowledge, 1965).

11 A. M. Allchin, *The Silent Rebellion. Anglican Religious Communities, 1845–1900* (London: Student Christian Movement Press, 1958), p. 49.

12 For an amusing and circumstantial account of founding and absorption, see Anson, *The Call of the Cloister*, pp. 220–42.

13 *Ibid.*, pp. 242–59. For a more hagiographical account of Butler and his foundation, see Mother Anne Louisa (Hoare), CSMV, *Butler of Wantage: His Inheritance and his Legacy: An Offering from his Community of S. Mary the Virgin* (London: Dacre Press, 1948).

14 As in David Newsome, *The Parting of Friends. The Wilberforces and Henry Manning* (Leominster: Gracewing, 2014).

15 Anson, *The Call of the Cloister*, p. 251.

16 C. S. Lewis, *Perelandra* (London: The Bodley Head, 1943).

17 Thomas Jay Williams, *Priscilla Lydia Sellon, the Restorer after Three Centuries of Religious Life in the English Church* (London: Society for Promoting Christian Knowledge, 1950).

18 Anson, *The Call of the Cloister*, pp. 259–79. Its original name was 'The Church of England Sisterhood of Mercy in Devonport and Plymouth'.

19 Chadwick, *The Victorian Church*, i, p. 506.

20 Anson, *The Call of the Cloister*, pp. 275–7.

21 *Ibid.*, pp. 280–5.

22 Cited in W. H. Hutchings, *Life and Letters of T. T. Carter* (London: Longmans, Green, 1903), p. 104.

23 Anson, *The Call of the Cloister*, pp. 317–27. See also Susan Mumm, *All Saints Sisters of the Poor. An Anglican Sisterhood in the Nineteenth Century* (London: Church of England Record Society, 2001).

24 Anson, *The Call of the Cloister*, pp. 304–17.

25 *Ibid.*, p. 305.

26 Allchin, *The Silent Rebellion*, p. 70.

27 Thomas T. Carter, *Harriet Monsell: A Memoir* (New York: Dutton, 1884).

28 James, *The Cowley Fathers*, p. 178.

29 Anson, *The Call of the Cloister*, pp. 336–54.

30 John Mason Neale, *Ayton Priory, or the Restored Monastery* (Cambridge: Deighton, and London: Rivington, 1843).

31 Rowell, *The Vision Glorious*, p. 111.

32 Allchin, *The Silent Rebellion*, p. 38.

33 The episode was one among many: see René Kollar, *A Foreign and Wicked Institution? The Campaign against Convents in Victorian England* (Cambridge: James Clarke, 2011). The unnatural character of independent female celibates was the dominant theme, as shown by Susan Mumm, *Stolen Daughters, Virgin Mothers: Anglican Sisterhoods in Victorian Britain* (Leicester: Leicester University Press, 1999).

34 Anson, *The Call of the Cloister*, pp. 355–63.

35 *Ibid.*, p. 356.

36 The claim of Chadwick, *The Victorian Church*, i, p. 511.

37 Anson, *The Call of the Cloister*, pp. 457–62.

38 Allchin, *The Silent Rebellion*, p. 167.

39 William Bright was expelled from his theological tutorship at Glenalmond for 'extreme' views but vindicated in spectacular manner when at Christ Church he became the colleague of Pusey, Liddon and King. See B. J. Kidd and Peter Goldsmith Medd, *Selected Letters of William Bright* (London: Gardner, Darton, & Co., 1903).

40 Hugh Allen, *New Llanthony Abbey. Father Ignatius's Monastery at Capel-y-ffin* (Tiverton: Peterscourt Press, 2011), pp. 4–5.

41 *Ibid.*, p. 8.

42 John Kersey, *Joseph-René Vilatte (1854–1929): Some Aspects of his Life, Work and Succession* (no place: European-American University Press, 2016).

43 Allen, *New Llanthony Abbey*, p. 358.

44 With characteristic lack of efficiency, Leycester Lyne had also left a document transferring the ownership, in specified circumstances, to the Abbot of Buckfast, a daughter house of Sainte Marie de la Pierre qui vire, in Burgundy. Anscar Vonier's claim was dismissed in the Court of Chancery in June 1911, *ibid.*, p. 385.

45 René Kollar, *Abbot Aelred Carlyle, Caldey Island, and the Anglo-Catholic Revival in England* (New York: Peter Lang, 1995), pp. 19–20.

46 Cited *ibid.*, p. 31.

47 *Ibid.*, pp. 133–5.

48 Emphasized (and exemplified) by Peter Anson, *Abbot Extraordinary. A Memoir of Aelred Carlyle, Monk and Missionary, 1874–1955* (London: Faith Press, 1958), whose personal memories of life on Caldey both assist and hamper an objective view. The author was more than a memorialist: Michael Yelton, *Peter Anson: Monk, Writer and Artist. An Introduction to his Life and Work*(London: Anglo-Catholic History Society, 2006).

49 Michael Yelton, *The Benedictines of Caldey. The Story of the Anglican Benedictines of Caldey and their Submission to the Catholic Church* (London: Burns, Oates & Washbourne, 1940), and more recently, and in brief, Aelred Baker, OSB, *Why did we do it? The Story of the Caldey Conversions in 1913* (Caldey: no publisher, 2012).

50 Quoted in Kollar, *Abbot Aelred Carlyle*, p. 242.

51 Petà Dunstan, *The Labour of Obedience. The Benedictines of Pershore, Nashdom and Elmore: A History* (Norwich: Canterbury Press, 2009).

52 For a personal memoir by a former monk of Nashdom, see Aidan Harker, *Anglican Abbot: Dom Denys Prideaux* (London: Anglo-Catholic History Society, 2016)

Notes

53 Sergius Bolshakoff, *Russian Mystics* (Kalamazoo, MI: Cistercian Publications, and London: Mowbray, 1977). The well-known Trappist monk-author Thomas Merton wrote an Introduction.

54 Dunstan, *The Labour of Obedience*, p. 118.

55 Harker, *Anglican Abbot*, p. 179.

56 Anonymous, *A Valiant Victorian. The Life and Times of Mother Emily Ayckbowm 1836–1900 of the Community of the Sisters of the Church* (London: Mowbray, 1964). See also Allchin, *The Silent Rebellion*, pp. 205–16. Founded in the parish of St Augustine's Kilburn and dedicated to the care of children, these Sisters paid an especially heavy price to sensationally minded journalists.

57 See Anson, *The Call of the Cloister*, pp. 398–404.

58 *Ibid.*, pp. 490–4.

59 Dunstan, *The Labour of Obedience*, p. 116.

60 See Anson, *The Call of the Cloister*, at respectively p. 529 and pp. 513–14.

61 *Ibid.*, p. 502.

62 M. V. Woodgate, *Father Benson, Founder of the Cowley Fathers* (London: Geoffrey Bles, 1953); Martin L. Smith, SSJE (ed,), *Benson of Cowley* (Oxford: Oxford University Press, 1980).

63 The Ignatian orientation was strongly renewed in the twentieth century by *Retreats for Priests according to the method and plan of the Spiritual Exercises of S. Ignatius* (London: Mowbray, 1930) by William Hawks Longridge, SSJE, a work praised by the Roman Jesuit publication *Civiltà Cattolica*, according to James, *The Cowley Fathers*, p. 297.

64 Cited in James, *The Cowley Fathers*, p. 41.

65 *Ibid.*, p. 104.

66 See for their role Peter Hinchliff, *The Anglican Church in South Africa. An Account of the History and Development of the Church of the Province of South Africa* (London: Darton, Longman & Todd, 1963).

67 Alan Wilkinson, *The Community of the Resurrection. A Centenary History* (London: Student Christian Movement, 2011).

68 Cited *ibid.*, p. 12.

69 James, *The Cowley Fathers*, pp.72–6.

70 Wilkinson, *The Community of the Resurrection*, p. 33.

71 *Ibid.*, p. 50.

72 *Ibid.*, p. 54. They would be resumed during the Great War, *ibid.*, p. 130.

73 Benjamin Gordon-Taylor and Nicholas Stebbing (eds.), *Walter Frere: Scholar, Monk, Bishop* (Norwich: Canterbury Press, 2011) provides a composite portrait of this many-sided man.

74 Wilkinson, *The Community of the Resurrection*, p. 92.

75 *Ibid.*, pp. 201–33, 297–320. This many-sided activity was replicated in a minor key in Southern Rhodesia/Zimbabwe.

76 Alistair Mason, *History of the Society of the Sacred Mission* (Norwich: Canterbury Press, 1993).

77 George Every (ed.), *No Pious Person. Autobiographical Recollections Drawn*

from the Writings of Herbert Kelly and his Brother Alfred (London: Faith Press, 1960).

78 Alistair Mason, *History of the Society of the Sacred Mission*, pp. 52–7.

79 *Ibid.*, p. 78.

80 *Ibid.*, p. 67.

81 For the wider history see Petà Dunstan, *This Poor Sort. History of the European Province of the Society of St Francis* (London: Darton, Longman & Todd, 2011).

82 George Potter, *Father Potter of Peckham. A South London Saga* (London: Hodder and Stoughton, 1955).

83 Father Denis of the Society of Saint Francis, *Father Algy [William Strowan Amherst Robertson], the story of one of the best known and best loved Anglican Franciscans* (London: Hodder and Stoughton, 1964).

84 A. Clifton Kelway, *A Franciscan Renewal. The Story of the Society of the Divine Compassion* (Plaistow: Society of the Divine Compassion, 1908); Kathleen E. Burne (ed.), *The Life and Letters of Father Andrew, S. D. C.* (London: Mowbray, 1956).

85 Geoffrey Curtis, CR, *William of Glasshampton, Friar, Monk, Solitary* (London: Society for Promoting Christian Knowledge, 1977).

86 Henry R. T. Brandreth, OGS, *The Oratory of the Good Shepherd. An Historical Sketch* (Cambridge: Oratory of the Good Shepherd, 1958); George Tibbatts, OGS, *The Oratory of the Good Shepherd. The First Seventy-five Years* (Windsor: The Almoner, 1988).

87 Allen Warren, *Dean Eric Milner-White. A very English Anglo-Catholic* (London: Anglo-Catholic History Society, 2022), p. 6. The Service had been invented in the 1880s at Truro by Edward White Benson but had never previously caught on. His prayer-compositions, *After the Third Collect. Prayers and Thanksgivings for Use in Public Worship* (London: Mowbray, 1952) combined contemporary relevance with classical English liturgical prose.

88 *Ibid.*, pp. 16–18. Compare Vernon Johnson, *One Lord, one Faith* (London: Sheed and Ward, 1929) and Eric Milner-White and Wilfred Knox, *One God and Father of All* (London: Mowbray, 1929).

89 Peter F. Anson, *Building Up the Waste Places. The Revival of Monastic Life on Medieval Lines in the Post-Reformation Church of England* (Leighton Buzzard: Faith Press, 1973).

Chapter 6

1 The case is made by Simon Skinner, 'Social and Political Commentary', in Brown, Nockles and Pereiro (eds.), *The Oxford Handbook of the Oxford Movement*, pp. 333–48, and at greater length in S. A. Skinner, *Tractarians and the 'Condition of England': The Social and Political Thought of the Oxford Movement* (Oxford: Oxford University Press, 2004).

2 W. G. Peck, *The Social Implications of the Oxford Movement* (New York and London: Charles Scribner, 1933). Peck, a former Methodist minister, was Rector of St John the Baptist, Hulme, in Manchester. A member of the League of the Kingdom of God, between his Methodism and his Anglicanism he had belonged to Dr Orchard's movement of 'Free Catholicism': see W. E. Orchard, *The New Catholicism and Other Sermons* (London: George Allen & Unwin, 1917), which also had its social reform agenda.

Notes

³ Ruth Kenyon, 'The Social Aspect of the Catholic Revival', in N. P. Williams and C. Harris (eds.), *Northern Catholicism*, Centenary Studies of the Oxford and Parallel Movements (London: Society for the Promotion of Christian Knowledge, 1933), pp. 367–97. Kenyon was Secretary of the Anglo-Catholic Summer School of Sociology.

⁴ Skinner, 'Social and Political Commentary', p. 338.

⁵ *Ibid.*, p. 339.

⁶ Cited *ibid.*, p. 344.

⁷ *Ibid.*, p. 345. For the early nineteenth century context of such reflections see Cyril K. Gloyn, *The Church in the Social Order: A Study of Anglican Social Theory from Coleridge to Maurice* (Forest Grove, OR: Pacific University, 1942).

⁸ Olive J. Brose, *Fredrick Denison Maurice: Rebellious Conformist* (Athens, OH: Ohio University Press, 1971); Jeremy Morris, *F. D. Maurice and the Crisis of Christian Authority* (Oxford: Oxford University Press, 2005).

⁹ Despite his defence of a visible Church with a threefold ministry, for Maurice 'national and ecclesial authorities were 'interlinked dimensions of the divine order', licensing the establishment at the Reformation of a national church, while his view of Catholicity was floating: 'a continuous presence in history, outworking itself even in the fragmentation of Christian churches and sects', Morris, *The High Church Revival in the Church of England*, p. 210.

¹⁰ For Maurice's 'Tracts on Christian Socialism', and the proposals of his disciple John Malcolm Forbes Ludlow (1821–1911) for 'Productive Associations' as well as 'Cooperative Stores' see Gray, *Earth and Altar*, pp. 82–8.

¹¹ A Group of Churchmen, *The Return of Christendom* (London: George Allen & Unwin, 1924). Reckitt himself had been a regular contributor to *G. K.'s Weekly* and he was a founder member of the Distributist League. Despite his dislike of the Roman Catholic Church, Reckitt expressed huge debts to both Chesterton and Belloc in *The World and the Faith. Essays of a Christian Sociologist* (London: Faith Press, 1954).

¹² Maurice B. Reckitt, *P. E. T. Widdrington. A Study in Vocation and Versatility* (London: Society for Promoting Christian Knowledge, 1961).

¹³ P. E. T. Widdrington, 'Epilogue', in Maurice B. Reckitt (ed.), *Prospect for Christendom. Essays in Catholic Social Reconstruction* (London: Faber & Faber, 1947 [1945]), pp. 250–5.

¹⁴ Peter d'Alroy Jones, *The Christian Socialist Revival, 1877–1914. Religion, Class, and Social Conscience in Victorian England* (Princeton, NY: Princeton University Press, 2015).

¹⁵ For his life, see E. G. Bettany, *Stewart Headlam. A Biography* (London: John Murray, 1926).

¹⁶ Gray, *Earth and Altar*, p. 90, the implications of 'Sacramental Socialism; for Eucharistic practice are spelled out on pp. 116–21.

¹⁷ Widdrington, 'Epilogue', p. 250.

¹⁸ Edward Lyttelton, *The Mind and Character of Henry Scott Holland* (London: Mowbray, 1926). Perhaps significantly for his choice of subject, Lyttelton was properly titled the 'Reverend the Honourable', and was Headmaster of Eton from 1908 to 1916.

¹⁹ Scott Holland is still a name to conjure with at English funerals, owing to

a schoolboy howler. Chosen to preach at Edward VII's funeral, his much-quoted account of death ('Death is nothing at all') is extracted from the portion of the sermon where he is criticizing the approach of wrong-thinking thanatologists.

[20] Gray, *Earth and Altar*, pp. 121–9.

[21] Arthur V. Woodworth, *Christian Socialism in England* (London: Swan Sonnenschein, 1903), pp. 140–1.

[22] *Ibid.*, p. 251.

[23] *Ibid.* Compare John Richard Orens, *Stewart Headlam's Radical Anglicanism. The Mass, the Masses, and the Music Hall* (Urbana, IL: University of Illinois Press, 2003).

[24] Compare Edward R. Norman, *The Victorian Christian Socialists* (Cambridge: Cambridge University Press, 2002).

[25] Widdrington, 'Epilogue', p. 252.

[26] F. W. Bussell, *Christian Theology and Social Progress* (London: Methuen, 1907). Frederick William Bussell was a Norfolk clergyman, Fellow of Brasenoze, and rector of Sisland, a village some ten miles south of Norwich.

[27] Widdrington, 'Epilogue', p. 252.

[28] Conrad Noel, *An Autobiography*, edited by Sidney Dark (London: Dent, 1945).

[29] Kenneth Leech (ed.), *Conrad Noel and the Catholic Crusade: A Critical Examination* (Croydon: Jubilee Group, 1993).

[30] Mark D. Chapman, *Liturgy, Socialism and Life. The Legacy of Conrad Noel* (London: Darton, Longman & Todd, 2001).

[31] Gray, *Earth and Altar*, p. 139.

[32] *Ibid.*, pp. 153–88.

[33] Widdrington, 'Epilogue', p. 252. See on this Maurice B. Reckitt and C. E. Bechhofer, *The Meaning of National Guilds* (London: Cecil Palmer and Hayward, 1918).

[34] Widdrington, 'Epilogue', p. 253.

[35] Maurice B. Reckitt, 'Introduction', in his *Prospect for Christendom*, pp. 7–9, and here at p. 7.

[36] [William Temple, ed.], *Politics and Citizenship: Being the Report Presented to the Conference on Christian Politics, Economics and Citizenship at Birmingham, April 5–12, 1924* (London: Longmans, Green & Co., 1924).

[37] [Malvern Conference], *Malvern 1941. The Life of the Church and the Order of Society, being the Proceedings of the Archbishop of York's Conference, 1941* (London: Longmans, Green & Co., 1941).

[38] Widdrington, 'Epilogue' p. 254.

[39] *Ibid.* See on Figgis, Paul Avis (ed.), *Neville Figgis, CR: His Life, Thought and Significance* (Leiden: Brill, 2022)

[40] Maurice B. Reckitt, *Faith and Society. A Study of the Structure, Outlook, and Opportunity of the Christian Social Movement in Great Britain and the United States of America* (London: Longmans, Green and C., 1932); Maurice B. Reckitt, *Religion in Social Action* (London: J. Heritage, 1937); Maurice B. Reckitt, *As it Happened. An Autobiography* (London: J. M. Dent, 1941). See also John S. Peart-Binns, *Maurice B. Reckitt: A Life* (London: Marshall Pickering, 1988).

[41] Peart-Binns, *Maurice B. Reckitt: A Life*, 'Introduction', p. 9.

Notes

42 Gordon Wakefield, *Francis Noel Davey. A Memoir* (London: Society for Promoting Christian Knowledge, 1981).

43 F. N. Davey, 'The Hope of Christendom Authentic', in Reckitt, *Prospect for Christendom*, pp. 11–26, and here at p. 17.

44 *Ibid.*, pp. 18–19.

45 V. A. Demant, 'The Idea of a Natural Order', in Reckitt, *Prospect for Christendom*, pp. 27–42.

46 Andrew Louth, *Vigo August Demant, 1893–1983* (London: Anglo-Catholic History Society, 2021), p. 3.

47 V. A. Demant, *God, Man, and Society. An Introduction to Christian Sociology* (London: Student Christian Movement Press, 1934).

48 V. A. Demant, *Christian Polity* (London: Faber & Faber, 1936).

49 *Ibid.*, p. 27.

50 T. S. Eliot, *The Idea of a Christian Society* (London: Faber & Faber, 1939), p. 34.

51 V. A. Demant, *The Religious Prospect* (London: Frederick Muller, 1939). It is also a *Leit-motiv* of his 'preachinments', underlying the curious title of their collected version: *Not One World but Two. A Miscellany of Preachments*, ed. Sławomir Nowosad (Lublin: John Paul II Catholic University, 2017).

52 Demant, 'The Idea of a Natural Order', p. 28.

53 *Ibid.*, p. 31.

54 *Ibid.*, pp. 28–9.

55 *Ibid.*, p. 32.

56 *Ibid.*, pp. 32, 33.

57 *Ibid.*, p. 33.

58 *Ibid.*, p. 34.

59 *Ibid.*

60 *Ibid.*, pp. 34–5.

61 R. H. Tawney, *Religion and the Rise of Capitalism. A Historical Study* (London: John Murray, 1926). Tawney's book was dedicated to Gore, who wrote the Introduction.

62 V. A. Demant, *Religion and the Decline of Capitalism* (London: Faber & Faber, 1949).

63 Demant, 'The Idea of a Natural Order', p. 39. Italics original.

64 E. L. Mascall, 'The Person and the Family', in Reckitt, *Prospect for Christendom*, pp. 45–56, and here at p. 39.

65 V. A. Demant, *Theology of Society. More Essays in Christian Polity* (London: Faber & Faber, 1947).

66 Mascall, 'The Person and the Family', p. 55.

67 Jacques Maritain, *Scholasticism and Politics* (New York: Macmillan, 1940).

68 E. L. Mascall, *Man: His Origin and Destiny* (London: Dacre Press, 1940).

69 E. L. Mascall's summary of the argument of *Man* in *Saraband. The Memoirs of E. L. Mascall* (Leominster: Gracewing, 1992), p. 192

70 T. S. Eliot, 'Cultural Forces in the Human Order', in Reckitt, *Prospect for Christendom*, pp. 57–60.

71 T. S. Eliot, *Notes toward the Definition of Culture* (London: Faber & Faber, 1948).

72 Eliot, 'Cultural Forces in the Human Order', p. 68.

73 Philip Mairet, *Autobiographical and Other Papers* (London: Carcanet, 1981).

74 Philip Mairet, 'A Civilisation of Technics', in Reckitt, *Prospect for Christendom*, pp. 70–84, and here at p. 78.

75 *Ibid.*, pp. 78–9.

76 *Ibid.*, p. 84.

77 Fiona MacCarthy, *Eric Gill* (London: Faber & Faber, 1990); Fiona MacCarthy, *The Simple Life. C. R. Ashbee in the Cotswolds* (London: Faber & Faber, 2014 [1981]). Ashbee had been the founder, in 1888, of the Guild of Handicrafts.

78 Maurice B. Reckitt, 'Catholic Sociology and the English Situation', in his *Prospect for Christendom*, pp. 85–98.

79 Henri de Lubac, SJ, *Catholicisme. Les aspects sociaux du dogme* (Paris: Editions du Cerf, 1938).

80 Reckitt, 'Catholic Sociology and the English Situation', p. 87.

81 V. A. Demant, *The Just Price. An Outline of the Mediaeval Doctrine and an Exploration of its Possible Equivalent Today* (London: Student Christian Movement Press, 1930).

82 Reckitt, 'Catholic Sociology and the English Situation', p. 96.

83 *Ibid.*, p. 97.

84 John McQuillan et al., *Flee to the Fields. The Faith and Works of the Catholic Land Movement* (London: Heath Cranton, 1934).

85 Reckitt, 'Catholic Sociology and the English Situation', p. 97.

86 Frances Hutchinson, *The Political Economy of Social Credit and Guild Socialism* (London: Routledge, 1997).

87 Reckitt, 'Catholic Sociology and the English Situation', p. 98.

88 *Ibid.*, p. 99.

89 Reckitt, *Maurice to Temple: A History of the Social Movement in the Church of England*.

90 For her life see Barbara Reynolds, *Dorothy L. Sayers. Her Life and Soul* (London: Hodder and Stoughton, 1993).

91 Barbara Reynolds, *The Passionate Intellect. Dorothy L. Sayers's Encounter with Dante* (Kent, OH: Kent State University Press, 1989). Reynolds, the General Editor of the Cambridge Italian Dictionary, also finished the translation of Dante's *Paradiso*, left incomplete at her death.

92 T. S. Eliot, *Dante* (London: Faber & Faber, 1929).

93 Dorothy L. Sayers, *Begin Here: A War-time Essay Collection* (London: Gollancz, 1940); Dorothy L. Sayers, *Creed or Chaos, and Other Essays in Popular Theology* (London: Methuen, 1940); Dorothy L. Sayers, *The Other Six Deadly Sins* (London: Methuen, 1943).

Chapter 7

1 Mark Chapman, 'The Evolution of Anglican Theology, 1910–2000', in Jeremy Morris (ed.), *The Oxford History of Anglicanism. IV. Global Anglicanism, 1910-Present*

Notes

(Oxford: Oxford University Press, 2017), pp. 25–50.

2 Michael Chandler, *The Life and Work of Henry Parry Liddon* (Leominster: Gracewing, 2000).

3 See for this figure Andrew Atherstone, *Oxford's Protestant Spy. The Controversial Career of Charles Golightly* (Exeter: Paternoster Press, 2007).

4 H. P. Liddon, *Essays and Addresses* (London and New York: Longmans, Green & Co., 1892).

5 H. P. Liddon, *Explanatory Analysis of St Paul's Epistle to the Romans* (London and New York: Longmans, Green & Co., 1893); *Explanatory Analysis of St Paul's First Epistle to Timothy* (London and New York: Longmans, Green & Co., 1897).

6 J. O. Johnston, *Life and Letters of Henry Parry Liddon* (London: Longmans, Green, 1904), p. 365. Emphasis is original.

7 Cited in Mark D. Chapman, *The Fantasy of Reunion. Anglicans, Catholics, and Ecumenism, 1833–1882* (Oxford: Oxford University Press, 2014), p. 240.

8 H. P. Liddon, *The Divinity of Our Lord and Saviour Jesus Christ* (London: Rivington, 1867), p. 24.

9 *Ibid.*, p. 28.

10 *Ibid.*, p. 64.

11 *Ibid.*, p. 67.

12 *Ibid.*, p. 145.

13 *Ibid.*, pp. 151, 152.

14 *Ibid.*, p. 183.

15 *Ibid.*, p. 193.

16 *Ibid.*, p. 237.

17 *Ibid.*, p. 238.

18 *Ibid.*, pp. 251–2.

19 *Ibid.*, p. 256.

20 *Ibid.*, p. 261.

21 *Ibid.*, p. 305.

22 *Ibid.*, p. 381.

23 *Ibid.*, p. 386.

24 *Ibid.*, p. 387.

25 *Ibid.*, p. 419.

26 *Ibid.*, p. 415.

27 *Ibid.*, pp. 535–6.

28 Charles Gore, *The Incarnation of the Son of God* (London: John Murray, 1891).

29 Charles Gore, *Dissertations on Subjects Connected with the Incarnation* (London: John Murray, 1895).

30 Charles Gore, *The Body of Christ. An Enquiry into the Institution and Doctrine of Holy Communion* (London: John Murray, 1901).

31 Charles Gore, *The New Theology and the Old Religion* (London: John Murray, 1907).

32 Charles Gore, *The Reconstruction of Belief* (London: John Murray, 1921), three volumes.

33 Charles Gore, *The Philosophy of the Good Life* (London: John Murray, 1930).

34 Avis, *Gore: Construction and Conflict*, p. 7.

35 Jeremy Morris, 'Liberalism Protestant and Catholic', in Brown, Nockles and Pereiro, *The Oxford Handbook of the Oxford Movement*, pp. 585–604, and here at p. 598. Italics are original.

36 For a good discussion, see Avis, *Gore*, pp. 68–75.

37 Charles Gore, *The Basis of Anglican Fellowship* (London: Mowbray, 1914).

38 Charles Gore, with Henry Leighton Goudge and Alfred Guillaume (eds.), *A New Commentary in Holy Scripture, including the Apocrypha* (London: Society for Promoting Christian Knowledge, 1928).

39 Christopher Dawson, *The Spirit of the Oxford Movement* (Washington, DC: Catholic University of America Press, 2023 [1923]), p. xxiii.

40 Ibid., p. 104.

41 F. W. Puller, SSJE, *What is the Distinctive Grace of Confirmation?* (London: Rivington, 1880); compare L. S. Thornton, *Confirmation: Its Place in the Baptismal Mystery* (London: Dacre Press, 1954), who rather doubted whether, lacking the 'seal of Confirmation from a bishop the baptisms administered by Protestant Dissenters could be certainly valid. The book was dedicated to Gregory Dix.

42 Harold Ellis, 'Lionel Spencer Thornton', *CR. Quarterly Review of the Community of the Resurrection*, 230 (1960), pp. 10–13.

43 Timothy Maxwell Gouldstone, *The Rise and Decline of Anglican Idealism in the Nineteenth Century* (New York: Palgrave Macmillan, 2005).

44 Compare L. S. Thornton, 'The Christian Concept of God', in E. G. Selwyn (ed.), *Essays Catholic and Critical* (London and New York: Macmillan, 1926), pp. 121–50.

45 L. S. Thornton, *The Incarnate Lord. An essay concerning the doctrine of the Incarnation in its relation to organic conceptions* (London: Longmans, Green & Co., 1928).

46 Alfred North Whitehead, *Process and Reality. An Essay in Cosmology* (Cambridge: Cambridge University Press, 1929).

47 *Doctrine in the Church of England. The Report of the Commission on Chrisan Doctrine appointed by the Archbishops of Canterbury and York in 1922* (London: Society for Promoting Christian Knowledge, 1938).

48 L. S. Thornton, *The Doctrine of the Atonement* (London: John Heritage, 1937).

49 L. S. Thornton, *The Common Life in the Body of Christ* (London: Dacre Press, 1942), p. 3.

50 Yngve Brilioth, *Eucharistic Faith and Practice, Evangelical and Catholic* (London: Society for Promoting Christian Knowledge, 1930), Brilioth, professor at Lund at the time of the translation, was an obvious choice: he had already written on the Oxford Movement. Gustaf Aulèn's *Christus Victor. An Historical Study of the Three Main Tyles of Theory of the Atonement* (London: Macmillan, 1931) was professor of dogmatics at Lund, and would later write on such 'hot button' themes (for other Lutherans) as 'Eucharist and Sacrifice' and the relation between 'Reformation and Catholicity', both produced in the later 1950s and quickly translated; Anders Nygren, author of *Agape and Eros* (London: Society for Promoting Christian Knowledge, 1932), was also

Notes

at Lund. The location of the three writers gave currency in England to the notion of a High Church Lutheran 'Lund School'. In 1936 Nygren published a sequel to his best-known book, deemed Part Two of a now composite work and subsequently put into English by a different translator, Philip Watson.

[51] Gunnar Rosendal, *The Catholic Movement in the Swedish Church* (Evanston, IL: Seabury-Western Theological Seminary, 1951).

[52] Bengt Ingmar Kilström, *Högkyrkligheten i Sverige och Finland under 1900-talet* (Helsingborg: Asak, 1990).

[53] Gabriel Hebert, *Liturgy and Society* (London: Faber & Faber, 1935); Gabriel Hebert (ed.), *The Parish Communion. A Book of Essays* (London: Society for Promoting Christian Knowledge, 1936). Austin Farrer and Gregory Dix were among the contributors.

[54] Mason, *History of the Society of the Sacred Mission*, p. 169. In 1933 some adjustment was made to the rite, following the cue of the 'Interim Rite' which proposed to re-order the 1662 service by appeal to the 1549 Prayer Book, with some Roman ceremonial indications, see Christopher Irvine, *Worship, Church, and Society. An exposition of the work of Arthur Gabriel Hebert* (Norwich: Canterbury Press, 1993), p. 93. The Interim Rite, suggested by N. P. Williams, in 1928, is explained in Mark Dalby, *Anglican Missals and their Canons: 1549, Interim Rite, and Roman* (Cambridge: Grove Books, 1998).

[55] Cited in Irvine, *Worship, Church, and Society*, p. 109.

[56] *Ibid.*, p. 110.

[57] Quoted Mason, *History of the Society of the Sacred Mission*, p. 181.

[58] Gray, *Earth and Altar*, p. 201.

[59] Gabriel Hebert, *The Throne of David. A Study of the Fulfilment of the Old Testament in Jesus Christ and his Church* (London: Faber & Faber, 1941); *The Authority of the Old Testament* (London: Faber & Faber, 1947); *The Old Testament from Within* (London: Oxford University Press, 1961).

[60] Gabriel Hebert, *The Form of the Church* (London: Faber & Faber, 1944); *Fundamentalism and the Church of God* (London: Westminster Press, 1957); *The Christ of Faith and the Jesus of History* (London: Student Christian Movement Press, 1962).

[61] I have made use of the Hebertian version of this familiar (because truthful) schema in Chapters 5 and 6 of my own 'biblical theology', *Lovely, Like Jerusalem, The Fulfilment of the Old Testament in Christ and the Church* (San Francisco, CA: Ignatius Press, 2007).

[62] Simon Bailey, *A Tactful God. Gregory Dix, Priest, Monk and Scholar* (Leominster: Gracewing, 2002), p. 47.

[63] *Ibid.*, p. 118.

[64] *Open Letter of Superiors of Religious Communities to the Archbishop of Canterbury* (London: Dacre Press, 1946).

[65] Bailey, *A Tactful God*, p. 124.

[66] Auctores varii, *Catholicity. A Study in the Conflict of Christian Traditions in the West, being a report presented to His Grace the Archbishop of Canterbury* (London: Dacre Press, 1947).

[67] Gregory Dix, *The Apostolic Tradition of St Hippolytus* (London: Society for

Promoting Christian Knowledge, 1937). A second edition, by Henry Chadwick, came from the same publisher in 1968.

68 Gregory Dix, *The Idea of the Church in Primitive Liturgies* (London: Society for Promoting Christian Knowledge, 1937)

69 Gregory Dix, 'Jurisdiction Episcopal and Papal in the Early Church', in *Laudate* XV/XVI for 1937/1938, re-published as *Jurisdiction in the Early Church* (London: Church Literature Association, 1975).

70 Gregory Dix, *Jurisdiction in the Early Church* (London: Dacre Press, 1942).

71 Gregory Dix, *The Question of Anglican Orders: Letters to a Layman* (London Dacre Press, 1944).

72 Gregory Dix, *The Theology of Confirmation in relation to Baptism* (London: Dacre Press, 1946).

73 Gregory Dix, *The Shape of the Liturgy* (London: Dacre Press, 1945).

74 Simon Jones (ed.), *The Sacramental Life. Gregory Dix and his Writings* (Norwich: Canterbury Press, 2007), pp. 11–12.

75 Cited from a later twentieth century liturgist, Kenneth Stevenson, in Bailey, *A Tactful God*, p. 191.

76 Gregory Dix, *Jew and Greek. A Study in the Primitive Church* (London: Dacre Press, 1953).

77 Mascall, *Saraband*, p. 138.

78 Bailey, *A Tactful God*, pp. 161–2.

79 For Farrer's life see Philip Curtis, *A Hawk among Sparrows.: A Biography of Austin Farrer* (London: Society for Promoting Christian Knowledge, 1985).

80 Austin Farrer, *Finite and Infinite. A Philosophical Essay* (Westminster: Dacre Press, 1959 [1943]).

81 For example, Robert Boak Slocum, *Light in a Burning-Glass. A Systematic Presentation of Austin Farrer's Theology* (Columbia, SC: University of South Carolina Press, 2007).

82 Austin Farrer, *Faith and Speculation. An Essay in Philosophical Theology* (London: Adam and Charles Black, 1967), p. 67.

83 *Ibid.*, p. 65. Farrer's view of 'action' invites comparison with that of his older French contemporary Maurice Blondel, for Blondel too, action (generously conceived) is the creative moment which opens up a metaphysical dimension where Uncreated Light can shine.

84 Austin Farrer, *Saving Belief. A Discussion of Essentials* (London: Hodder and Stoughton, 1964).

85 Austin Farrer, *A Science of God?* (London: Geoffrey Bles, 1966), p. 123.

86 Austin Farrer, *The Essential Sermons*, ed. Leslie Houlden (London: Society for Promoting Christian Knowledge, 1991), p. 18.

87 Austin Farrer, *Love Almighty and Ills Unlimited. An Essay on Providence and Evil* (London: Collins, 1962).

88 Austin Farrer, *The Essential Sermons*, p. 204.

89 Austin Farrer, *The Glass of Vision* (Westminster: Dacre Press, 1948).

90 *Ibid.*, p. 134.

Notes

⁹¹ An admirable perspective for holding spirituality and theology together: see Charles Hefling, *Jacob's Ladder: Theology and Spirituality in the Thought of Austin Farrer* (Cambridge, MA: Cowley Publications, 1979).

⁹² E. L. Mascall, *He Who Is. A Study in Traditional* Theism (London: Longmans, Green, 1943); *Existence and Analogy. A Sequel to 'He Who Is'* (London: Longmans, Green, 1949).

⁹³ E. L. Mascall, *A Guide to Mount Carmel, being a summary and an analysis of The Ascent of Mount Carmel of St John of the Cross, with some introductory notes* (London: Dacre Press, 1944).

⁹⁴ E. L. Mascall, *Words and Images. A Study in Theological Discourse* (London: Longmans, Green & Co., 1959, reprinted by Darton, Longman & Todd in 1966).

⁹⁵ E. L. Mascall, *Christ, the Christian and the Church* (London: Longmans, 1965).

⁹⁶ For Mascall, excepting the question of the mode of the Eucharistic presence which Gore expressed in terms of a 'Kantian quasi-idealism', 'his thought was remarkably free from what one might describe as conventional Anglican inhibitions', *Corpus Christi. Essays on the Church and the Eucharist* (London: Longmans, Green, 1955), p. 155.

⁹⁷ See E. L. Mascall, *Up and Down in Adria. Some Considerations of the Volume Entitled 'Soundings'* (London: Faith Press, 1963).

⁹⁸ E. L. Mascall, *Theology and Natural Science. Some Questions on their Relations* (London: Longmans, 1956).

⁹⁹ E. L. Mascall, *The Secularization of Christianity. An Analysis and a Critique* (London: Darton, Longman & Todd, 1965); *The Christian Universe* (London: Darton, Longman & Todd, 1968); *Whatever Happened to the Human Mind? Essays in Christian Orthodoxy* (London: Society for Promoting Christian Knowledge, 1980); *Theology and the Gospel of Christ. An Essay in Reconstruction* (London: Society for Promoting Christian Knowledge, 1980); *Jesus: Who He is and how we know Him* (London: Darton, Longman & Todd, 1986).

¹⁰⁰ Mascall, *The Christian Universe*, pp. 10–11.

¹⁰¹ E. L. Mascall, *Via Media. An Essay in Theological Synthesis* (London: Longmans, Green & Co., 1956).

¹⁰² Tracts 38 and 41 were entitled, respectively, *Via Media I*, and *Via Media II*, and the concept was central to Newman's *Lectures on the Prophetical Office of the Church, viewed relatively to Romanism and Popular Protestantism* (London: J. G. and F. Rivington, 1838) the chief ecclesiological work of his Anglican period.

¹⁰³ Mascall, *Via Media*, p. xiii.

¹⁰⁴ Mascall, *Corpus Christi*; *Grace and Glory* (London: Faith Press, 1961); *The Triune God: An Ecumenical Study* (Worthing: Churchman, 1986).

¹⁰⁵ E. L. Mascall, *The Openness of Being* (London: Westminster Press, 1971).

¹⁰⁶ Mascall, *Saraband*, p. 82.

¹⁰⁷ *Ibid.*, p. 125, and cf. p. 147 where he extends the explanation of non-preferment to his views of ecumenism, liturgical revision, extra-liturgical devotions, 'Catholic sociology' and 'basic doctrinal orthodoxy itself'.

¹⁰⁸ K. E. Kirk, *Some Principles of Moral Theology and their Application* (London: Longmans, 1921).

109   W. J. Brown, *Jeremy Taylor* (London: Society for Promoting Christian Knowledge, 1925).

110   See H. B. McAdoo, *The Structure of Caroline Moral Theology* (London: Longmans, Green & Co., 1942).

111   K. E. Kirk, *Conscience and its Problems. An Introduction to Casuistry* (London: Longmans, 1927).

112   K. E. Kirk, *The Vision of God. The Christian Doctrine of the Summum Bonum* (London: Longmans, 1931).

113   K. E. Kirk, *The Threshold of Ethics* (London: Skeffington, 1933).

114   Eric Waldren Kemp (ed.), *The Life and Letters of Kenneth Escop Kirk, Bishop of Oxford, 1937–1954* (London: Hodder and Stoughton, 1959).

115   James, *The Cowley Fathers*, p. 312, who depends for these reports on Colin Stephenson, *Merrily on High. An Anglo-Catholic Memoir* (London: Darton, Longman & Todd, 1972), pp. 61, 86.

116   Owen Chadwick, *Michael Ramsey: A Life* (Oxford: Clarnedon Press, 1990); more briefly and unofficially, Michael De-la-Noy, *Michael Ramsey. A Portrait* (London: Fount, 1991).

117   Chitty's role in Ramsey's orientation to the East is stressed (along with the place of the Fellowship of St Alban and St Sergius) by A. M. Allchin, 'Michael Ramsey and the Orthodox Tradition', in Robin Gill and Lorna Kendall (eds.), *Michael Ramsey as Theologian* (London: Darton, Longman & Todd, 1998), pp. 47–62.

118   A. M. Ramsey, *The Gospel and the Catholic Church* (Peabody, MA: Hendrickson Publishing, 2009 [1935, 2nd edition, 1956]).

119   *Ibid.*, p. 120.

120   *Ibid.*, p. xxiii.

121   *Ibid.*, p. xxiv.

122   *Ibid.*, p. 38.

123   Cited from P. T. Forsyth, *Lectures on the Church and the Sacraments* (London and New York: Longmans, Green, 1917), *ibid.*, p. 39.

124   *Ibid.*, p. 60.

125   *Ibid.*, p. 184.

126   P. T. Forsyth, *The Resurrection of Christ. An Essay in Biblical Theology* (London: Centenary Press, 1945); *The Glory of God and the Transfiguration of Christ* (London: Longmans, Green, 1949).

127   Jared C. Cramer, *Safeguarded by Glory. Michael Ramsey's Ecclesiology and the Struggle of Contemporary Anglicanism* (Lanham, MD: Lexington Books, 2010).

128   Mark Chapman, 'The Evolution of Anglican Theology, 1910–2000', in Morris, *Oxford History of Anglicanism. IV*, pp. 25–50, and here at p. 42.

129   *Ibid.*

130   A. M. Ramsey, *F. D. Maurice and the Conflicts of Modern Theology* (Cambridge: Cambridge University Press, 1951); *From Gore to Temple. The Development of Anglican Theology between 'Lux Mundi' and the Second World War, 1889–1939* (London: Longmans Green, 1960).

131   A. M. Ramsey, *Image Old and New* (London: Society for Promoting Chris-

tian Knowledge, 1963); *Sacred and Secular: a study in the otherworldly and this-worldly aspects of Christianity* (London: Longmans, 1965); *God, Christ and the World: a study in contemporary theology* (London Student Christian Movement Press, 1969). For a thought experiment in how Ramsey and Mascall might have responded in contrasting ways to the 'Christian atheism' or 'Non-objective theism' of the Sea of Faith movement, see Robin Gill, 'Michael Ramsey: A Speculation', in Gill and Kendall, *Michael Ramsey as Theologian*, pp. 176–95.

132   Douglas Dales (ed.), *Glory Descending, Michael Ramsey and his Writings* (Norwich: Canterbury Press, 2005).

Chapter 8

1   Reed, *Glorious Battle*, p. 84. Reed points out, however, that some organizations founded before 1860 were unstable alliances of Anglo-Catholics with moderate high churchmen. Thus the *Association for Making Known upon the Continent the Principles of the Anglican Church*, later the Anglo-Continental Society, became too anti-Roman for most Anglo-Catholics. The official aim of the Society at its foundation in 1855 was to 'make the principles of the Church of England, her doctrine, discipline, and status, better known on the Continent', but by the 1870s it had started to make common cause with Old Catholics and seek out Italian clergy who might be open to a Reformation of some kind whereupon Anglo-Catholics fled from it as liable to foment schism in Roman Catholic lands, *ibid.*, p. 114.

2   George Bayfield-Roberts, *The History of the English Church Union, 1859–1894* (London: Church Printing, 1895).

3   Gunstone, *Lift High the Cross*, p. 148.

4   J. Embry, *The Catholic Movement and the Society of the Holy Cross* (London: Faith Press, 1931); Owen Higgs et al., *In This Sign Conquer: A History of the Society of the Holy Cross, 1855–2005* (London: Continuum, 2006).

5   *The Priest in Absolution. A manual for such as are called unto the higher ministries of the English Church* (London: Joseph Masters, 1866).

6   Joannes Reuter, SJ, *Neo-Confessarius practice inductus seu Methodus rite obeundi munus confessoris* (Cologne: Metternich, 1750), was constantly reprinted throughout the nineteenth century. The ninth edition appeared from the Parisian publishing house Lethielleux in 1890. The Abbé Jean-Joseph Gaume's *Manuel des Confesseurs* (Liège: Lardinois, 1837) was an anthology of advice to confessors mainly taken from canonized authors of the sixteenth to eighteenth centuries. Gaume was best known for campaigning to remove pagan authors from the teaching of classics in church schools, in which he was opposed by Bishop Dupanloup of Orleans.

7   G. A. C. Whatton, *The Priest's Companion. A Manual of Instructions and Prayers for Priests and Religious* (London: E. Knott & Son, 1939). A second edition appeared in 1946. For Whatton, sometime Master of the Societas Sancti Crucis, briefly a (Roman) Catholic and Benedictine novice at Downside, see Yelton, *Anglican Papalism*, pp. 96–7.

8   Luke Miller, 'The Winds of Change, 1914–1945', in Higgs et al., *In This Sign Conquer*, p. 123.

9   Cited *ibid.*, p. 124.

10   Members of the Ecclesiological late Cambridge Camden Society (ed.), *Hierurgia*

Anglicana. Documents and Extracts illustrative of the Ritual of the Church of England after the Reformation (London: J. G. F. and J. Rivington & J. Masters, 1848), p. ix. The book was published simultaneously in Cambridge and Oxford as well.

[11] *The Society of the Faith, 1905–1955. A Commemorative Tribute to the Society and its Founders* (London: Faith Press, 1955). For the founders see also Robert Gage, *The Douglas Brothers and the Society of the Faith* (London: Anglo-Catholic History Society, 2019).

[12] Julian W. S. Litten, 'Foreword', in Yelton, *Anglican Papalism*, p. ix.

[13] Edmund S. Wood, *The Regal Power of the Church or the Fundamentals of the Canon Law. A Dissertation* (Cambridge: Macmillan and Bowes, 1888), reprinted by Dacre Press in 1948. Wood was several times Master of the Society of the Holy Cross and much involved in both the English Church Union and the Confraternity of the Blessed Sacrament.

[14] See Brian Doolan, *The First Fifty Years: The Catholic League from 1913–1966* (London: Crux Press, 1967).

[15] Michael Walsh, *Look to the Rock. The Catholic League and the Anglican Papalist Quest for Reunion* (Norwich: Canterbury Press, 2019), pp. 11–13.

[16] *Ibid.*, p. 15.

[17] Cited *ibid.*, p. 20.

[18] Cited *ibid.*, p. 24.

[19] Cited *ibid.*, p. 27.

[20] *The Creed of the Council of Trent with Explanations* (London: Catholic League, 1954), p. 4.

[21] Spencer Jones, *England and the Holy See. An Essay towards Reunion* (London: Longmans, Green, & Co., 1902).

[22] Yelton, *Anglican Papalism*, pp. 24–6.

[23] Photograph and caption in Walsh, *Look to the Rock*, between pp. 66 and 67.

[24] Kenneth E. Kirk, *The Story of the Woodard Schools* (London: Hodder and Stoughton, 1937), pp. 12–13,

[25] Ollard, *A Short History of the Oxford Movement*, pp. 167–8. But Addington came eventually to oppose the advanced Ritualism of Alexander Mackonochie whom he had personally appointed. The son of an English merchant in St Petersburg, he rose to become Governor of the Bank of England, and naturally did not wish to see his appointee a gaol-bird.

[26] For Woodard's life, and the beginnings of his work, see Kenneth E. Kirk, *The Story of the Woodard Schools*, pp. 22–45.

[27] *Ibid.*, pp. 94–5.

[28] Reed, *Glorious Battle*, p. 162.

[29] Requirements of membership were laid out in the *Manual of the Confraternity of the Blessed Sacrament of the Body and Blood of Christ with the Objects and Rules and the Laws as revised in 1934*, 2nd edn (London: W. Knott & Son, 1934).

[30] Anson, *The Call of the Cloister*, pp. 429–31. See also Michael Yelton, *The Community of Reparation to Jesus in the Blessed Sacrament and the Church of St Alphege, Southwark* (London: Anglo-Catholic History Society, 2022). The Sisterhood had a Scottish precedent, the Community of St Mary and St John, founded in Perth in

Notes

1870, *ibid.*, p. 2.

31 Morris, *The High Church Revival in the Church of England*, p. 101, fn. 105.

32 John Betjeman, *Collected Poems* (London: John Murray, 2003 [1970]), p. 162.

33 See Alfred H. Simmons, *To All that Be in Rome. A Treatise on Ecumenical Relations* (Aldershot: no publisher, 1965), p. 13.

34 Alan Parkinson and Richard McEwan, *The Society of Mary: people, places and things* (no place: Society of Mary, 2006).

35 Michael Yelton, *Alfred Hope Patten and the Shrine of Our Lady of Walsingham* (Norwich: Canterbury Press, 2006).

36 Michael Rear. *Walsingham Pilgrims and Pilgrimage* (Leominster: Gracewing, 2019), 2nd edition, p. 197.

37 Yelton, *Anglican Papalism*, p. 135.

38 A suitably devised scheme for the vivacious author of *Merrily on High. An Anglo-Catholic Memoir* (Norwich; Canterbury Press, 2010), 2nd edition. Enjoyable religion.

39 Mascall, *Saraband*, p. 77.

40 As quoted by Simon Skinner, 'The *British Critic*: Newman and Mozley, Oakeley and Ward', in Brown, Nockles and Pereiro, *The Oxford Handbook of the Oxford Movement*, pp. 289–303. Skinner comments, 'It was a fitting epitaph to the breach between Phalanx and Tractarian churchmanship, epitomized in the struggle for the *Critic*, that on the final page in its fifty-year history is inscribed this dispute between the old and the new', p. 299.

41 Ollard, *A Short History of the Oxford Movement*, pp. 152–4.

42 Reed, *Glorious Battle*, pp. 90–2.

43 Cited in Gunstone, *Lift High the Cross*, p. 344.

44 William Davage, 'The Congress Movement: The High-Water Mark of Anglo-Catholicism', in Brown, Nockles and Pereiro, *The Oxford Handbook of the Oxford Movement*, pp. 517–29.

45 Gunstone, *Lift High the Cross*, p. 2.

46 William Davage, 'The Congress Movement', p. 518.

47 Cited *ibid*.

48 *Ibid.*, p. 519.

49 *Ibid.*, p. 522. See John Gunstone, *Anglo-Catholic Congresses in the Provinces* (London: Anglo-Catholic History Society, 2004), and Gunstone, *Lift High the Cross*, pp. 108–21.

50 *Ibid.*, p. 91.

51 William Davage, 'The Congress Movement', p. 523.

52 H. Maynard Smith, *Frank, Bishop of Zanzibar* (London: Society for Promoting Christian Knowledge, 1926).

53 *Ibid.*, pp. 145–70.

54 S. C. Carpenter, *Winnington-Ingram. The Biography of Arthur Foley Winnington-Ingram, Bishop of London, 1901–1939* (London: Hodder and Stoughton, 1949).

55 Quoted in Davage, 'The Congress Movement', p. 524.

56 *Ibid*.

After Newman

57 For a contemporary assessment of how things looked to Anglo-Catholics at this juncture, see Sheila Kaye-Smith, *Anglo-Catholicism* (London: Chapman & Hall, 1925).
58 Davage, 'The Congress Movement', p. 526.
59 Gunstone, *Lift High the Cross*, p. 248.
60 Quoted in Davage, 'The Congress Movement ', p. 528.

Chapter 9

1 Basil F. L. Clarke, *Church Builders of the Nineteenth Century. A Study of the Gothic Revival in England* (New York: Augustus Kelly, 1969), 2nd edition, p. 78
2 Ibid. See further Christopher Webster and John Elliott (eds.), *A Church as it Should Be. The Cambridge Camden Society and its Influence* (Donnington: Shaun Tyas, 2001).
3 For the Society's *Tracts* see Leon Litvack, *John Mason Neale and the Quest for Sobornost* (Oxford: Clarendon, 1994), p. 11.
4 Peter Anson, *Fashions in Church Furnishings, 1840–1940* (London: Faith Press, 1965), p. 61.
5 [John Mason Neale], *Church Enlargement and Church Arrangement* (Cambridge: Cambridge University Press, 1843), p. 2.
6 The appeal broadens in A. W. Pugin, *An Apology for the Revival of Christian Architecture in England* (London: Weale, 1843).
7 Ward, *Ward and the Oxford Movement*, pp. 154–5.
8 Joseph P. Chinnici, *The English Catholic Enlightenment: John Lingard and the Cisalpine Movement, 1770–1850* (Shepherdstown, WV: Patmos Press, 1980).
9 For his life in context, see Nicholas Olsberg, *The Master Builder: William Butterfield and his Times* (London: Lund Humphries, 2021).
10 Yetton, *Anglican Papalism.*, p. 56. An example of both would be St Saviour's, Hoxton: both ruined by War damage and also depopulated, *ibid.*, pp. 152–62.
11 Geoff Brandwood, 'High Anglicanism in High Places', in Peter Howell and Andrew Saint (ed.), *Butterfield Revisited*, Studies in Victorian Architecture and Design 6 (London: Victorian Society, 2017).
12 Anthony Quiney, *John Loughborough Pearson* (New Haven, CT: Yale University Press, 1979), pp. 4, 229.
13 *Ibid.*, pp. 105–24 (the London area churches), pp. 133–48 (Truro).
14 *Ibid.*, p. 201. For the outreach of the Gothic Revival into the British Empire, see G. A. Bremner, *Imperial Gothic. Religious Architecture and High Anglican Culture in the British Empire, 1840–1870* (New Haven, CT: Yale University Press, 2013).
15 Charles Locke Eastlake, *A History of the Gothic Revival* (London: Longmans, Green & Co., 1872), pp. 303–4.
16 George Gilbert Scott, *A Plea for the Faithful Restoration of our Ancient Churches* (London and Oxford: John Henry Parker, 1850). For his life see Gavin Stamp (ed.), *Personal and Professional Recollections. The Autobiography of the Victorian Architect George Gilbert Scott* (Stamford: Paul Watkins, 1995).
17 Geoff Brandwood, *George Edmund Street*, ed. P. Howell and P. C. W. Taylor

Notes

(Liverpool: Liverpool University Press, 2024).

18 George Edmund Street, *Brick and Marble in the Middle Ages. Notes of a Tour in the North of Italy* (no place: no publisher, 1855); *Some Account of Gothic Architecture in Spain* (London: Hohn Murray, 1865). Both these works were republished by Cambridge University Press in 2017.

19 George Edmund Street, 'On the Future of Art in England', *The Ecclesiologist* 19 (1858), pp. 232–40, and here at p. 234.

20 Michael Hall, *George Frederick Bodley and the Later Gothic Revival in Britain and America* (New Haven, CT: Yale University Press, 2014), p. 25.

21 *Ibid.*, p. 3.

22 For Bodley's 'idea of a cathedral', the completed buildings in Australia and the United States and the design for Liverpool, see *ibid.*, pp. 395–415. Bodley's design for a reredos in the Lady Chapel of Liverpool was, however accepted.

23 *Ibid.*, p. 168.

24 Cited in *The Church of the Holy Angels, Hoar Cross* (Hoar Cross Parish Church Council: Hoar Cross, no date), no pagination but p. 21.

25 Hall, *George Frederick Bodley*, p. 43.

26 Cited *ibid.*, p. 44.

27 For an overview of his life and work, see Anthony Symondson [with, for the Gazetteer, S. A. Bucknall], *Sir Ninian Comper. An introduction to his life and work* (Reading: Spire Books, 2006), pp. 19–205.

28 Michael Fisher, *Guarding the Pugin Flame: John Hardman Powell, 1827–1895* (Reading: Spire Books, 2017).

29 For a survey of this unexpected renaissance, see Mary Schoeser, *English Church Embroidery, 1833–1953* (London: Watts & Co., 1998). Her fifth chapter, 'Convents and their Embroidery schools', deals with the Sisterhood of the Holy Cross (Park Village West), the Society of the Most Holy Trinity, the Society of All Saints, Sisters of the Poor, the Community of St John the Baptist (Clewer), the Community of the Sisters of the Church, the Community of St Mary the Virgin (Wantage), all described in Chapter 5; the Society of the Sisters of Bethany, mentioned *à propos* of the Wagners of Brighton in Chapter 4, and due to enter the picture again in connexion with Sir Ninian Comper in Chapter 9; the Community of All Hallows at Ditchingham, in Suffolk, the Community of St Peter's, Horbury (a rare Northern foundation, near Wakefield, in Yorkshire), the Sisters of Charity at St Raphael's, Bristol, and the Missionary Community of St Denys at Warminster in Wiltshire, for which quartet of Sisterhoods see Anson, *The Call of the Cloister*, pp. 328–31, 364–70, 414–18, 453. It will be noted that the starting point of Schoeser's study is the year of Keble's Assize Sermon.

30 Peter F. Anson, *Fashions in Church Furnishing, 1840–1960* (London: Faith Press, 1960).

31 Symondson and Bucknall, *Sir Ninian Comper*, pp. 231–48.

32 For the revival of mural painting in English churches, both Anglican and Catholic, see Aidan Nichols, OP, *In Search of the Sacred Image* (Leominster: Gracewing, 2020), pp. 116–21.

33 Dennis Farr (ed.), *Thomas Gambier Parry (1816–1888) as Artist and Collector* (London: Courtauld Institute Galleries, 1993).

34 A. T. John Salter, *The Anglican Papalist*, p. 13. He was simultaneously General Secretary of the Anglican and Eastern Orthodox Churches Union and Priest Director of the (strongly Papalist) Catholic League, until in 1933 his signature on an Anglo-Papalist petition (described in Chapter 1) led to his ejection from the committee of the former. Fynes-Clinton's transformation of St Magnus the Martyr, London Bridge from a condition he described as hardly more iconic than a synagogue, to the fit object of T. S. Eliot's acclamation in *The Waste Land*, is described *ibid.*, pp. 88–101.

35 Nichols, OP, *In Search of the Sacred Image*, pp. 111–16.

36 Adrian Barlow, *The Life and Legacy of Charles Eamer Kempe* (Cambridge: Lutterworth Press, 2018).

37 Rowell, *The Vision Glorious*, p. 22.

38 Barlow, *The Life and Legacy of Charles Eamer Kempe*, p. 16.

39 *Ibid.*, p. 95.

40 *Ibid.*, p. 28.

41 *Ibid.*, pp. 47–8.

42 For the 'maelstrom in a mole hole' of his time as churchwarden, see *ibid.*, pp. 195–8.

43 *Ibid.*, p. 229.

44 *Ibid.*, p. 256.

45 T. S. Eliot, *For Lancelot Andrews* (London: Faber & Faber, 1970 [1928]), p. 11.

46 Joseph Ellis Baker, *The Novel and the Oxford Movement* (Princeton, NJ: Princeton University Press, 1932).

47 According to the research of Barbara Dennis, *Charlotte Yonge, Novelist of the Oxford Movement: A Literature of Victorian Customs and Society* (Lewiston, NY: Edwin Mellen Press, 1992).

48 Ellen Jordan, Charlotte Mitchell, and Helen Schinske, '"A Handmaid to the Church": How John Keble shaped the career of Charlotte Yonge, the "Novelist of the Oxford Movement"', in Blair (ed.), *John Keble in Context*, pp. 175–91.

49 The 'National Society for Promoting the Education of the Poor in the Principles of the Established Church in England and Wales', founded in 1811, sought to become the foundation of the primary education system nation-wide, in which it was challenged by the Nonconformist British and Foreign Schools Society. See H. J. Burgess, *Enterprise in Education. The Story of the Work of the Established Church in the Education of the People prior to 1870* (London: Society for Promoting Christian Knowledge, 1958).

50 Charlotte Yonge, *Musings over 'The Christian Year' and 'Lyra Innocentium', together with a few gleanings of recollections of the Rev. John Keble, gathered by several friends* (Oxford and London: James Parker, 1874).

51 Alethea Hayter, *Charlotte Yonge* (London: Northcote House, 1996), p. 2.

52 *Ibid.*, p. 1.

53 Charlotte Yonge, *Life of John Coleridge Patteson, Missionary Bishop of the Melanesian Islands* (London: Macmillan, 1875), two volumes.

54 Yonge's absorption in the progress of missionary work is highlighted in Barbara Dennis, *Charlotte Yonge (1823–1901), Novelist of the Oxford Movement: A*

Notes

Literature of Victorian Customs and Society (Lewiston, NY: Edwin Mellen Press, 1992) as one dimension of the confidence of religious culture in High Victorian England.

55 Hayter, *Charlotte Yonge*, p. 16.

56 W. H. Hutton, 'The Oxford Movement', in A. W. Ward and A. R. Waller (ed.), *The Cambridge History of English Literature* XII (Cambridge: Cambridge University Press, 1915), p. 277.

57 See Lynda Palazzo, *Christina Rossetti's Feminist Theology* (Basingstoke: Palgrave Macmillan, 2002), and more mildly Diane D'Amico, *Christina Rossetti. Faith, Gender and Time* (Baton Rouge, LA: Louisiana State University Press, 1999).

58 A lesson to be unlearned as in Kathleen Jones, *Learning Not to be First. A Biography of Christina Rossetti* (Oxford: Oxford University Press, 1991).

59 Dinah Roe, *The Rossettis in Wonderland. A Victorian Family History* (London: Haus Publishing, 2011).

60 Richard Frederick Littledale, *Catholic Ritual in the Church of England: Scriptural, Reasonable, Lawful* (London: Palmer, 1865).

61 Christina Rossetti, *Annus Domini. A Prayer for Each Day of the Year, Founded on Holy Scripture* (London: James Parker, 1874).

62 Henry W. Burrows, *The Half-Century of Christ Church, St Pancras, Albany Street* (London: Skeffington, 1887).

63 Orby Shipley (ed.), *Lyra Mystica: Hymns and Verses on Sacred Subjects* (London: Longmans, Green, 1869). Shipley was on the staff of St Alban's, Holborn.

64 Orby Shipley (ed.), *Lyra Eucharistica: Hymns and Verse on the Holy Communion, ancient and modern, with other poems* London: Longmans, Green, 1864).

65 Tennyson, *Victorian Devotional Poetry*, pp. 199–200.

66 *Ibid.*, p. 202.

67 *Ibid.*, p. 201.

68 Christina Rossetti, *The Face of the Deep. A Devotional Commentary on the Apocalypse* (London: James Parker, 1892).

69 Elizabeth Ludlow, 'Christina Rossetti and the Pre-Raphaelites', in Brown, Nockles and Pereiro, *The Oxford Handbook of the Oxford Movement*, pp. 427–38, and here at p. 432.

70 Christina Rossetti, *Verses* (London: Society for Promoting Christian Knowledge, 1893).

71 Ludlow, 'Christina Rossetti and the Pre-Raphaelites', p. 435. The key phrase there mirrors the title of Rossetti's *Called to be Saints: The Minor Festivals Devotionally Considered* (London: Society for Promoting Christian Knowledge, 1881).

72 Emma Mason, *Christina Rossetti. Poetry, Ecology, Faith* (Oxford: Oxford University Press, 2018), p. 35. Mason's study contains a wealth of factual detail but its ecotheology ('green grace') should be taken *cum [magno] grano salis*.

73 Manning was vice-president of the Victoria Street Society for the Protection of Animals from Vivisection. See for the context, A. W. H. Bates, *Anti-Vivisection in Britain. A Social History* (London: Palgrave Macmillan, 2017), chapter 1, 'Christians and Anti-Vivisection in the Nineteenth Century'. Newman and Manning were aligned on the matter, unlike Pius IX. Bates ascribes this to their shared Anglican background.

74 T. S. Eliot, *The Complete Poems and Plays* (London: Faber & Faber, 1986 [1969]), pp. 59–80, 169–98.

75 *Ibid.*, pp. 103–4.

76 James Matthew Wilson, 'An "Organ for a Frenchified Doctrine": Jacques Maritain and *The Criterion*'s Neo-Thomism', in Benjamin G. Lockerd (ed.), *T. S. Eliot and Christian Tradition* (Madison, WI: Fairleigh Dickinson Press, 2014), pp. 99–117. As Maritain's thought developed Eliot came to consider its manner of expression as much Romantic as classic.

77 William James, *The Varieties of Religious Experience. A Study in Human Nature* (London: Longmans, Green, 1902).

78 Evelyn Underhill, *Mysticism. A Study in the Nature and Development of Spiritual Consciousness* (London: Longmans, 1911), cited in Barry Spurr, *'Anglo-Catholic in Religion': T. S. Eliot and Christianity* (Cambridge: Lutterworth Press, 2010), p. 24. Her initial approach to mysticism was religiously eclectic but became more fully Christian after the Great War when she returned to Anglican practice, eventually self-identifying as Anglo-Catholic, Dana Greene, *Evelyn Underhill. Artist of the Infinite Life* (London: Darton, Longman & Todd, 1991), p. 100. Her importance for Anglo-Catholics is signalled in Jane Shaw, *Mysticism and Anglo-Catholicism. Evelyn Underhill and her Circle* (London: Anglo-Catholic History Society, 2023). 'The new life which entered the Church of England with the Tractarian movement, changing its appearance as it grew and spread, has now penetrated and transformed in varying ways and degrees the whole temper of her worship, and brought it back into harmony with Catholic tradition', cited *ibid.*, p. 3, from Evelyn Underhill, *Worship* (London: Nisbet & Co., 1936), p. 334.

79 Spurr, *'Anglo-Catholic in Religion'*, p. 87.

80 *Ibid.*, p. 31.

81 Cited *ibid.*, p. 113.

82 Eliot, *The Complete Poems and Plays*, p. 89–100.

83 Eliot, 'Introduction', in John Baillie and Hugh Martin (ed.), *Revelation* (London: Faber & Faber, 1937), pp. 1–2.

84 Jeremy Morris, 'An Infallible Fact-Factory Going Full Blast': Austin Farrer. Marian Doctrine and the Travails of Anglo-Catholicism', in R. N. Swanson (ed.), *The Church and Mary*, Studies in Church History 39 (Cambridge: Cambridge University Press, 2004), pp. 358–67.

85 Eliot, *The Complete Poems and Plays*, pp. 237–82. For an account by its producer see C. Martin Browne, *The Making of T. S. Eliot's Plays* (Cambridge: Cambridge University Press, 1969).

86 James Matthew Wilson, 'Style and Substance: T. S. Eliot, Jacques Maritain, and Neo-Thomism', *Religion and Literature* 42. 3 (2010), pp. 43–71.

87 Grevel Lindop, *Charles Williams. The Third Inkling* (Oxford: Oxford University Press, 2015).

88 Cited *ibid.*, p. 408.

89 Charles Williams, *Seed of Adam, and Other Plays* (Oxford: Oxford University Press, 1948).

90 The claim of Thomas Howard, *The Novels of Charles Williams* (New York and London: Oxford University Press, 1983).

Notes

⁹¹ Lindop, a highly sympathetic biographer, does not hesitate to ascribe to these relationships a sado-masochistic element: *Charles Williams*, p. 340. He suggests it as the reason Williams does not seem to have frequented the sacrament of Penance: fear a confessor would make him 'change course', *ibid.*, p. 348.

⁹² For a composite account see Humphrey Carpenter, *The Inklings. C. S. Lewis, J. R. R. Tolkien, Charles Williams and their Friends* (London: Allen & Unwin, 1978).

⁹³ Charles Williams, *He Came Down from Heaven* (London: Heinemann, 1938).

⁹⁴ Charles Williams, *The Descent of the Dove. A History of the Holy Spirit in the Church* (London: Longmans, Green, 1939).

⁹⁵ Charles Williams, *The Forgiveness of Sins* (London: Geoffrey Bles, 1942).

⁹⁶ Lindop, *Charles Williams*, p. 193.

⁹⁷ Charles Williams, *The Figure of Beatrice* (London: Faber & Faber, 1943).

⁹⁸ For her background and life, see Jane Emery, *Rose Macaulay, A Writer's Life* (London: John Murray, 1991), a wonderful biography.

⁹⁹ Rose Macaulay, *The World my Wilderness* (London: Collins, 1950).

¹⁰⁰ Rose Macaulay, *The Towers of Trebizond* (London: Collins, 1956).

¹⁰¹ *Ibid.*, p. 6. Compare David Hein, 'Faith and Doubt in Rose Macaulay's *The Towers of Trebizond*', *Anglican Theological Review* 88 (2006), pp. 47–78.

¹⁰² Rose Macaulay, *Letters to a Friend, 1950–1952*, edited Constance Babington-Smith (London: Collins, 1961); Rose Macaulay, *Last Letters to a Friend, 1952–1958*, edited Constance Babington-Smith (London: Collins, 1964). A much younger but contemporary woman novelist struck a similar acidulous note about the Roman Catholic clergy, writing of Ronald Knox's secession, it 'must be beastly to be a *Roman* priest', Barbara Pym, *A Very Private Eye. An Autobiography in Diaries and Letters* (London: Macmillan, 1984), ed. Hazel Holt and Hilary Pym, p. 323. Emphasis is original. Pym's Anglo-Catholicism is apparent from her choice of churches during her professional life in London: St Mary Magdalene, Paddington; All Saints, Notting Hill; St Alban's, Holborn, St Gabriel's, Warwick Square: places that (in Pym's words) smell of old incense, not floor polish.

¹⁰³ Macaulay, *The Towers of Trebizond*, p. 12.

¹⁰⁴ Michael Chandler, *The Life and Work of John Mason Neale, 1818–1866* (Leominster: Gracewing, 1995).

¹⁰⁵ Ollard, *A Short History of the Oxford Movement*, p. 132.

¹⁰⁶ J. M. Neale, 'On the History of Hymnology', *The Ecclesiologist* 12 (1851), p. 241.

¹⁰⁷ J. M. Neale, *Hymni ecclesiae, e breviariis at missalibus gallicanis, germanis, hispanis, lusitanis desumpti* (Oxford: John Henry Parker, 1851).

¹⁰⁸ J. M. Neale, *Sequentiae e missalibus germanicis, anglicis, gallicanis, aliisque Medii Aevi collectae* (London: John William Parker & Son, 1852).

¹⁰⁹ J. M. Neale, *Mediaeval Hymns and Sequences* (London: Joseph Masters, 1851).

¹¹⁰ *The Hymnal Noted, Parts I and II* (New York: Novello, and London: Joseph Masters, 1851).

¹¹¹ *The Psalter Noted* (New York, Novello, and London: Joseph Masters, 1850).

¹¹² J. M. Neale, *Hymns of the Eastern Church* (London: Hayes, 1862).

113 Ibid., p. xii.
114 Litvack, *John Mason Neale and the Quest for Sobornost*, p. 105.
115 Ian Bradley, *Abide with me. The World of Victorian Hymns* (London: Faber & Faber, 1997), pp. 25–6.
116 Andrw Chandler, *The Place of John Mason Neals* (London: Anglo-Catholic History Society, 2024), p. 12.
117 J. R. Watson, *The English Hymn: A Critical and Historical Study* (Oxford: Clarendon Press, 1997), p. 380.
118 Ibid., p. 379.
119 Ibid., p. 336.
120 Ibid., p. 386.
121 Ibid., p. 388–9, citing W. K. Lowther-Clarke, *A Hundred Years of Hymns Ancient and Modern* (London: William Clowes, 1960), p. 31. The hymns from the German, chosen from Catherine Winkworth's translations in her 1855 *Lyra Germanica*, drew largely on the Lutheran chorale tradition.
122 William Chatterton Dix, *Altar Songs: Verses for the Holy Eucharist* (London: G. J. Palmer, 1867). See on the Anglo-Catholic contribution Hilary Davidson, *Hymns and the Anglo-Catholic Revival* (London: Anglo-Catholic History Society, 2008).
123 William Chatterton Dix, *A Vision of All Saints, and Other Poems* (London: John Hodges, 1871).
124 B. H. C. Dickinson, *Sabine Baring-Gould: Squarson, Writer, and Folklorist, 1834–1924* (Newton Abbot: David & Charles, 1970), p. 64.
125 Cecil Sharp, *English Folk Song: Some Conclusions* (London: Simpkin, 1907).
126 Dickinson, *Sabine Baring-Gould*, pp. 123–40.
127 John E. Barnes, *George Ratcliffe Woodward, 1848–1934, Priest, Poet, Musician* (Norwich: Canterbury Press, 2012).
128 G. R. Woodward (compiled and arranged), *Carols for Christmastide* (London: Pickering & Chatto, 1892); *Carols for Easter and Ascensiontide* (London: Pickering & Chatto, 1895); *The Cowley Carol Book: Carols for Christmas, Easter and Ascensiontide* (London: Mowbray, 1901).
129 G. R. Woodward, *Songs of Syon. A collection of hymns and sacred poems mostly translated from ancient Greek, Latin and German sources* (London: Schott, 1904).
130 G. R. Woodward and Charles Wood, *Carols for Christmas, Easter and Ascensiontide, Second Series* (London: Mowbray, 1919). A 1947 'complete' edition came from the same Anglo-Catholic publishing house.
131 G. R. Woodward and Charles Wood, *The Cambridge Carol Book* (London: Society for the Promotion of Christian Knowledge, 1924).
132 G. R. Woodward (ed.), *Piae Cantiones. A collection of church and school songs, chiefly ancient Swedish, originally published in A. D. 1582 by Theodoric Petri of Nyland* (London: Plainsong and Mediaeval Music Society, 1910).
133 Percy Dearmer, with Martin Shaw and Ralph Vaughan Williams, *Songs of Praise* (London: Oxford University Press, 1925).
134 Maria Hackett later produced her *Brief Account of Cathedral and Collegiate Schools, with an Abstract of their Statutes and Endowments* (London: John Nichols, 1824), taking copies personally to each cathedral.

Notes

¹³⁵ W. J. Jebb, *The Choral Service of the United Church of England and Ireland being an inquiry into the liturgical system of the cathedral and collegiate foundations of the Anglican Communion* (London: J. W. Parker, 1843). See more widely Bernard Rainbow, *The Choral Revival in the Anglican Church, 1839–1872* (New York: Oxford University Press, 1970).

¹³⁶ Robert Druitt, *A Popular Tract on Church Music, and a Practical Scheme for its Reformation* (London: Rivington, 1845).

¹³⁷ Zon Bennett, *The English Plainchant Revival* (Oxford: Oxford University Press, 1999).

¹³⁸ Dale Adelmann, *The Contribution of Cambridge Ecclesiologists to the Revival of Anglican Choral Worship, 1839–62* (Aldershot: Ashgate, 1997).

¹³⁹ A. W. Pugin, *An Earnest Appeal for the Revival of Ancient Plain* (London and Edinburgh: Charles Dolman, 1850); Anson, *The Call of the Cloister*, p. 318, fn 3.

¹⁴⁰ *Plainsong for Schools. Masses and Occasional Chants* (Liverpool: Rushworth and Dreaper, 1930), two volumes, with many subsequent printings.

¹⁴¹ Jeremy Dibble, 'Music and Anglicanism in the Nineteenth Century', in Strong, *The Oxford History of Anglicanism. III*, pp. 388–400, and here at p. 393.

¹⁴² *Ibid.*, p. 394.

¹⁴³ See further Walter Hillsman, 'The Victorian Revival of Plainsong in English: its usage under Tractarians and Ritualists', in Diana Word (ed.), *The Church and the Arts*, Studies in Christ History 28 (Cambridge: Cambridge University Press, 1992), pp. 405–15.

¹⁴⁴ Dibble, 'Music and Anglicanism in the Nineteenth Century', pp. 395–6.

Chapter 10

¹ Henry Parry Liddon, *The Life of Edward Bouverie Pusey* (London: Longmans Green, 1894–8), III, pp. 148–9.

² E. B. Pusey, *The Articles Treated on in Tract 90 Reconsidered and their Interpretation Vindicated* (Oxford: John Henry Parker, and London: Rivington, 1841).

³ Rowan Williams, *Looking East in Winter. Contemporary Thought and the Eastern Christian Tradition* (London: Bloomsbury, 2021).

⁴ E. B. Pusey, *Letter to His Grace the Archbishop of Canterbury, on some Circumstances Connected with the Present Crisis in the English Church* (Oxford: John Henry Parker, and London: Rivington, 1842).

⁵ J. H. Newman, 'Introduction', in William Palmer, *Notes of a Visit to the Russian Church in the Years 1840, 1841*, selected and arranged by Cardinal Newman (London: Kegan Paul Trench & Co., 1882), pp. vi-vii.

⁶ Its classic early nineteenth century expression is by William Palmer of Worcester (not, then, his Magdalen sound-alike), *A Treatise on the Church of Christ, designed chiefly for the use of students of theology* (London: Rivington, 1838).

⁷ J. M. Neale, 'Introduction', in Antonio Pereira de Figueiredo, *Tentativa Theologica. Episcopal Rights and Ultra-montane Usurpations*, tr. E. H. Landon (London: Joseph Masters, 1847), p. viii.

⁸ *Ibid.*, p. xvii.

9 *Ibid.*, p. xix.

10 Johnston, *Life and Letters of Henry Parry Liddon*, p. 127.

11 For overviews, see P. E. Shaw, *The Early Tractarians and the Eastern Church* (Milwaukee: Moorhouse, 1930); Tatiana Soloviova, 'Anglican-Orthodox Dialogue in the Nineteenth Century and Gladstone's Interest in the Reunion of Christendom', in Peter Francis (ed.), *The Gladstone Umbrella* (Hawarden: Monad Press, 2001), pp. 50–72.

12 Their expedition is described in Stuart Dodgson Collingwood, *The Life and Letters of Lewis Carroll* (New York: Century, 1899), pp. 111–26.

13 J. O. Johnston, *Life and Letters of Henry Parry Liddon*, p. 102.

14 Randall Davidson, *The Lambeth Conferences of 1867, 1878 and 1888: with the Official Reports and Resolutions, together with the Sermons preached at the Conferences* (London: Society for Promoting Christian Knowledge, 1896), pp.94–6.

15 Cited in Reed, *Glorious Battle*, p. 269.

16 W. R. Inge, *The Church and the Age* (London: Longmans, Green & Co., 1912), p 62.

17 Cited in Wilkinson, *The Community of the Resurrection*, p. 144.

18 *Ibid.*

19 See Jeffrey Bibbee, *Anglo-Catholicism and the Orthodox East. William Birkbeck and the Quest for Unity, 1888–1916* (London: Anglo-Catholic History Society, 2017).

20 Bryn Geffert, *Eastern Orthodox and Anglicans. Diplomacy, Theology, and the Politics of Interwar Ecumenism* (Notre Dame, IN: University of Notre Dame Press, 2010), p. 4.

21 Ibid, pp. 83–5.

22 A. C. Headlam, *The Doctrine of the Church and Christian Reunion* (London: John Murray, 1920). See Ronald Jasper, *A. C. Headlam. Life and Letters of a Bishop* (London: Faith Press, 1960).

23 James Good, *The Church of England and the Ecumenical Movement*, pp. 71–80.

24 Geffert, *Eastern Orthodox and Anglicans*, p. 33.

25 *Ibid.*, p. 141.

26 For this body, still extant, see John Burley and Jack Witten 'The Society of St. Willibrord', in Gordon Huelin (ed.), *Old Catholics and Anglicans, 1931–1981* (Oxford: Oxford University Press, 1983), pp. 62–85.

27 Edward Every, 'Canon John Albert Douglas, R. I. P.', *Sobornost* 3 [21] (1957), pp. 496–8.

28 Geffert, *Eastern Orthodox and Anglicans*, p. 141.

29 *Ibid.*, p. 185. For the (to varying degrees) inconclusive doctrinal discussions after Lausanne (Lambeth, 1930; Bucharest, 1935–6 — the most positive, but ill received by Evangelicals at home; Edinburgh, 1937; Moscow, 1948 — the latter without Anglican representatives though taking up the question of Anglican Orders raised by Geoffrey Fisher of Canterbury, 1887–1972), see *ibid.*, pp. 184–217, 252–5.

30 Dimitrios Filippos Salapatas, *The Fellowship of St Alban and St Sergius. Orthodox and Anglican Ecumenical Relations, 1927–2012* (Cambridge: Cambridge Scholars Publishing, 2018).

31 Aidan Nichols, OP, *Alban and Sergius. The Story of a Journal* (Leominster: Gracewing, 2018).

Notes

32 C. B. Moss, *The Old Catholic Movement, its Origins and History* (London: Society for Promoting Christian Knowledge, 1964, 2nd edition).

33 Though in his book-length study, which first alerted Anglicans to the existence of Old Catholics, he sought to qualify the adjective: this John Mason Neale, *A History of the So-called Jansenist Church of Holland* (Oxford and London: John Henry and James Parker, 1858).

34 W. J. Sparrow-Simpson, *Roman Catholic Opposition to Papal Infallibility* (London: John Murray, 1909).

35 Charlotte Yonge, *Reasons why I am a Catholic but not a Roman Catholic* (London: Wells Gardner, 1901).

36 Chapman, *The Fantasy of Reunion*, p. 207.

37 It was originally published as *Is the Church of Rome the Babylon of the Book of Revelation?* (London: Rivington, 1850).

38 Chapman, *The Fantasy of Reunion*, pp. 213–19.

39 Cited *ibid.*, p. 221.

40 W. E. Gladstone, *The Vatican Decrees in their Bearing on Civil Allegiance: A Political Expostulation* (London: John Murray, 1874).

41 Chapman, *The Fantasy of Reunion*, p. 249.

42 *Ibid.*, p. 261.

43 Quoted in Good, *The Church of England and the Ecumenical Movement*, p. 81.

44 Cited in Chapman, *The Fantasy of Reunion*, p. 293.

45 Henry R. T. Brandreth, *Episcopi Vagantes and the Anglican Church* (London: Society for Promoting Christian Knowledge, 1961), 2nd edition, pp 12–18; John Kersey, *Arnold Harris Mathew and the Old Catholic Movement in England, 1908–52* (no place: European-American University Press, 2010).

46 For the remarkably short text, see Huelin, *Old Catholics and Anglicans*, p. 164 — if we exclude its title and the names of the signatories, sixty-seven words.

47 Robert Runcie, 'An Assessment of the Bonn Agreement', *ibid.*, pp. 1–9, and here at p. 9.

48 See Chapman, *The Fantasy of Reunion*, pp. 36–66.

49 Margaret Pawley, *Faith and Family: The Life and Circle of Ambrose Phillips de Lisle* (Norwich: Canterbury Press, 2017).

50 Henry R. T. Brandreth, *Dr Lee of Lambeth. A Chapter in Parenthesis in the History of the Oxford Movement* (London: Society for Promoting Christian Knowledge, 1951). Lee was minister at the Berkeley Chapel in Mayfair when the Association was created but in 1867 he became Vicar of All Saints, Lambeth. He had emerged from Liddon's Cuddesdon College, one of its earliest ordinands, in 1854.

51 Donald J. Mackey, *Bishop Forbes: A Memoir* (London: Kegan, Trench & Co., 1888); Rowan Strong, *Alexander Forbes of Brechin. The First Tractarian Bishop* (Oxford: Clarendon Press, 1995).

52 Ambrose Phillips de Lisle, *The Future Unity of Christendom* (London: Charles Dolman, 1857).

53 Charles Stephen Dessain (ed.), *Letters and Diaries of John Henry Newman. New Beginnings in England, April 1857 to December 1858* (Oxford: Oxford University Press, 2016), pp. 70–1.

54 Alexander Forbes, *An Explanation of the Thirty-Nine Articles* (Oxford and London: James Parker, 1867–8). The book, a reading of the Articles in terms of second-generation Tractarianism, was re-published in 2024 by Nashotah House Press, with a Preface by Dr Clinton Collister. For a brief presentation of the work see Chapman, *The Fantasy of Reunion*, pp. 135–41.

55 G. F. Cobb's *The Kiss of Peace, or England and Rome at One on the Doctrine of the Holy Eucharist* (London: J. T. Hayes, 1867). For Cobb, see Chapman, *The Fantasy of Reunion*, pp. 182–8.

56 J. H. Newman, *A Letter to the Rev. E. B. Pusey, D. D. on his Recent Eirenicon* (London: Longmans, 1866), later incorporated in his *Certain Difficulties felt by Anglicans in Catholic Teaching* (London: Longmans, 1888), two volumes, ii, pp. 1–170.

57 I draw here on the excellent analysis of the ongoing debate between Pusey and Newman in Chapman, *The Fantasy of Reunion*, pp. 76–130, who points out that Newman's 'method' in his replies to Pusey would never satisfy those for whom patristic proof remained the functional equivalent of the *sola scriptura* of the Reformation', *ibid.*, p. 99.

58 E. B. Pusey, *First Letter to the Very Rev. J. H. Newman in Explanation chiefly in regard to the Reverential Love due to the Ever-blessed Theotokos, and the Doctrine of the Immaculate Conception with an analysis of Cardinal de Turrecremata's Work on the Immaculate Conception* (Oxford; Parker, and London; Rivington, 1869).

59 E. B. Pusey., *Is Healthful Reunion Impossible: The Second Letter to the Very Rev. J. H. Newman, D. D.* (Oxford: Parker, and London: Rivington, 1980). A second edition appeared in 1876.

60 Chapman, *The Fantasy of Reunion*, p. 116.

61 Pusey, *Is Healthful Reunion Impossible?*, p. 306.

62 Rowell, *The Vision Glorious*, p. 197.

63 Pawley, *Faith and Family*, pp. 380–4.

64 Cited in Rowell, *The Vision Glorious*, p. 203.

65 Ollard, *A Short History of the Oxford Movement*, pp. 180–1.

66 Brandreth, *Dr Lee of Lambeth*, p. 139.

67 Owing to Belgian Anglophilia (the 1830 Treaty of London created modern Belgium), there had been a significant, if fluctuating, level of interest in the rise of Anglo-Catholicism: see Jan de Maeyer and Karl Strobbe, 'The Oxford Movement: reception and perception in Catholic circles in nineteenth century Belgium', in Stewart J. Brown and Peter B. Nockles (eds.), *The Oxford Movement: Europe and the Wider World, 1830–1930* (Cambridge: Cambridge University Press, 2014), pp. 185–202.

68 Paul Avis, 'Anglicanism and Christian Unity in the Twentieth Century', in Morris, *Oxford History of Anglicanism. IV*, pp. 189–213, and here at p. 206.

69 Cited in Rowell, *The Vision Glorious*, p. 206.

70 *Ibid.*, p. 208.

71 As quoted in Walter Frere, *Recollections of Malines. A Contribution to the Cause of Christian Reunion* (London: Centenary Press, 1935), p. 117.

72 Anselm Bolton, *A Catholic Memorial of Lord Halifax and Cardinal Mercier* (London: Williams and Norgate, 1935); Walter Frere, *Recollections of Malines. A contribution to the cause of Christian reunion* (London: Centenary Press, 1935).

Notes

73 Henry Fynes-Clinton and William Robert Courbould, *The Church of England and the Holy See: What are we to Say?* (London: Council for Promoting Christian Unity, 1933).

74 'Father Clement', *Catholic Reunion. An Anglican Plea for a Uniate Patriarchate of Canterbury and for an Anglican Ultramontanism* (Oxford: Basil Blackwell, 1935).

75 Yelton, *Anglican Papalism*, p. 7.

76 *Ibid.*, p. 47.

77 *Ibid.*, pp. 42–5.

78 Embry, *The Catholic Movement and the Society of the Holy Cross*, p. 309.

79 'Father Clement', p. 44.

80 Salter, *The Anglican Papalist*, p. 21.

81 Yelton, *Anglican Papalism*, p. 8, though Yelton also notices the possible usefulness to Anglo-Papalists of the role of Dutch and Swiss Old Catholics in the conferring of Anglican Orders.

82 H. E. W. Slade, SSJE, *A Work Begun: The Story of the Cowley Fathers in India, 1874–1967* (London: Society for Promoting Christian Knowledge, 1970), p. 36; see also on the progressive establishment of the Bombay and Poona mission, James, *The Cowley Fathers*, pp. 65–7, 94–6, 110–14, 157–64; 165–6.

83 *Ibid.*, p. 113.

84 *Ibid.*, pp. 184–92.

85 George Congreve and William H. Longridge (ed.), *Letters of Richard Meux Bension* (London: Mowbray, 1916), pp. 227–9.

86 Rowan Strong, 'Origins of Anglo-Catholic Missions: Fr Richard Benson and the initial missions of the Society of St John the Evangelist, 1869–1882', *Journal of Ecclesiastical History* 66 (2015), pp. 90–115.

87 Rowan Strong, 'The Oxford Movement and Missions', in Brown, Nockles and Pereiro, *The Oxford Handbook of the Oxford Movement*, pp. 485–97, and here at p. 490.

88 G. Studdert-Kennedy, 'Theology and Authority, Constitution and Improvisation. The Colonial Church in India', in Judith M. Browne and Robert E. Frykenberg (eds.), *Christians, Cultural Interactions, and India's Religious Traditions* (Grand Rapids, MI: Eerdmans, 2002), pp. 154–82. See further on this subject, Mildred E. Gibbs, *The Anglican Church in India, 1600–1970* (New Dehi, Society for Promoting Christian Knowledge, 1972); Bernard Palmer, *Imperial Vineyard: The Anglican Church in India under the Raj from the Mutiny to the Partition* (London: Book Guild, 1999).

89 George Herbert Wilson, *The History of the Universities' Mission to Central Africa* (London: Universities' Mission to Central Africa, 1936), pp. 1–3. Wilson's work is in part a revised and compressed version of A. E. M. Anderson-Morshead, *The History of the Universities' Mission to Central Africa, 1859–1909* (London: Universities' Mission to Central Africa, 1909). Her work was taken further in Arthur Gordon Blood, *The History of the Universities' Mission to Central Africa, Volume II, 1907–1932* (London: Universities' Mission to Central Africa, 1957), and his *The History of the Universities' Mission to Central Africa, Volume III, 1957–1965* (London: Universities' Mission to Central Africa, 1965).

90 C. Brad Faught, 'Tractarianism on the Zambezi. Bishop Mackenzie and the Beginnings of the Universities' Mission to Central Africa', *Anglican and Episcopal*

History LXXII, 3 (1997), pp. 298–323.

91 Wilson, *The History of the Universities' Mission to Central Africa*, p. 66.

92 See Steven Maughan, *Mighty England do Good. Culture, Faith, Empire, and World in the Foreign Missions of the Church of England, 1850–1915* (Grand Rapids, MI: Eerdmans, 2014).

93 John Stuart, *Anglo-Catholicism and the Universities' Mission to Central Africa* (London: Anglo-Catholic History Society, 2011), p. 4.

94 *Ibid.*, p. 8.

95 Robert Marshall Heanley, *A Memoir of Edward Steere, D. D. LL. D* (London: Universities' Mission to Central Africa, 1898).

96 Masasi would become a see-city in 1926 when, after the death of Bishop Weston, the southern archdeaconries of the Zanzibar diocese were hived off to form a new entity.

97 Cited in H. Maynard-Smith, *Frank, Bishop of Zanzibar* (London: Society for Promoting Christian Knowledge, 1926), p. 100.

98 In Frank Weston, *Conquering and to Conquer* (London: Society for Promoting Christian Knowledge, 1918).

99 Cited in Gunstone, *Lift High the Cross*, p. 55.

100 Frank Weston, *The Christ and his Critics An Open Pastoral Letter to the European Missionaries of his Diocese* (London: Mowbray, 1919).

101 For the Community of the Mission Sisters of the Holy Name of Jesus, see Anson, *The Call of the Cloister*, pp. 394–6. For the Sisters of the Society of Saint Margaret in Aberdeen, see above, Chapter 5.

102 For his life, see J. H. Evans, *Militant Churchman: George Augustus Selwyn, bishop of New Zealand and Lichfield* (London: Allen & Unwin, 1964); R. W. K. Williams, *George Augustus Selwyn (1809–1878): Theological Formation, Life and Work* (Farnham: Routledge, 2014).

103 Michael Gladwin, 'Anglicanism in Oceania since 1914', in William L. Sachs (ed.), *The Oxford History of Anglicanism. V. Global Anglicanism, c. 1910–2000* (Oxford: Oxford University Press, 2018), pp. 50–75, and here at p. 51.

104 Ian Breward, 'Anglicanism in Australia and New Zealand', in Morris, *Oxford History of Anglicanism. IV*, pp. 331–61 and here at pp. 335–6.

105 David Hilliard, 'The Making of an Anglican Martyr: Bishop John Coleridge Patteson of Melanesia', in Diana Woods (ed.), *Studies in Church History 30: Martyrs and Martyrologies* (Cambridge: Cambridge University Press, 1993), pp. 333–45.

106 Thorgeir Kolshus and Even Hovdhaugen, 'Reassessing the Death of Bishop John Coleridge Patteson', *Journal of Pacific History* 45. 3 (2010), pp. 331–51.

107 Charlotte Yonge, *Life of John Coleridge Patteson, Missionary Bishop of the Melanesian Islands* (London: Macmillan, 1875), two volumes.

108 Breward, 'Anglicanism in Australia and New Zealand', p. 335.

109 Brian Macdonald-Milne, *The True Way of Service: The Pacific Story of the Melanesian Brotherhood, 1925–2000* (Leicester: Christians Aware, 2003).

110 For Anglo-Catholicism in Australia, see David Hilliard, *Anglo-Catholicism in Australia and New Zealand: A Short History* (London: Anglo-Catholic History Society, 2024), pp. 1–74. Its most striking feature was the 'Bush Brotherhoods', pp. 29–31,

Notes

though Religious communities of a more conventional kind were also found, *ibid.*, pp. 26–8, as they were indeed in New Zealand, pp. 94–7.

111 Gladwin, 'Anglicanism in Oceania since 1914', pp. 62, 63.

112 Cited *ibid.*, p. 63, from David Wetherell, *Reluctant Mission. The Anglican Church in Papua New Guinea, 1891–1942* (St Lucia: University of Queensland Press, 1977).

113 Sarah Stockwell, 'Anglicanism in the Era of Decolonization', in Morris, *Oxford History of Anglicanism. IV*, pp. 160–85.

114 Andrew Porter, 'The Universities' Mission to Central Africa: Anglo-Catholicism and the Twentieth Century Colonial Encounter', in Brian Stanley (ed.), *Missions, Nationalism and the End of Empire* (Grand Rapids, MI ,and Cambridge: Eerdmans, 2003), pp. 79–108.

115 Cited in Rowell, *The Vision Glorious*, pp. 163–4.

Chapter 11

1 Cited in Litvack, *John Mason Neale and the Quest for Sobornost*.

2 Rowan Strong, 'Series Introduction', in Morris, *Oxford History of Anglicanism. IV*, p. xviii.

3 Z. N. Brooke, *The English Church and the Papacy. From the Conquest to the Reign of John* (Cambridge: Cambridge University Press, 1952).

4 James Good, *The Church of England and the Ecumenical Movement. A Catholic Appreciation* (Cork: Cork University Press, and London: Burns & Oates, 1961), p. 1.

5 Colin Podmore, 'The Development of the Instruments of Communion', in Morris, *The Oxford History of Anglicanism. IV*, pp. 271–302, and here at p. 301.

6 Simmons, *To All that Be in Rome*, p. 7.

7 *Ibid.*

8 William Stubbs, *A Charge Delivered to the Clergy and Churchwardens* (Oxford: Oxford University Press, 1899), p. 54.

www.ingramcontent.com/pod-product-compliance
Lightning Source LLC
Chambersburg PA
CBHW020944230426
43666CB00005B/163